ARCHITECTURAL DRAFTSMAN'S REFERENCE HANDBOOK

JACK R. LEWIS FCSI

Architect, Professor
School of Architecture and Environmental Design
California Polytechnic State University
San Luis Obispo, California

ARCHITECTURAL DRAFTSMAN'S REFERENCE HANDBOOK

PRENTICE-HALL, INC., *Englewood Cliffs, New Jersey 07632*

Library of Congress Cataloging in Publication Data

Lewis, Jack R., date—
    Architectural draftsman's reference handbook.

    1. Structural drawing—Handbooks, manuals,
etc. 2. Architectural drawing—Handbooks,
manuals, etc. I. Title.
T355.L48   692'.3'02472   81-10687
ISBN 0-13-044164-3   AACR2

Editorial/production supervision by *Virginia Huebner*
Cover design by *Edsal Enterprises*
Manufacturing buyer: *Joyce Levatino*

Printed in the United States of America

10 9 8 7

Prentice-Hall International, Inc., *London*
Prentice-Hall of Australia Pty. Limited, *Sydney*
Prentice-Hall of Canada, Ltd., *Toronto*
Prentice-Hall of India Private Limited, *New Delhi*
Prentice-Hall of Japan, Inc., *Tokyo*
Prentice-Hall of Southeast Asia Pte. Ltd., *Singapore*
Whitehall Books Limited, Wellington, *New Zealand*

TABLE OF CONTENTS

TABLE OF CONTENTS 2

TABLE OF CONTENTS

PREFACE

As a draftsman, practicing architect, and university instructor, I have found that quick reference material useful to the draftsman is not always easily available or perhaps reasonably up to date. There are many texts written on the theory and practice of drafting, indicating weight of lines, dimensioning, perspective principles, and the like. The average draftsman will have been exposed to these and individual or local requirements in classes that he or she may attend, but in only a very few references will other information required to properly indicate in drawings the sizes and other qualities for materials or conditions be easily found.

This book is, therefore, a collection of information from manufacturers, trade associations, and individuals that will help to reduce the amount of time and effort required to find usable data. A great deal of the included information is from previously published material, however, much has been condensed or rearranged, and part has never been published before. This collection of data in one reference source should shorten the time spent searching, even if the draftsman knows where to look, and will thus increase productive time.

An effort has been made to limit this reference to everyday questions that could arise in drafting residential or small commercial work or in student work. There are undoubtedly specialized items that could have been included, but large commercial projects, hospitals, schools and other such construction will usually have special details. With the continuing proliferation of new materials and methods, it is probably better to retain the more standard data and research the extraordinary when the occasion presents itself.

My special thanks go to the numerous and very generous manufacturing firms, trade associations, and publishers who have allowed the use of their copyrighted material. The user of this book is urged to correspond with them if the material included herein is not sufficient and can be sure of a knowledgeable and cooperative answer. My thanks also go to my students, who have, by their questions, caused this book to be compiled, and to my family and friends whose encouragement has resulted in its completion.

JACK R. LEWIS

San Luis Obispo, California

ACKNOWLEDGEMENTS

The author and publisher wish to acknowledge the assistance of individuals, organizations, and companies listed below.

Acoustic Materials Association
American Institute of Graphic Arts
American Institute of Steel Construction
American Institute of Timber Construction
American Plywood Association
American Society for Testing and Materials
American Woodpreservers' Association

Bawden Brothers Inc,—Sernoll Division
Bethlehem Steel Corporation

California Cooperage
California Lathing and Plastering Contractors
    Association
California, State of
Carrier Corporation
Cast Iron Pipe Research Association
Construction Specifications Institute

Environmental Services Administration

Federal Housing Administration

Indiana Limestone Institute
Inland Steel Company

Masonry Institute of America
MOTORCAMPING—Times Mirror Magazines, Inc.

National Association of Architectural Metal
    Manufacturers
National Oceanic and Atmospheric Administration

Red Cedar Shingle and Handsplit Shake Bureau

SMACNA Architectural Manual
Sheet Metal and Air Conditioning National Association
Steel Deck Institute

Tile Council of America

United States Army—Corps of Engineers
United States Bureau of Public Roads
United States Department of Housing and Urban
    Development
United States Department of Interior
United States Department of Transportation
United States League of Savings Associations
United States Weather Bureau

Vermiculite Institute

Western Concrete Reinforcing Steel Institute
Western Pine Association
Weyerhaeuser Company
Wheeling Corrugating Company

Special thanks to Anne Mosnier, Rob Mowat and David Tsao, students at California Polytechnic State University, San Luis Obispo, California, who did the finished drawing and hand lettering from the rough sketches by the author.

ARCHITECTURAL DRAFTSMAN'S REFERENCE HANDBOOK

GENERAL INFORMATION   DIVISION 1

ABBREVIATION	ABBREV	BARREL	BBL
ACCESS PANEL	AP	BASEMENT	BSMT
ACOUSTIC	ACST	BATHROOM	B
ACOUSTIC TILE	AT	BEAM	BM
AGGREGATE	AGGR	BEDROOM	BR
AIR CONDITIONING	AIR COND	BENCH MARK	BM
ALTERNATING CURRENT	AC	BENDING MOMENT	M
ALUMINUM	AL	BETTER	BTR
AMERICAN CONCRETE		BEVELED	BEV
INSTITUTE	ACI	BLOCK	BLK
AMERICAN GAS INSTITUTE	AGA	BLOCKING	BLKG
AMERICAN INSTITUTE OF		BLUEPRINT	BP
ARCHITECTS	AIA	BOARD	BD
AMERICAN INSTITUTE OF		BOARD FOOT	BD FT
STEEL CONSTRUCTION	AISC	BOARD MEASURE	BM
AMERICAN SOCIETY FOR		BOLT	BLT
TESTING AND MATERIALS	ASTM	BRACKET	BRKT
AMERICAN STANDARDS		BRICK	BRK
ASSOCIATION	ASA	BRITISH THERMAL UNIT	BTU
AMERICAN WATER WORK		BUILDING	BLDG
ASSOCIATION	AWWA	BULKHEAD	BLKHD
AMERICAN WELDING		BUNDLE	BDL
SOCIETY	AWS	BUREAU OF STANDARD	
AMPERE	AMP		BU STAN
ANGLE	∠ OR ANGL	BY (AS 2" x 4")	X
APARTMENT	APT		
APPROXIMATE	APPROX	CABINET	CAB
ASBESTOS	ASB	CADMIUM	CAD
ASPHALT	ASPH	CALKING	CLKG
ASPHALT TILE	AT	CANDLEPOWER	CP
ASSEMBLE	ASSEM	CASING	CSG
ASSOCIATE	ASSOC	CAST IRON	CI
AUTOMATIC	AUTO	CAST STEEL	CS
AVENUE	AVE	CEILING	CLG
AVERAGE	AVG	CEMENT	CEM
AXIS	AX	CEMENT PLASTER	CEM PLAS

CENTER	CTR	CUBIC YARD	YD³ CU YD
CENTER LINE	₵ or CL	CYLINDER	CYL
CENTER TO CENTER	C to C		
CERAMIC	CER	DEAD LOAD	DL
CHALKBOARD	CH BD	DEGREE	° or DEG
CHAMFER	CHAM	DEGREE CELSIUS	°C
CHANNEL	[or CHAN	DEGREE FAHRENHEIT	°F
CIRCUT	CKT	DEPARTMENT	DEPT
CIRCUT BREAKER	CIR BKR	DETAIL	DET
CIRCULAR	CIR	DIAGRAM	DIAG
CIRCUMFERENCE	CIRC	DIAMETER	φ or DIAM
CLEAN OUT	CO	DIMENSION	DIM
CLEAR	CLR	DINING ROOM	DR
CLOSET	CLO	DIRECT CURRENT	DC
COATED	CTD	DISCONNECT	DISC
COEFFICIENT	COEF	DITTO	" or DO
COLD WATER	CW	DIVISION	DIV
COLUMN	COL	DOUBLE-HUNG (WINDOW) DH	
COMBINATION	COMB		
COMMERCIAL STANDARD	CS	DOUGLAS FIR	DF
COMPANY	CO	DOWEL	DWL
CONCRETE	CONC	DOWN	DN
CONCRETE BLOCK	CONC BLK	DOWNSPOUT	DS
CONDUIT	CND	DOZEN	DOZ
CONNECTION	CONN	DRAWING	DWG
CONSTRUCTION	CONST	DRINKING FOUNTAIN	DF
CONSTRUCTION SPECIFICATIONS INSTITUTE	CSI	DUPLEX	DX
		DUPLICATE	DUP
CONTRACTOR	CONTR		
COUNTER	CTR	EACH	EA
COUNTERSINK	CSK	EAST	E
CROSS SECTION	X-SECT	ELBOW	ELL
CUBIC FOOT	FT³ or CU FT	ELECTRIC	ELEC
CUBIC FEET PER MINUTE CFM		ELEVATION	ELEV
		ENCLOSURE	ENCL
CUBIC INCH	IN³ or CU IN	END TO END	E to E

ENGINEER	ENGR	GALVANIZED	GALV
EQUIPMENT	EQUIP	GALVANIZED IRON	GI
ESTIMATE	EST	GAUGE	GA
EXTRA HEAVY	EX HVY	GENERAL CONTRACTOR	
		GEN CONTR	
FABRICATE	FAB	GLASS	GL
FAHRENHEIT	F	GOVERNMENT	GOVT
FEDERAL	FED	GRADE	GRD
FEDERAL SPECIFICATION		GRADE LINE	GL
FED SPEC		GYPSUM	GYP
FEET	' or FT		
FEET PER MINUTE	FPM	HARDWARE	HDW
FEET PER SECOND	FPS	HEAD	HD
FINISH	FIN	HEATER	HTR
FINISH FLOOR	FIN FL	HEIGHT	HT
FIREBRICK	FBRK	HEXAGONAL	HEX
FIRE HOSE	FH	HORIZONTAL	HORIZ
FIXTURE	FIX	HORSEPOWER	HP
FLANGE	FLG	HOSE BIBB	HB
FLASHING	FLG	HOT WATER	HW
FLAT HEAD	FH	HOT WATER HEATER	HWH
FLOOR	FL		
FLOOR DRAIN	FD	INCH	" or IN
FLOORING	FLG	INCORPORATED	INC
FOOT	' or FT	INFORMATION	INFO
FOOT POUND	FT LB	INSIDE DIAMETER	ID
FOOTING	FTG	INSULATE	INSUL
FOUNDATION	FDN	INTERIOR	INT
FULL SIZE	FS	INVERT	INV
		IRON	I
GALLON	GAL		
GALLONS PER HOUR	GPH	JANITOR'S CLOSET	JAN
GALLONS PER MINUTE	GPM	JOINT	JNT
GALLONS PER SECOND	GPS	JUNCTION BOX	J

KILN DRIED	KD	NATIONAL	NATL
KILO	K	NATIONAL BUREAU	
KILOWATT	KW	OF STANDARDS	NBS
KIP (1000 LB)	K	NOMINAL	NOM
KITCHEN	K	NORTH	N
KNOCKED DOWN	KD	NUMBER	# or NO
LABORATORY	LAB	OCTAGONAL	OCT
LATITUDE	LAT	OFFICE	OFF
LAVATORY	LAV	ON CENTER	OC
LEFT HAND	LH	ONE THOUSAND	M
LEFT HAND REVERSED	LHR	OPENING	OPNG
LEVEL	LEV	OUNCE	OZ
LIBRARY	LIB	OUT TO OUT	O TO O
LIGHTWEIGHT	LW	OUTSIDE DIAMETER	OD
LINEAR FEET	LIN. FT	OVERALL	OA
LINOLEUM	LINO		
LIVE LOAD	LL	PAGE	PG
LIVING ROOM	LR	PAIR	PR
LONGITUDE	LONG	PARTS PER MILLION	PPM
LUMBER	LBR	PASSENGER	PASS
LUMEN	L	PENNY (NAIL SIZE)	d
		PERCENT	%
MANUFACTURE	MFGR	PI (CIRCULAR MEASURE)	π
MARK	MK	PLASTER	PLAS
MAXIMUM	MAX	PLATE GLASS	PL GL
MEDIUM	MED	PLUMBING	PLMB
METAL	MET	PLYWOOD	PLY
METER	M	POINT	PT
MINIMUM	MIN	POLISH	POL
MINUTE	' or MIN	POUND	# or LB
MODULAR	MOD	PULL CHAIN	PC
MODULUS OF ELASTCITY	E	PUSH BUTTON	PB

QUANTITY	QTY	STREET	ST
QUART	QT	SUBSTITUTE	SUB
		SUPPLEMENT	SUPP
RADIUS	R or RAD	SURFACED FOUR SIDES	S4S
RANDOM	RDM	SURFACED ONE SIDE	
REFLECTIVE	REFL	AND ONE EDGE	S1S1E
RETURN	RET	SUSPEND	SUSP
RIGHT HAND	RH	SWITCH	SW
RIGHT HAND REVERSED	RHR	SYMBOL	SYM
RISER	R		
ROOFING	RFG	TANGENT	TAN
ROOM	RM	TELEPHONE	TEL
ROUGH	RO or RGH	TEMPERATURE	TEMP
ROUND	Ø or RND	TERRAZZO	TER
		THICK	THK
SCALE	SC	THOUSAND	M
SECOND	SEC	THOUSAND POUNDS	KIP
SECTION	SECT	TONGUE AND GROOVE	T&G
SELECT	SEL	TYPICAL	TYP
SEWER	SEW		
SHEATHING	SHTG	UNDERWRITERS	
SHEET	SH or SHT	LABORATORY	UL
SIDING	SDG	UNITED STATES	
SINK	SK or S	STANDARD	USS
SOIL PIPE	SP	URINAL	UR
SOUTH	S		
SPEAKER	SPKR	VACUUM	VAC
SQUARE	□ or SQ	VANISHING POINT	VP
SQUARE FOOT	□′ or SQ FT	VAPOR PROOF	VAP. PRF.
STAINLESS STEEL	SST	VENT	V
STANDARD	STD	VOLT	V
STATION	STA	VOLUME	VOL
STEEL	STL		

WATER	W
WATERCLOSET	WC
WATER HEATER	WH
WATERPROOF	WP
WATT	W
WATTHOUR	WHR
WEATHERPROOF	WP
WEIGHT	WT
WEST	W
WESTERN PINE	WP
WIRE GLASS	W GL
WITH	W/
WITHOUT	W/O
WOOD	WD
WROUGHT IRON	WI
YARD	YD
YELLOW PINE	YP
ZINC	Z

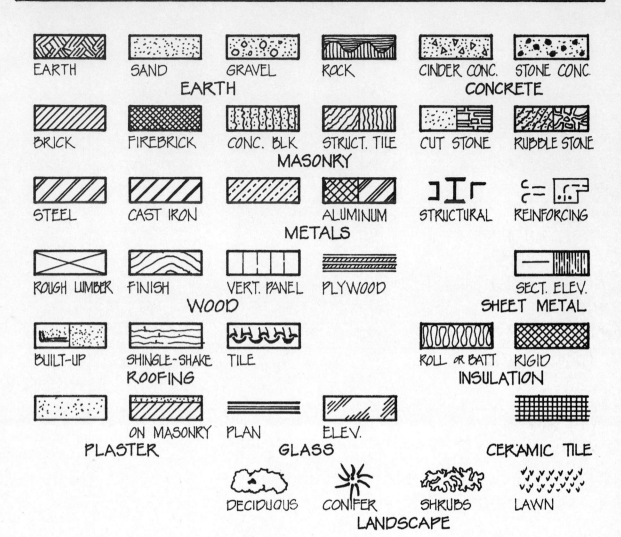

EARTH SAND GRAVEL ROCK CINDER CONC. STONE CONC.

EARTH **CONCRETE**

BRICK FIREBRICK CONC. BLK STRUCT. TILE CUT STONE RUBBLE STONE

MASONRY

STEEL CAST IRON ALUMINUM STRUCTURAL REINFORCING

METALS

ROUGH LUMBER FINISH VERT. PANEL PLYWOOD SECT. ELEV.

WOOD **SHEET METAL**

BUILT-UP SHINGLE-SHAKE TILE ROLL OR BATT RIGID

ROOFING **INSULATION**

ON MASONRY PLAN ELEV.

PLASTER **GLASS** **CERAMIC TILE**

DECIDUOUS CONIFER SHRUBS LAWN

LANDSCAPE

MASONRY CONCRETE MARBLE SLUMP CONC. BK.

HORIZ. SIDING VERT. SIDING PLYWOOD

TYPICAL ELEVATION INDICATION

FOR TYPICAL PLUMBING AND HEATING SYMBOLS SEE
PLATE 15-1; FOR ELECTRICAL SYMBOLS, PLATE 16-1.

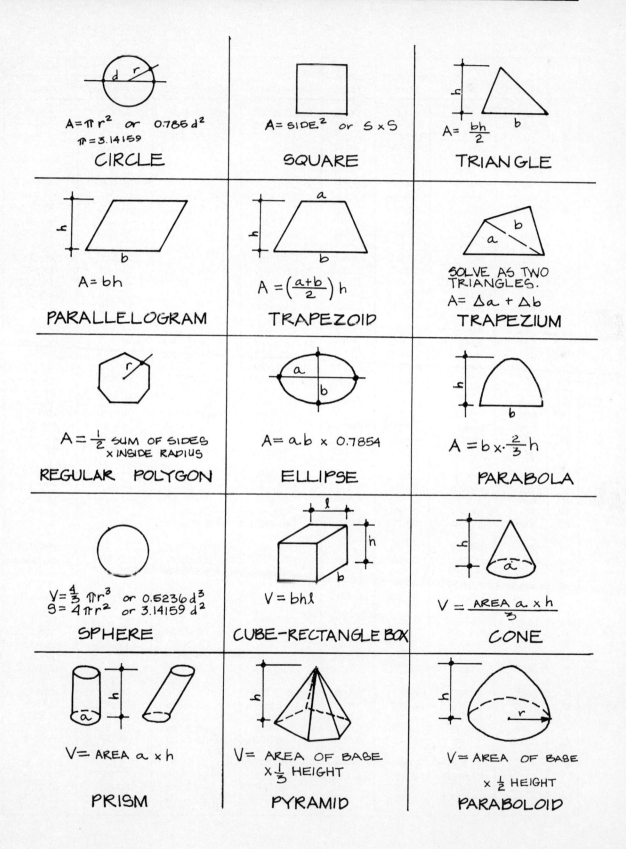

CIRCLE
$$A = \pi r^2 \text{ or } 0.785 d^2$$
$$\pi = 3.14159$$

SQUARE
$$A = SIDE^2 \text{ or } S \times S$$

TRIANGLE
$$A = \frac{bh}{2}$$

PARALLELOGRAM
$$A = bh$$

TRAPEZOID
$$A = \left(\frac{a+b}{2}\right) h$$

TRAPEZIUM
SOLVE AS TWO TRIANGLES.
$$A = \Delta a + \Delta b$$

REGULAR POLYGON
$$A = \frac{1}{2} \text{ SUM OF SIDES} \times \text{INSIDE RADIUS}$$

ELLIPSE
$$A = a \cdot b \times 0.7854$$

PARABOLA
$$A = b \times \cdot \frac{2}{3} h$$

SPHERE
$$V = \frac{4}{3} \pi r^3 \text{ or } 0.5236 d^3$$
$$S = 4 \pi r^2 \text{ or } 3.14159 d^2$$

CUBE-RECTANGLE BOX
$$V = bhl$$

CONE
$$V = \frac{AREA \ a \times h}{3}$$

PRISM
$$V = AREA \ a \times h$$

PYRAMID
$$V = AREA \ OF \ BASE \times \frac{1}{3} HEIGHT$$

PARABOLOID
$$V = AREA \ OF \ BASE \times \frac{1}{2} HEIGHT$$

NO.	SQUARE	CUBE	SQUARE ROOT	CUBE ROOT	LOGARITHM	1000 X RECIPROCAL	NO.= DIAMETER	
							CIRCUM.	AREA
1	1	1	1.0000	1.0000	0.00000	1000.000	3.142	0.7854
2	4	8	1.4142	1.2599	0.30103	500.000	6.283	3.1416
3	9	27	1.7321	1.4422	0.47712	333.333	9.425	7.0686
4	16	64	2.0000	1.5874	0.60206	250.000	12.566	12.5664
5	25	125	2.2361	1.7100	0.69897	200.000	15.708	19.6350
6	36	216	2.4495	1.8171	0.77815	166.667	18.850	28.2743
7	49	343	2.6458	1.9129	0.84510	142.857	21.991	38.4845
8	64	512	2.8284	2.0000	0.90309	125.000	25.133	50.2655
9	81	729	3.0000	2.0801	0.95424	111.111	28.274	63.6173
10	100	1000	3.1623	2.1544	1.00000	100.000	31.416	78.5398
11	121	1331	3.3166	2.2240	1.04139	90.9091	34.558	95.0332
12	144	1728	3.4641	2.2894	1.07918	83.3333	37.699	113.097
13	169	2197	3.6056	2.3513	1.11394	76.9231	40.841	132.732
14	196	2744	3.7417	2.4101	1.14613	71.4286	43.982	153.938
15	225	3375	3.8730	2.4662	1.17609	66.6667	47.124	176.715
16	256	4096	4.0000	2.5198	1.20412	62.5000	50.265	201.062
17	289	4913	4.1231	2.5713	1.23045	58.8235	53.407	226.980
18	324	5832	4.2426	2.6207	1.25527	55.5556	56.549	254.469
19	361	6859	4.3589	2.6684	1.27875	52.6316	59.690	283.529
20	400	8000	4.4721	2.7144	1.30103	50.0000	62.832	314.159
21	441	9261	4.5826	2.7589	1.32222	47.6190	65.973	346.361
22	484	10648	4.6904	2.8020	1.34242	45.4545	69.115	380.133
23	529	12167	4.7958	2.8439	1.36173	43.4783	72.257	415.476
24	576	13824	4.8990	2.8845	1.38021	41.6667	75.398	452.389
25	625	15625	5.000	2.9240	1.39794	40.0000	78.540	490.874
26	676	17576	5.0990	2.9625	1.41497	38.4615	81.681	530.929
27	729	19683	5.1962	3.0000	1.43136	37.0370	84.823	572.555
28	784	21952	5.2915	3.0366	1.44716	35.7143	87.965	615.752
29	841	24389	5.3852	3.0723	1.46240	34.4828	91.106	660.520
30	900	27000	5.4772	3.1072	1.47712	33.3333	94.248	706.858
31	961	29791	5.5678	3.1414	1.49136	32.2581	97.389	754.768
32	1024	32768	5.6569	3.1748	1.50515	31.2500	100.531	804.248
33	1089	35937	5.7446	3.2075	1.51851	30.3030	103.673	855.299
34	1156	39304	5.8310	3.2396	1.53148	29.4118	106.814	907.920
35	1225	42875	5.9161	3.2711	1.54407	28.5714	109.956	962.113
36	1296	46656	6.0000	3.3019	1.55630	27.7778	113.097	1017.88
37	1369	50653	6.0828	3.3322	1.56820	27.0270	116.239	1075.21
38	1444	54872	6.1644	3.3620	1.57978	26.3158	119.381	1134.11
39	1521	59319	6.2450	3.3912	1.59106	25.6410	122.522	1194.59
40	1600	64000	6.3246	3.4200	1.60206	25.0000	125.66	1256.64
41	1681	68921	6.4031	3.4482	1.61278	24.3902	128.81	1320.25
42	1764	74088	6.4807	3.4760	1.62325	23.8095	131.95	1385.44
43	1849	79507	6.5574	3.5034	1.63347	23.2558	135.09	1452.20
44	1936	85184	6.6332	3.5303	1.64345	22.7273	138.23	1520.53
45	2025	91125	6.7082	3.5569	1.65321	22.2222	141.37	1590.43
46	2116	97336	6.7823	3.5830	1.66276	21.7391	144.51	1661.90
47	2209	103823	6.8557	3.6088	1.67210	21.2766	147.65	1734.94
48	2304	110592	6.9282	3.6342	1.68124	20.8333	150.80	1809.56
49	2401	117649	7.0000	3.6593	1.69020	20.4082	153.94	1885.74

AMERICAN INSTITUTE OF STEEL CONSTRUCTION.

NO.	SQUARE	CUBE	SQUARE ROOT	CUBE ROOT	LOGARITHM	1000 x RECIPROCAL	NO. = DIAMETER	
							CIRCUM.	AREA
50	2500	125000	7.0711	3.6840	1.69897	20.0000	157.08	1963.50
51	2601	132651	7.1414	3.7084	1.70757	19.6078	160.22	2042.82
52	2704	140608	7.2111	3.7325	1.71600	19.2308	163.36	2132.72
53	2809	148877	7.2801	3.7563	1.72428	18.8679	166.50	2206.18
54	2916	157464	7.3485	3.7798	1.73239	18.5185	169.65	2290.22
55	3025	166375	7.4162	3.8030	1.74036	18.1818	172.79	2375.83
56	3136	175616	7.4833	3.8259	1.74819	17.8571	175.93	2463.01
57	3249	185193	7.5498	3.8485	1.75587	17.5439	179.07	2551.76
58	3364	195112	7.6158	3.8709	1.76343	17.2414	182.21	2642.08
59	3481	205379	7.6811	3.8930	1.77085	16.9492	185.35	2733.97
60	3600	216000	7.7460	3.9149	1.77815	16.6667	188.50	2827.43
61	3721	226981	7.8102	3.9365	1.78533	16.3934	191.64	2922.47
62	3844	238328	7.8740	3.9579	1.79239	16.1290	194.78	3019.07
63	3969	250047	7.9373	3.9791	1.79934	15.8730	197.92	3117.25
64	4096	262144	8.0000	4.0000	1.80618	15.6250	201.06	3216.99
65	4225	274625	8.0623	4.0207	1.81291	15.3846	204.20	3318.31
66	4356	287496	8.1240	4.0412	1.81954	15.1515	207.35	3421.19
67	4489	300763	8.1854	4.0615	1.82607	14.9254	210.49	3525.65
68	4624	314432	8.2462	4.0817	1.83251	14.7069	213.63	3631.68
69	4761	328509	8.3066	4.1016	1.83885	14.4928	216.77	3739.28
70	4900	343000	8.3666	4.1213	1.84510	14.2857	219.91	3848.45
71	5041	357911	8.4261	4.1408	1.85126	14.0845	223.05	3959.19
72	5184	373248	8.4853	4.1602	1.85733	13.8889	226.19	4071.50
73	5329	389017	8.5440	4.1793	1.86332	13.6986	229.34	4185.39
74	5476	405224	8.6023	4.1983	1.86923	13.5135	232.48	4300.84
75	5625	421875	8.6603	4.2172	1.87506	13.3333	235.62	4417.86
76	5776	438976	8.7178	4.2358	1.88081	13.1579	238.76	4536.46
77	5929	456533	8.7750	4.2543	1.88649	12.9870	241.90	4656.63
78	6084	474552	8.8318	4.2727	1.89209	12.8205	245.04	4778.36
79	6241	493039	8.8882	4.2908	1.89763	12.6582	248.19	4901.67
80	6400	512000	8.9443	4.3089	1.90309	12.5000	251.33	5026.55
81	6561	531441	9.0000	4.3267	1.90849	12.3457	254.47	5153.00
82	6724	551368	9.0554	4.3445	1.91381	12.1951	257.61	5281.02
83	6889	571787	9.1104	4.3621	1.91908	12.0482	260.75	5410.61
84	7056	592704	9.1652	4.3795	1.92428	11.9048	263.89	5541.77
85	7225	614125	9.2195	4.3968	1.92942	11.7647	267.04	5674.50
86	7396	636056	9.2736	4.4140	1.93450	11.6279	270.18	5808.80
87	7569	658503	9.3274	4.4310	1.93952	11.4943	273.32	5944.68
88	7744	681472	9.3808	4.4480	1.94448	11.3636	276.46	6082.12
89	7921	704969	9.4340	4.4647	1.94939	11.2360	279.60	6221.14
90	8100	729000	9.4868	4.4814	1.95424	11.1111	282.74	6361.73
91	8281	753571	9.5394	4.4979	1.95904	10.9890	285.88	6503.88
92	8464	778688	9.5917	4.5144	1.96379	10.8696	289.03	6647.61
93	8649	804357	9.6437	4.5307	1.96848	10.7527	292.17	6792.91
94	8836	830584	9.6954	4.5468	1.97313	10.6383	295.31	6939.78
95	9025	857375	9.7468	4.5629	1.97772	10.5263	298.45	7088.22
96	9216	884736	9.7980	4.5789	1.98227	10.4167	301.59	7238.23
97	9409	912673	9.8489	4.5947	1.98677	10.3093	304.73	7389.81
98	9604	941192	9.8995	4.6104	1.99123	10.2041	307.88	7542.96
99	9801	970299	9.9499	4.6261	1.99564	10.1010	311.02	7697.69

AMERICAN INSTITUTE OF STEEL CONSTRUCTION.

LINEAR MEASURE

1 INCH .... 2.54 CENTIMETERS
1 FOOT .... .3048 METERS
1 YARD .... .9144 METERS
1 ROD .... 5.0292 METERS
1 MILE ...... 1.6093 KILOMETERS
1 CENTIMETER.. .3937 INCHES
1 DECIMETER .. 3.9370 INCHES
1 DECIMETER ..... .3281 FOOT
1 METER..... 39.370 INCHES
1 METER..... 3.2808 FEET
1 METER .... 1.0936 YARDS
1 KILOMETER .. 3280.83 FEET
1 KILOMETER ... 1093.61 YARDS
1 KILOMETER ... 198.838 RODS
1 KILOMETER ... .62137 MILES

SQUARE MEASURE

1 SQ. INCH 6.4516 SQ. CENTIMETERS
1 SQ. FOOT .... .0929 SQ. METERS
1 SQ. YARD .... .8361 SQ. METERS
1 SQ. ROD.... 25.2930 SQ. METERS
1 ACRE... 4046.873 SQ. METERS
1 ACRE... .40468 HECTARE
1 SQ. MILE .. 258.9998 HECTARE
1 SQ. MILE ... 2.5900 KILOMETERS
1 SQ. CENTIMETER.. 1550 SQ. INCHES
1 SQ. DECIMETER.. 15.500 SQ. INCHES
1 SQ. METER ... 1550.0 SQ. INCHES
1 SQ. METER .... 10.764 SQ. FEET
1 SQ. METER .... 1.1960 SQ. YARDS
1 HECTARE ..... 2.4710 ACRES
1 HECTARE ..... 395.36 SQ. RODS
1 HECTARE .... 24.710 CHAINS
1 SQ. KILOMETER 247.104 ACRES
1 SQ. KILOMETER.. .3861 MILES

WEIGHT

1 GRAIN .... .0648 GRAM
1 OUNCE TROY .... 31.103 GRAMS
1 OUUND TROY ... .3732 KILOGRAM
1 OUNCE AVOIR. .... 28.350 GRAMS
1 POUND AVOIR. .... .4536 KILOGRAM
1 SHORT TON ... .9072 TONNEAU
1 LONG TON ... 1.0160 TONNEAU
1 GRAM ..... 15.4324 GRAINS
1 GRAM .... .0322 OZ. TROY
1 GRAM .... .0353 OZ. AVOIR
1 KILOGRAM.. 2.6792 POUNDS TROY
1 KILOGRAM.. 2.2046 POUNDS AVOIR
1 TONNEAU ..... 1.1023 SHORT TONS
1 TONNEAU .... .9843 LONG TON
1 TONNEAU 2204.622 POUNDS AVOIR

CAPACITY

1 MINIM .... .0616 MILLILITER
1 FLUID DRAM .... 3.6966 MILLILITERS
1 FLUID OUNCE .. 29.5730 MILLILITERS
1 GILL .... 118.292 MILLILITERS
1 LIQUID PINT .... .4732 LITER
1 LIQUID QUART ...... .9463 LITER
1 GALLON .... 3.7853 LITERS
1 MILLILITER .... 16.2311 MINIMS
1 MILLILITER ... .2705 FLUID DRAM
1 MILLILITER ... .0338 FLUID OUNCE
1 LITER ...... 2.1134 LIQUID PINTS
1 LITER .... 1.0567 LIQUID QUARTS
1 LITER .... .2642 GALLON
1 DRY QUART... 1.1012 LITERS
1 DRY PECK... 8810 DEKALITER
1 BUSHEL .... .3523 HECTOLITER
1 LITER ..... .9081 DRY QUART
1 DEKALITER 1.1351 DRY PECKS

CUBIC MEASURE

1 CU. INCH . . . 16.387 CU. CENTIMETERS	1 CU. CENTIMETER . . .0610 CU. INCH
1 CU. FOOT . . 28.347 CU. DECIMETERS	1 CU. DECIMETER . . . .0353 CU. FOOT
1 CU. YARD . . . . .7645 CU. METER	1 CU. METER . . . 1.3079 CU. YARDS
1 CORD . . . . 3.624 CU. METERS	1 CU. METER . . . . .2759 CORD

FRACTION	1/64 THS	DECIMAL	MILLIMETER (APPROX)	FRACTION	1/64 THS	DECIMAL	MILLIMETER (APPROX)
...	1	.015625	0.397	...	33	.515625	13.097
1/32	2	.03125	0.794	17/32	34	.53125	13.494
...	3	.046875	1.191	...	35	.546875	13.891
1/16	4	.0625	1.588	9/16	36	.5625	14.288
...	5	.078125	1.984	...	37	.578125	14.684
3/32	6	.09375	2.381	19/32	38	.59375	15.081
...	7	.109375	2.778	...	39	.609375	15.478
1/8	8	.125	3.175	5/8	40	.625	15.875
...	9	.140625	3.572	...	41	.640625	16.272
5/32	10	.15625	3.969	21/32	42	.65625	16.669
...	11	.171875	4.366	...	43	.671875	17.066
3/16	12	.1875	4.763	11/16	44	.6875	17.463
...	13	.203125	5.159	...	45	.703125	17.859
7/32	14	.21875	5.556	23/32	46	.71875	18.256
...	15	.234375	5.953	...	47	.734375	18.653
1/4	16	.250	6.350	3/4	48	.750	19.050
...	17	.265625	6.747	...	49	.765625	19.447
9/32	18	.28125	7.144	25/32	50	.78125	19.844
...	19	.296875	7.541	...	51	.796875	20.241
5/16	20	.3125	7.938	13/16	52	.8125	20.638
...	21	.328125	8.334	...	53	.828125	21.034
11/16	22	.34375	8.731	27/32	54	.84375	21.431
...	23	.359375	9.128	...	55	.859375	21.828
3/8	24	.375	9.525	7/8	56	.875	22.225
...	25	.390625	9.922	...	57	.890625	22.622
13/32	26	.40625	10.319	29/32	58	.90625	23.019
...	27	.421875	10.716	...	59	.921875	23.416
7/16	28	.4375	11.113	15/16	60	.9375	23.813
...	29	.453125	11.509	...	61	.953125	24.205
15/32	30	.46875	11.905	31/32	62	.96875	24.606
...	31	.484375	12.303	...	63	.984375	25.003
1/2	32	.500	12.700	1	64	1.000	25.400

BEAM DIAGRAMS AND FORMULAS

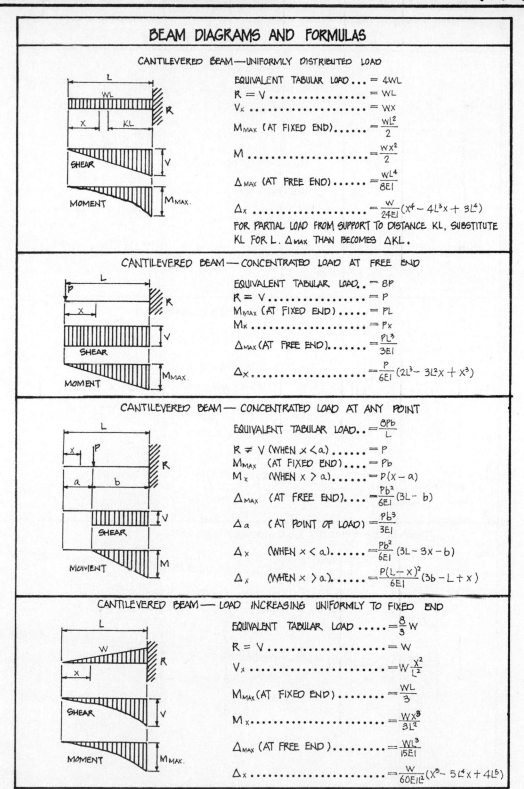

CANTILEVERED BEAM—UNIFORMLY DISTRIBUTED LOAD

EQUIVALENT TABULAR LOAD ... $= 4WL$

$R = V$ .... $= WL$

V_x .... $= Wx$

M_{MAX} (AT FIXED END) ...... $= \dfrac{WL^2}{2}$

M .... $= \dfrac{Wx^2}{2}$

Δ_{MAX} (AT FREE END) ...... $= \dfrac{WL^4}{8EI}$

Δ_x .... $= \dfrac{W}{24EI}(x^4 - 4L^3x + 3L^4)$

FOR PARTIAL LOAD FROM SUPPORT TO DISTANCE KL, SUBSTITUTE KL FOR L. Δ_{MAX} THAN BECOMES ΔKL.

CANTILEVERED BEAM—CONCENTRATED LOAD AT FREE END

EQUIVALENT TABULAR LOAD.. $= 8P$

$R = V$ .... $= P$

M_{MAX} (AT FIXED END) ..... $= PL$

M_x .... $= Px$

Δ_{MAX} (AT FREE END) .... $= \dfrac{PL^3}{3EI}$

Δ_x .... $= \dfrac{P}{6EI}(2L^3 - 3L^2x + x^3)$

CANTILEVERED BEAM—CONCENTRATED LOAD AT ANY POINT

EQUIVALENT TABULAR LOAD.. $= \dfrac{8Pb}{L}$

$R = V$ (WHEN $x < a$) ...... $= P$

M_{MAX} (AT FIXED END) .... $= Pb$

M_x (WHEN $x > a$) ...... $= P(x - a)$

Δ_{MAX} (AT FREE END) .... $= \dfrac{Pb^2}{6EI}(3L - b)$

Δ_a (AT POINT OF LOAD) $= \dfrac{Pb^3}{3EI}$

Δ_x (WHEN $x < a$) ...... $= \dfrac{Pb^2}{6EI}(3L - 3x - b)$

Δ_x (WHEN $x > a$) ...... $= \dfrac{P(L-x)^2}{6EI}(3b - L + x)$

CANTILEVERED BEAM—LOAD INCREASING UNIFORMLY TO FIXED END

EQUIVALENT TABULAR LOAD ..... $= \dfrac{8}{3}W$

$R = V$ .... $= W$

V_x .... $= W\dfrac{x^2}{L^2}$

M_{MAX} (AT FIXED END) .... $= \dfrac{WL}{3}$

M_x .... $= \dfrac{Wx^3}{3L^2}$

Δ_{MAX} (AT FREE END) .... $= \dfrac{WL^3}{15EI}$

Δ_x .... $= \dfrac{W}{60EIL^2}(x^5 - 5L^4x + 4L^5)$

BEAM DIAGRAMS AND FORMULAS

SIMPLE BEAM—UNIFORMLY DISTRIBUTED LOAD

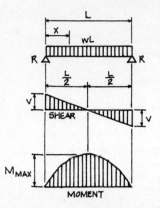

EQUIVALENT TABULAR LOAD $\dots\dots = WL$

$R = V \dots\dots\dots\dots\dots = \dfrac{WL}{2}$

$V_x \dots\dots\dots\dots\dots\dots = W\left(\dfrac{L}{2} - x\right)$

M_{MAX} (AT CENTER)$\dots\dots\dots = \dfrac{WL^2}{8}$

$M_x \dots\dots\dots\dots\dots\dots = \dfrac{Wx}{2}(L - x)$

Δ_{MAX} (AT CENTER)$\dots\dots\dots = \dfrac{5WL^4}{384EI}$

$\Delta_x \dots\dots\dots\dots\dots\dots = \dfrac{Wx}{24EI}(L^3 - 2Lx^2 + x^3)$

SIMPLE BEAM—UNIFORM LOAD PARTIALLY DISTRIBUTED

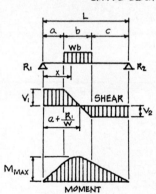

$R_1 = V_1$ (MAX WHEN $a < c$)$\dots = \dfrac{Wb}{2L}(2c + b)$

$R_2 = V_2$ (MAX WHEN $a > c$)$\dots = \dfrac{Wb}{2L}(2a + b)$

V_x [WHEN $x < a$ AND $> (a+b)$] $= R_1 - W(x - a)$

$M_{MAX}\left(\text{AT } x = a + \dfrac{R_1}{W}\right)\dots\dots = R_1\left(a + \dfrac{R_1}{2W}\right)$

M_x (WHEN $x < a$)$\dots\dots\dots = R_1 x$

M_x [WHEN $x > a$ AND $< (a+b)$] $= R_1 x - \dfrac{W}{2}(x - a)^2$

M_x [WHEN $x > (a+b)$]$\dots\dots = R_2(L - x)$

SIMPLE BEAM—UNIFORM LOAD PARTIALLY DISTRIBUTED AT ONE END

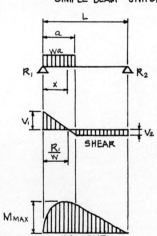

$R_1 = V_{1MAX} \dots\dots = \dfrac{Wa}{2L}(2L - a)$

$R_2 = V_2 \dots\dots\dots = \dfrac{Wa^2}{2L}$

V (WHEN $x < a$) $= R_1 - Wx$

$M_{MAX}\left(\text{AT } x = \dfrac{R_1}{W}\right)\dots = \dfrac{R_1^2}{2W}$

M_x (WHEN $x < a$) $= R_1 x - \dfrac{Wx^2}{2}$

M_x (WHEN $x > a$)$.= R_2(L - x)$

Δ_x (WHEN $x < a$)$.= \dfrac{Wx}{24EIL}[a^2(2L - a)^2 - 2ax^2(2L - a) + Lx^3]$

Δ_x (WHEN $x > a$)$.= \dfrac{Wa^2(L - x)}{24EIL}(4xL - 2x^2 - a^2)$

CONCRETE REINFORCING STEEL INSTITUTE

BEAM DIAGRAMS AND FORMULAS

SIMPLE BEAM—UNIFORM LOAD PARTIALLY DISTRIBUTED AT EACH END

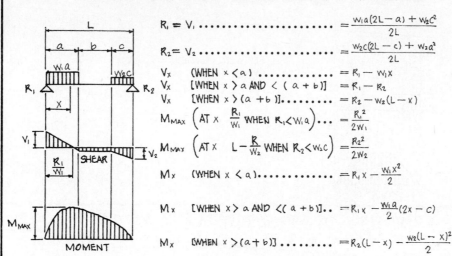

$$R_1 = V_1 \dots\dots\dots\dots\dots = \frac{w_1a(2L - a) + w_2c^2}{2L}$$

$$R_2 = V_2 \dots\dots\dots\dots\dots = \frac{w_2c(2L - c) + w_2a^2}{2L}$$

$$V_x \quad (\text{WHEN } x < a) \dots\dots\dots = R_1 - w_1x$$

$$V_x \quad [\text{WHEN } x > a \text{ AND } < (a + b)] = R_1 - R_2$$

$$V_x \quad [\text{WHEN } x > (a+b)] \dots\dots = R_2 - w_2(L - x)$$

$$M_{MAX} \left(\text{AT } x \ \frac{R_1}{w_1} \text{ WHEN } R_1 < w_1a\right) \dots = \frac{R_1^2}{2w_1}$$

$$M_{MAX} \left(\text{AT } x \quad L - \frac{R}{w_2} \text{ WHEN } R_2 < w_2c\right) = \frac{R_2^2}{2w_2}$$

$$M_x \quad (\text{WHEN } x < a) \dots\dots\dots = R_1x - \frac{w_1x^2}{2}$$

$$M_x \quad [\text{WHEN } x > a \text{ AND } < (a + b)] \dots = R_1x - \frac{w_1a}{2}(2x - c)$$

$$M_x \quad [\text{WHEN } x > (a+b)] \dots\dots = R_2(L - x) - \frac{w_2(L - x)^2}{2}$$

SIMPLE BEAM—CONCENTRATED LOAD AT CENTER

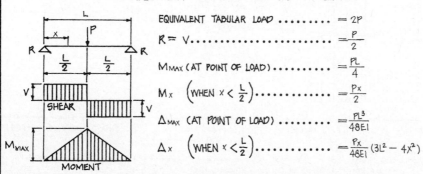

$$\text{EQUIVALENT TABULAR LOAD} \dots\dots = 2P$$

$$R = V \dots\dots\dots\dots\dots\dots = \frac{P}{2}$$

$$M_{MAX} (\text{AT POINT OF LOAD}) \dots\dots\dots = \frac{PL}{4}$$

$$M_x \left(\text{WHEN } x < \frac{L}{2}\right) \dots\dots\dots = \frac{Px}{2}$$

$$\Delta_{MAX} (\text{AT POINT OF LOAD}) \dots\dots = \frac{PL^3}{48EI}$$

$$\Delta_x \left(\text{WHEN } x < \frac{L}{2}\right) \dots\dots\dots = \frac{Px}{48EI}(3L^2 - 4x^2)$$

SIMPLE BEAM   CONCENTRATED LOAD AT ANY POINT

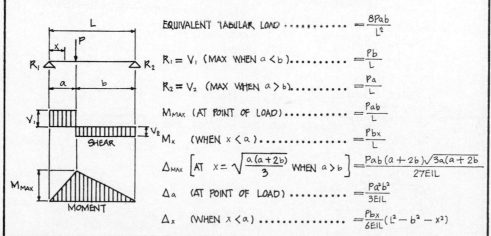

$$\text{EQUIVALENT TABULAR LOAD} \dots\dots\dots = \frac{8Pab}{L^2}$$

$$R_1 = V_1 \ (\text{MAX WHEN } a < b) \dots\dots\dots = \frac{Pb}{L}$$

$$R_2 = V_2 \ (\text{MAX WHEN } a > b) \dots\dots\dots = \frac{Pa}{L}$$

$$M_{MAX} (\text{AT POINT OF LOAD}) \dots\dots\dots = \frac{Pab}{L}$$

$$M_x \quad (\text{WHEN } x < a) \dots\dots\dots\dots = \frac{Pbx}{L}$$

$$\Delta_{MAX} \left[\text{AT } x = \sqrt{\frac{a(a+2b)}{3}} \text{ WHEN } a > b\right] = \frac{Pab(a + 2b)\sqrt{3a(a + 2b)}}{27EIL}$$

$$\Delta_a \quad (\text{AT POINT OF LOAD}) \dots\dots\dots = \frac{Pa^2b^2}{3EIL}$$

$$\Delta_x \quad (\text{WHEN } x < a) \dots\dots\dots\dots = \frac{Pbx}{6EIL}(L^2 - b^2 - x^2)$$

BEAM DIAGRAMS AND FORMULAS

SIMPLE BEAM — TWO EQUAL CONCENTRATED LOADS SYMMETRICALLY PLACED

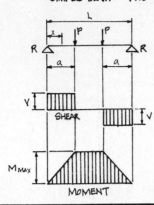

$$\text{EQUIVALENT TABULAR LOAD} \ldots \ldots = \frac{8Pa}{L}$$

$$R = V \qquad = P$$

$$M_{MAX} \text{ (BETWEEN LOADS)} \ldots \ldots = Pa$$

$$M_x \text{ (WHEN } x < a) \ldots \ldots = Px$$

$$\Delta_{MAX} \text{ (AT CENTER)} \ldots \ldots = \frac{Pa}{24EI}(3L^2 - 4a^2)$$

$$\Delta_x \text{ (WHEN } x < a) \ldots \ldots = \frac{Px}{6EI}(3La - 3a^2 - x^2)$$

$$\Delta_x \text{ [WHEN } x > a \text{ AND } < (L-a)] \ldots = \frac{Pa}{6EI}(3Lx - 3x^2 - a^2)$$

SHEAR

MOMENT

SIMPLE BEAM — TWO EQUAL CONCENTRATED LOADS UNSYMMETRICALLY PLACED

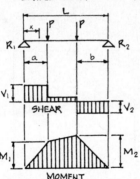

$$R_1 = V_1 \text{(MAX. WHEN } a < b) \ldots \ldots = \frac{P}{L}(L - a + b)$$

$$R_2 = V_2 \text{(MAX. WHEN } a < b) \ldots \ldots = \frac{P}{L}(L - b + a)$$

$$V_x \text{ [WHEN } x > a \text{ AND } < (L-b)] \ldots = \frac{P}{L}(b - a)$$

$$M_1 \text{ (MAX. WHEN } a > b) \ldots \ldots = R_1 a$$

$$M_2 \text{ (MAX. WHEN } a < b) \ldots \ldots = R_2 b$$

$$M_x \text{ (WHEN } x < a) \qquad = R_1 x$$

$$M_x \text{ [WHEN } x > a \text{ AND } < (L-b)] \qquad = R_1 x - P(x-a)$$

SHEAR

MOMENT

SIMPLE BEAM — TWO UNEQUAL CONCENTRATED LOADS UNSYMMETRICALLY PLACED

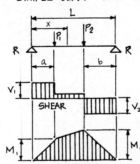

$$R_1 = V_1 \ldots \ldots = \frac{P_1(L-a) + P_2 b}{L}$$

$$R_2 = V_2 \ldots \ldots = \frac{P_1 a + P_2(L-b)}{L}$$

$$V_x \text{ [WHEN } x > a \text{ AND } < (L-b)] \ldots = R_1 - P_1$$

$$M_1 \text{ (MAX. WHEN } R_1 < P_1) \ldots \ldots = R_1 a$$

$$M_2 \text{ (MAX. WHEN } R_2 < P_2) \ldots \ldots = R_2 b$$

$$M_x \text{ (WHEN } x < a) \ldots \ldots = R_1 x$$

$$M_x \text{ [WHEN } x > a \text{ AND } < (L-b)] \cdot = R_1 x - P_1(x-a)$$

SHEAR

MOMENT

SIMPE BEAM — TWO EQUAL CONCENTRATED MOVING LOADS

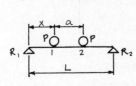

$$R_{MAX} \quad V_{1MAX} \text{ (AT } x = 0) \ldots \ldots = P\left(2 - \frac{a}{L}\right)$$

$$M_{MAX} \begin{cases} \left[\begin{array}{l} \text{WHEN } a < (2-\sqrt{2})L = .586L \\ \text{UNDED LOAD I AT } x = \frac{1}{2}\left(L - \frac{a}{2}\right) \end{array}\right] \ldots = \frac{P}{2L}\left(L - \frac{a}{2}\right)^2 \\[2em] \left[\begin{array}{l} \text{WHEN } a > (2-\sqrt{2})L = .586L \\ \text{WITH ONE LOAD AT CENTER OF SPAN} \end{array}\right] = \frac{PL}{4} \end{cases}$$

CONCRETE REINFORCING STEEL INSTITUTE

BEAM DIAGRAMS AND FORMULAS

SIMPLE BEAM—TWO UNEQUAL CONCENTRATED MOVING LOAD

$$R_{1\,max} = V_{1\,max} \quad (\text{AT } x=0) \ldots\ldots\ldots\ldots = P_1 + P_2\left(\frac{-a}{L}\right)$$

$P_1 = P_2$

$M_{max}\begin{cases} \left[\text{UNDER } P_1 \text{ AT } x=\frac{1}{2}\left(L - \frac{P_2 a}{P_1+P_2}\right)\right] = (P_1+P_2)\frac{x^2}{L} \\[2mm] \left[\begin{array}{l}M_{max} \text{ MAY OCCUR WITH LARGER LOAD} \\ \text{AT CENTER OF SPAN AND OTHER} \\ \text{LOAD OFF SPAN}\end{array}\right] = \frac{P_1 L}{4} \end{cases}$

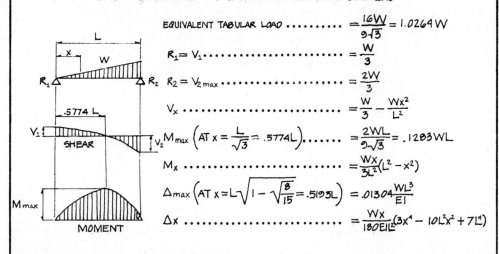

SIMPLE BEAM—LOAD INCREASING UNIFORMLY TO ONE END

EQUIVALENT TABULAR LOAD $\ldots\ldots\ldots = \dfrac{16W}{9\sqrt{3}} = 1.0264\,W$

$R_1 = V_1 \ldots\ldots\ldots\ldots\ldots\ldots\ldots = \dfrac{W}{3}$

$R_2 = V_{2\,max} \ldots\ldots\ldots\ldots\ldots\ldots = \dfrac{2W}{3}$

$V_x \ldots\ldots\ldots\ldots\ldots\ldots\ldots\ldots = \dfrac{W}{3} - \dfrac{Wx^2}{L^2}$

$M_{max}\left(\text{AT } x=\dfrac{L}{\sqrt{3}} = .5774L\right)\ldots\ldots = \dfrac{2WL}{9\sqrt{3}} = .1283\,WL$

$M_x \ldots\ldots\ldots\ldots\ldots\ldots\ldots\ldots = \dfrac{Wx}{3L^2}(L^2 - x^2)$

$\Delta_{max}\left(\text{AT } x=L\sqrt{1-\sqrt{\dfrac{8}{15}}} = .5193L\right) = .01304\dfrac{WL^3}{EI}$

$\Delta x \ldots\ldots\ldots\ldots\ldots\ldots\ldots = \dfrac{Wx}{180EIL^2}(3x^4 - 10L^2 x^2 + 7L^4)$

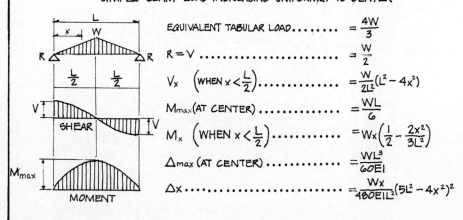

SIMPLE BEAM—LOAD INCREASING UNIFORMLY TO CENTER

EQUIVALENT TABULAR LOAD $\ldots\ldots\ldots = \dfrac{4W}{3}$

$R = V \ldots\ldots\ldots\ldots\ldots\ldots\ldots = \dfrac{W}{2}$

$V_x \quad \left(\text{WHEN } x < \dfrac{L}{2}\right)\ldots\ldots\ldots = \dfrac{W}{2L^2}(L^2 - 4x^2)$

$M_{max}\,(\text{AT CENTER}) \ldots\ldots\ldots\ldots = \dfrac{WL}{6}$

$M_x \quad \left(\text{WHEN } x < \dfrac{L}{2}\right)\ldots\ldots\ldots = Wx\left(\dfrac{1}{2} - \dfrac{2x^2}{3L^2}\right)$

$\Delta_{max}\,(\text{AT CENTER}) \ldots\ldots\ldots = \dfrac{WL^3}{60EI}$

$\Delta x \ldots\ldots\ldots\ldots\ldots\ldots\ldots = \dfrac{Wx}{480EIL^2}(5L^2 - 4x^2)^2$

BEAM DIAGRAMS AND FORMULAS

BEAM OVERHANGING ONE SUPPORT—UNIFORMLY DISTRIBUTED LOAD

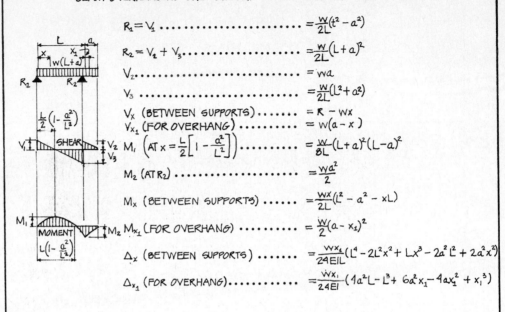

$$R_1 = V_1 \dots\dots\dots\dots\dots\dots = \frac{w}{2L}(L^2 - a^2)$$

$$R_2 = V_2 + V_3 \dots\dots\dots\dots = \frac{w}{2L}(L+a)^2$$

$$V_2 \dots\dots\dots\dots\dots\dots\dots = wa$$

$$V_3 \dots\dots\dots\dots\dots\dots\dots = \frac{w}{2L}(L^2 + a^2)$$

$$V_x \text{ (BETWEEN SUPPORTS)} \dots\dots = R - wx$$

$$V_{x_1} \text{ (FOR OVERHANG)} \dots\dots\dots = w(a - x)$$

$$M_1 \left(\text{AT } x = \frac{L}{2}\left[1 - \frac{a^2}{L^2}\right] \right) \dots\dots = \frac{w}{8L}(L+a)^2(L-a)^2$$

$$M_2 \text{ (AT } R_2) \dots\dots\dots\dots\dots = \frac{wa^2}{2}$$

$$M_x \text{ (BETWEEN SUPPORTS)} \dots\dots = \frac{wx}{2L}(L^2 - a^2 - xL)$$

$$M_{x_1} \text{ (FOR OVERHANG)} \dots\dots\dots = \frac{w}{2}(a - x_1)^2$$

$$\Delta_x \text{ (BETWEEN SUPPORTS)} \dots\dots = \frac{wx_1}{24EIL}(L^4 - 2L^2x^2 + Lx^3 - 2a^2L^2 + 2a^2x^2)$$

$$\Delta_{x_1} \text{ (FOR OVERHANG)} \dots\dots\dots = \frac{wx_1}{24EI}(4a^2L - L^3 + 6a^2x_1 - 4ax_1^2 + x_1^3)$$

BEAM OVERHANGING ONE SUPPORT—UNIFORMLY DISTRIBUTED LOAD ON OVERHANG

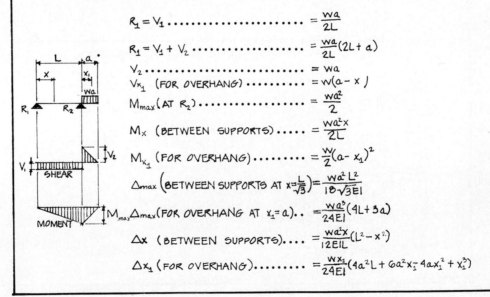

$$R_1 = V_1 \dots\dots\dots\dots\dots\dots = \frac{wa}{2L}$$

$$R_1 = V_1 + V_2 \dots\dots\dots\dots\dots = \frac{wa}{2L}(2L + a)$$

$$V_2 \dots\dots\dots\dots\dots\dots\dots = wa$$

$$V_{x_1} \text{ (FOR OVERHANG)} \dots\dots\dots = w(a - x)$$

$$M_{max} \text{ (AT } R_2) \dots\dots\dots\dots\dots = \frac{wa^2}{2}$$

$$M_x \text{ (BETWEEN SUPPORTS)} \dots\dots = \frac{wa^2x}{2L}$$

$$M_{x_1} \text{ (FOR OVERHANG)} \dots\dots\dots = \frac{w}{2}(a - x_1)^2$$

$$\Delta_{max}\left(\text{BETWEEN SUPPORTS AT } x = \frac{L}{\sqrt{3}}\right) = \frac{wa^2L^2}{18\sqrt{3}EI}$$

$$M_{max}\Delta_{max} \text{ (FOR OVERHANG AT } x_1 = a) \dots = \frac{wa^3}{24EI}(4L + 3a)$$

$$\Delta_x \text{ (BETWEEN SUPPORTS)} \dots\dots = \frac{wa^2x}{12EIL}(L^2 - x^2)$$

$$\Delta_{x_1} \text{ (FOR OVERHANG)} \dots\dots\dots = \frac{wx_1}{24EI}(4a^2L + 6a^2x_1 - 4ax_1^2 + x_1^3)$$

CONCRETE REINFORCING STEEL INSTITUTE

BEAM DIAGRAMS AND FORMULAS

BEAM OVERHANGING ONE SUPPORT—UNIFORMLY DISTRIBUTED LOAD BETWEEN SUPPORTS

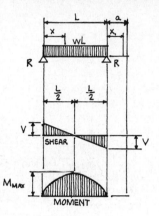

$$\text{EQUIVALENT TABULAR LOAD} \dots = wL$$

$$R = V \dots = \frac{wL}{2}$$

$$V_x \dots = w\left(\frac{L}{2} - x\right)$$

$$M_{MAX} \text{ (AT CENTER)} \dots = \frac{wL^2}{8}$$

$$M_x \dots = \frac{wx}{2}(L - x)$$

$$\Delta_{MAX} \text{ (AT CENTER)} \dots = \frac{5wL^4}{384EI}$$

$$\Delta x \dots = \frac{wx}{24EI}(l^3 - 2Lx^2 + x^3)$$

$$\Delta x_1 \dots = \frac{wL^3 x_1}{24EI}$$

BEAM OVERHANGING ONE SUPPORT—CONCENTRATED LOAD AT END OF OVERHANG

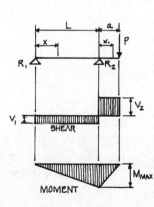

$$R_1 = V_1 \dots = \frac{Pa}{L}$$

$$R_2 = V_1 + V_2 \dots = \frac{P}{L}(L + a)$$

$$V_2 \dots = P$$

$$M_{MAX} \text{(AT } R_2) \dots = Pa$$

$$M_x \text{ (BETWEEN SUPPORTS)} \dots = \frac{Pax}{L}$$

$$M_{x_1} \text{ (FOR OVERHANG)} \dots = P(a - x_1)$$

$$\Delta_{MAX}\left(\text{BETWEEN SUPPORTS AT } x = \frac{L}{\sqrt{3}}\right) \dots = \frac{PaL^2}{9\sqrt{3}EI} = .06415\frac{PaL^2}{EI}$$

$$\Delta_{MAX} \text{ (FOR OVERHANG AT } x_1 = a) \dots = \frac{Pa^2}{3EI}(L + a)$$

$$\Delta x \text{ (BETWEEN SUPPORTS)} \dots = \frac{Pax}{6EIL}(L^2 - x^2)$$

$$\Delta x_1 \text{ (FOR OVERHANG)} \dots = \frac{Px}{6EI}(2aL + 3ax_1 - x_1^2)$$

CONCRETE REINFORCING STEEL INSTITUTE

BEAM DIAGRAMS AND FORMULAS

BEAM OVERHANGING ONE SUPPORT—CONCENTRATED LOAD AT ANY POINT BETWEEN SUPPORTS

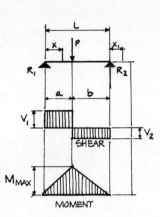

EQUIVALENT TABULAR LOAD . . . . $= \dfrac{8Pab}{L^2}$

$R_1 = V_1$ (MAX WHEN $a < b$) . . . . $= \dfrac{Pb}{L}$

$R_2 = V_2$ (MAX WHEN $a > b$) . . . . $= \dfrac{Pa}{L}$

M_{MAX} (AT POINT OF LOAD) . . . . $= \dfrac{Pab}{L}$

M_x (WHEN $x < a$) . . . . $= \dfrac{Pbx}{L}$

$\Delta_{MAX} \left[\text{AT } x = \sqrt{\dfrac{a(a+2b)}{3}} \text{ WHEN } a > b \right] = \dfrac{Pab(a+2b)\sqrt{3a(a+2b)}}{27EIL}$

Δ_a (AT POINT OF LOAD) . . . . $= \dfrac{Pa^2 b^2}{3EIL}$

Δ_x (WHEN $x < a$) . . . . $= \dfrac{Pbx}{6EIL}(L^2 - b^2 - x^2)$

Δ_x (WHEN $x > a$) . . . . $= \dfrac{Pa(L-x)}{6EIL}(2Lx - x^2 - a^2)$

Δ_{x_1} . . . . $= \dfrac{Pabx_1}{6EIL}(L+a)$

BEAM FIXED AT ONE END, SUPPORTED AT OTHER—UNIFORMLY DISTRIBUTED LOAD

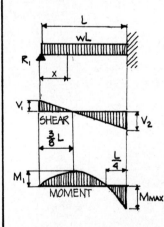

EQUIVALENT TABULAR LOAD . . . . $= wL$

$R_1 = V_1$ . . . . $= \dfrac{3wL}{8}$

$R_2 = V_2 \, MAX$ . . . . $= \dfrac{5wL}{8}$

V_x . . . . $= R_1 - wx$

M_{MAX} . . . . $= \dfrac{wL^2}{8}$

$M_1 \ \left(\text{AT } x = \dfrac{3}{8}L \right)$ . . . . $= \dfrac{9}{128}wL^2$

M_x . . . . $= R_1 x - \dfrac{wx^2}{2}$

$\Delta_{MAX} \left[\text{AT } x = \dfrac{1}{16}(1 + \sqrt{33}) = .4215L \right]. = \dfrac{wL^4}{185EI}$

Δ_x . . . . $= \dfrac{wx}{48EI}(L^3 - 3Lx^2 + 2x^3)$

CONCRETE REINFORCING STEEL INSTITUTE

BEAM DIAGRAMS AND FORMULAS

BEAM FIXED AT ONE END, SUPPORTED AT OTHER—CONCENTRATED LOAD AT CENTER

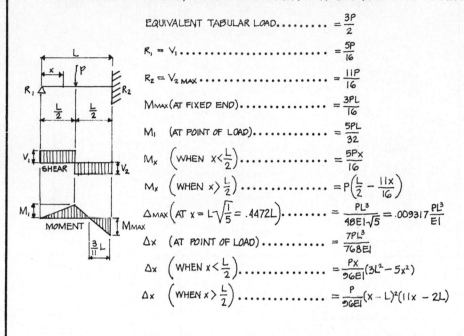

$$\text{EQUIVALENT TABULAR LOAD} = \frac{3P}{2}$$

$$R_1 = V_1 = \frac{5P}{16}$$

$$R_2 = V_{2\,MAX} = \frac{11P}{16}$$

$$M_{MAX} \text{(AT FIXED END)} = \frac{3PL}{16}$$

$$M_1 \text{ (AT POINT OF LOAD)} = \frac{5PL}{32}$$

$$M_x \left(\text{WHEN } x < \frac{L}{2}\right) = \frac{5Px}{16}$$

$$M_x \left(\text{WHEN } x > \frac{L}{2}\right) = P\left(\frac{L}{2} - \frac{11x}{16}\right)$$

$$\Delta_{MAX} \left(\text{AT } x = L\sqrt{\frac{1}{5}} = .4472L\right) = \frac{PL^3}{48EI\sqrt{5}} = .009317\frac{PL^3}{EI}$$

$$\Delta_x \text{ (AT POINT OF LOAD)} = \frac{7PL^3}{768EI}$$

$$\Delta_x \left(\text{WHEN } x < \frac{L}{2}\right) = \frac{Px}{96EI}(3L^2 - 5x^2)$$

$$\Delta_x \left(\text{WHEN } x > \frac{L}{2}\right) = \frac{P}{96EI}(x - L)^2(11x - 2L)$$

BEAM FIXED AT ONE END, SUPPORTED AT OTHER—CONCENTRATED LOAD AT ANY POINT

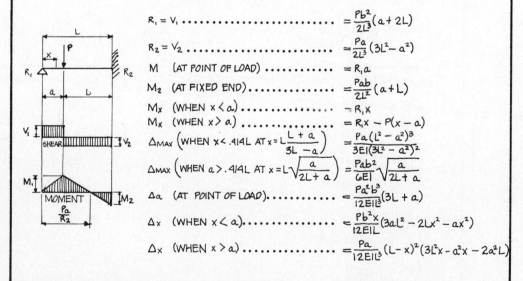

$$R_1 = V_1 = \frac{Pb^2}{2L^3}(a + 2L)$$

$$R_2 = V_2 = \frac{Pa}{2L^3}(3L^2 - a^2)$$

$$M \text{ (AT POINT OF LOAD)} = R_1 a$$

$$M_2 \text{ (AT FIXED END)} = \frac{Pab}{2L^2}(a + L)$$

$$M_x \text{ (WHEN } x < a) = R_1 x$$

$$M_x \text{ (WHEN } x > a) = R_1 x - P(x - a)$$

$$\Delta_{MAX} \left(\text{WHEN } x < .414L \text{ AT } x = L\frac{L + a}{3L - a}\right) = \frac{Pa(L^2 - a^2)^3}{3EI(3L^2 - a^2)^2}$$

$$\Delta_{MAX} \left(\text{WHEN } a > .414L \text{ AT } x = L\sqrt{\frac{a}{2L + a}}\right) = \frac{Pab^2}{6EI}\sqrt{\frac{a}{2L + a}}$$

$$\Delta_a \text{ (AT POINT OF LOAD)} = \frac{Pa^2 b^3}{12EIL^3}(3L + a)$$

$$\Delta_x \text{ (WHEN } x < a) = \frac{Pb^2 x}{12EIL}(3aL^2 - 2Lx^2 - ax^2)$$

$$\Delta_x \text{ (WHEN } x > a) = \frac{Pa}{12EIL^3}(L - x)^2(3L^2 x - a^2 x - 2a^2 L)$$

CONCRETE REINFORCING STEEL INSTITUTE

BEAM DIAGRAMS AND FORMULAS

BEAM FIXED AT BOTH ENDS — UNIFORMLY DISTRIBUTED LOADS

EQUIVALENT TABULAR LOAD $\dots\dots = \dfrac{2wL}{3}$

$R = V \dots\dots\dots = \dfrac{wL}{2}$

$V_x \dots\dots\dots = w\left(\dfrac{L}{2} - x\right)$

M_{MAX} (AT ENDS) $\dots\dots = \dfrac{wL^2}{12}$

M_1 (AT CENTER) $\dots\dots = \dfrac{wL^2}{24}$

$M_x \dots\dots\dots = \dfrac{w}{12}(6Lx - L^2 - 6x^2)$

Δ_{MAX} (AT CENTER) $\dots\dots = \dfrac{wL^4}{384EI}$

$\Delta_x \dots\dots\dots = \dfrac{wx^2}{24EI}(L-x)^2$

BEAM FIXED AT BOTH ENDS — CONCENTRATED LOAD AT CENTER

EQUIVALENT TABULAR LOAD $\dots\dots = P$

$R = V \dots\dots\dots = \dfrac{P}{2}$

M (AT CENTER AND ENDS) $\dots\dots = \dfrac{PL}{8}$

M_x $\left(\text{WHEN } x < \dfrac{L}{2}\right) \dots\dots = \dfrac{P}{8}(4x - L)$

Δ_{MAX} (AT CENTER) $\dots\dots = \dfrac{PL^3}{192EI}$

$\Delta_x \dots\dots\dots = \dfrac{Px^2}{48EI}(3L - 4x)$

BEAM FIXED AT BOTH ENDS — CONCENTRATED LOAD AT ANY POINT

$R_1 = V_1$ (MAX WHEN $a < b$) $\dots\dots = \dfrac{Pb^2}{L^3}(3a + b)$

$R = V$ (MAX WHEN $a > b$) $\dots\dots = \dfrac{Pa^2}{L^3}(a + 3b)$

M_1 (MAX WHEN $a < b$) $\dots\dots = \dfrac{Pab^2}{L^2}$

M_2 (MAX WHEN $a > b$) $\dots\dots = \dfrac{Pa^2b}{L^2}$

M_a (AT POINT OF LOAD) $\dots\dots = \dfrac{2Pa^2b^2}{L^3}$

M_x (WHEN $x < a$) $\dots\dots = R_1 x - \dfrac{Pab^2}{L^2}$

Δ_{MAX} $\left(\text{WHEN } a > b \text{ AT } x = \dfrac{2aL}{3a+b}\right) = \dfrac{2Pa^3b^2}{3EI(3a + b)}$

Δ_a AT POINT OF LOAD $\dots\dots = \dfrac{Pa^3b^3}{3EIL^3}$

Δ_x (WHEN $x < a$) $\dots\dots = \dfrac{Pb^2x^2}{6EIL^3}(3aL - 3ax - bx)$

CONCRETE REINFORCING STEEL INSTITUTE

OCCUPANCY OR USE	LIVE LOAD (PSF)
ARMORIES AND DRILL ROOMS	150
ASSEMBLY HALLS	
FIXED SEATS	60
MOVABLE SEATS	100
BALCONY (EXTERIOR)	100
BOWLING ALLEY, POOLROOMS, ETC.	75
CORRIDORS	
FIRST FLOOR	100
OTHER FLOORS SAME AS OCCUPANCY SERVED.	
DANCE HALLS	100
DINING ROOMS AND RESTAURANTS	100
DWELLINGS (SEE RESIDENTIAL)	
GARAGES (PASSENGER CARS)	
150% OF MAX. WHEEL LOAD	
GYMNASIUMS	100
HOSPITALS	
OPERATING ROOMS	60
PRIVATE ROOMS	40
WARDS	40
HOTELS (SEE RESIDENTIAL)	
LIBRARIES	
READING ROOMS	60
STACKS	150
MANUFACTURING	125
MARQUEES	75
OFFICE BUILDINGS	
OFFICES	80
LOBBIES	100
PENAL INSTITUTIONS	
CELL BLOCKS	40
CORRIDORS	100

OCCUPANCY OR USE	LIVE LOAD (PSF)
RESIDENTIAL	
MULTIFAMILY HOUSING	
PRIVATE APTS	40
PUBLIC ROOMS	100
CORRIDORS	60
DWELLINGS	
FIRST FLOOR	40
SECOND FLOOR	30
ATTICS	20
ROOF LOADS	20
HOTELS	
GUEST ROOMS	40
PUBLIC ROOMS	100
CORRIDORS	100
PRIVATE CORRIDORS	60
REVIEWING STANDS AND BLEACHERS	100
SCHOOLS	
CLASS ROOMS	40
CORRIDORS	100
SIDEWALKS, DRIVEWAYS, AND AREAS SUBJECT TO VEHICULAR TRUCKING	250
SKATING RINKS	100
STAIRS, FIRE ESCAPES, AND EXITWAYS	100
STORAGE WAREHOUSES	
LIGHT LOADS	125
HEAVY LOADS	250
(SEE FOLLOWING PAGES FOR WEIGHTS OF STORED ITEMS)	
STORES	
RETAIL	

LIVE LOADS FOR VARIOUS OCCUPANCIES 1.25

OCCUPANCY OR USE	LIVE LOAD (PSI)
FIRST FLOOR	100
UPPER FLOORS	75
WHOLESALE	125
THEATERS	
AISLES, CORRIDORS, AND LOBBIES	100
ORCHESTRA FLOORS	60
BALCONIES	60
STAGE FLOORS	150
YARDS AND TERRACES	100

(CHECK LOCAL BUILDING CODES FOR REQUIRED LIVE LOADS THAT MAY BE DIFFERENT FROM THOSE GIVEN ABOVE.)

UNITED STATES DEPARTMENT OF COMMERCE, NATIONAL BUREAU OF STANDARDS

MATERIAL	WEIGHT PER CUBIC FOOT OF SPACE LB.	HEIGHT OF PILE FEET	WEIGHT PER SQUARE FOOT OF FLOOR LB.	RECOMMENDED LIVE LOAD LB. PER SQ. FOOT
BUILDING MATERIALS				
ASBESTOS	50	6	300	
BRICKS, BUILDING	45	6	270	
BRICKS, FIRE CLAY	75	6	450	
CEMENT, NATURAL	59	5	354	300
CEMENT, PORTLAND	72 TO 105	6	432 TO 630	TO
GYPSUM	50	6	300	400
LIME AND PLASTER	53	5	265	
TILES	50	6	300	
WOODS, BULK	45	6	270	
DRUGS, PAINTS, OIL, ETC.				
ALUM, PEARL, IN BARRELS	33	6	198	
BLEACHING POWDER, IN HOGSHEADS	31	3½	102	
BLUE VITRIOL, IN BARRELS	45	5	226	
GLYCERINE, IN CASES	52	6	312	
LINSEED OIL, IN BARRELS	36	6	216	
LINSEED OIL, IN IRON DRUMS	45	4	180	
LOGWOOD EXTRACT, IN BOXES	70	5	350	
ROSIN, IN BARRELS	48	6	288	
SHELLAC, GUM	38	6	228	200
SOAPS	50	6	300	TO
SODA ASH, IN HOGSHEADS	62	2¾	167	300
SODA, CAUSTIC, IN IRON DRUMS	88	3⅜	294	
SODA, SILICATE, IN BARRELS	53	6	318	
SULPHURIC ACID	60	1⅝	100	
TOILET ARTICLES	35	6	210	
VARNISHES	55	6	330	
WHITE LEAD PASTE, IN CANS	174	3½	610	
WHITE LEAD, DRY	86	4¾	408	
RED LEAD AND LITHARGE, DRY	132	3¾	495	
DRY GOODS, COTTON, WOOL, ETC.				
BURLAP, IN BALES	43	6	258	
CARPETS AND RUGS	30	6	180	
COIR YARN, IN BALES	33	8	264	
COTTON, IN BALES, AMERICAN	30	8	240	
COTTON, IN BALES, FOREIGN	40	8	320	
COTTON, BLEACHED GOODS, IN CASES	28	8	224	
COTTON FLANNEL, IN CASES	12	8	96	
COTTON SHEETING, IN CASES	23	8	184	
COTTON YARN, IN CASES	25	8	200	
EXCELSIOR, COMPRESSED	19	8	152	200
HEMP, ITALIAN, COMPRESSED	22	8	176	TO
HEMP, MANILA, COMPRESSED	30	8	240	250
JUTE, COMPRESSED	42	8	328	
LINEN DAMASK, IN CASES	50	5	250	
LINEN GOODS, IN CASES	30	8	240	
LINEN TOWELS, IN CASES	40	6	240	
SILK AND SILK GOODS	45	8	350	
SISAL, COMPRESSED	21	8	168	
TOW, COMPRESSED	29	8	232	
WOOL, IN BALES, COMPRESSED	48			
WOOL, IN BALES, NOT COMPRESSED	13	8	104	
WOOL, WORSTEDS, IN CASES	27	8	216	

AMERICAN INSTITUTE OF STEEL CONSTRUCTION

MATERIAL	WEIGHT PER CUBIC FOOT OF SPACE LB.	HEIGHT OF PILE FEET	WEIGHT PER SQUARE FOOT OF FLOOR LB.	RECOMMENDED LIVE LOAD LB. PER SQ. FT
GROCERIES , WINES , LIQUORS , ETC.				
BEANS , IN BAGS	40	8	320	
BEVERAGES	40	8	320	
CANNED GOODS , IN CASES	58	6	348	
CEREALS	45	8	360	
COCOA	35	8	280	
COFFEE , ROASTED , IN BAGS	33	8	264	
COFFEE , GREEN , IN BAGS	39	8	312	
DATES , IN CASES	55	6	330	
FIGS , IN CASES	74	5	370	
FLOUR , IN BARRELS	40	5	200	250
FRUITS , FRESH	35	8	280	TO
MEAT AND MEAT PRODUCTS	45	6	270	300
MILK , CONDENSED	50	6	300	
MOLASSES , IN BARRELS	48	5	240	
RICE , IN BAGS	58	6	348	
SAL SODA , IN BARRELS	46	5	230	
SALT , IN BAGS	70	5	350	
SOAP POWDER , IN CASES	38	8	304	
STARCH , IN BARRELS	25	6	150	
SUGAR , IN BARRELS	43	5	215	
SUGAR , IN CASES	51	6	306	
TEA , IN CHESTS	25	8	200	
WINES AND LIQUORS , IN BARRELS	38	6	228	
HARDWARE , ETC.				
AUTOMOBILE PARTS	40	8	320	
CHAIN	100	6	600	
CUTLERY	45	8	360	
DOOR CHECKS	45	6	270	
ELECTRICAL GOODS AND MACHINERY	40	8	320	
HINGES	64	6	384	
LOCKS , IN CASES , PACKED	31	6	186	
MACHINERY , LIGHT	20	8	160	
PLUMBING , FIXTURES	30	8	240	300
PLUMBING , SUPPLIES	55	6	336	TO
SASH FASTENERS	48	6	288	400
SCREWS	101	6	606	
SHAFTING STEEL	125			
SHEET TIN , IN BOXES	278	2	556	
TOOLS , SMALL , METAL	75	6	450	
WIRE CABLES ON REELS			425	
WIRE , INSULATED COPPER , IN COILS	63	5	315	
WIRE , GALVANIZED IRON , IN COILS	74	4½	333	
WIRE , MAGNET , ON SPOOLS	75	6	450	
MISCELLANEOUS				
AUTOMOBILE TIRES	30	6	180	
AUTOMOBILES , UNCRATED	8		64	
BOOKS (SOLIDLY PACKED)	65	6	390	
FURNITURE	20			
GLASS AND CHINAWARE , IN CRATES	40	8	320	
HIDES AND LEATHER , IN BALES	20	8	160	
LEATHER AND LEATHER GOODS	40	8	320	
PAPER , NEWSPAPER , AND STRAWBOARDS	35	6	210	
PAPER , WRITING AND CALENDARED	50	6	360	
ROPE , IN COILS	32	6	192	
RUBBER , CRUDE	50	8	400	
TOBACCO , BALES	35	8	280	

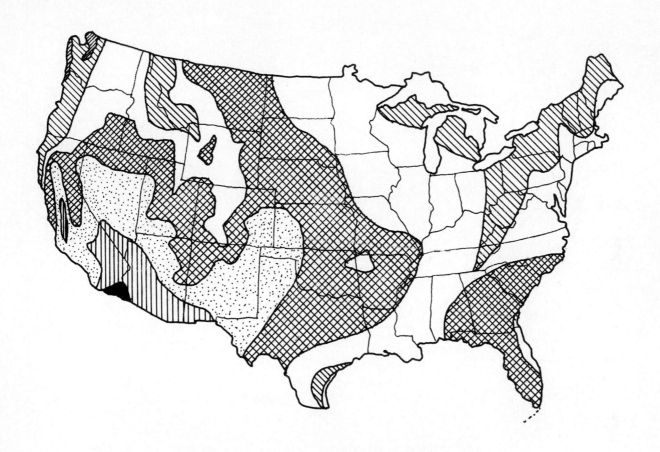

AVERAGE HOURS OF SUNSHINE PER YEAR

1600   2000   2400

2800   3200   3600

4000

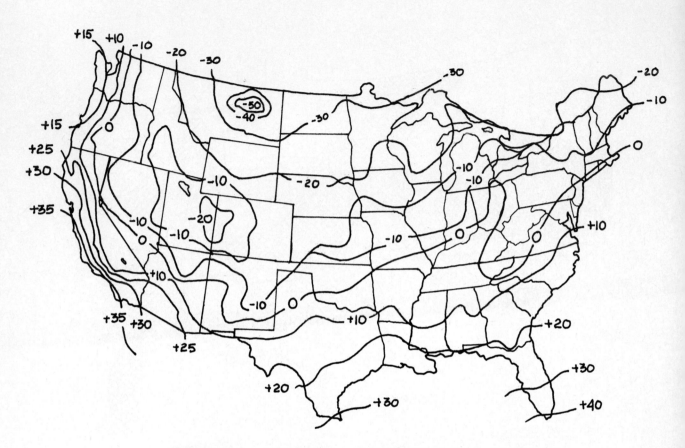

AVERAGE OUTSIDE TEMPERATURE ZONES
FOR DESIGN OF THERMAL INSULATION

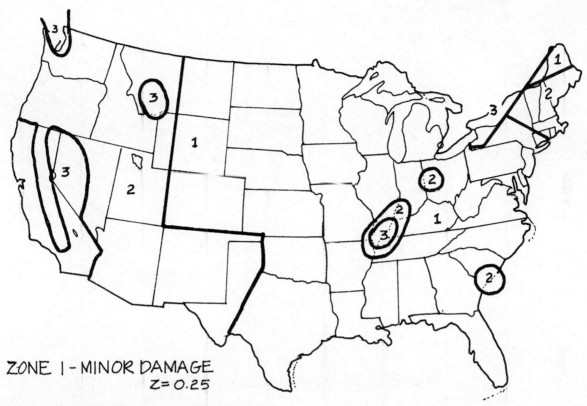

ZONE 1 - MINOR DAMAGE
        Z= 0.25

ZONE 2 - MODERATE DAMAGE
        Z= 0 50

ZONE 3 - MAJOR DAMAGE
        Z= 1.00

ZONES OF APPROXIMATELY EQUAL SEISMIC PROBABILITY.
BASED ON EARTHQUAKE DATA COMPILED BY THE ENVIRON-
-MENTAL SCIENCE SERVICES ADMINISTRATION.

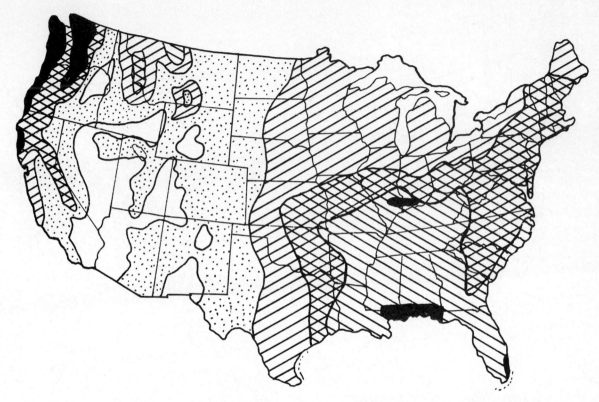

INCHES OF RAINFALL / AVERAGE YEAR

MORE THAN 60"		20-40"	
50-60"		10-20"	
40-50"		LESS THAN 10"	

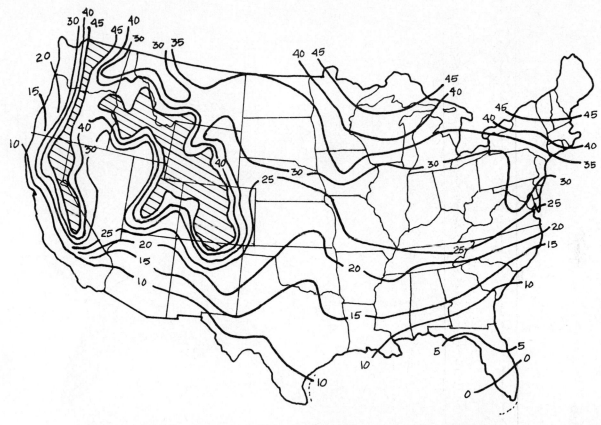

ISOTHERM LINES OF EQUAL SNOW WEIGHT

SNOW WEIGHT DATA FOR SHADED AREAS SHOULD
BE DETERMINED FROM LOCAL WEATHER SOURCES.

SNOW LOAD lb. per sq.ft.	SNOW LOAD OR LIVE LOAD ON HORIZONTAL PROJECTION lb./sq. ft. for roof slopes (°F)			
	0° to 15°	16° to 30°	31° to 45°	46° to 60°
40	40	30	15	10
30	30	25	12	10
25	25	20	12	10
20	20	15	10	10
15	15	12	10	10

U.S. WEATHER BUREAU

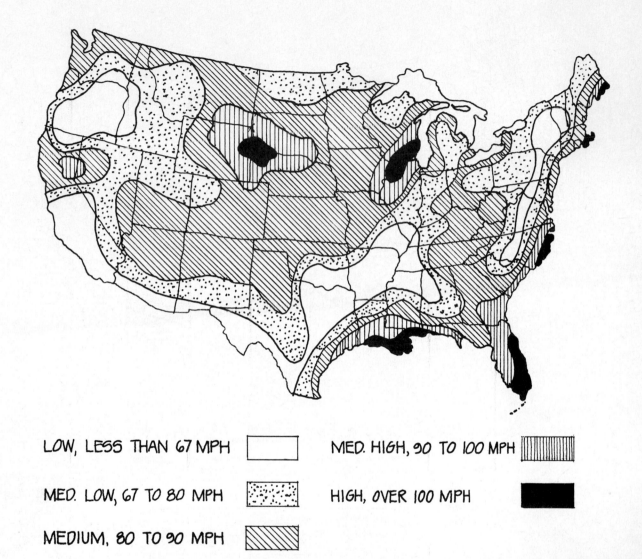

LOW, LESS THAN 67 MPH

MED. LOW, 67 TO 80 MPH

MEDIUM, 80 TO 90 MPH

MED. HIGH, 90 TO 100 MPH

HIGH, OVER 100 MPH

U.S. WEATHER BUREAU

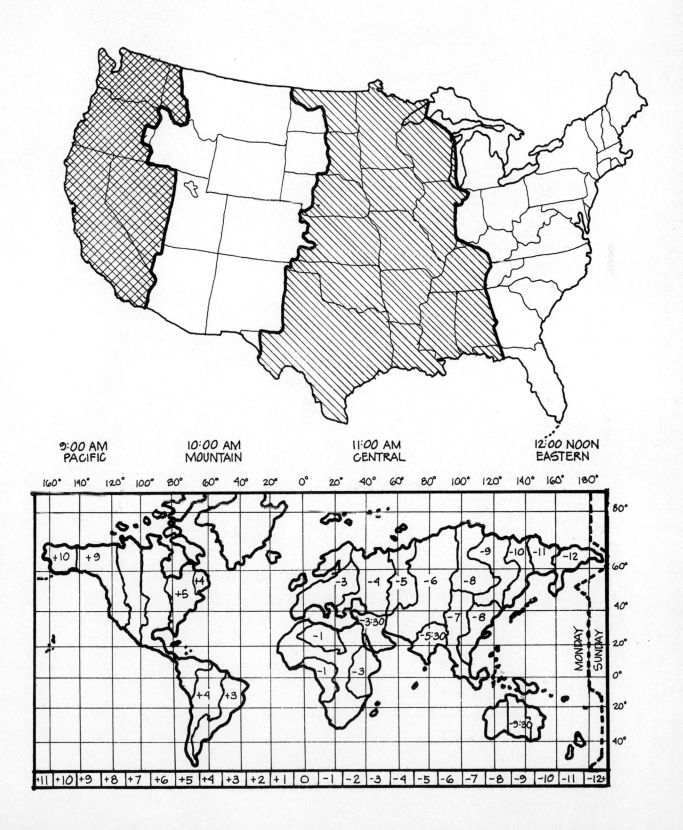

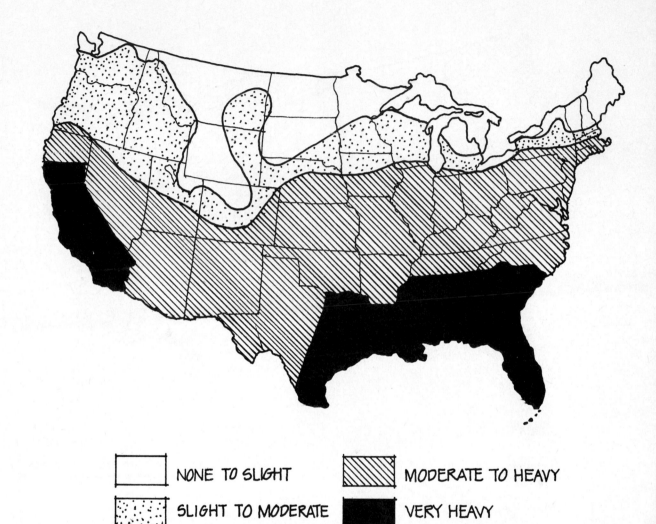

NONE TO SLIGHT   MODERATE TO HEAVY

SLIGHT TO MODERATE   VERY HEAVY

LINES DEFINING AREAS ARE APPROXIMATE ONLY. CONTACT
LOCAL AUTORITIES FOR SPECIFIC CONDITIONS.

U.S. DEPARTMENT OF HOUSING AND URBAN DEVELOPMENT,
FEDERAL HOUSING ADMINISTRATION (FHA)

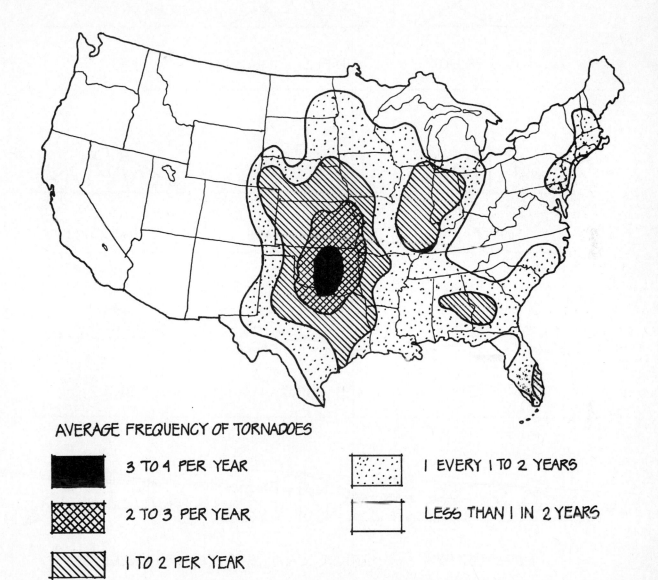

AVERAGE FREQUENCY OF TORNADOES

- ■ 3 TO 4 PER YEAR
- ▨ 2 TO 3 PER YEAR
- ▧ 1 TO 2 PER YEAR
- ⋯ 1 EVERY 1 TO 2 YEARS
- ☐ LESS THAN 1 IN 2 YEARS

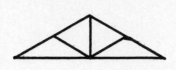

KING POST

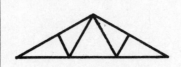

SIMPLE FINK

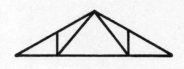

PRATT

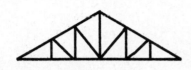

HOWE

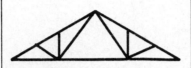

SIMPLE FAN

BELGIAN

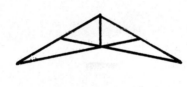

SCISSORS

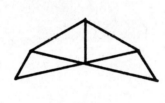

CURB

SHED

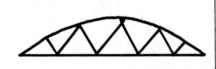

BOWSTRING

PARKER CAMELBACK

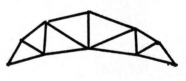

CRESCENT

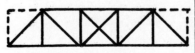

PRATT
(PARALLEL CHORDS)

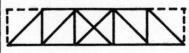

HOWE
(PARALLEL CHORDS)

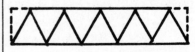

WARREN
(PARALLEL CHORDS)

FLAT TRUSSES MAY ALSO HAVE SLIGHTLY CAMBERED OR PITCHED TOPS

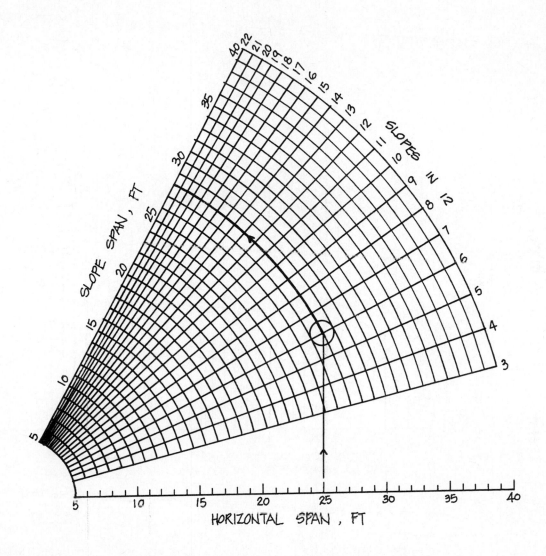

SPAN CONVERSION. EXAMPLE: 25 FT HORIZONTAL SPAN = 28 FT SLOPE SPAN WHEN SLOPE IS 6 IN 12. USE 28 FT IN DETERMINING FOOTAGE.

AMERICAN INSTITUTE OF TIMBER CONSTRUCTION

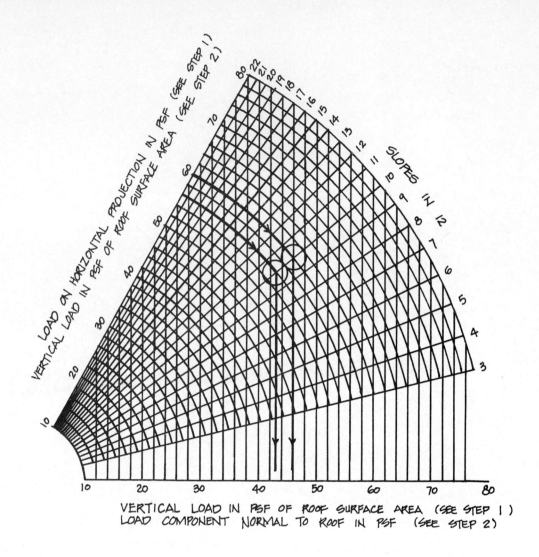

VERTICAL LOAD IN PSF OF ROOF SURFACE AREA (SEE STEP 1)
LOAD COMPONENT NORMAL TO ROOF IN PSF (SEE STEP 2)

LOAD CONVERSION. EXAMPLE: 60 PSF LIVE LOAD AND 10 PSF DEAD LOAD ON 10 IN 12 SLOPE. STEP 1: 60 PSF LIVE LOAD ON HORIZONTAL PROJECTION = 46 PSF OF ROOF SURFACE AREA VERTICAL LOAD ON 10 IN 12 ROOF SLOPE. STEP 2: 10 PSF OF ROOF SURFACE AREA DEAD LOAD PLUS 46 PSF OF ROOF SURFACE AREA LIVE LOAD = 56 PSF OF ROOF SURFACE AREA COMBINED LOAD ACTING VERTICALLY ; 56 PSF OF ROOF SURFACE AREA VERTICAL TOTAL LOAD = 43 PSF NORMAL TO ROOF CAUSING BENDING AND DEFLECTION.

AMERICAN INSTITUTE OF TIMBER CONSTRUCTION

	LENGTH	WIDTH	HEIGHT	WEIGHT
ALFA ROMEO VOLARE	171.1	65.5	52.5	2710
AMC PACER	172.7	77.0	52.8	3204
AMC SPIRIT	166.8	71.1	51.7	2517
BUICK ELECTRA	222.1	77.2	55.9	3985
BUICK LA SABRE	218.2	77.2	55.7	3570
BUICK SKYLARK	200.2	72.7	53.1	3414
CADILLAC DE VILLE	221.2	76.4	55.3	4344
CHEVROLET CHEVETTE	162.6	61.8	52.8	
CHEVROLET MALIBU	192.7	71.5	54.2	3210
CHEVROLET MONTE CARLO	200.4	71.5	53.9	
CHEVROLET MONZA	174.2	65.4	50.2	
CHRYSLER LA BARON 2 DR.	206.1	72.8	55.3	3429
DATSUN 210	169.9	63.0		
DODGE ASPEN	201.2	72.9	55.3	3141
DODGE COLT	162.6	60.4	52.8	2025
DODGE OMNI	164.8	66.2	53.7	2195
DODGE ST. REGIS	220.2	77.1	54.5	3675
FORD FAIRMONT	195.8	71.0	52.3	2670
FORD FIESTA	147.1	61.7	52.5	1770
FORD GRANADA	197.8	71.0	53.3	3249
FORD MUSTANG	179.1	67.4	51.6	2750
FORD THUNDERBIRD	217.7	78.5	52.8	4028
HONDA ACCORD	163.2	53.8	52.6	2108
HONDA CIVIC	148.6	63.8		
* LINCOLN CONTINENTAL	230.3	79.7	54.1	4787
LINCOLN VERSAILLES	201.0	74.5	54.1	3848
MAZDA GLC	154.0	64.0	48.5	2000
MERCEDES BENZ 300 CD	191.0	70.0	51.5	3210
MERCURY CAPRI	179.1	69.1	51.5	2548
MERCURY COUGAR	215.5	78.6		
OLDSMOBILE CUTLASS	197.7	71.9	54.5	3172
OLDSMOBILE DELTA 88	217.5	76.8	55.2	3624
OLDSMOBILE OMEGA	199.6	72.9	53.7	3258
PLYMOUTH HORIZON	164.8	66.2	53.7	2197
PONTIAC FIREBIRD	198.1	73.0	47.0	3445
PONTIAC GRAND PRIX	201.4	72.7	50.5	3245
SUBARU 4 DR.	164.2	61.4		
TOYOTA CELICA	173.6	64.6	50.8	2015
TOYOTA COROLLA	170.0	63.6	50.6	2530
VOLKSWAGEN RABBIT	155.3	63.4	55.5	1950
VOLKSWAGEN SCIROCCO	155.7	63.9	55.7	2050

*   LONGEST AND WIDEST

	LENGTH	WIDTH	HEIGHT	WEIGHT
ALFA ROMEO SPIDER	161.1	64.4		
AMC PACER	173.9	77.2	52.6	3200
AMC SPIRIT	167.0	72.0	50.0	2700
AUDI 5000	190.1	70.0	50.5	2700
BUICK ELECTRA	220.2	78.1	51.5	3720
BUICK LE SABRE 2 DR.	217.4	78.1	51.5	3520
BUICK SKYLARK	181.1	67.7	49.0	2620
* CADILLAC DE VILLE	221.0	76.1	51.5	4320
CHEVROLET CHEVETTE	161.9	61.8	49.0	2120
CHEVROLET MALIBU	192.7	71.5	51.5	3180
CHEVROLET MONTE CARLO	200.4	71.5	51.0	3280
CHEVROLET MONZA	174.3	65.4	46.5	2770
CHRYSLER LE BARON 2 DR.	201.2	74.2	51.5	3460
DATSUN 210	165.0	62.2	49.0	2020
DODGE ASPEN 2 DR.	200.3	72.4	52.0	3330
DODGE COLT	157.0	62.0	49.0	1880
DODGE OMNI 4 DR.	164.8	65.8	50.5	2140
DODGE ST. REGIS	220.2	77.6	51.0	3830
FIAT BRAVA	172.0	65.0	50.0	2550
FORD FAIRMONT	197.4	71.0	51.0	2800
FORD FIESTA	147.0	61.7	50.0	1790
FORD GRANADA	199.7	74.5	51.0	3410
FORD MUSTANG 4 CY.	179.2	69.1	49.0	3610
FORD THUNDERBIRD	200.4	74.2	51.0	3340
HONDA ACCORD	171.9	63.8	48.5	2290
HONDA CIVIC	148.0	62.2	48.0	1850
** LINCOLN CONTINENTAL	219.0	78.1	52.0	4090
LINCOLN VERSAILLES	200.8	74.5	51.0	
MAZDA GLC	156.5	63.2	49.0	1980
MERCEDES BENZ 300 CD	187.5	70.3	51.5	
MERCURY CAPRI	179.2	69.1	49.0	
MERCURY COUGAR XR-7	200.4	74.2	50.0	3340
OLDSMOBILE CUTLASS 4 DR.	199.1	71.9	51.0	3240
OLDSMOBILE DELTA 88	218.4	76.3	52.0	3710
OLDSMOBILE OMEGA	181.8	69.8	49.0	2610
PLYMOUTH ARROW	170.1	63.0	47.0	
PLYMOUTH HORIZON 2 DR.	172.8	66.7	51.0	
PONTIAC FIREBIRD	198.1	73.0	47.0	3390
PONTIAC GRAND PRIX	201.4	72.7	50.5	3340
SUBARU DL	168.1	53.7		2150
TOYOTA CELICA	175.5	64.6	47.0	2410
TOYOTA COROLLA	166.3	63.4	49.0	2000
VOLKSWAGEN RABBIT	155.3	63.4	51.0	1870
VOLKSWAGEN	155.7	63.9	47.0	1990

*   LONGEST
**   WIDEST

	LENGTH	WIDTH	HEIGHT	WEIGHT
AMC EAGLE	183.2	72.3	55.8	3209
AMC SPIRIT	167.2	71.9	51.5	2665
BMW 528i	190.0	67.2	55.9	4210
* BUICK ELECTRA	221.3	75.9	55.0	4010
BUICK LE SABRE	218.4	75.9	55.0	4000
BUICK SKYLARK	181.1	69.1	53.5	2900
CADILLAC DE VILLE	221.1	75.4	54.6	4200
CHEVROLET CAMARO	197.6	74.5	50.1	
CHEVROLET CAPRICE SEDAN	212.1	75.3	55.2	
CHEVROLET CHEVETTE 4 DR.	164.9	61.8	52.9	
CHEVROLET CITATION X-11	176.7	68.3	53.1	2626
CHEVROLET MONTE CARLO	200.4	71.8	53.9	3350
CRYSLER CORDOBA	210.1	72.7	53.3	3446
CRYSLER LE BARON	205.7	74.2	55.3	3368
DATSUN 510	169.5	63.0	54.7	2195
DODGE COLT	156.8	62.4	50.5	1950
DODGE OMNI	164.8	65.8	53.1	2118
DODGE ST. REGIS	220.2	77.6	54.5	3644
FORD ESCORT	163.9	65.9	53.3	1987
FORD FAIRMONT 2 DR.	195.5	71.0	52.9	2673
FORD GRANADA	196.5	71.0	52.9	2880
FORD MUSTANG	179.1	67.4	51.4	2583
FORD THUNDERBIRD	200.4	74.1	53.0	3468
HONDA ACCORD 4 DR.	171.9	63.8	52.3	2249
HONDA CIVIC 4 DR.	161.0	62.2	54.2	1990
** LINCOLN CONTNENTAL	219.0	78.1	56.1	4068
MAZDA GLC SPORT	151.9	64.2	54.1	1880
MERCEDES BENZ 240D	190.9	70.3	56.6	3120
MERCURY CAPRI	179.1	69.1	51.4	2623
MERCURY COUGAR	196.5	71.0	53.0	2804
MERCURY LYNX	163.9	65.9	53.3	2066
OLDSMOBILE CUTLASS	199.1	71.9	55.9	3200
OLDSMOBILE DELTA 88	218.1	76.3	56.0	3500
OLDSMOBILE OMEGA	181.1	69.8	53.1	2500
PLYMOUTH HORIZON	164.9	65.8	53.1	2118
PONTIAC FIREBIRD	198.1	73.1		3200
PONTIAC GRAN PRIX	201.9	72.1	54.0	3500
RENAULT 18i	178.7	66.5	55.3	2261
TOYOTA COROLLA SR5	168.3	64.0	50.8	
TOYOTA CELICA	175.5	64.6	50.8	
VOLVO BERTONE	192.5	67.3	53.9	3111
VOLKSWAGON JETTA	167.8	63.4	55.5	1892
VOLKSWAGON RABBIT	155.3	63.4	55.5	2170

* LONGEST
** WIDEST

	OVERALL LENGTH	WHEEL BASE		OVERALL LENGTH	WHEEL BASE
AMC PACER WAGON	177.7	100.0	JEEP CJ-5	138.0	83.5
BUICK ESTATE WAGON	216.7	115.9	JEEP CHEROKEE	183.5	109.0
CHEVROLET IMPALA	214.7	116.0	JEEP PICKUP J-10	192.5	119.0
DATSUN 620 HUSTLER	169.3	100.2	PLYMOUTH VOYAGER	194.0	127.0
DODGE D-50 SPORT	184.6	109.4	SUBARU STATION DL.	164.8	96.7
DODGE VAN	194.0	127.0	TOYOTA CRUISER	152.0	90.0
FORD BRONCO	180.0	104.0	VOLKSWAGEN BUS	177.0	94.5
GMC (CHEV.) VAN	202.0	125.0	VOLKSWAGEN DASHER	173.1	97.2
INTERNATIONAL TERRA	184.0	118.0			

4 WHEEL DELIVERY

SCHOOL BUS

6 WHEEL DELIVERY

17 PASSENGER

10 WHEEL AND 8 WHEEL TRAILER

24 PASSENGER

14 WHEEL HIGHWAY

48 PASSENGER CITY BUS

18 WHEEL TRANSPORT

CALIF. CODE: 8° MAX. WIDTH, 13⁶ MAX. HEIGHT, 60° MAX. LENGTH, 79,800 LB. MAX. LOAD.

MINIMOTORHOMES

	OVERALL LENGTH	WHEEL BASE	OVERALL WIDTH	OVERALL WEIGHT	GROSS WEIGHT	SLEEPS
APACHE — 21	250	127	93	108	10,200	4-6
APACHE — 23	274	145	93	108	10,500	6
APACHE HUNTER	250	127	93	108	10,200	5-8
APECO ROADCRUISER	276	145	95	122	8,180	4
APECO RC IV	276	145	95	122	8,200	4
ARNOLD CAPE COD	294	145	94	120	11,000	6
BARTH 22 M	264	146	93	106	10,000	6
BLAZON 220 RD	271	146	92	114	8,024	6
BONANZA 8202	242	127	96	113	7,000	6
BONANZA 8221	266	145	96	113	7,700	6
BROUGHAM 195	248	127	96	112	9,000	6
BROUGHAM 222	270	145	96	112	10,500	6
BROUGHAM 250	300	163	96	112	10,500	6
CASUAL 170 CADDY	211	109	85	117	7,700	4-6
CASUAL 180 CARIB	219	138	85	117	8,400	4-6
CASUAL CHIEF	252	138	85	117	10,500	6
CHAMPION 927	204	109	84	114	8,200	4
CHAMPION 913	276	145	93	115	10,200	4
CHINOOK GAZELLE	208	110	78	81	4,600	4
CHINOOK CONCRS.	240	127	77	104	9,000	5
CHINOOK FUTURA	246	127	96	112	9,000	6
COACHMAN 18 RD	216	127	84	112	8,200	4
COACHMAN CADET	240	127	90	112	9,000	6
COACHMAN 22 RB	264	145	92	112	10,500	6
COACHMAN RB&L	288	163	92	112	11,500	4
COMET 20 SB-U	246	127	93	120	9,000	6
COMET 22 SB	270	145	93	120	10,500	6
CRUISE AIR A200	253	127	90	120	7,000	6
CRUISE AIR A237	273	145	90	120	8,060	6
DIAMOND MICRO	204	138	93	117	10,250	4
DIAMOND MAXI 24	280	163	93	117	11,500	6
DODGEN 22 RK	268	158	95	114	10,250	2
DODGEN 22 CK	268	158	95	114	10,250	4
DODGEN REAR DR.	240	158	93	117	9,200	4-6
EL DORADO KONA	228	138	94	113	9,000	5
EL DORADO LANAI	280	158	94	120	10,500	6
EL DORADO MAJOR	280	158	94	120	10,500	4
EMPIRE 20 FLSB	241	127	93	108	10,200	4-6
EMPIRE 22 FPSB	265	145	93	108	10,500	6
FAR WEST 120	249	138	94	111	10,050	6
FAR WEST 222	273	158	93	111	10,050	6

CONDENSED FROM <u>MOTORCAMPING</u> (POPULAR SCIENCE)

© TIMES MIRROR MAGAZINES, INC.

MINIMOTORHOMES

	OVERALL LENGTH	WHEEL BASE	OVERALL WIDTH	OVERALL HEIGHT	GROSS WEIGHT	SLEEPS
FLAIR B	204	109	81	111	8,510	4
FLAIR M	240	127	93	114	9,000	4
FLAIR T OR G	270	145	93	114	10,500	4-5
FLEETWING 20 RG	250	145	96	NA	7,450	6
FLEETWING 22 DD	274	145	96	NA	7,800	6
FRANKLIN 22 RG	264	146	93	NA	10,500	6
GLOBESTAR 23	276	145	93	NA	7,860	6
HARVEST 2002	240	127	94	112	9,000	6
HARVEST 2300	276	163	94	112	10,500	6
HARVEST 2520	300	178	94	112	10,500	6
HIGHLAND 1900	228	127	93	120	8,300	6
HIGHLAND 2520	312	173	93	120	10,500	8
HOPCAP 210	257	146	93	114	10,500	6
HOPCAP 230	281	146	93	114	10,500	6
HUNTSMAN IMPERIAL	240	127	92	NA	7,600	6
HUNTSMAN 25	300	163	92	NA	8,400	6
ITASCA 420 RG	246	125	93	111	8,900	4-6
ITASCA 25 RB	302	158	92	126	12,300	6
JAMBOREE W	243	127	95	114	10,500	4
JAMBOREE M	258	145	95	114	10,500	6
JAYCO 2250	280	158	96	112	10,200	6
LANDAU ELF-CV	226	110	78	96	4,600	4
LEISURE TIME 21	254	138	91	117	10,050	6
LEISURE TIME 23	280	158	91	117	10,050	6
MALLARD 23	277	158	93	117	10,250	6
MARATHON 20 RB	250	127	93	116	7,065	6
MARATHON 25 RB	300	163	93	116	8,190	6
MIDAS 230-III	278	158	93	109	11,000	4-6
MIDAS 230 IV	280	158	93	111	11,000	6-8
NUWA 23 RB MINI	273	146	94	112	7,770	4
ROCKWOOD 1801	216	125	96	122	8,400	4
ROCKWOOD 2202	264	146	96	122	10,000	6
STARCRAFT 2202	266	146	96	110	10,500	6
TIOGA G	273	145	95	115	10,500	4
TIOGA R	286	163	95	115	11,500	6
TIOGA ARROW	262	145	95	112	10,500	5
TRAVELCRAFT 20	240	127	94	109	10,500	6
TRAVELCRAFT 23	282	145	94	109	10,500	6
WINNEBAGO 240RG	246	127	93	111	9,000	5-6
WINNEBAGO 424RH	280	163	94	111	11,500	5-6

CONDENSED FROM MOTORCAMPING (POPULAR SCIENCE)

© TIMES MIRROR MAGAZINES, INC.

MINIMOTORHOMES

	OVERALL LENGTH	WHEEL BASE	OVERALL WIDTH	OVERALL HEIGHT	GROSS WEIGHT	SLEEPS
YELLOWSTONE 350	284	146	96	121	10,500	6
YELLOWSTONE 460	279	158	96	121	11,000	6
XPLORER 228	228	127	79	107	7,000	6
XPLORER 272	272	145	90	109	10,500	7

MOTORCOACHES, 30 FT. PLUS

APOLLO 3000 RB	360	198	96	108	14,500	6
APOLLO 3000	396	208	96	108	16,000	6
AVCO 3200 RB	372	208	94	128	17,000	6
BARTH 30T	360	201	93	115	15,000	6
BARTH 34T	408	219	93	115	15,000	6
BLUEBIRD 33	396	194	93	138	34,000	6
BLUEBIRD 35 XV	420	217	96	144	34,000	6
CHAMPION 924	372	178	93	125	14,000	6
COACHMAN REGENCY	374	208	92	113	16,000	4
COBRA VENTURA	360	178	96	128	14,500	4-6
COBRA GRANDE II	396	208	96	128	14,500	6
COBRA V. ROYALE	424	208	96	128	14,500	4
CONCORD 825	372	178	93	129	14,000	8
CRUISE AIR 3201	398	208	93	129	12,000	6
FORETRAVEL 33 RB	396	208	96	113	16,000	6
KINGS HIWAY	384	208	96	125	16,000	4-6
LANDAU REGENCY	396	208	92	125	16,000	6
LANDAU IMPERIAL	420	208	95	126	18,500	4
OVERLAND ESTANCIA	384	208	94	125	16,000	6
PACE ARROW A	375	208	95	113	16,000	4-5
REVCON CAMELOT	360	202	95	113	10,700	4
SOUTHWIND L	390	208	95	115	16,000	5
SWINGER ISLANDER	390	208	93	125	12,800	7
TITAN 517	372	178	93	125	14,000	6
TRAVCO 320	384	208	96	122	16,000	4-6
VOGUE 33 RB	396	208	96	128	16,000	4-7
WINNEBAGO ELANDAN	390	208	92	128	16,000	4-6

CONDENSED FROM MOTORCAMPING (POPULAR SCIENCE)
© TIMES MIRROR MAGAZINES, INC.

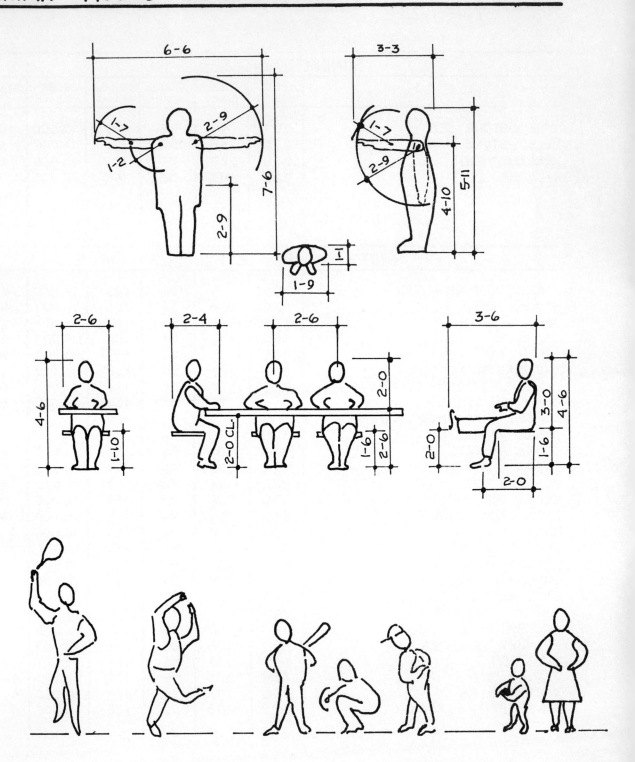

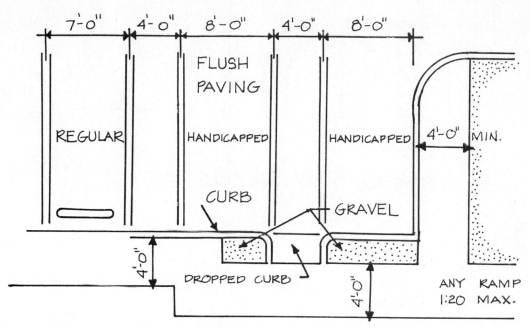

7'-0"   4'-0"   8'-0"   4'-0"   8'-0"

FLUSH PAVING

REGULAR   HANDICAPPED   HANDICAPPED   4'-0" MIN.

CURB   GRAVEL

4'-0"

DROPPED CURB   4'-0"

ANY RAMP 1:20 MAX.

5'-0" WALK PREFERRED TO ALLOW WHEELCHAIRS TO PASS EACH OTHER.

PARKING LAYOUT

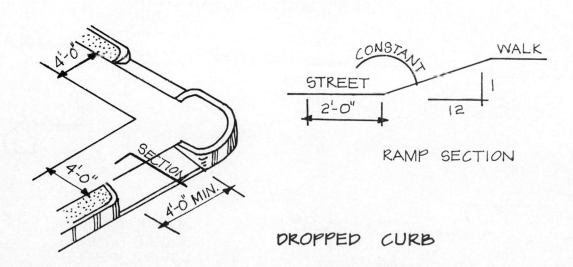

4'-0"

4'-0"

SECTION

4'-0" MIN.

DROPPED CURB

CONSTANT   WALK

STREET

2'-0"   12   1

RAMP SECTION

STATE OF CALIFORNIA

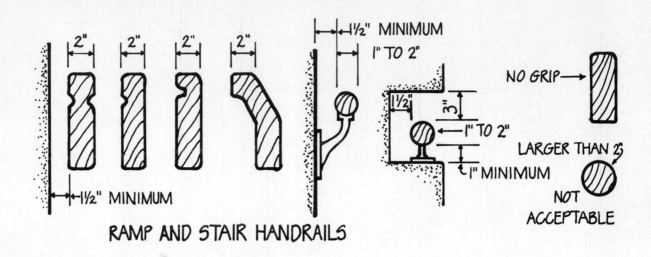

2"   **2"**   **2"**   **2"**

1½" MINIMUM

1" TO 2"

1½"

3"

1" TO 2"

1" MINIMUM

1½" MINIMUM

NO GRIP →

LARGER THAN 2"

NOT ACCEPTABLE

RAMP AND STAIR HANDRAILS

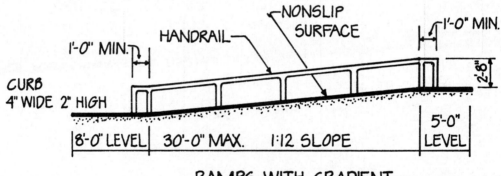

1'-0" MIN.

HANDRAIL

NONSLIP SURFACE

1'-0" MIN.

2'-8"

CURB 4" WIDE 2" HIGH

8'-0" LEVEL | 30'-0" MAX. | 1:12 SLOPE | 5'-0" LEVEL

RAMPS WITH GRADIENT

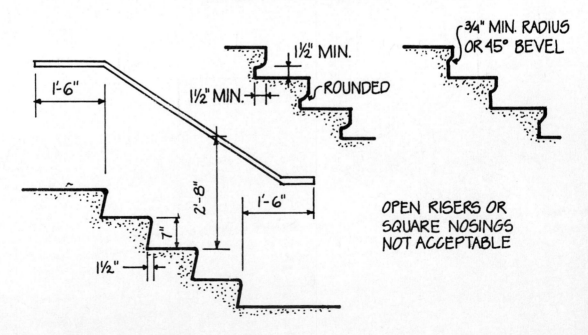

1'-6"

1½" MIN.

ROUNDED

1½" MIN.

¾" MIN. RADIUS OR 45° BEVEL

2'-8"

1'-6"

7"

1½"

OPEN RISERS OR SQUARE NOSINGS NOT ACCEPTABLE

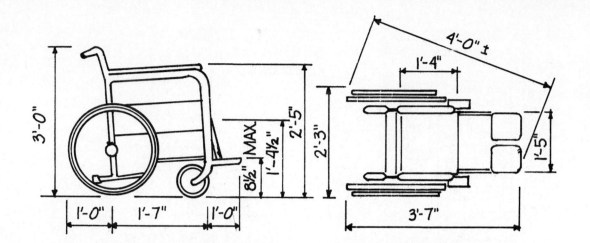

FUNCTIONS OF WHEELCHAIR

FIXED TURNING RADIUS, WHEEL TO WHEEL = 18"

FIXED TURNING RADIUS, FRONT TO REAR STRUCTURE = 31.5"

AVERAGE 180° AND 360°, TURNING AREA REQUIRED = 60" x 60"

WIDTH REQUIRED FOR TWO CHAIRS TO PASS = 60" MIN.

ADULT FUNCTIONS IN CHAIR

UNILATERAL VERTICAL REACH AVE. = 60", RANGE 54" TO 78"

HORIZONTAL WORKING REACH AVE = 30.8", RANGE 28" TO 33"

BILATERAL HORIZONTAL REACH AVE. = 64.5", RANGE 54" TO 71"

DIAGONAL REACH ON THE WALL AVE. = 48" FROM FLOOR

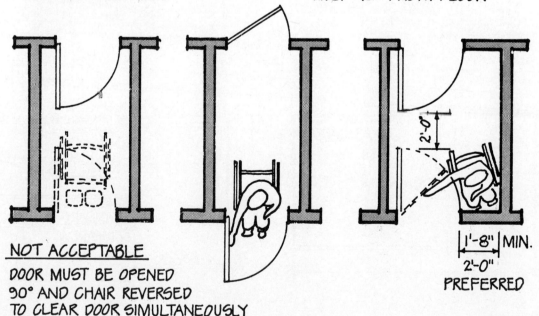

NOT ACCEPTABLE

DOOR MUST BE OPENED 90° AND CHAIR REVERSED TO CLEAR DOOR SIMULTANEOUSLY

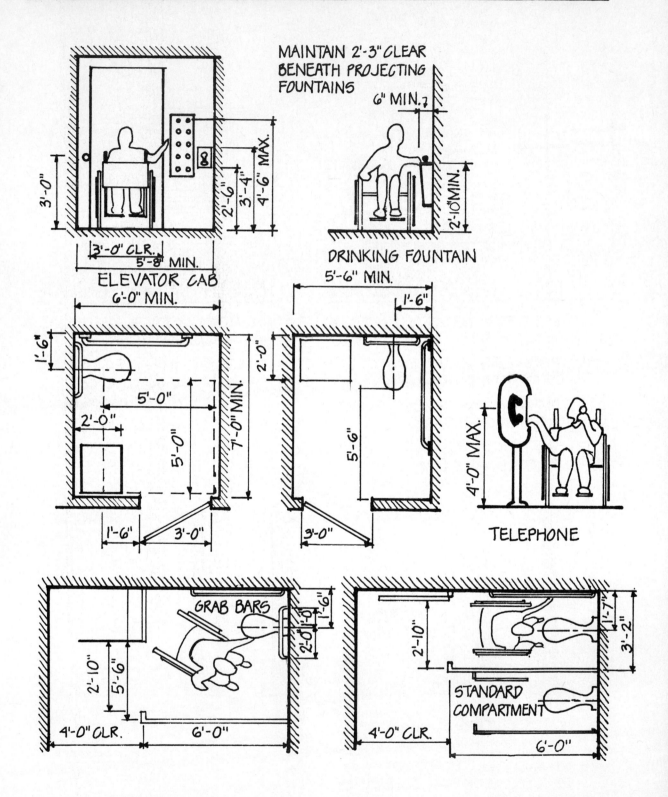

MAINTAIN 2'-3" CLEAR BENEATH PROJECTING FOUNTAINS

ELEVATOR CAB

DRINKING FOUNTAIN

TELEPHONE

GRAB BARS

STANDARD COMPARTMENT

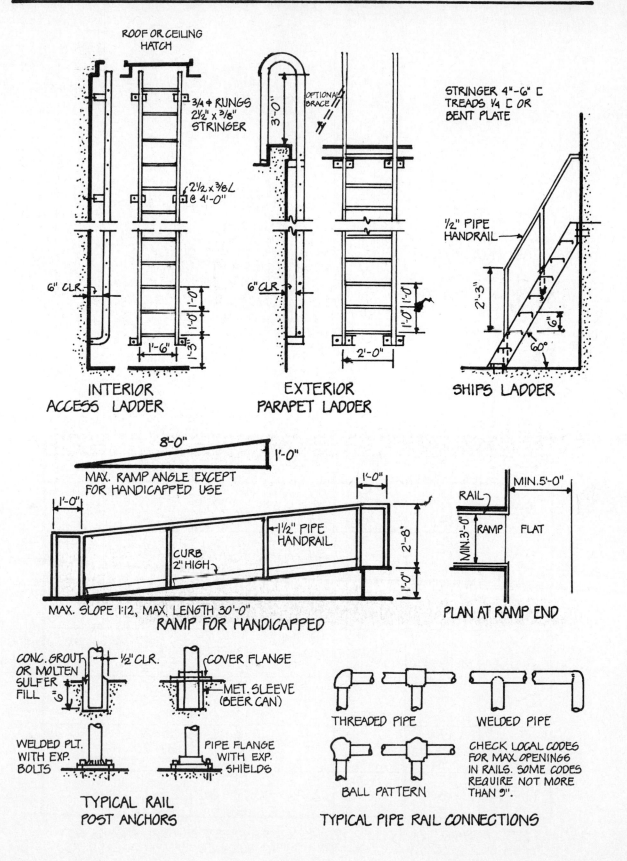

ROOF OR CEILING HATCH

3/4 ⌀ RUNGS
2½" x 3/8"
STRINGER

2½ x 3/8 L
@ 4'-0"

6" CLR.

1'-0" 1'-0"

1'-3"

1'-6"

**INTERIOR
ACCESS LADDER**

OPTIONAL BRACE

3'-0"

6" CLR.

1'-0" 1'-0"

2'-0"

**EXTERIOR
PARAPET LADDER**

STRINGER 4"-6" C
TREADS ¼ C OR
BENT PLATE

½" PIPE HANDRAIL

2'-3"

6"

60°

SHIPS LADDER

8'-0"

1'-0"

MAX. RAMP ANGLE EXCEPT
FOR HANDICAPPED USE

1'-0"

1'-0"

1½" PIPE HANDRAIL

CURB
2" HIGH

2'-8"

1'-0"

MAX. SLOPE 1:12, MAX. LENGTH 30'-0"
RAMP FOR HANDICAPPED

MIN. 5'-0"

RAIL

MIN. 3'-0"

RAMP

FLAT

PLAN AT RAMP END

CONC. GROUT
OR MOLTEN
SULFER
FILL

½" CLR.

6"

COVER FLANGE

MET. SLEEVE
(BEER CAN)

WELDED PLT.
WITH EXP.
BOLTS

PIPE FLANGE
WITH EXP.
SHIELDS

**TYPICAL RAIL
POST ANCHORS**

THREADED PIPE

WELDED PIPE

BALL PATTERN

CHECK LOCAL CODES
FOR MAX. OPENINGS
IN RAILS. SOME CODES
REQUIRE NOT MORE
THAN 9".

TYPICAL PIPE RAIL CONNECTIONS

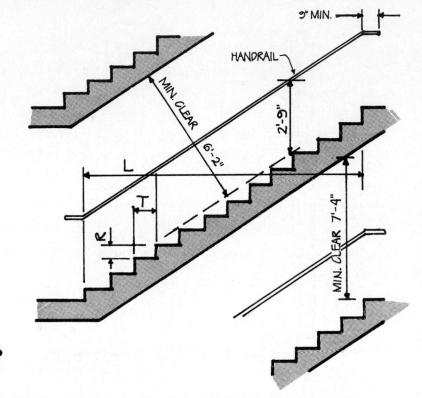

"RULE OF THUMB"
FOR STAIR PROPORTIONS

$$R + T = 17'' \pm \frac{1}{4}''$$

$$2R + T = 25'' \pm \frac{1}{4}''$$

$$R \times T = 75'' \pm \frac{1}{2}''$$

$$\frac{R}{T} = TAN(R-3) \times 8°$$

RECOMMENDED SAFE STAIR DIMENSIONS						
FLOOR TO FLOOR HT.	NUMBER OF RISERS	RISER	TREAD	TOTAL RUN	APPROXIMATE ANGLE	
8-0	13	7 3/8	10 1/4	10 - 3	36 - 0	
	14	6 7/8	11 1/2	12 - 5 1/2	31 - 0	
	15	6 13/32	12 1/2	14 - 7	26 - 45	
8-6	13	7 7/8	9 1/4	9 - 3	40 - 30	
	14	7 5/16	10 1/2	11 - 4 1/2	33 - 30	
	15	6 13/16	11 1/2	13 - 8 1/2	29 - 0	
9-0	14	7 23/32	9 1/2	10 - 3 1/2	39 - 0	
	15	7 7/32	10 1/2	12 - 3	34 - 30	
	16	6 3/4	11 3/4	14 - 8 1/4	30 - 0	
9-6	15	7 19/32	9 3/4	11 - 4 1/2	37 - 30	
	16	7 1/8	10 3/4	13 - 5 1/4	33 - 30	
	17	6 23/32	11 3/4	15 - 8	29 - 30	
10-0	16	7 1/2	10	12 - 6	36 - 0	
	17	7 1/16	11	14 - 8	32 - 0	
	18	6 21/32	12	17 - 0	29 - 15	
10-6	17	7 13/32	10	13 - 4	35 - 30	
	18	7	11	15 - 7	32 - 20	
	19	6 5/8	12	18 - 0	29 - 30	
11-0	17	7 3/4	9 1/2	12 - 8	39 - 15	
	18	7 11/32	10 1/4	14 - 6 1/2	36 - 0	
	19	6 15/16	11	16 - 6	32 - 20	

ANGLE OF STAIRS PREFERRED BETWEEN 20° AND 35°. CRITICAL ANGLES NOT RECOMMENDED BELOW 20° NOR FROM 35° TO 50°. SEE RAMPS OR LADDERS.

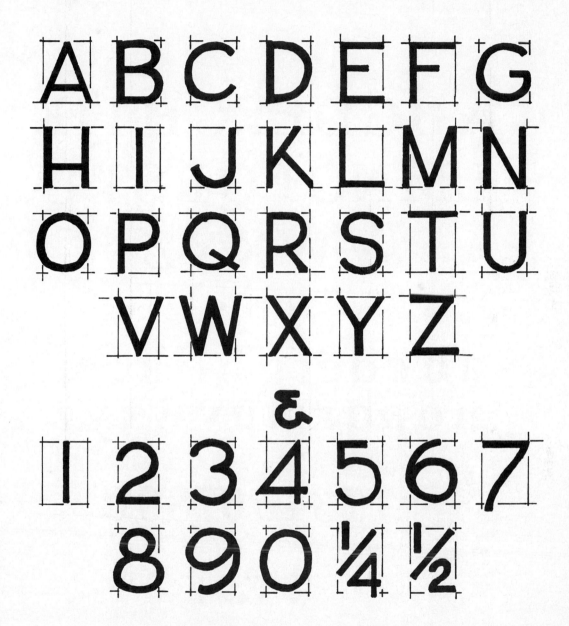

SINGLE STROKE VERTICAL

ABCDEFGHIJK LMNOPQRSTU VWXYZ

⟨>: :<⟩

abcdefghijklm
nopqrstuvwxyz

1234567890

! & ?

BASKERVILLE SEMIBOLD

OLD ENGLISH

ENGRAVERS SCRIPT

MODERN STENCIL

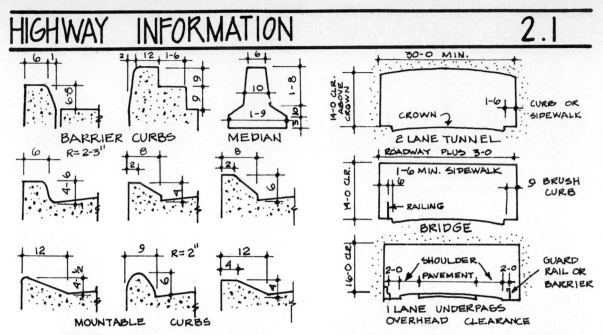

BARRIER CURBS

MEDIAN

2 LANE TUNNEL

BRIDGE

MOUNTABLE CURBS

1 LANE UNDERPASS OVERHEAD CLEARANCE

SPEED, TIME, DISTANCE FOR PASSING: TWO LANE ROAD

DESIGN SPEED	ACTUAL SPEEDS		ASSUMED SPEEDS			TOTAL TIME REQD. (SEC.)	DISTANCE TRAVELED (FEET)					TOTAL FEET ROUNDED
MPH	LOW	INTER	PASS'D MPH	PASS'G. MPH	AVE. PASS'G.		INITIAL	PASSING	CLEAR	OPPOSING	TOTAL	
30	28	26	26	36	34.9	16.5	145	475	100	315	1035	1100
40	36	34	34	44		18.0	215	640	180	425	1460	1500
50	44	41	41	51	43.8	19.3	290	825	250	550	1915	2000
60	52	47	47	57	52.6							
65	55	50	50	60	62.0	20.3	370	1030	300	680	2380	2500
70	58	54	54	64								

MINIMUM STOPPING SIGHT DISTANCE

DESIGN SPEED	ASSUMED SPEED		BRAKE REACTION				COEFF. OF FRICTION		BRAKING DISTANCE		STOPPING SIGHT DISTANCE	
			WET		DRY				WET (FT.)	DRY (FT.)	WET (FT.)	DRY (FT.)
MPH	WET	DRY	(SEC.)	(FT.)	(SEC.)	(FT.)	WET	DRY				
30	28	30	2.5	103	2.5	110	.36	.62	73	48	176	158
40	36	40	2.5	132	2.5	147	.33	.60	131	89	263	236
50	44	50	2.5	161	2.5	183	.31	.58	208	144	369	327
60	52	60	2.5	191	2.5	220	.30	.56	300	214	491	434
65	55	65	2.5	202	2.5	238	.30	.56	336	251	538	489
70	58	70	2.5	213	2.5	257	.29	.55	387	297	600	554
75	61	75	2.5	224	2.5	275	.28	.54	443	347	667	622

CROSS ROADS · INTERSECT SIDE ROAD · MERGING SIDE ROAD · DIMINISH ROAD WIDTH · "S" CURVE · WINDING ROAD

CURVE 50 MPH · SLIPPERY WHEN WET · DIVIDED HIGHWAY · TWO-WAY TRAFFIC · EXIT ONLY · SCHOOL AHEAD

NO PARKING · NO TURN · WRONG WAY · STOP · YIELD RIGHT OF WAY · SIGNAL AHEAD

LOCATION – DISTANCE SIGN · BIKE ROUTE · HOSPITAL · CAMPING · INFORMATION

U TURN LEFT TURN · NO U TURN · NO PASSING · NO TRUCKS · KEEP RIGHT

BLACK  RED

WHITE GREEN

YELLOW  BLUE

HIGHWAY CONSTRUCTION SIGNS AND
BARRIERS ARE BLACK ON ORANGE.

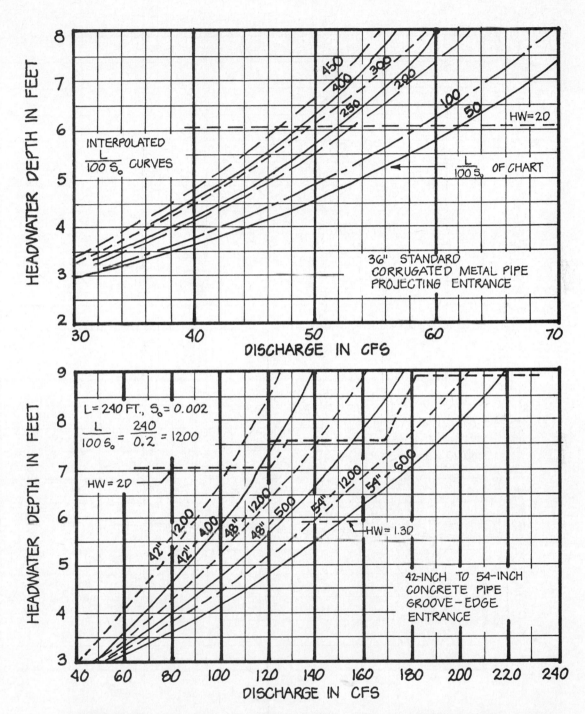

EXAMPLE: ASSURE CULVERT LENGTH 240 FT WITH SLOPE 0.002, $\frac{L}{100 S_o}$ = 1200, DISCHARGE 100 CFS AND HEADWATER DEPTH 6.0 FT REQUIRES 48-INCH PIPE.

EXAMPLE: ASSUME DISCHARGE 120 CFS, HEADWATER DEPTH 6.0 FT. 42-INCH NOT ADEQUATE FOR LENGTH-SLOPE AS MIN. HEADWATER IS 7.4 FT FOR 120 CFS. REQUIRES 48-INCH PIPE.

U.S. BUREAU OF PUBLIC ROADS

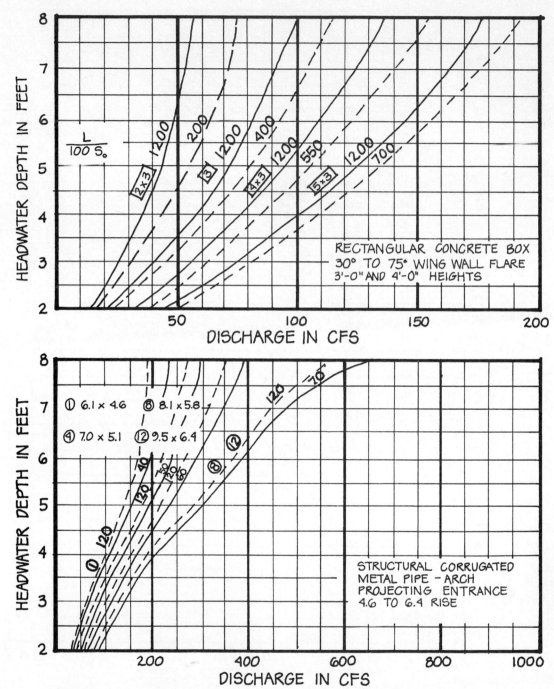

Upper chart:

HEADWATER DEPTH IN FEET (vertical axis, 2 to 8)

$\dfrac{L}{100\,S_o}$

1200, 200, 1200, 400, 1200, 550, 1200, 700

2×3, 3, 4×3, 5×3

RECTANGULAR CONCRETE BOX
30° TO 75° WING WALL FLARE
3'-0" AND 4'-0" HEIGHTS

DISCHARGE IN CFS (50, 100, 150, 200)

Lower chart:

HEADWATER DEPTH IN FEET (vertical axis, 2 to 8)

① 6.1 × 4.6   ⑧ 8.1 × 5.8
④ 7.0 × 5.1   ⑫ 9.5 × 6.4

120, 76

STRUCTURAL CORRUGATED
METAL PIPE – ARCH
PROJECTING ENTRANCE
4.6 TO 6.4 RISE

DISCHARGE IN CFS (200, 400, 600, 800, 1000)

EXAMPLE : ASSUME CULVERT LENGTH 400 FT WITH SLOPE
0.004, DISCHARGE 125 CFS, AND HW AT 7.5 FT.   SELECT 4'-0" x 3'-0"
= HW 6.8 FT OR USE 3'-6" x 4'-0" = HW 6.3 FT.

ALLOWABLE BEARING CAPACITY OF VARIOUS FOUNDATION BEDS.

TYPE	LB/FT^2	TONS/FT^2
ALLUVIAL SOIL	1,000	$\frac{1}{2}$
SOFT CLAY	2,000	1
FIRM CLAY	4,000	2
WET SAND	4,000	2
SAND AND CLAY MIXED	4,000	2
FINE DRY SAND	6,000	3
HARD CLAY	8,000	4
COARSE DRY SAND	8,000	4
GRAVEL	12,000	6
COMPACTED SAND AND GRAVEL	16,000	8
HARDPAN OR HARD SHALE	20,000	10
MEDIUM ROCK	40,000	20
ROCK UNDER CASSIONS	50,000	25
BED ROCK	160,000	80

VALUES ARE FOR MATERIAL CONFINED TO LOCATION. USE SPECIAL PRECAUTIONS WHEN SAND OR SIMILAR MATERIAL IS NOT COMPLETELY CONFINED AND MAY MOVE BY EXCAVATION OR EROSION, WIND, ETC.

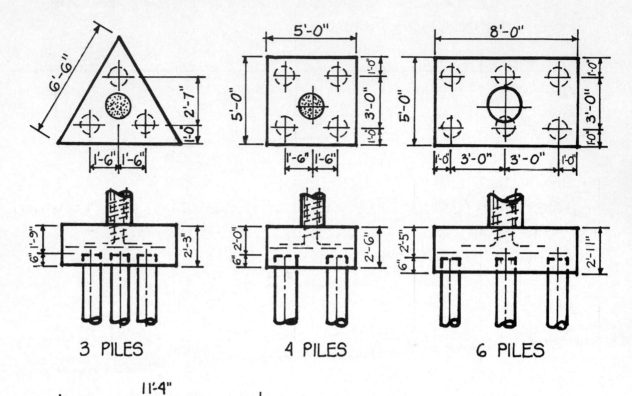

3 PILES   4 PILES   6 PILES

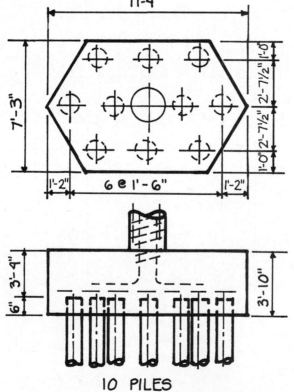

10 PILES

DIAGRAMS ARE BASED UPON 12" DIAMETER CONCRETE PILES. NUMBER OF PILES REQUIRED IS DETERMINED BY FRICTION VALUE, SOIL CONDITION, AND PILE CAPACITY. COLUMNS UPON PILE CAPS MAY BE WOOD, CONCRETE, OR STEEL WITH APPROPRIATE CONNECTING BASE.

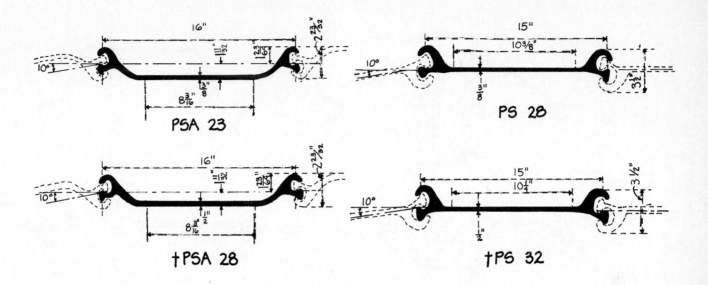

PSA 23

PS 28

†PSA 28

†PS 32

AISI STANDARDIZED SECTION DESIGNATION	AREA SQ. IN.	NOMINAL WIDTH IN.	WEIGHT IN POUNDS		MOMENT OF INERTIA IN⁴	SECTION MODULUS IN.³		SURFACE AREA SQ. FT. PER LIN. FT. OF WALL	
			PER LIN. FT OF BAR	PER SQ FT OF WALL		SINGLE SECTION	PER LIN. FT. OF WALL	TOTAL AREA	NORMAL COATING AREA
PZ 38	16.77	18	57.0	38.0	421.2	70.2	46.8	5.52	5.06
PZ 32	16.47	21	56.0	32.0	385.7	67.0	38.3	5.52	5.06
PZ 27	11.91	18	40.5	27.0	276.3	45.3	30.2	4.94	4.48
PDA 27	10.59	16	36.0	27.0	53.0	14.3	10.7	4.52	3.86
PMA 22	10.59	19⅝	36.0	22.0	26.0	8.8	5.4	4.54	3.88
PSA 23	8.99	16	30.7	23.0	5.5	3.2	2.4	3.76	3.08
PSA 28	10.98	16	37.3	23.0	6.0	3.3	2.5	3.74	3.06
PS 28	10.29	15	35.0	28.0	4.6	3.0	2.4	3.70	2.86
PS 32	11.76	15	40.0	32.0	4.6	3.0	2.4	3.66	2.82

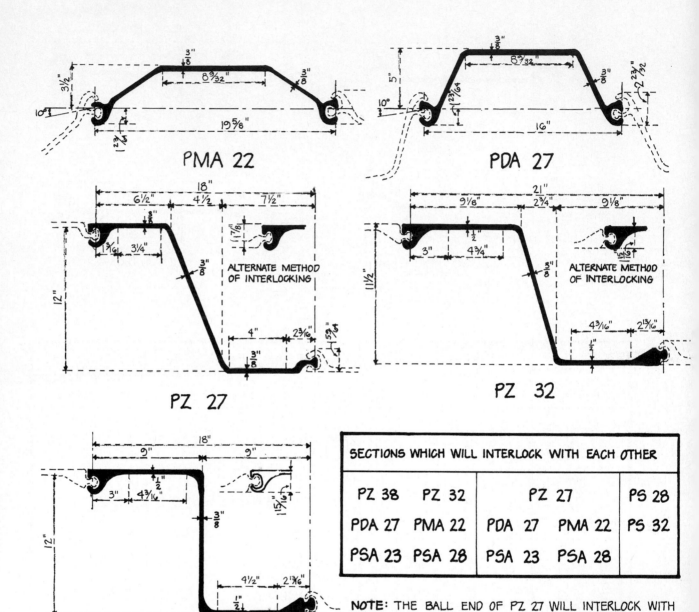

PMA 22

PDA 27

PZ 27

ALTERNATE METHOD OF INTERLOCKING

PZ 32

ALTERNATE METHOD OF INTERLOCKING

PZ 38

SECTIONS WHICH WILL INTERLOCK WITH EACH OTHER		
PZ 38 PZ 32	PZ 27	PS 28
PDA 27 PMA 22	PDA 27 PMA 22	PS 32
PSA 23 PSA 28	PSA 23 PSA 28	

NOTE: THE BALL END OF PZ 27 WILL INTERLOCK WITH THE SOCKET END OF PZ 38 AND PZ 32; HOWEVER, THE SOCKET END OF PZ 27 WILL NOT INTERLOCK WITH THE BALL END OF PZ 38 AND PZ 32.

EVERGREEN TREES

PALMS

AILANTHUS H=50'-75' D=2'-3' S=40'-60' O.C.=30'-40'	**CATALPA NORTHERN** H=80'-100' D=3'-4' S=50'-60' O.C.=50'-60'
MAPLE NORTHERN H=60-80' D=2'-3' S=60'-70' O.C.=50'-60'	**APPLE** H=20'-40' D=1'-2' S=20'-40' O.C.=25'
ASH, WHITE H=70'-80' D=2'-3' S=35'-50' O.C.=40'-50'	**GINKGO BILOBA** H=60'-80' D=2'-3' S=50'-60' O.C.=50'-60'
MAPLE, RED H=50'-75' D=2'-3' S=40'-50' O.C.=40'-50'	**WEEPING WILLOW** H=30'-40' D=1'-2' S=30'-40' O.C.=30'-40'
BEECH AMERICAN H=50'-75' D=6"-4' S=40'-50' O.C.=30'-40'	**ELM AMERICAN** H=80'-100' D=4'-8' S=70'-80' O.C.=60'-70'
MAPLE SUGAR H=70'-100' D=2'-4' S=50'-60' O.C.=50'-60'	**WALNUT BLACK** H=75'-100' D=3'-5' S=40'-50' O.C.=30'-40'
BEECH EUROPEAN H=50'-75' D=3'-4' S=50'-70' O.C.=50'-60'	**ELM ENGLISH** H=75'-100' D=3'-4' S=50'-60' O.C.=50'-60'
OAK, PIN H=60'-80' D=3'-4' S=40'-50' O.C.=40'-50'	**POPLAR CAROLINA** H=75'-100' D=3'-5' S=40'-50' O.C.=30'-40'
BIRCH WHITE H=50'-75' D=1'-3' S=30'-50' O.C.=30'-40'	**HORSECHESTNUT** H=60'-70' D=2'-3' S=40'-50' O.C.=40'-50'
OAK NORTHREN RED H=60'-80' D=2'-6' S=50'-70' O.C.=50'-60'	**POPLAR LOMBARDY** H=75'-100' D=2'-6' S=20'-30' O.C.=20'-30'
BALD CYPRESS H=100'-150' D=3'-5' S=50'-100' O.C.=60'-70' MATURE TREE / YOUNG TREE	**LOCUST BLACK** H=40'-70' D=2'-4' S=30'-40' O.C.=30'-40'
OAK, WHITE H=80'-100' D=3'-6' S=80'-100' O.C.=100'	**SWEET GUM** H=80'-120' D=3'-5' S=40'-50' O.C.=40'-50'
DOUGLAS FIR H=100'-200' D=10'-12' S=50'-60' O.C.=50'-60' MATURE TREE / YOUNG TREE	**LOCUST HONEY** H=40'-60' D=2'-3' S=20'-30' O.C.=30'-40'
PLANE TREE (ORIENTAL) H=70'-80' D=2'-4' S=50'-60' O.C.=50'-60'	**TULIP TREE** H=60'-80' D=2'-3' S=30'-40' O.C.=40'-50'
	LINDEN H=70'-90' D=2'-4 S=50'-60' O.C.=40'-50'
MAGNOLIA, SOUTHERN H=70'-80' D=2'-3' S=50'-60' O.C.=50'-60'	**PINE AUSTRIAN** H=60'-80' D=2'-3' S=30'-40' O.C.=40'-50'
YEW, IRISH H=50'-60' D=4'-6' S=30'-40' O.C.=30'-40'	**MAGNOLIA** H=70'-90' D=3'-4' S=60'-70' O.C.=50'-60'
LIVE OAK H=50'-60' D=4'-6' S=60'-70' O.C.=60'-70'	**PINE MONTEREY** H=50'-60' D=4'-6' S=50'-60' O.C.=50'-60'

DEODAR CEDAR H=60'-100' D=2'-3' S=40'-50' O.C.=40'-50'	ARBOR VITAE 25'-50' 1'-2' 10'-20' 10'-20	BRISTLE -CONE PINE H=20'-25' D=12" S=10'-15' O.C.=20'	BOX TREE 20'-30' 1'-2' 25'-30 20-25'	AMER. HOLLY 40'-50' 1'-2' 25'-35' 30'-40'	PINYON PINE H=25'-50' 1'-2' 30'-40'	RED CEDAR 25'-50' 1'-2' 10'-15' 20'-30'	SCOP. JUNIPER H=15'-30' D=1'-2' S=6'-12' O.C.=20'
PINE, RED (NORWAY) H=60'-80' D=2'-3' S=30'-40' O.C.=40'-50'		SPRUCE COLO. H=70'-90' D=18"-3' S=30'-40' O.C.=40'-50'		HEMLOCK CANADA H=60'-80' D=2'-4' S=40'-60' O.C.=40'-50'		CYPRESS SAWARA H=20'-40' D=9"-15" S=15'-20' O.C.=20-30'	
PINE WHITE H=80'-100' D=4'-5' S=60'-80' O.C.=50'-60'		SPRUCE NORWAY H=50'-100' D=2'-3' S=30'-40' O.C.=40'-50'		LARCH. EUR. H=50'-60' D=1'-3' S=30'-40' O.C.=40'-50'		FIR WHITE H=100'-150' D=3'-4' S=50'-60' O.C.=50'-60'	

DATE PALM H=80'-100' D=3'-5' S=50'-60' O.C.=50'-60'	WINDMILL PALM H=15'-20' D=12"-18" S=10' O.C.=20'
COCONUT PALM H=40'-100' D=12"-18" S=40'-50' O.C.=40'-60'	WASHINGTON PALM H=60'-90' D=3'-4' S=25'-35' O.C.=20'-40'
ROYAL PALM H=100' D=18"-2' S=30'-40' O.C.=40'-50'	BANANA TREE H=20' D=18"-24" S=15' O.C.=15'-20'

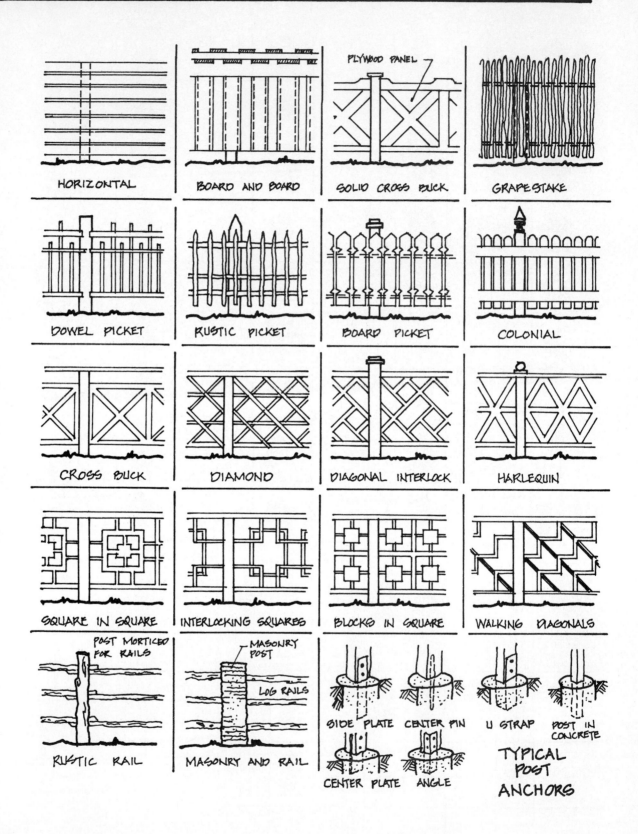

HORIZONTAL

BOARD AND BOARD

SOLID CROSS BUCK — PLYWOOD PANEL

GRAPESTAKE

DOWEL PICKET

RUSTIC PICKET

BOARD PICKET

COLONIAL

CROSS BUCK

DIAMOND

DIAGONAL INTERLOCK

HARLEQUIN

SQUARE IN SQUARE

INTERLOCKING SQUARES

BLOCKS IN SQUARE

WALKING DIAGONALS

RUSTIC RAIL — POST MORTICED FOR RAILS

MASONRY AND RAIL — MASONRY POST, LOG RAILS

SIDE PLATE   CENTER PIN   U STRAP   POST IN CONCRETE

CENTER PLATE   ANGLE

TYPICAL POST ANCHORS

MERIDIANS AND BASE LINES OF THE UNITED STATES RECTANGULAR SURVEYS

RECTANGULAR SYSTEM IS USED IN STATES SHOWN UNSHADED, HAWAII AND ALASKA. EACH PRINCIPAL MERIDIAN AND ITS BASE LINE IS SHOWN ON THE MAP WITH LOCATION AND LATITUDE IN TABLE ON FOLLOWING PAGE; SHADED AREAS USE METES AND BOUNDS SURVEYS.

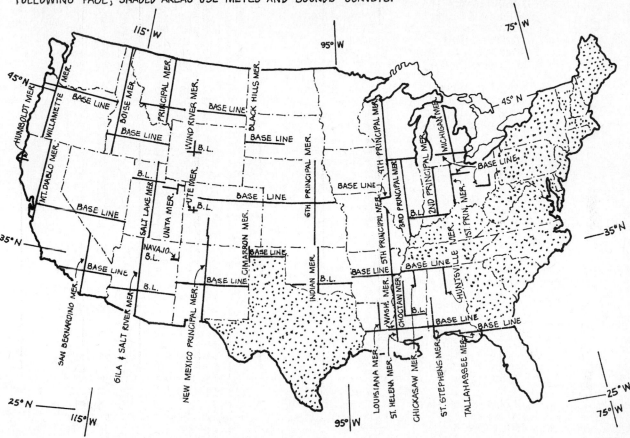

FROM CONSTRUCTION: PRINCIPALS, MATERIALS AND METHODS
UNITED STATES LEAGUE OF SAVINGS ASSOCIATIONS

MERIDIAN	GOVT. SURVEY FOR ALL OR PART OF STATE	LONGITUDE WEST FROM GREENWICH			LATITUDE NORTH OF EQUATOR		
BLACK HILLS	SOUTH DAKOTA	104	03	00	44	00	00
BOISE	IDAHO	116	24	15	43	22	31
CHICKASAW	MISSISSIPPI	89	15	00	34	59	00
CHOCTAW	MISSISSIPPI	90	14	45	31	54	40
CIMARRON	OKLAHOMA	103	00	00	36	30	00
COPPER RIVER	ALASKA	145	18	42	61	49	11
FAIRBANKS	ALASKA	147	38	33	64	51	49
FIFTH PRINCIPAL	ARK., IOWA, MINN., MO., N. DAK., & S. DAK.	91	03	42	34	44	00
FIRST PRINCIPAL	OHIO & INDIANA	84	48	50	41	00	00
FOURTH PRINCIPAL	ILLINOIS[1]	90	28	45	40	00	30
FOURTH PRINCIPAL	MINN. & WISC.	90	28	45	40	30	00
GILA AND SALT RIVER	ARIZONA	112	18	24	32	22	33
HUMBOLDT	CALIFORNIA	124	07	11	40	25	04
HUNTSVILLE	ALA. & MISS.	86	34	45	35	00	00
INDIAN	OKLAHOMA	97	14	30	34	30	00
LOUISIANA	LOUISIANA[2]	92	24	15	31	00	00
MICHIGAN	MICH. & OHIO	84	22	24	42	26	30
MOUNT DIABLO	CALIF. & NEV.	121	54	48	37	51	30
NAVAJO	ARIZ. & N. MEX.	108	32	45	35	45	00
NEW MEX. PRINCIPAL	NEW MEXICO	106	52	41	34	15	25
NEW MEX. PRINCIPAL	COLORADO	106	53	36			
PRINCIPAL	MONTANA	111	38	50	45	46	48
SALT LAKE	UTAH	111	54	00	40	46	04
SAN BERNARDINO	CALIFORNIA	116	56	15	34	07	10
SECOND PRINCIPAL	ILL. & IND.	86	28	00	38	28	20
SEWARD	ALASKA	149	21	53	60	07	26
SIXTH PRINCIPAL	COLO., KANS. NEBR., S. DAK & WYO.	97	23	00	40	00	00
ST. HELENA	LOUISIANA	91	09	15	31	00	00
ST. STEPHENS	ALA. & MISS.	88	02	00	31	00	00
TALLAHASSEE	FLORIDA	84	16	42	30	28	00
THIRD PRINCIPAL	ILLINOIS	89	10	15	38	28	20
UINTA	UTAH	109	57	30	40	26	20
UTE	COLORADO	108	33	20	39	06	40
WASHINGTON	MISSISSIPPI	91	09	15	31	00	00
WILLAMETTE	ORE. & WASH.	122	44	20	45	31	00
WIND RIVER	WYO.	108	48	40	43	01	20

1. NUMBERS ARE CARRIED TO FRACTIONAL TOWNSHIP 29 NORTH IN ILLINOIS, AND ARE REPEATED IN WISC., BEGINNING WITH SOUTH BOUNDARY OF THE STATE; RANGE NUMBERS ARE IN REGULAR ORDER.
2. LATITUDE DOUBTFUL; IS TO BE VERIFIED.

NOTE: EAST BOUNDARY OF OHIO, KNOWN AS "ELLICOTT'S LINE", LONGITUDE 80°32'20", WAS THE FIRST REFERENCE MERIDIAN, WITH TOWNSHIP NUMBERS COUNTING FROM OHIO RIVER, AND RANGE NUMBERS IN REGULAR ORDER. TOWNSHIP AND RANGE NUMBERS WITHIN THE U.S. MILITARY LAND IN OHIO ARE COUNTED FROM SOUTH AND EAST BOUNDARIES OF TRACT.

FROM CONSTRUCTION: PRINCIPALS, MATERIALS AND METHODS
UNITED STATES LEAGUE OF SAVINGS ASSOCIATION

SECTION = 1 SQ. MILE = 640 ACRES

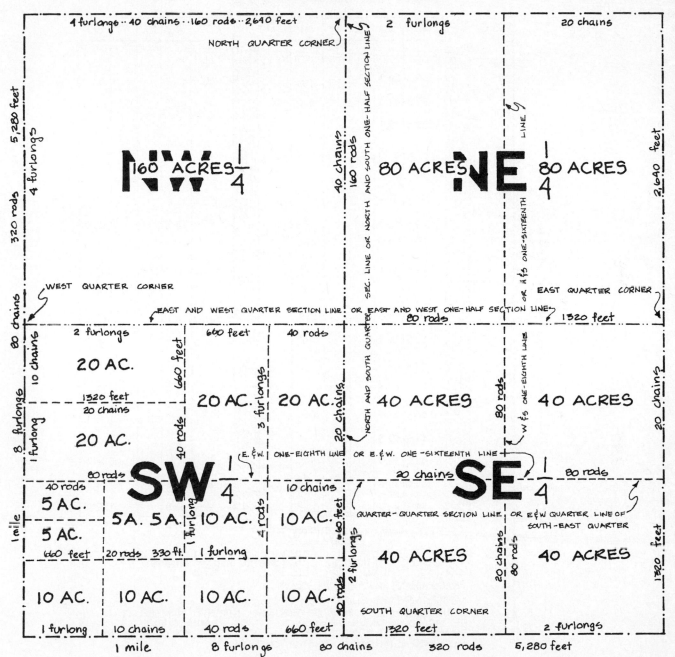

SECTIONS, ONE MILE SQUARE, ARE SUBDIVIDED BY FEDERAL ACT DOWN TO 40 ACRE-QUARTER QUARTERS.
LAND ACREAGE AND DISTANCES WITHIN THE SECTION ARE SHOWN HERE

FROM CONSTRUCTION: PRINCIPLES, MATERIALS AND METHODS.
UNITED STATES LEAGUE OF SAVINGS ASSOCIATIONS.

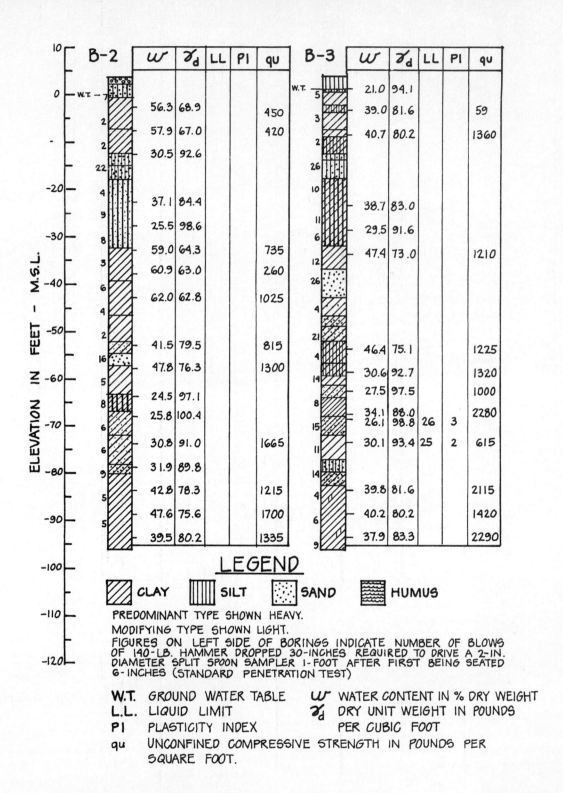

B-2	w	γ_d	LL	PI	qu
	56.3	68.9			450
	57.9	67.0			420
	30.5	92.6			
	37.1	84.4			
	25.5	98.6			
	59.0	64.3			735
	60.9	63.0			260
	62.0	62.8			1025
	41.5	79.5			815
	47.8	76.3			1300
	24.5	97.1			
	25.8	100.4			
	30.8	91.0			1665
	31.9	89.8			
	42.8	78.3			1215
	47.6	75.6			1700
	39.5	80.2			1335

B-3	w	γ_d	LL	PI	qu
	21.0	94.1			
	39.0	81.6			59
	40.7	80.2			1360
	38.7	83.0			
	29.5	91.6			
	47.4	73.0			1210
	46.4	75.1			1225
	30.6	92.7			1320
	27.5	97.5			1000
	34.1	88.0			2280
	26.1	98.8	26	3	
	30.1	93.4	25	2	615
	39.8	81.6			2115
	40.2	80.2			1420
	37.9	83.3			2290

LEGEND

CLAY   SILT   SAND   HUMUS

PREDOMINANT TYPE SHOWN HEAVY.
MODIFYING TYPE SHOWN LIGHT.
FIGURES ON LEFT SIDE OF BORINGS INDICATE NUMBER OF BLOWS OF 140-LB. HAMMER DROPPED 30-INCHES REQUIRED TO DRIVE A 2-IN. DIAMETER SPLIT SPOON SAMPLER 1-FOOT AFTER FIRST BEING SEATED 6-INCHES (STANDARD PENETRATION TEST)

W.T. GROUND WATER TABLE w WATER CONTENT IN % DRY WEIGHT
L.L. LIQUID LIMIT γ_d DRY UNIT WEIGHT IN POUNDS
PI PLASTICITY INDEX   PER CUBIC FOOT
qu UNCONFINED COMPRESSIVE STRENGTH IN POUNDS PER SQUARE FOOT.

CONCRETE   DIVISION 3

ASTM STANDARD REINFORCING BARS

BAR SIZE DESIGNATION	WEIGHT POUNDS PER FOOT	NORMAL DIMENSIONS — ROUND SECTIONS		
		DIAMETER INCHES	CROSS SECTIONAL AREA - SQ. INCHES	PERIMETER INCHES
# 3	.376	.375	.11	1.178
# 4	.668	.500	.20	1.571
# 5	1.043	.625	.31	1.963
# 6	1.502	.750	.44	2.356
# 7	2.044	.875	.60	2.749
# 8	2.670	1.000	.79	3.142
# 9	3.400	1.128	1.00	3.544
# 10	4.303	1.270	1.27	3.990
# 11	5.313	1.410	1.56	4.430
# 14	7.65	1.693	2.25	5.32
# 18	13.60	2.257	4.00	7.09

SIZES #14 AND #18 ARE LARGE BARS GENERALLY NOT CARRIED IN REGULAR STOCK. THESE SIZES AVAILABLE ONLY BY ARRANGEMENT WITH YOUR SUPPLIER.

CONCRETE REINFORCING STEEL INSTITUTE

IDENTIFICATION MARKS — ASTM STANDARD BARS

THE ASTM SPECIFICATIONS FOR BILLET STEEL, RAIL STEEL, AXLE STEEL AND LOW ALLOY STEEL REINFORCING BARS (A615, A616, A617 AND A706) REQUIRE IDENTIFICATION MARKS TO BE ROLLED INTO THE SURFACE OF ONE SIDE OF THE BAR TO DENOTE THE PRODUCER'S MILL DESIGNATION, BAR SIZE, TYPE OF STEEL AND, FOR GRADE 60, A GRADE MARK INDICATING YIELD STRENGTH.* GRADE 40 AND GRADE 50 BARS SHOW ONLY THREE MARKS (NO GRADE MARK) IN FOLLOWING ORDER:

1st — PRODUCING MILL (USUALLY AN INITIAL)

2nd — BAR SIZE NUMBER (#3 THROUGH #18)

3rd — TYPE STEEL: **N** FOR NEW BILLET (S FOR SUPPLEMENTARY REQUIREMENTS A615 — #14 AND #18 ONLY)

               A FOR AXLE

               ⊥ FOR RAIL

               W FOR LOW ALLOY

GRADE 60 BARS MUST ALSO SHOW A MINIMUM YIELD DESIGNATION GRADE MARK OF EITHER THE NUMBER 60 OR ONE (1) GRADE MARK LINE.

A GRADE MARK LINE IS SMALLER AND BETWEEN THE TWO MAIN RIBS WHICH ARE ON OPPOSITE SIDES OF ALL U.S. MADE BARS. WHEN A NUMBER GRADE MARK IS USED, IT IS 4th IN ORDER.

LINE SYSTEM — GRADE MARKS

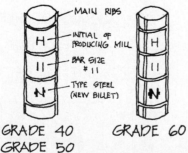

GRADE 40 GRADE 50   GRADE 60

NUMBER SYSTEM — GRADE MARKS

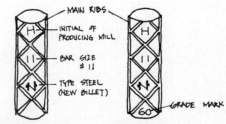

GRADE 40 GRADE 50   GRADE 60

VARIATIONS: BAR IDENTIFICATION MARKS MAY ALSO BE ORIENTED TO READ HORIZONTALLY (90° TO THOSE ILLUSTRATED ABOVE). GRADE MARK LINES MUST BE CONTINUED AT LEAST 5 DEFORMATION SPACES. GRADE MARK NUMBERS MUST BE PLACED WITHIN SEPARATE CONSECUTIVE DEFORMATION SPACES TO READ VERTICALLY OR HORIZONTALLY.

CONCRETE REINFORCING STEEL INSTITUTE

STANDARD HOOKS

ALL SPECIFIC SIZES RECOMMENDED BY CRSI BELOW MEET REQUIREMENTS OF ACI 318-71

RECOMMENDED END HOOKS
ALL GRADES

D = 6d FOR #3 THROUGH #8

D = 8d FOR #9, #10 AND #11

D = 10d FOR #14 AND #18

BAR SIZE	180° HOOKS*		90° HOOKS
	A OR G	J	A OR G
#3	5	3	6
#4	6	4	8
#5	7	5	10
#6	8	6	1-0
#7	10	7	1-2
#8	11	8	1-4
#9	1-3	11¼	1-7
#10	1-5	1-0¾	1-10
#11	1-7	1-2¼	2-0
#14	2-2	1-8½	2-7
#18	2-11	2-3	3-5

*WITH GRADE 40 ONLY, WHERE AVAILABLE DEPTH IS LIMITED. BARS MAY BE BENT WITH D = 5d FOR #3 THROUGH #11.

STIRRUP AND TIE HOOKS

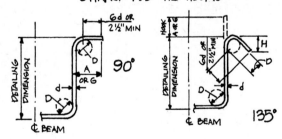

90°

135°

STIRRUPS
(TIES SIMILAR)
STIRRUP AND TIE HOOK DIMENSIONS
GRADES 40·50·60 KSI

BAR SIZE	D (IN.)	90° HOOK	135° HOOK	
		HOOK A OR G	HOOK A OR G	H APPROX.
#3	1½	4	4	2½
#4	2	4½	4½	3
#5	2½	6	5½	3¾

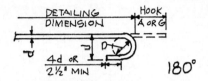

180°

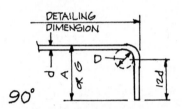

90°

135° SEISMIC STIRRUP / TIE HOOKS

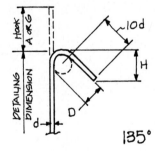

135°

135° SEISMIC STIRRUP / TIE HOOK DIMENSIONS

GRADES 40·50·60 KSI

BAR SIZE	D (IN.)	135° HOOK	
		HOOK A OR G	H APPROX.
#3	1½	5	3½
#4	2	6½	4½
#5	2½	8	5½
#6	4½	11	6¾

CONCRETE REINFORCING STEEL INSTITUTE

TYPICAL BAR BENDS

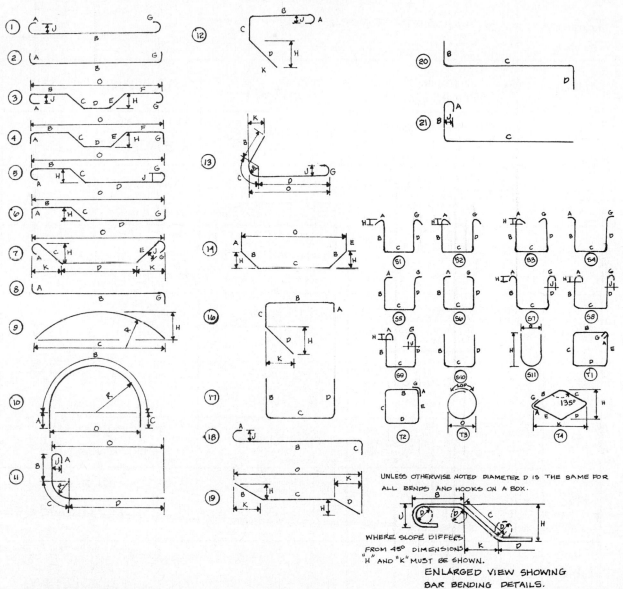

UNLESS OTHERWISE NOTED DIAMETER D IS THE SAME FOR ALL BENDS AND HOOKS ON A BOX.

WHERE SLOPE DIFFERS FROM 45° DIMENSIONS "H" AND "K" MUST BE SHOWN.

ENLARGED VIEW SHOWING BAR BENDING DETAILS.

NOTES:

1. ALL DIMENSIONS ARE OUT TO OUT OF BAR EXCEPT "A" AND "G" ON STANDARD 180° AND 135° HOOKS.
2. "J" DIMENSIONS ON 180° HOOKS TO BE SHOWN ONLY WHERE NECESSARY TO RESTRICT HOOK SIZE, OTHERWISE STANDARD HOOKS ARE TO BE USED.
3. WHERE "J" IS NOT SHOWN, "J" WILL BE KEPT EQUAL TO OR LESS THAN "H". WHERE "J" CAN EXCEED "H", IT SHOULD BE SHOWN.
4. "H" DIMENSIONS STIRUPS TO BE SHOWN WHERE NECESSARY TO FIT WITHIN CONCRETE.
5. WHERE BARS ARE TO BE BENT MORE ACCURATELY THAN STANDARD BENDING TOLERANCES, BENDING DIMENSIONS WHICH REQUIRE CLOSER WORKING SHOULD HAVE LIMITS INDICATED.
6. FIGURES IN CIRCLES SHOW TYPES.
7. FOR RECOMMENDED DIAMETER "D", OF BENDS, HOOKS, ETC. SEE TABLES.

CONCRETE REINFORCING STEEL INSTITUTE.

TABLE 1   STANDARD TYPES AND SIZES

SYMBOL	BAR SUPPORT ILLUSTRATION	TYPE OF SUPPORT	STANDARD SIZES
SB	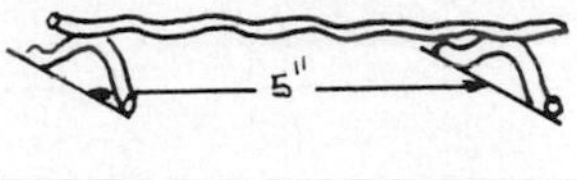	SLAB BOLSTER	¾, 1, 1½, AND 2 INCH HEIGHT IN 5 FT. AND 10 FT. LENGTHS.
SBR*	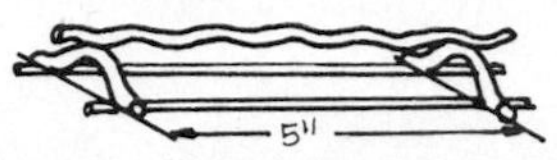	SLAB BOLSTER WITH RUNNERS	SAME AS SB.
BB	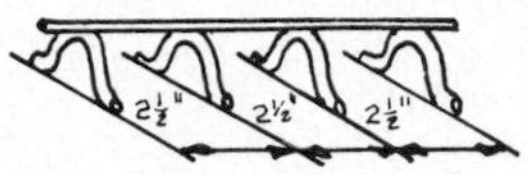	BEAM BOLSTER	1, 1½, 2; OVER 2" TO 5" HEIGHTS IN INCREMENTS OF ¼" IN LENGTHS OF 5 FT.
UBB*	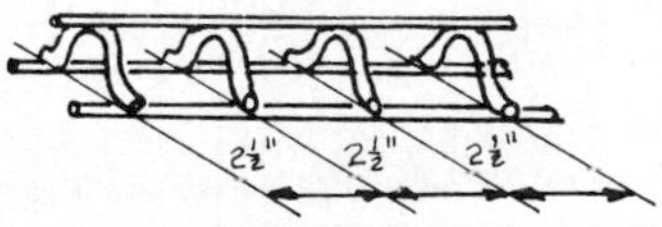	UPPER BEAM BOLSTER	SAME AS BB.
BC	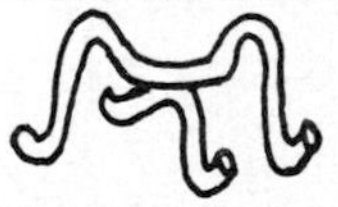	INDIVIDUAL BAR CHAIR	¾, 1, 1½, AND 1¾" HIEGHTS.
JC		JOIST CHAIR	4, 5, AND 6 INCH WIDTHS. ¾, 1, AND 1½ INCH HEIGHTS.
HC		INDIVIDUAL HIGH CHAIR	2 TO 15 INCH HEIGHTS IN INCREMENTS OF ¼ IN.
CHC	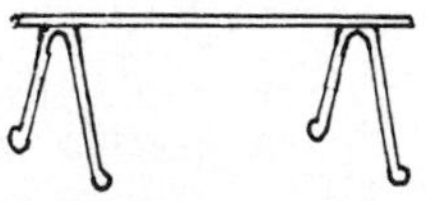	CONTINUOUS HIGH CHAIR	SAME AS HC IN 5 FOOT AND 10 FOOT LENGTHS.
UCHC*	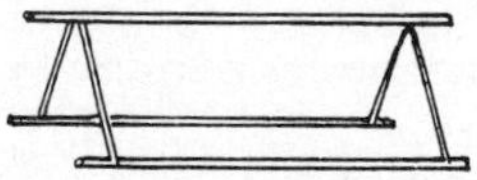	UPPER CONTIN--UOUS HIGH CHAIR	SAME AS CHC.

* AVAILABLE IN CLASS "A" ONLY EXCEPT ON SPECIAL ORDER.

CONCRETE REINFORCING STEEL INSTITUTE.

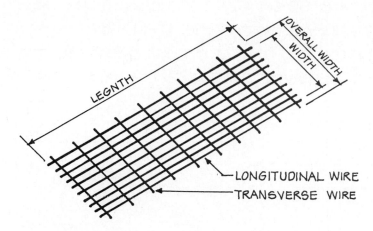

LEGNTH

OVERALL WIDTH

WIDTH

LONGITUDINAL WIRE
TRANSVERSE WIRE

INDUSTRY METHOD
OF DESIGNATING

EXAMPLE: WWF6 x 12 - W16 x W26
LONGITUDINAL WIRE SPACING   6"
TRANSVERSE WIRE SPACING   12"
LONGITUDINAL WIRE SIZE   16"
TRANSVERSE WIRE SIZE   26"

MIN. LAP IS
ONE SPACE
PLUS 2 INCHES

2"

SMOOTH WIRE CONFORMS TO ASTM-A82.
DEFORMED WIRE CONFORMS TO ASTM-A496.
SMOOTH WELDED FABRIC CONFORMS TO ASTM-A185.
DEFORMED WELDED FABRIC CONFORMS TO ASTM-A497.
SMOOTH WIRE IS INDICATED BY THE LETTER **W**.
DEFORMED WIRE IS INDICATED BY THE LETTER **D**.
FABRIC WITH WIRE SIZES SMALLER THAN W1.4
AVAILABLE IN ROLLS. FABRIC WITH WIRE SIZES
LARGER THAN W5.5 AVAILABLE ONLY IN SHEETS.

STYLE DESIGNATION		SPACING OF WIRE (INCH)		DIAM. OF WIRE (INCH)		SECTION AREA (SQ.IN. PER FT.)		WEIGHT (LBS.)
OLD BY STL. WIRE SIZE	NEW BY W NUMBER	LONG.	TRANS.	LONG.	TRANS.	LONG.	TRANS.	100 SQ.FT.
6 x 6 —10 x 10	6 x 6 -W1.4 x W1.4	6	6	.135	.135	.029	.029	21
6 x 6 — 8 x 8	6 x 6 - W2.1 x W2.1	6	6	.162	.162	.041	.041	30
6 x 6 — 6 x 6	6 x 6 - W2.9 x W29	6	6	.192	.192	.058	.058	42
6 x 6 — 4 x 4	6 x 6 - W4 x W4	6	6	.225	.225	.080	.080	58
4 x 4 —10 x 10	4 x 4 -W1.4 x W1.4	4	4	.135	.135	.043	.043	31
4 x 4 — 8 x 8	4 x 4 -W2.1 x W2.1	4	4	.162	.162	.062	.062	44
4 x 4 — 6 x 6	4 x 4 -W2.9 x W29	4	4	.192	.192	.087	.087	62
4 x 4 — 4 x 4	4 x 4 -W4 x W4	4	4	.225	.225	.120	.120	85
4 x 12 - 8 x 12	4 x 12-W2.1 x W0.9	4	12	.162	.1055	.062	.009	25
4 x 12 - 7 x 11	4 x 12-W2.5 x W1.1	4	12	.177	.1205	.074	.011	31

CONCRETE REINFORCING STEEL INSTITUTE

CHARTS GIVEN BELOW CONSIDER ONLY THE NORMAL USE OF A SINGLE SYSTEM AND DO NOT CONSIDER EXTREME POSSIBILITIES. CHARTS SHOULD BE USED FOR PRELIMINARY DESIGN ONLY. IF GREATER THAN NORMAL LOADS ARE ANTICIPATED, OR WIDER THAN NORMAL SPACING, USE UPPER PORTION OF CHART. USE LOWER PORTION FOR LIGHT LOADS. FOR CANTILEVERS USE THREE TIMES CANTILEVER LENGTH TO DETERMINE THICKNESS OR DEPTH.

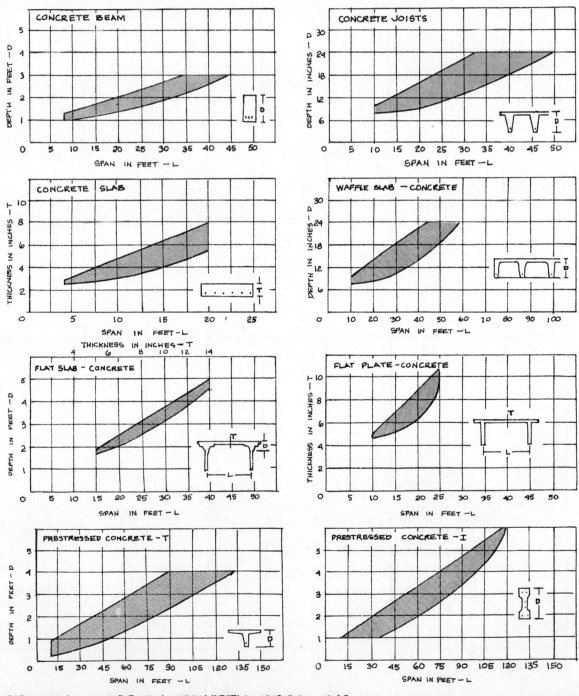

SERNOLL DIVISION: BAWDEN BROS. INC.

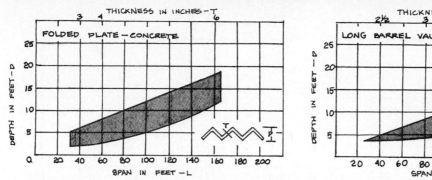

CHARTS GIVEN BELOW ASSUME UNSUPPORTED HEIGHT FROM 1 TO 50 FEET
AND PRIMARILY SUPPORT ONLY A ROOF OR ONE-STORY LOAD **OR** ARE
STRUCTURAL SUPPORTS WHICH HAVE A NORMAL ONE-STORY HEIGHT AND
MUST SUPPORT FROM 1 TO 50 STORIES. NORMAL UNSUPPORTED STORY
HEIGHT IS ASSUMED 8 TO 12 FEET. MIDDLE RANGE OF CHART SHOULD
BE USED FOR NORMAL LOADING. USE FOR PRELIMINARY DESIGN ONLY.

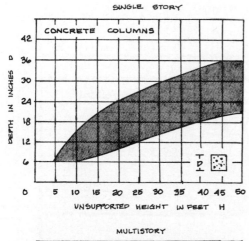

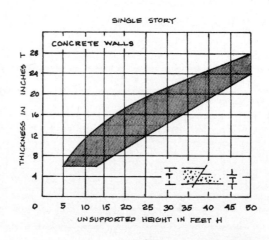

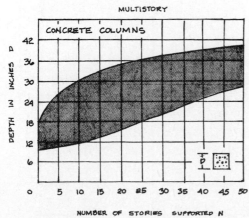

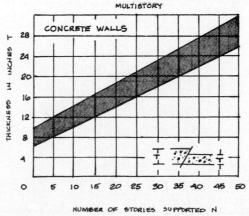

SERNOLL DIVISION: BAWDEN BROS. INC.

DEPTH	12			14			16			18		
FLANGE		3.0		3.0	3.3	3.3	3.0	3.3	4.0	3.0	3.3	4.3
WIDTH	6	8	10	8	10	12	8	10	12	8	10	12
STR. STL.	2#4	2#4	2#6	2#4	2#6	3#6	2#5	2#6	3#6	2#5	2#6	3#6
TRUSS STL.	—	1#5	2#5	—	2#5	2#7	—	2#5	2#7	—	2#5	2#7
ULTIMATE USABLE LOAD (Plf)												
8-0	2052	3550	6562	2537	7932	11918	4519	9486	13900			
10-0	1313	2271	4576	1624	5529	9253	2892	6609	10796			
12-0	912	1577	3177	1127	3839	6426	2008	4589	7497			
14-0	670	1160	2334	828	2820	4721	1475	3372	5508	1703	3923	6273
16-0	513	887	1787	634	2159	3614	1129	2581	4217	1304	3003	4880
18-0	405	701	1412	501	1706	2856	892	2039	3332	1020	2373	3855
20-0	328	567	1144	406	1382	2313	723	1652	2699	834	1922	3123
22-0	271	469	945	335	1142	1911	597	1365	2230	689	1588	2581
24-0	228	394	794	281	959	1606	502	1147	1874	579	1334	2168
26-0	194	336	676	240	817	1368	427	977	1596	493	1137	1848
28-0										425	980	1593
30-0										370	854	1388

DEPTH	20			22			24			26		
FLANGE	3.0	3.3	4.7	4.6	4.7	5.5	4.7	6.0	5.8	4.7	6.8	6.3
WIDTH	8	10	12	10	12	14	12	14	16	12	14	16
STR. STL.	2#5	2#6	3 6	2#7	3#6	3#9	3#6	3#9	4#11	3#6	3#9	4#10
TRUSS STL	—	2#5	2#7	2#6	2#7	2#9	2#7	2#8	4#9	2#7	2#8	4#9
ULTIMATE USABLE LOAD (Plf)												
14-0	1931	4474	7229	6735	8155	11374						
16-0	1478	3425	5534	5157	6243	9953						
18-0	1168	2706	4373	4074	4933	8847						
20-0	946	2192	3542	3300	3995	7687	4449	7799	11698	4963	8484	12860
22-0	782	1811	2927	2727	3302	6353	3677	6446	10635	4052	7012	11691
24-0	657	1522	2459	2292	2774	5338	3089	5416	9748	3404	5892	10717
26-0	559	1297	2096	1953	2364	4548	2632	4615	3998	2901	5020	9538
28-0	482	1118	1807	1683	2038	3922	2270	3979	8356	2501	4329	8224
30-0	420	974	1574	1466	1775	3416	1977	3466	7347	2180	3771	7164
32-0		856	1383	1289	1560	3002	1738	3046	6457	1915	3314	6298
34-0		758	1225	1142	1382	2660	1539	2698	5720	1696	2935	5577
36-0							1373	2407	5100	1513	2618	4975

THICKNESS	4	5	6	7	8	9	10
BOTTOM BAR	#3 @ 12	#3 @ 12	#4 @ 12	#4 @ 12	#4 @ 12	#4 @ 12	
TOP BAR	#3 @ 12	#3 @ 12	#4 @ 12	#4 @ 12	#4 @ 12	#4 @ 12	
TEMP.	#3 @ 15	#3 @ 12	#4 @ 18	#4 @ 15	#4 @ 13	#4 @ 12	
ULTIMATE USABLE LOAD (PSF)							
4 - 0	661	890					
5 - 0	396	536					
6 - 0	252	343	856	1037			
7 - 0	165	227	599	727	855	983	
8 - 0	109	152	432	526	619	713	
9 - 0	70	100	318	388	458	528	
10 - 0	42	63	236	289	342	395	
11 - 0			129	160	192	223	
12 - 0			65	83	101	119	
14 - 0					42	51	
16 - 0							
18 - 0							

THICKNESS	4	5	6	7	8	9	10
BOTTOM BAR	#4 @ 12	#4 @ 10	#4 @ 8	#5 @ 10	#6 @ 12	#6 @ 11	#6 @ 10
TOP BAR	#3 @ 12	#3 @ 12	#4 @ 12	#4 @ 12	#4 @ 12	#4 @ 12	#4 @ 12
TEMP.	#3 @ 15	#3 @ 12	#4 @ 18	#4 @ 15	#4 @ 13	#4 @ 12	#5 @ 17
ULTIMATE USABLE LOAD (PSF)							
4 - 0	1204						
5 - 0	743	1223					
6 - 0	493	821					
7 - 0	342	578	937				
8 - 0	244	420	691	1050			
9 - 0	177	312	522	802	1126		
10 - 0	129	235	402	624	884		
12 - 0	67	134	244	393	568	731	929
14 - 0		74	150	254	377	492	633
16 - 0			88	164	254	337	440
18 - 0			46	102	169	231	308
20 - 0				57	108	155	214

THICKNESS	4	5	6	7	8	9	10
BOTTOM BAR	#4 @ 8	#4 @ 6	#4 @ 5	#5 @ 7	#5 @ 6	#6 @ 7	#7 @ 8
TOP BAR	#3 @ 12	#3 @ 12	#4 @ 12	#4 @ 12	#4 @ 11	#4 @ 9	#4 @ 8
TEMP.	#3 @ 15	#3 @ 12	#4 @ 18	#4 @ 15	#4 @ 13	#4 @ 12	#5 @ 17
ULTIMATE USABLE LOAD (PSF)							
4 - 0							
5 - 0	1119						
6 - 0	754						
7 - 0	534	989					
8 - 0	391	735	1135				
9 - 0	293	561	873				
10 - 0	223	437	686	927			
12 - 0		274	442	607	856		
14 - 0			295	413	592	840	
16 - 0				287	421	603	838
18 - 0				201	304	441	623
20 - 0					220	325	469

THICKNESS	4	5	6	7	8	9	10
BOTTOM AND TRUSS	#4 @ 12	#4 @ 12	#4 @ 12	#4 @ 12	#4 @ 12	#4 @ 12	
TOP BAR	#4 @ 12	#4 @ 12	#4 @ 12	#4 @ 12	#4 @ 12	#4 @ 12	
TEMP.	#3 @ 15	#3 @ 12	#4 @ 18	#4 @ 15	#4 @ 13	#4 @ 12	
ULTIMATE USABLE LOAD (PSF)							
4 - 0	1315				MIN. REINF. ≥ 0.0018 bt		
5 - 0	815	1103					
6 - 0	542	737	931	1126			
7 - 0	379	517	654	792			
8 - 0	272	373	474	576	909	1044	
9 - 0	199	275	351	427	686	789	
10 - 0	147	205	263	321	528	607	
12 - 0	79	114	148	183	277	321	
14 - 0		58	79	99	164	191	
16 - 0				45	90	106	
18 - 0					40	49	
20 - 0							

THICKNESS	4	5	6	7	8	9	10
BOTTOM AND TRUSS	#4 #5 @ 11	#4 #5 @ 9	#4 #5 @ 7	#4 #5 @ 6	#5 #6 @ 7	#5 #6 @ 6	#5 #6 @ 5
TOP BAR	#4 @ 12	#4 @ 12	#4 @ 9	#5 @ 12	#6 @ 14	#6 @ 12	#6 @ 10
TEMP.	#3 @ 15	#3 @ 12	#4 @ 18	#4 @ 15	#4 @ 13	#4 @ 12	#5 @ 17
ULTIMATE USABLE LOAD (PSF)							
4 - 0							
5 - 0			BOTTOM STEEL +M: $\rho \sim 0.0075$				
6 - 0	956		TOP STEEL FOR -M: $\rho \leq 0.00833$				
7 - 0	682	1119					
8 - 0	505	835					
9 - 0	383	640	1086				
10 - 0	296	500	858				
12 - 0	182	319	561	843			
14 - 0		209	382	585	827		
16 - 0		138	266	417	598	815	
18 - 0			187	302	441	608	838
20 - 0				219	328	461	643

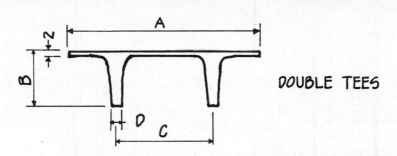

DOUBLE TEES

A	B	C	D	WEIGHT SQ. FT.	MAX. ROOF SPAN	MAX. FLOOR SPAN	
7-11¾	14	4-0	3¾	39.8	30-0	26-0	
7-11¾	14	4-0	5⅞	44.6	45-0	36-0	
7-11¾	24	4-0	4¾	57.9	64-0	53-0	
7-11¾	28	4-0	6½	80.0	88-0	70-0	
11-11¾	26	6-0	7¼	67.0	70-0	60-0	
11-11¾	36	6-0	7¼	79.6	90-0	80-0	BRIDGE SPAN TO 48-0
11-11¾	41	6-0	7¼	85.9	94-0	90-0	BRIDGE SPAN TO 65-0

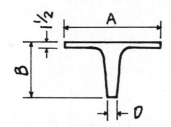

SINGLE TEES

A	B	D		WEIGHT SQ. FT.	MAX. ROOF SPAN	MAX. FLOOR SPAN	
9-11½	26	6½		49.9	59.0		
3-11¾	41	10		139.0		63.0*	* BRIDGE SPANS

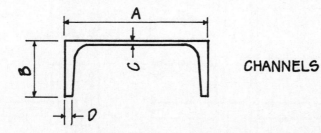

CHANNELS

A	B	C	D	WEIGHT	MAX. ROOF SPAN	MAX. FLOOR SPAN
9-11⅝	29½	4½	5½	71.4	61.0	58.0
9-11½	16	3½	5½	60.8	38.0	32.0

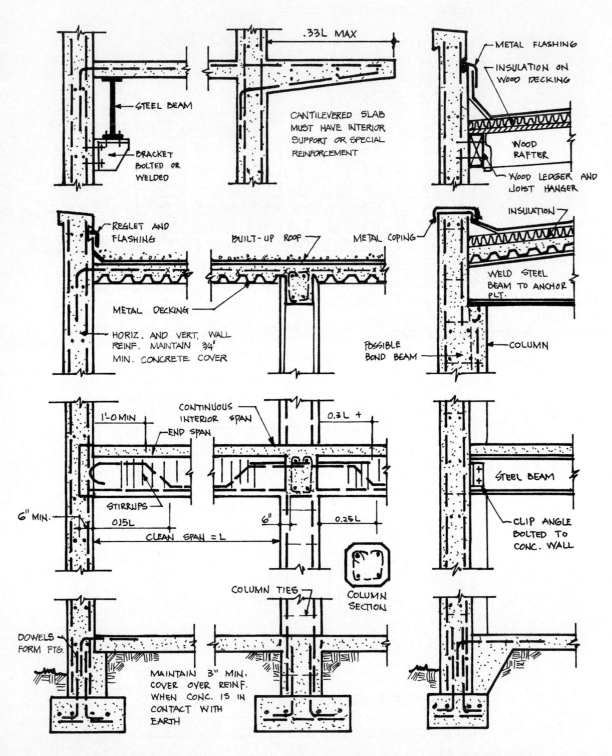

- STEEL BEAM
- BRACKET BOLTED OR WELDED
- .33L MAX
- CANTILEVERED SLAB MUST HAVE INTERIOR SUPPORT OR SPECIAL REINFORCEMENT
- METAL FLASHING
- INSULATION ON WOOD DECKING
- WOOD RAFTER
- WOOD LEDGER AND JOIST HANGER

- REGLET AND FLASHING
- METAL DECKING
- HORIZ. AND VERT. WALL REINF. MAINTAIN 3/4" MIN. CONCRETE COVER
- BUILT-UP ROOF
- METAL COPING
- INSULATION
- WELD STEEL BEAM TO ANCHOR PLT.
- POSSIBLE BOND BEAM
- COLUMN

- 1'-0 MIN
- END SPAN
- CONTINUOUS INTERIOR SPAN
- 0.3L +
- 6" MIN.
- STIRRUPS 0.15L
- CLEAN SPAN = L
- 6"
- 0.25L
- STEEL BEAM
- CLIP ANGLE BOLTED TO CONC. WALL

- DOWELS FORM FTG.
- MAINTAIN 3" MIN. COVER OVER REINF. WHEN CONC. IS IN CONTACT WITH EARTH
- COLUMN TIES
- COLUMN SECTION

FOR ONE WAY, TWO WAY, WAFFLE PAN, AND CONCRETE JOIST SYSTEMS, SEE FOLLOWING SYSTEMS.

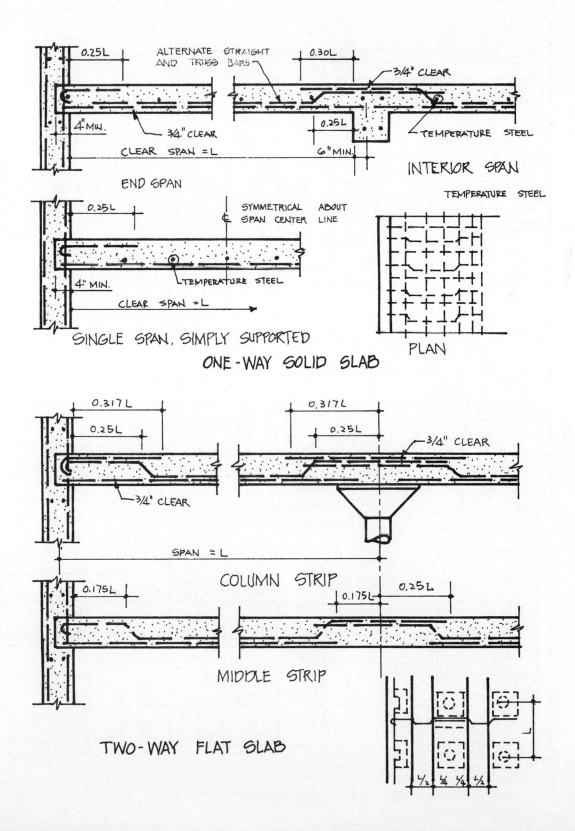

0.25L ALTERNATE STRAIGHT AND TRUSS BARS

0.30L

3/4" CLEAR

3/4" CLEAR

4" MIN.

CLEAR SPAN = L

0.25L

6" MIN.

TEMPERATURE STEEL

END SPAN

INTERIOR SPAN

0.25L

SYMMETRICAL ABOUT SPAN CENTER LINE

TEMPERATURE STEEL

TEMPERATURE STEEL

4" MIN.

TEMPERATURE STEEL

CLEAR SPAN = L

SINGLE SPAN, SIMPLY SUPPORTED

PLAN

ONE-WAY SOLID SLAB

0.317L

0.317L

0.25L

0.25L

3/4" CLEAR

3/4" CLEAR

SPAN = L

COLUMN STRIP

0.175L

0.175L

0.25L

MIDDLE STRIP

TWO-WAY FLAT SLAB

L/2 L/4 L/4 L/2

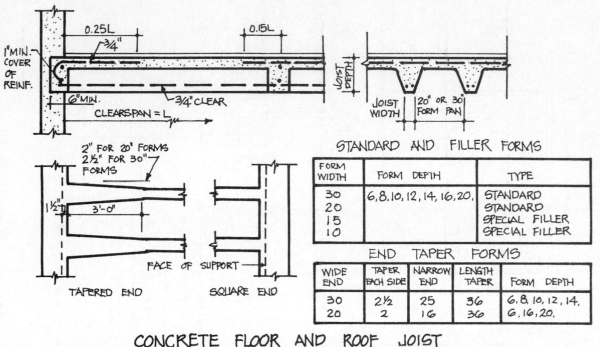

STANDARD AND FILLER FORMS

FORM WIDTH	FORM DEPTH	TYPE
30	6,8,10,12,14,16,20,	STANDARD
20		STANDARD
15		SPECIAL FILLER
10		SPECIAL FILLER

END TAPER FORMS

WIDE END	TAPER EACH SIDE	NARROW END	LENGTH TAPER	FORM DEPTH
30	2½	25	36	6,8,10,12,14,
20	2	16	36	6,16,20,

CONCRETE FLOOR AND ROOF JOIST

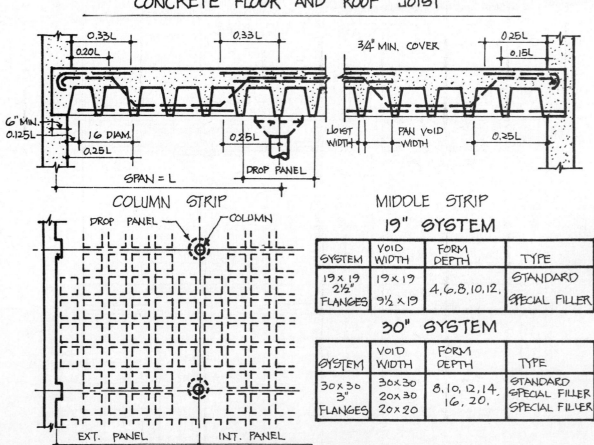

COLUMN STRIP   MIDDLE STRIP

19" SYSTEM

SYSTEM	VOID WIDTH	FORM DEPTH	TYPE
19 x 19 2½" FLANGES	19 x 19	4,6,8,10,12,	STANDARD
	9½ x 19		SPECIAL FILLER

30" SYSTEM

SYSTEM	VOID WIDTH	FORM DEPTH	TYPE
30 x 30 3" FLANGES	36 x 30	8,10,12,14, 16, 20,	STANDARD
	20 x 30		SPECIAL FILLER
	20 x 20		SPECIAL FILLER

WAFFLE-PAN CONSTRUCTION

WESTERN CONCRETE REINFORCING STEEL INSTITUTE

WALL PANEL / COLUMN INTERSECTIONS

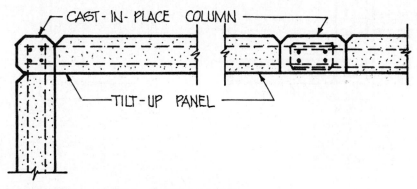

COLUMN FLUSH BOTH FACES

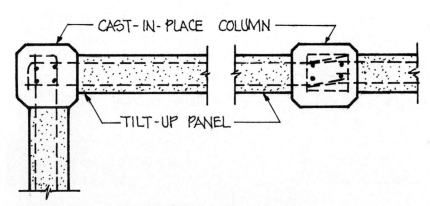

COLUMN PROTRUDING BOTH FACES

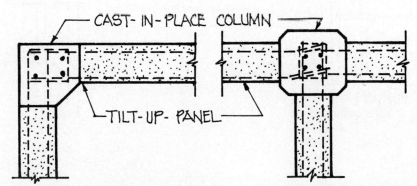

FLUSH DIAGONAL CORNER   INTERSECTING WALL

EDGE OF PANELS MAY BE SHAPED TO PROVIDE BETTER BOND
WITH COLUMN OR TO ADD WEATHER TIGHTNESS.

FOUNDATIONS

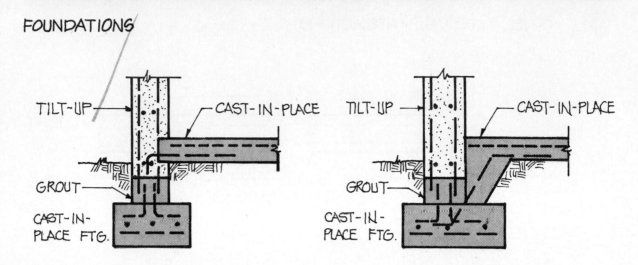

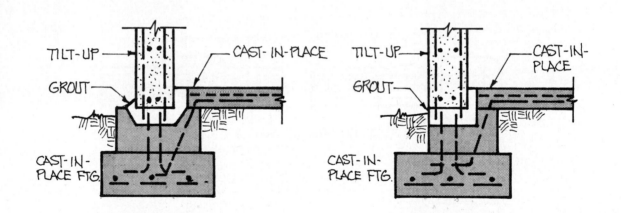

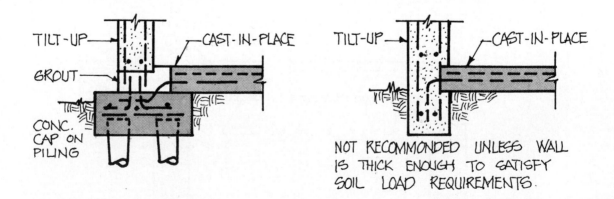

NOT RECOMMONDED UNLESS WALL
IS THICK ENOUGH TO SATISFY
SOIL LOAD REQUIREMENTS.

DOWELS MUST OCCUR AT ALL GROUTED CONNECTIONS AND MUST
EXTEND FROM PRECAST TILT-UP PANELS INTO MORE PLASTIC PARTS
THAT ARE CAST-IN-PLACE, EXCEPT FOUNDATIONS AS SHOWN ABOVE.

ROOF-TO-WALL CONNECTIONS

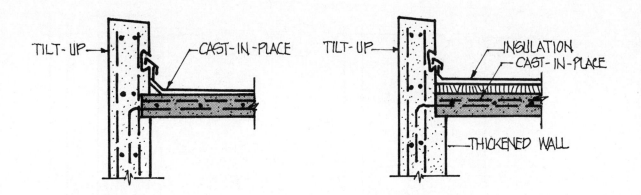

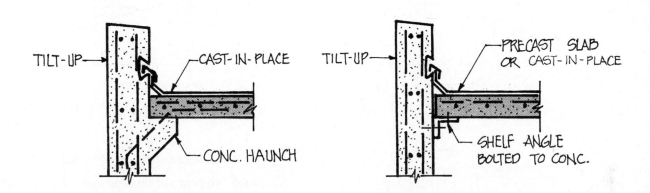

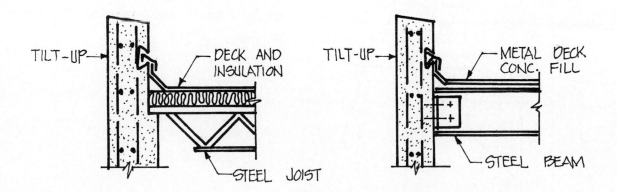

DOWELS AND/OR BOLTS MUST BE INSTALLED IN TILT-UP PANELS
TO CONNECT CAST-IN-PLACE CONCRETE OR OTHER MATERIALS.

GRAVITY TYPE—NOT REINFORCED

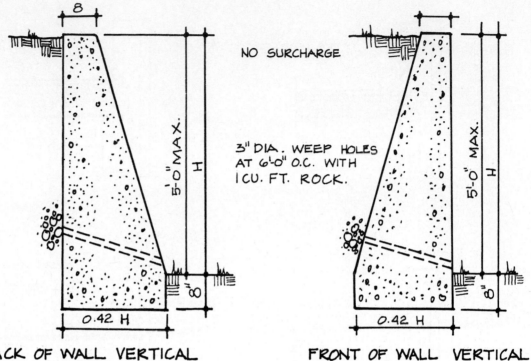

NO SURCHARGE

3" DIA. WEEP HOLES AT 6'-0" O.C. WITH 1 CU. FT. ROCK.

8

5'-0" MAX.

H

8"

0.42 H

BACK OF WALL VERTICAL

8

5'-0" MAX.

H

8"

0.42 H

FRONT OF WALL VERTICAL

GRAVITY-TYPE RETAINING WALLS ARE NOT REINFORCED SO ARE DEPENDENT UPON MASS ALONE TO HOLD THE EARTH.

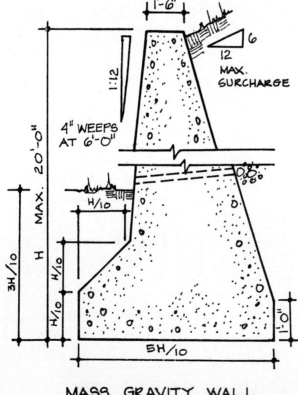

1'-6"

1:12

6

12

MAX. SURCHARGE

4" WEEPS AT 6'-0"

MAX. 20'-0"

H

H/10

3H/10

H/10

H/10

H/10

1'-0"

5H/10

MASS GRAVITY WALL

CONCRETE RETAINING WALLS 3.20

WALLS CALCULATED ON THE
FOLLOWING:

    CONCRETE DESIGN $f_c = 2000$ psi

    MAX. SOIL PRESSURE 1500 #/SQ. FT.

    FLUID PRESSURE 30# CU. FT

    OVERTURN FACTOR 1:5

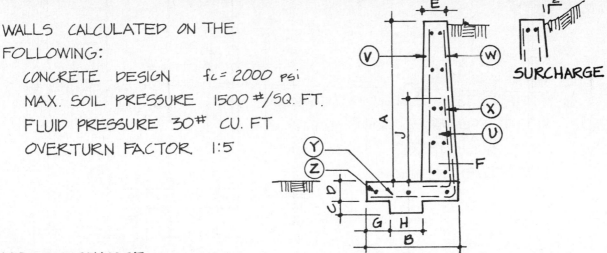

SURCHARGE

NO SURCHARGE

A	B	C	D	E	F	G	H	J	REINFORCEMENT					
									U	V	W	X	Y	Z
4-0	2-8	1-0	1-0	8	9	6	1-0	—	—	—	4e16	4e24	4e16	3#4
5-0	2-10	1-0	1-0	8	10	8	1-0	—	—	—	4e16	4e24	4e16	3#4
6-0	3-2	1-0	1-0	8	10	1-0	1-0	—	—	—	4e16	4e24	4e16	3#4
7-0	3-6	1-0	1-0	8	1-0	1-2	1-0	—	—	4e24	5e16	5e24	5e16	3#5
8-0	4-4	1-0	1-0	8	1-0	1-8	1-2	5-0	5e11	4e24	5e11	5e24	5e11	3#5
9-0	4-8	1-2	1-2	10	1-2	1-4	1-2	5-0	5e8	4e24	4e8	5e24	5e8	3#5
10-0	5-2	1-2	1-2	10	1-2	1-6	1-2	5-0	5e8	4e24	5e8	5e24	5e8	3#5

1:2 SURCHARGE

A	B	C	D	E	F	G	H	J	REINFORCEMENT					
									U	V	W	X	Y	Z
4-0	2-8	1-0	1-0	8	9	8	1-0	—	—	—	4e16	4e24	4e16	3#4
5-0	3-2	1-0	1-0	8	10	1-4	1-0	—	—	—	5e16	4e24	5e16	3#4
6-0	3-8	1-0	1-0	8	10	1-6	1-0	—	—	—	5e16	4e24	5e16	3#5
7-0	4-0	1-0	1-0	10	1-0	1-6	1-0	—	5e10	4e24	4e10	4e16	5e16	3#5
8-0	4-6	1-2	1-2	10	1-2	1-8	1-2	2-0	6e12	4e24	5e12	4e16	6e12	3#6
9-0	5-0	1-6	1-2	10	1-2	2-0	1-6	5-0	6e9	4e24	5e9	4e16	6e9	3#6
10-0	5-8	1-6	1-2	1-0	1-2	2-8	1-6	6-0	7e9	5e24	6e9	4e12	7e9	3#6

95

WALLS CALCULATED ON THE
FOLLOWING:

    CONCRETE DESIGN $f_c = 2000$ psi
    FLUID PRESSURE $30^\#$ CU. FT.
    MAX. SOIL PRESSURE $1500^\#$/SQ. FT.
    OVERTURN FACTOR   1:5

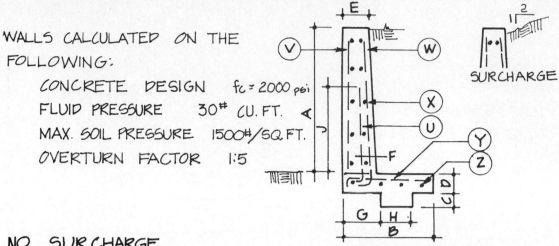

SURCHARGE

NO SURCHARGE

A	B	C	D	E	F	G	H	J	REINFORCEMENT					
									U	V	W	X	Y	Z
4-0	2-4	10	1-0	8	9	1-0	10	—	—	—	4@24	4@24	4@24	3#4
5-0	2-8	1-0	1-0	8	1-0	1-0	1-0	1-6	4@12	4@24	4@12	4@24	4@24	3#4
6-0	3-6	1-0	1-0	8	1-0	1-2	1-0	3-0	4@16	4@24	4@16	4@24	4@16	4#4
7-0	4-0	1-0	1-2	8	1-0	1-6	1-0	3-6	4@16	4@24	4@16	4@24	5@16	4#5
8-0	4-6	1-2	1-2	10	1-2	1-6	1-2	4-0	4@16	4@24	4@16	4@24	5@16	4#5
9-0	5-0	1-2	1-2	10	1-2	1-8	1-2	4-6	5@16	4@24	4@16	4@24	5@16	4#5
10-0	5-6	1-2	1-4	10	1-4	2-0	1-2	5-0	5@12	4@24	4@16	4@24	5@12	5#5

1:2 SURCHARGE

A	B	C	D	E	F	G	H	J	REINFORCEMENT					
									U	V	W	X	Y	Z
4-0	3-2	1-0	1-0	8	9	1-2	1-0	—	—	—	4@24	4@24	4@24	3#4
5-0	3-10	1-0	1-0	8	10	1-4	1-0	—	—	—	4@16	4@24	4@16	4#4
6-0	4-6	1-0	1-0	10	1-0	1-6	1-0	—	—	4@24	4@12	4@24	4@16	4#4
7-0	5-4	1-2	1-2	10	1-0	1-8	1-2	3-6	4@16	4@24	5@16	4@24	5@16	5#5
8-0	6-0	1-2	1-2	10	1-2	2-0	1-2	4-0	5@16	4@24	5@16	4@16	5@16	5#5
9-0	6-10	1-2	1-4	10	1-4	2-4	1-2	4-6	5@12	4@24	5@12	5@24	5@12	5#5
10-0	7-6	1-4	1-4	1-0	1-6	2-6	1-4	6-0	5@12	4@24	5@12	5@24	5@12	6#5

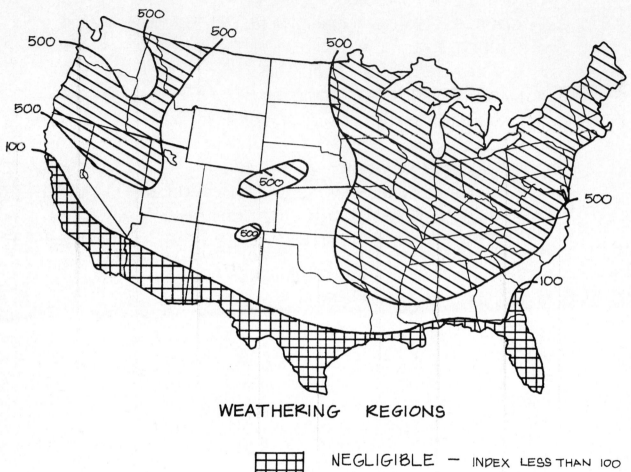

WEATHERING REGIONS

NEGLIGIBLE — INDEX LESS THAN 100

MODERATE — INDEX 100 TO 500

SEVERE — INDEX 500 OR MORE

WEATHERING INDEX IS THE PRODUCT OF THE AVERAGE ANNUAL FREEZING CYCLE DAYS AND THE AVERAGE ANNUAL WINTER RAINFALL IN INCHES. GRADE SW BRICK SHOULD BE USED IN SEVERE AREAS AND IN ANY LOCATION IN CONTACT WITH THE EARTH.

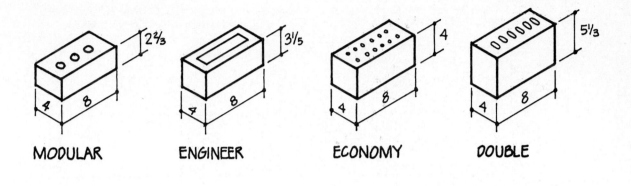

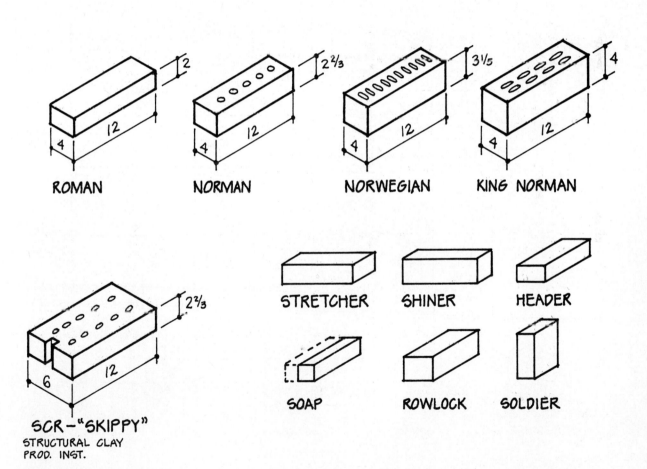

MODULAR ENGINEER ECONOMY DOUBLE

ROMAN NORMAN NORWEGIAN KING NORMAN

STRETCHER SHINER HEADER

SOAP ROWLOCK SOLDIER

SCR-"SKIPPY"
STRUCTURAL CLAY
PROD. INST.

BRICK ARE CLASSIFIED AS **SW** WHERE HIGH RESISTANCE TO WEATHERING IS REQUIRED, **MW** WHERE MODERATE WEATHERING IS EXPECTED, AND **NW** FOR BACKING OR INTERIOR USE. FACE OF BRICK MAY BE SMOOTH, WIRECUT, STIPPLED, RUFFLED, SANDMOLD, OR MANY OTHER TEXTURES.

CONCRETE MASONRY UNITS 4.3

DIMENSIONS AS SHOWN ARE ACTUAL UNIT SIZES. A 7⅝" x 7⅝" x 15⅝" UNIT IS COMMONLY KNOWN AS AN 8" x 8" x 16" CONCRETE BLOCK.
HALF LENGTH UNITS ARE USUALLY AVAILABLE FOR MOST OF THE UNITS SHOWN BELOW. SEE CONCRETE PRODUCTS MANUFACTURER FOR SHAPES AND SIZES OF UNITS LOCALLY AVAILABLE.

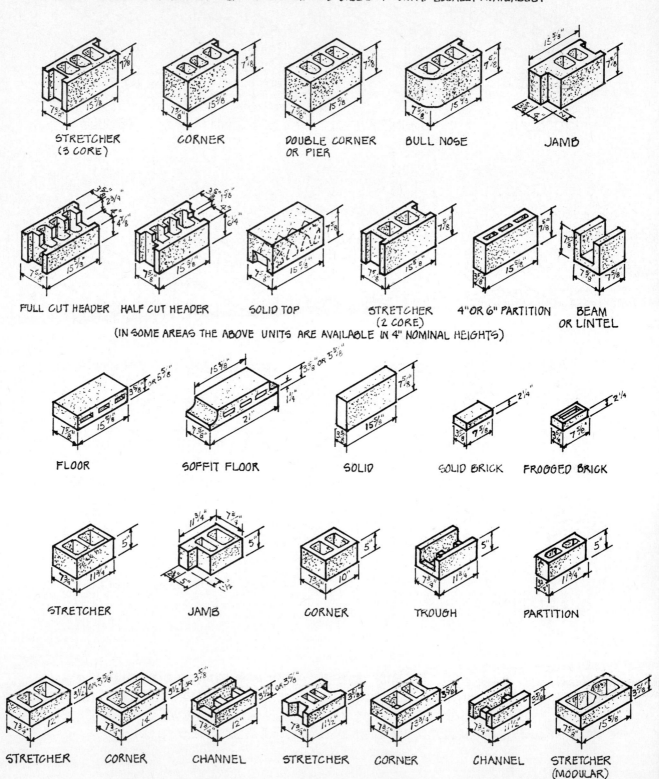

STRETCHER (3 CORE)   CORNER   DOUBLE CORNER OR PIER   BULL NOSE   JAMB

FULL CUT HEADER   HALF CUT HEADER   SOLID TOP   STRETCHER (2 CORE)   4" OR 6" PARTITION   BEAM OR LINTEL

(IN SOME AREAS THE ABOVE UNITS ARE AVAILABLE IN 4" NOMINAL HEIGHTS)

FLOOR   SOFFIT FLOOR   SOLID   SOLID BRICK   FROGGED BRICK

STRETCHER   JAMB   CORNER   TROUGH   PARTITION

STRETCHER   CORNER   CHANNEL   STRETCHER   CORNER   CHANNEL   STRETCHER (MODULAR)

COURSE HEIGHTS FOR CONCRETE BLOCKS 4.4

	WALL HEIGHT			
	3/8" JOINT		1/2" JOINT	
	4" BLOCK	8" BLOCK	4" BLOCK	8" BLOCK
1	4"	8	4⅛"	8⅛"
2	8"	1'-4"	8¼"	1'-4¼"
3	1'-0"	2'-0"	1'-0⅝"	2'-0⅜"
4	1'-4"	2'-8"	1'-4½"	2'-8½"
5	1'-8"	3'-4"	1'-8⅝"	3'-4⅝"
6	2'-0"	4'-0"	2'-0¾"	4'-0¾"
7	2'-4"	4'-8"	2'-4⅞"	4'-8⅞"
8	2'-8"	5'-4"	2'-9"	5'-5"
9	3'-0"	6'-0"	3'-1⅛"	6'-1½"
10	3'-4"	6'-8"	3'-5¼"	6-9¼"
15	5'-0"	10'-0"	5'-1⅞"	10'-1⅞"
20	6'-8"	13'-4"	6'-10½"	13'-6½"
25	8'-4"	16'-8"	8'-7⅛"	16'-11⅛"
30	10'-0"	20'-0"	10'-3¾"	20'-3¾"
35	11'-8"	23'-4"	12'-0⅜"	23'-8⅜"
40	13'-4"	26'-8"	13'-9"	27'-1"
45	15'-0"	30'-0"	15'-5⅝"	30'-5⅝"
50	16'-8"	33'-4"	17'-2¼"	33'-10¼"

STRUCTURAL CLAY TILE

4" WALL THICKNESS

12 × 12   8 × 8 OR 12   10²/₃ × 12   5¹/₃ × 12   5¹/₃ × 12

6" WALL THICKNESS

12 × 12   12 × 12   8 × 12   8 × 12

8" WALL THICKNESS

12 × 12   12 × 12   8 × 12   5¹/₃ × 12   8 × 8   5¹/₃ × 12

8 × 12   5¹/₃ × 12   10²/₃ × 12   6²/₃ × 12   8 × 12 OR 16   8 × 12

10" WALL THICKNESS

5¹/₃ OR 8 × 12 OR 16   12 × 12   12 × 12

12" WALL THICKNESS

12 × 12   12 × 12   8 × 12   8 × 12   8 × 12

STRUCTURAL FACING TILE

STRETCHER

SCORED OR UNSCORED   SOAP

5¹/₁₆"   11³/₄"   3³/₄"
5¹/₁₆"   11³/₄"   3³/₄"
5¹/₁₆"   11³/₄"   1¾"

SOAP

6" STRETCHER   8" STRETCHER
SCORED OR UNSCORED

5¹/₁₆"   11³/₄"   1¾"
5¹/₁₆"   5³/₄"   11³/₄"
5¹/₁₆"   7³/₄"   11³/₄"

STRETCHER

2³/₈"   11³/₄"   3³/₄"
2³/₈"   7³/₄"   3³/₄"   1¾"
2³/₈"   11³/₄"   1¾"

STRETCHER   SOAP

SOAP

2³/₈"   7³/₄"   1¾"
7³/₄"   15³/₄"   3³/₄"
7³/₄"   15³/₄"   1¾"

GLAZED STRUCTURAL UNITS 4.6

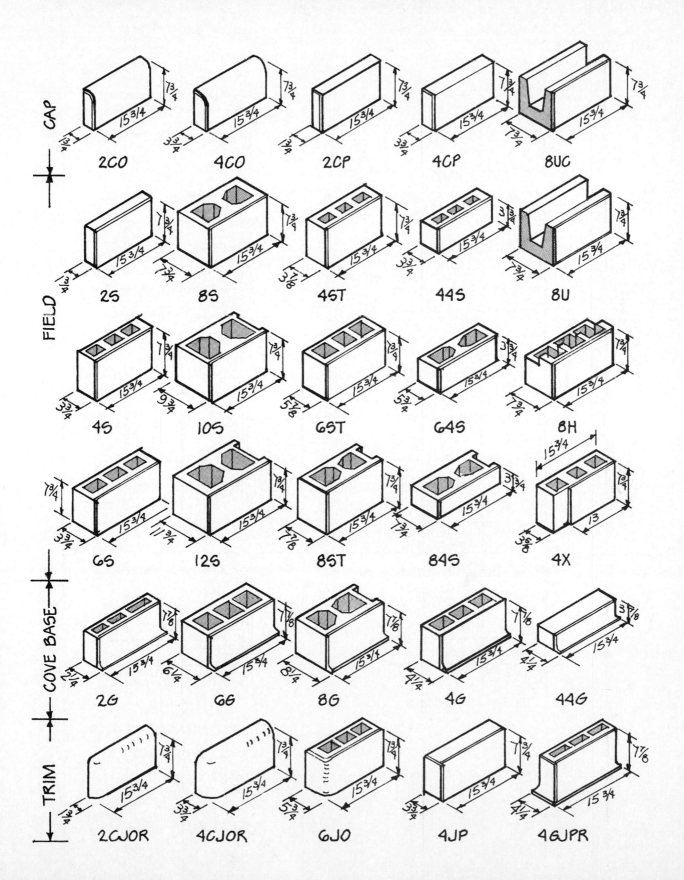

CAP

2CO   4CO   2CP   4CP   8UC

FIELD

2S   8S   4ST   44S   8U

4S   10S   6ST   64S   8H

6S   12S   8ST   84S   4X

COVE BASE

2G   6G   8G   4G   44G

TRIM

2CJOR   4CJOR   6JO   4JP   4GJPR

CONCAVE
RECOMMENDED: TOOLING WORKS
MORTAR TIGHT TO PRODUCE A
GOOD WEATHER JOINT.

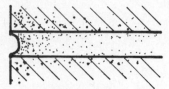

FLUSH
QUESTIONABLE: SPECIAL CARE
REQUIRED TO MAKE WEATHER-
TIGHT AND CLEAN JOINT.

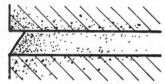

"V" JOINT
RECOMMENDED: TOOLING WORKS
MORTAR TIGHT TO PRODUCE A
GOOD WEATHER JOINT.

RAKED
NOT RECOMMENDED: GIVES A
STRONG HORIZONTAL SHADOW
BUT MAY LEAK AT BOTTOM.

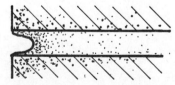

WEATHER
RECOMMENDED: TOOLING WORKS
MORTAR TIGHT TO PRODUCE A
GOOD WEATHER JOINT.

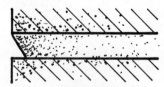

SQUEEZED
NOT RECOMMENDED: GIVES A
RUSTIC EFFECT BUT MORTAR IS
NOT TOOLED TIGHT.

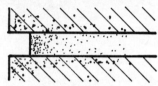

DEEP CONCAVE
RECOMMENDED: GIVES SOME
APPEARANCE OF RAKED JOINT.
MORTAR IS TOOLED TIGHT.

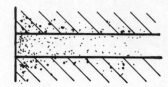

STRUCK
NOT RECOMMENDED: RAIN IS
CHANNELED INTO BOTTOM
OF JOINT.

CHARTS GIVEN BELOW ASSUME AN UNSUPPORTED HEIGHT OF FROM 1 TO 50 FEET AND PRIMARILY SUPPORT ONLY A ROOF OR ONE STORY LOAD **OR** ARE STRUCTURAL SUPPORTS WHICH HAVE A NORMAL ONE STORY HEIGHT AND MUST SUPPORT FROM 1 TO 50 STORIES. NORMAL UNSUPPORTED STORY HEIGHT IS ASSUMED 8 TO 12 FEET. MIDDLE RANGE OF CHART SHOULD BE USED FOR NORMAL LOADING: UPPER PORTION FOR HEAVY LOADS AND LOWER PORTION FOR LIGHT LOADS. USE FOR PRELIMINARY DESIGN ONLY.

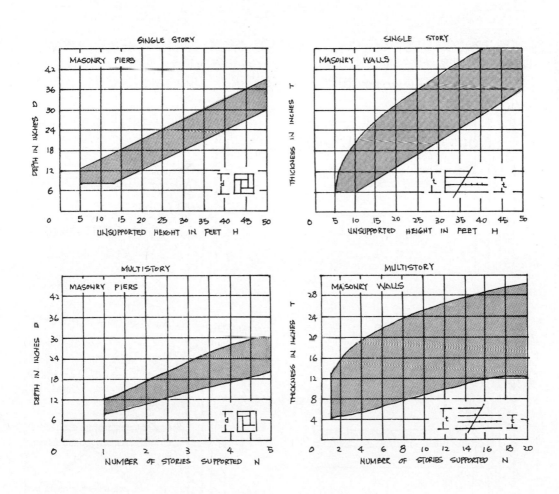

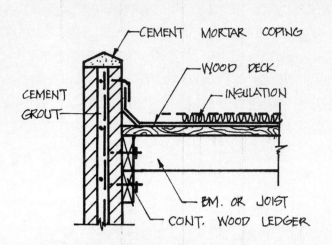

CEMENT MORTAR COPING

CEMENT GROUT

WOOD DECK

INSULATION

BM. OR JOIST

CONT. WOOD LEDGER

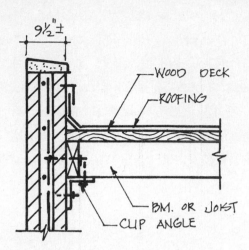

9½"±

WOOD DECK

ROOFING

BM. OR JOIST

CLIP ANGLE

FULLY REINFORCED AND SOLIDLY GROUTED BRICK WALLS SHOWN ABOVE ARE REQUIRED FOR SEISMIC ACTIVITY IN CALIFORNIA. WALLS BUILT WITHOUT REINFORCED - GROUTED SPACE ARE TERMED "CAVITY WALLS".

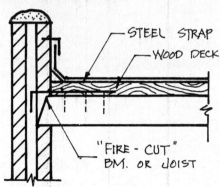

STEEL STRAP

WOOD DECK

"FIRE - CUT" BM. OR JOIST

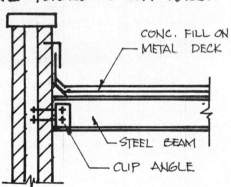

CONC. FILL ON METAL DECK

STEEL BEAM

CLIP ANGLE

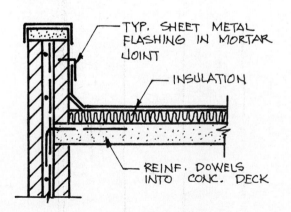

TYP. SHEET METAL FLASHING IN MORTAR JOINT

INSULATION

REINF. DOWELS INTO CONC. DECK

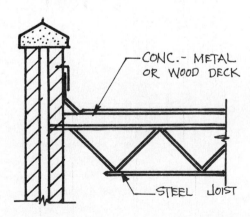

CONC.- METAL OR WOOD DECK

STEEL JOIST

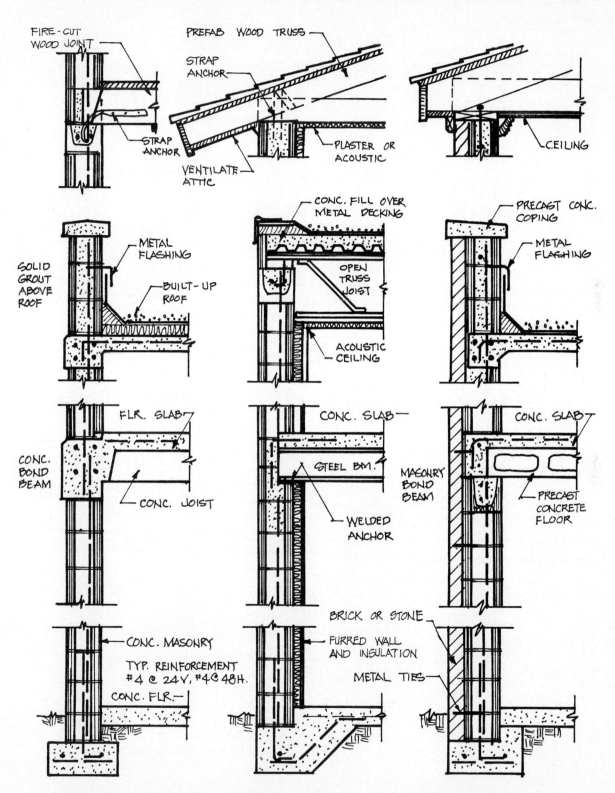

FIRE-CUT WOOD JOINT

STRAP ANCHOR

PREFAB WOOD TRUSS

STRAP ANCHOR

VENTILATE ATTIC

PLASTER OR ACOUSTIC

CEILING

SOLID GROUT ABOVE ROOF

METAL FLASHING

BUILT-UP ROOF

CONC. FILL OVER METAL DECKING

OPEN TRUSS JOIST

ACOUSTIC CEILING

PRECAST CONC. COPING

METAL FLASHING

CONC. BOND BEAM

FLR. SLAB

CONC. JOIST

CONC. SLAB

STEEL BM.

WELDED ANCHOR

MASONRY BOND BEAM

CONC. SLAB

PRECAST CONCRETE FLOOR

CONC. MASONRY

TYP. REINFORCEMENT #4 @ 24V, #4 @ 48H.

CONC. FLR.

BRICK OR STONE

FURRED WALL AND INSULATION

METAL TIES

REINFORCEMENT SHOWN VARIES. CONSULT LOCAL BUILDING CODES.

STEEL WINDOW INSTALLATION DETAILS

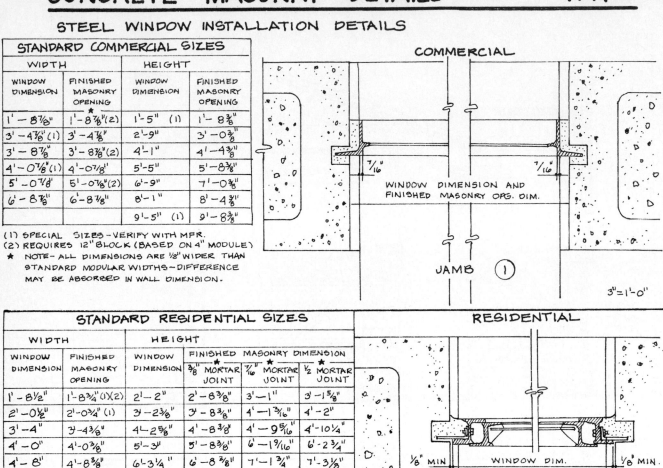

STANDARD COMMERCIAL SIZES			
WIDTH		HEIGHT	
WINDOW DIMENSION	FINISHED MASONRY OPENING ★	WINDOW DIMENSION	FINISHED MASONRY OPENING
1'-8 7/8"	1'-8 7/8" (2)	1'-5" (1)	1'-8 3/8"
3'-4 7/8" (1)	3'-4 7/8"	2'-9"	3'-0 3/8"
3'-8 7/8"	3'-8 7/8" (2)	4'-1"	4'-4 3/8"
4'-0 7/8" (1)	4'-0 7/8"	5'-5"	5'-8 3/8"
5'-0 7/8"	5'-0 7/8" (2)	6'-9"	7'-0 3/8"
6'-8 7/8"	6'-8 7/8"	8'-1"	8'-4 3/8"
		9'-5" (1)	9'-8 3/8"

(1) SPECIAL SIZES - VERIFY WITH MFR.
(2) REQUIRES 12" BLOCK (BASED ON 4" MODULE)
★ NOTE - ALL DIMENSIONS ARE 1/2" WIDER THAN STANDARD MODULAR WIDTHS - DIFFERENCE MAY BE ABSORBED IN WALL DIMENSION.

COMMERCIAL

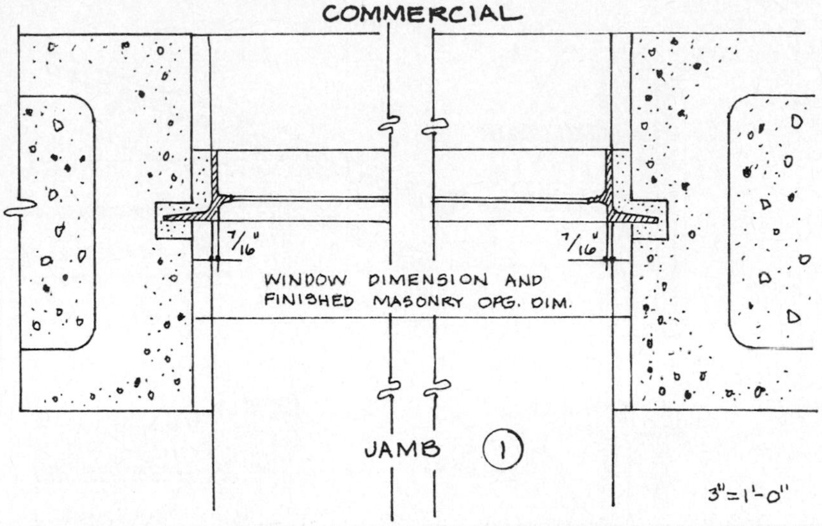
7/16"
7/16"
WINDOW DIMENSION AND FINISHED MASONRY OPG. DIM.

JAMB (1)

3" = 1'-0"

STANDARD RESIDENTIAL SIZES					
WIDTH		HEIGHT			
WINDOW DIMENSION	FINISHED MASONRY OPENING	WINDOW DIMENSION	FINISHED MASONRY DIMENSION ★ 3/8" MORTAR JOINT	★ 7/16" MORTAR JOINT	★ 1/2" MORTAR JOINT
1'-8 1/2"	1'-8 3/4" (1)(2)	2'-2"	2'-8 3/8"	3'-1"	3'-1 5/8"
2'-0 1/2"	2'-0 3/4" (1)	3'-2 3/8"	3'-8 3/8"	4'-1 3/16"	4'-2"
3'-4"	3'-4 3/8"	4'-2 5/8"	4'-8 3/8"	4'-9 5/16"	4'-10 1/4"
4'-0"	4'-0 3/8"	5'-3"	5'-8 3/8"	6'-1 9/16"	6'-2 3/4"
4'-8"	4'-8 3/8"	6'-3 1/4"	6'-8 3/8"	7'-1 3/4"	7'-3 1/8"
6'-0"	6'-0 3/8"				
6'-8"	6'-8 3/8"				
8'-0"	8'-0 3/8"				

★ NOTE - FINISHED MASONRY DIMENSIONS ARE BASED ON 4" BLOCK HEIGHT.

(1) DIMENSIONS ARE 3/8" WIDER THAN STANDARD MODULAR WIDTHS. DIFFERENCE MAY BE ABSORBED IN WALL DIMENSION.
(2) REQUIRES 12" BLOCK (BASED ON 4" MODULE).

RESIDENTIAL

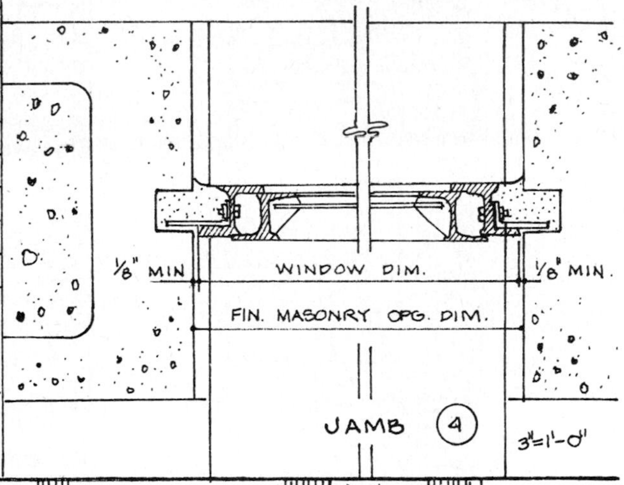
1/8" MIN
WINDOW DIM.
1/8" MIN.
FIN. MASONRY OPG. DIM.

JAMB (4)

3" = 1'-0"

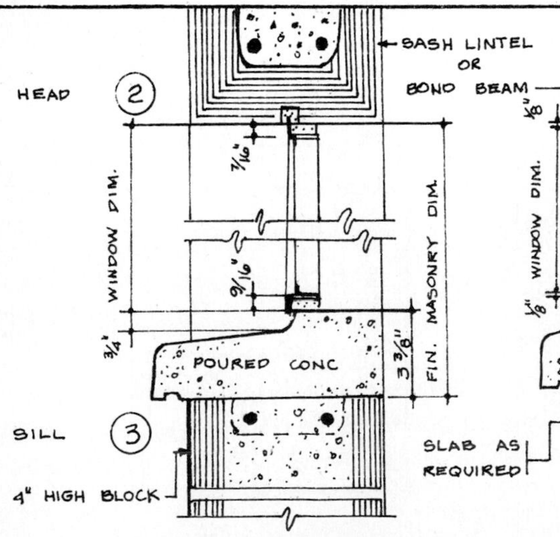
SASH LINTEL OR BOND BEAM
HEAD (2)
7/16"
WINDOW DIM.
9/16"
FIN. MASONRY DIM.
3/4"
POURED CONC
3 3/8"
SILL (3)
4" HIGH BLOCK

COMMERCIAL

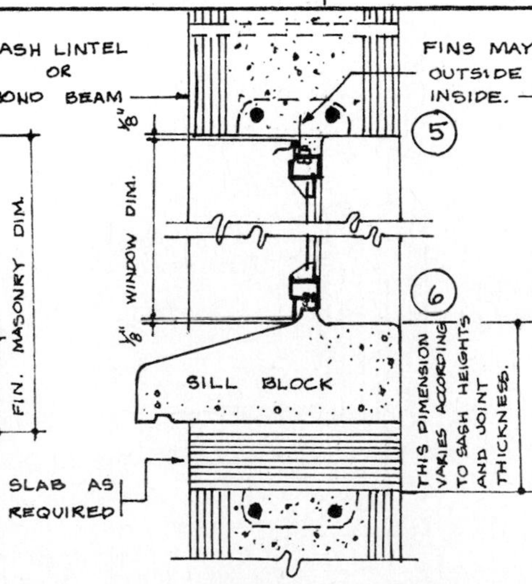
FINS MAY BE ON OUTSIDE OR INSIDE.
5/8"
(5)
WINDOW DIM.
(6)
1/8"
SILL BLOCK
SLAB AS REQUIRED
THIS DIMENSION VARIES ACCORDING TO SASH HEIGHTS AND JOINT THICKNESS.

RESIDENTIAL

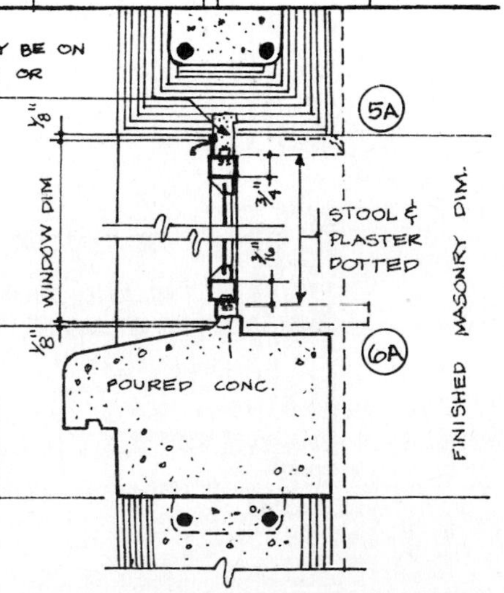
(5A)
1/8"
3/4"
STOOL & PLASTER DOTTED
3/16"
WINDOW DIM
1/8"
(6A)
POURED CONC.
FINISHED MASONRY DIM.

RESIDENTIAL

MASONRY INSTITUTE OF AMERICA.

WOOD DOUBLE-HUNG WINDOW DETAILS

DOUBLE HUNG WOOD WINDOW SIZES USING 2 3/16" JAMB AND HEAD THICKNESS WHICH WILL HARMONIZE WITH GROUP 1 DOORS.

WIDTH		HEIGHT USING 3/8" HORIZ. MORTAR JOINT	
WINDOW DIMENSION	FINISHED MAS. OPG.	WINDOW DIMENSION	FINISHED MAS. OPG.
1'-8"	2'-0 3/8"	2'-0"	2'-8 3/8"
2'-4"	2'-8 3/8"	2'-8"	3'-4 3/8"
3'-0"	3'-4 3/8"	3'-4"	4'-0 3/8"
3'-8"	4'-0 3/8"	4'-0"	4'-8 3/8"
4'-4"	4'-8 3/8"	4'-8"	5'-4 3/8"
5'-0"	5'-4 3/8"	5'-4"	6'-0 3/8"
——	——	ABOVE 3/8" MORTAR JOINT BASED ON 4" AND 8" HI. BLOCK	

HEIGHT USING 7/16 HORIZ. MORTAR JOINT		HEIGHT USING 1/2" HORIZ. MORTAR JOINT	
WINDOW DIMENSION	FINISHED MAS OPG.	WINDOW DIMENSION	FINISHED MAS. OPG.
1'-4 3/8"	2'-0 13/16"	1'-4 3/4"	2'-1 1/4"
2'-0 1/2"	2'-8 15/16"	2'-1"	2'-9 1/2"
2'-6 5/8"	3'-5 1/16"	2'-9 1/4"	3'-5 3/4"
3'-4 3/4"	4'-1 3/16"	3'-5 1/2"	4'-2"
4'-0 7/8"	4'-9 5/16"	4'-1 3/4"	4'-10 1/4"
4'-9"	5'-5 7/16"	4'-10"	5'-6 1/2"

ABOVE 7/16" AND 1/2" MORTAR JOINT BASED ON 4" HIGH BLOCK.

DOUBLE HUNG WOOD WINDOW SIZES USING 1 3/16" JAMB AND HEAD THICKNESS WHICH WILL HARMONIZE WITH GROUP 2 DOORS.

WIDTH		HEIGHT USING 3/8" HORIZ. MORTAR JOINT	
WINDOW DIMENSION	FINISHED MAS. OPG.	WINDOW DIMENSION	FINISHED MAS. OPG.
1'-10"	2'-0 3/8"	2'-1"	2'-8 3/8"
2'-6"	2'-8 3/8"	2'-9"	3'-4 3/8"
3'-2"	2'-4 3/8"	3'-5"	4'-0 3/8"
3'-10"	4'-0 3/8"	4'-1"	4'-8 3/8"
4'-6"	4'-8 3/8"	4'-9"	5'-4 3/8"
5'-2"	5'-4 3/8"	5'-5"	6'-0 3/8"
——	——	ABOVE 3/8" MORTAR JOINT BASED ON 4" AND 8" HI. BLOCK	

HEIGHT USING 7/16 HORIZ. MORTAR JOINT		HEIGHT USING 1/2" HORIZ. MORTAR JOINT	
WINDOW DIMENSION	FINISHED MAS. OPG.	WINDOW DIMENSION	FINISHED MAS. OPG.
1'-5 3/8"	2'-0 13/16"	1'-5 3/4"	2'-1 1/4"
2'-1 1/2"	2'-8 15/16"	2'-2"	2'-9 1/2"
3'-9 5/8"	3'-5 1/16"	2'-10 1/4"	3'-5 3/4"
3'-5 3/4"	4'-1 3/16"	3'-6 1/2"	4'-2"
4'-1 7/8"	4'-9 5/16"	4'-2 3/4"	4'-10 1/4"
4'-10"	5'-5 7/16"	4'-11"	5'-6 1/2"

ABOVE 7/16" AND 1/2" MORTAR JOINT BASED ON 4" HIGH BLOCK.

3" = 1'-0"

HEAD (JAMB SIM)

SILL

HEAD (JAMB SIMILAR)

SILL

FINISHED MASONRY OPG. DIM.

WINDOW DIM.

MORTAR JOINT THICKNESS

MASONRY INSTITUTE OF AMERICA

WALLS CALCULATED ON THE
FOLLOWING:

   CONCRETE DESIGN fc = 2000 psi
   CONCRETE BLOCK "A" GRADE 8 x 16
   MAX. SOIL PRESSURE 1000#/SQ. FT.
   ALL CELLS SOLIDLY GROUTED

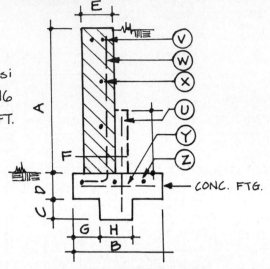

CONC. FTG.

NO SURCHARGE

A	B	C	D	E	F	G	H	J	REINFORCEMENT					
									U	V	W	X	Y	Z
3-4	2-0	—	1-0	6	6	—	—	—	—	2#4	4@24	4@24	3@32	2#4
4-0	2-6	—	1-0	8	8	—	—	—	—	2#4	4@24	4@24	4@48	2#4
5-4	3-6	9	1-0	8	8	9	1-0	1-4	4@24	2#4	4@24	4@32	4@24	3#4
6-0	3-10	9	1-0	8	1-0	9	1-0	1-4	4@24	2#4	4@24	4@48	4@24	3#4
7-4	4-8	1-0	1-0	8	1-0	1-0	1-2	2-0	4@16	2#4	4@24	4@48	4@16	3#4
8-0	5-4	1-0	1-2	8	1-0	1-0	1-2	2-0	5@16	2#4	4@24	4@48	5@16	3#4

NO SURCHARGE

A	B	C	D	E	REINFORCEMENT			
					V	W	X	Y
3-4	1-10	9	6	8	2#3	3@16	3@24	4@36
4-0	2-4	10	7	8	2#3	4@24	4@24	4@32
4-8	2-6	11	8	8	2#4	4@16	4@24	4@24
5-4	2-8	12	9	8	2#4	5@16	4@16	4@16

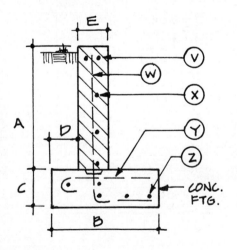

CONC. FTG.

CONCRETE DESIGN fc = 2000 psi
CONCRETE BLOCK "A" GRADE 8" x 16"
ALL CELLS SOLIDLY GROUTED
PROVIDE CONTINUOUS 1½ x 3 KEY BETWEEN
WALL AND CONCRETE FOOTING
"Z" BARS ARE #4 FOR ALL WALL HEIGHTS

WALLS CALCULATED ON THE FOLLOWING:
   CONCRETE DESIGN $f_c = 2000$ psi
   CONCRETE BLOCK "A" GRADE 8"x16"
   MAX. SOIL PRESSURE 1000 lb./sq.ft.

"U" BARS MAY BE TERMINATED AT
HEIGHT INDICATED OR EVERY
THIRD BAR AT 2/3 HEIGHT OF
THE WALL. ALL CELLS SOLID
GROUTED.

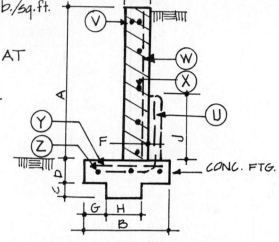

CONC. FTG.

NO SURCHARGE

A	B	C	D	E	F	G	H	J	U	V	W	X	Y	Z
									REINFORCEMENT					
3-4	2-3	—	1-0	6	6	—	—	—	—	2#4	4@24	4@24	3@24	2#4
4-0	2-6	—	1-0	8	8	—	—	—	—	2#4	4@24	4@24	4@48	2#4
5-4	2-9	10	1-0	8	8	1-0	1-0	1-4	4@24	2#4	4@24	4@32	4@32	2#4
6-0	3-3	10	1-2	8	1-0	1-0	1-0	1-4	4@24	2#4	4@24	4@48	4@24	3#4
7-4	3-10	1-0	1-2	8	1-0	1-2	1-2	2-0	4@16	2#4	5@24	4@48	4@16	3#4
8-0	4-6	1-0	1-2	8	1-0	1-2	1-2	2-0	5@16	2#5	6@24	4@48	5@16	4#4
9-4	6-4	1-0	1-2	1-0	1-4	1-4	1-4	2-8	6@16	2#6	8@12	4@48	6@24	5#5

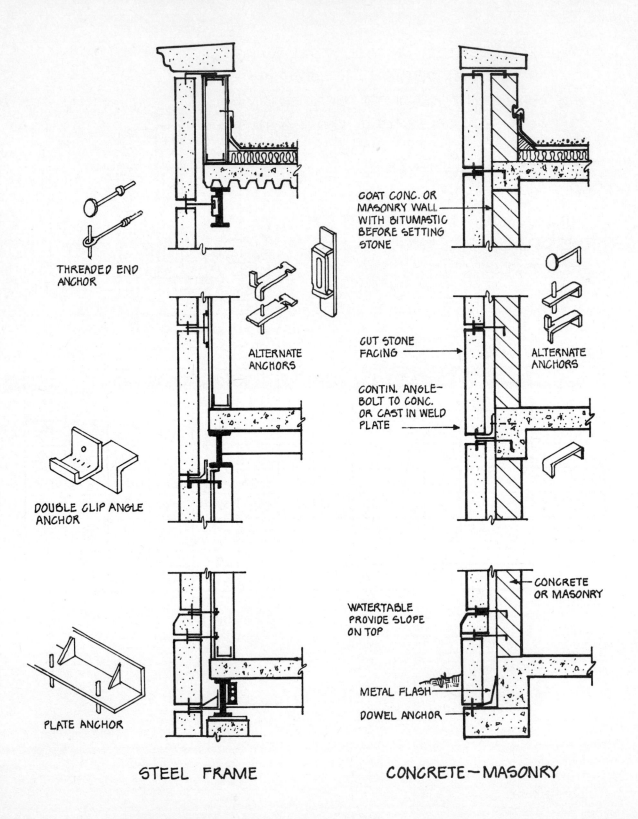

THREADED END
ANCHOR

ALTERNATE
ANCHORS

DOUBLE CLIP ANGLE
ANCHOR

PLATE ANCHOR

STEEL FRAME

COAT CONC. OR
MASONRY WALL
WITH BITUMASTIC
BEFORE SETTING
STONE

CUT STONE
FACING

CONTIN. ANGLE-
BOLT TO CONC.
OR CAST IN WELD
PLATE

ALTERNATE
ANCHORS

WATERTABLE
PROVIDE SLOPE
ON TOP

CONCRETE
OR MASONRY

METAL FLASH

DOWEL ANCHOR

CONCRETE—MASONRY

INDIANA LIMESTONE INSTITUTE

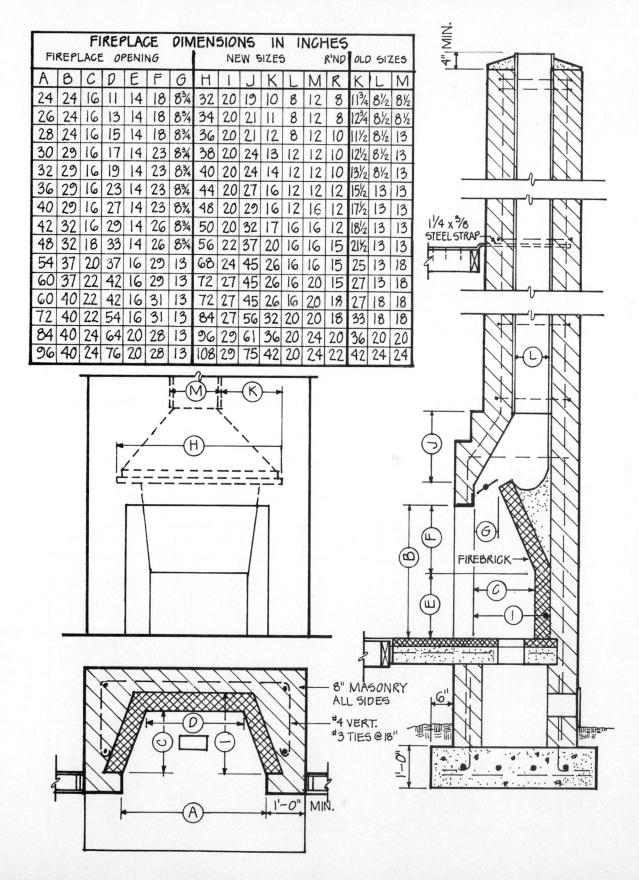

FIREPLACE DIMENSIONS IN INCHES

FIREPLACE OPENING							NEW SIZES						R'ND	OLD SIZES		
A	B	C	D	E	F	G	H	I	J	K	L	M	R	K	L	M
24	24	16	11	14	18	8¾	32	20	19	10	8	12	8	11¾	8½	8½
26	24	16	13	14	18	8¾	34	20	21	11	8	12	8	12¾	8½	8½
28	24	16	15	14	18	8¾	36	20	21	12	8	12	10	11½	8½	13
30	29	16	17	14	23	8¾	38	20	24	13	12	12	10	12½	8½	13
32	29	16	19	14	23	8¾	40	20	24	14	12	12	10	13½	8½	13
36	29	16	23	14	23	8¾	44	20	27	16	12	12	12	15½	13	13
40	29	16	27	14	23	8¾	48	20	29	16	12	16	12	17½	13	13
42	32	16	29	14	26	8¾	50	20	32	17	16	16	12	18½	13	13
48	32	18	33	14	26	8¾	56	22	37	20	16	16	15	21½	13	13
54	37	20	37	16	29	13	68	24	45	26	16	16	15	25	13	18
60	37	22	42	16	29	13	72	27	45	26	16	20	15	27	13	18
60	40	22	42	16	31	13	72	27	45	26	16	20	18	27	18	18
72	40	22	54	16	31	13	84	27	56	32	20	20	18	33	18	18
84	40	24	64	20	28	13	96	29	61	36	20	24	20	36	20	20
96	40	24	76	20	28	13	108	29	75	42	20	24	22	42	24	24

4" MIN.

1¼ x ⅜ STEEL STRAP

FIREBRICK

8" MASONRY ALL SIDES

#4 VERT.
#3 TIES @ 18"

1'-0" MIN.

6"

1'-0"

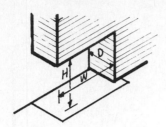

TWO FACE ADJACENT

H	W × D	FLUE
26	32 × 16	12 × 16
29	40 × 16	16 × 16
29	48 × 20	16 × 16

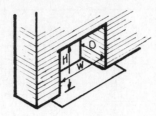

TWO FACE OPPOSITE

H	W × D	FLUE
29	32 × 28	16 × 16
29	36 × 28	16 × 20
29	40 × 28	16 × 20

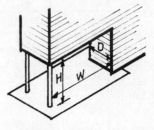

THREE FACE, 2 LONG

H	W × D	FLUE
27	36 × 32	20 × 20
27	36 × 36	20 × 20
27	36 × 40	20 × 20

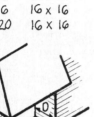

ONE FACE, HOOD

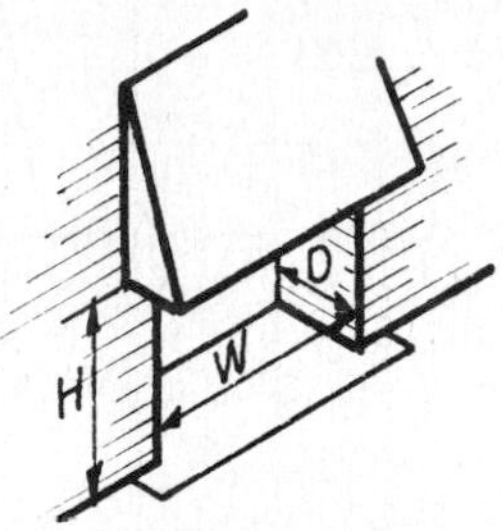

H	W × D	FLUE
26	32 × 20	16 × 16
29	40 × 20	16 × 16
29	48 × 20	16 × 20

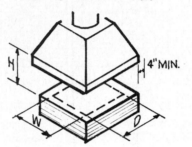

SQUARE, OPEN 4 SIDES

H	W × D	SQ FLUE	R'ND.
26	24 × 24	16 × 16	15
26	28 × 28	13 × 21	15
28	32 × 32	17 × 21	18

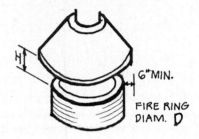

ROUND, OPEN ALL SIDES

H	D	SQ. FLUE	R'ND.
26	32	16 × 20	15
28	36	17 × 21	18
28	42	20 × 20	18

	NOMINAL SIZE	OUTSIDE SIZE	FLUE AREA (SQ. IN.)	FIREPLACE OPEN. (SQ. IN.)		NOMINAL SIZE	OUTSIDE SIZE	FLUE AREA (SQ. IN.)	FIREPLACE OPEN. (SQ. IN.)
SQUARE	8 × 8	8½ × 8½	50	440	**RECTANGULAR**	8½ × 13	8½ 12¾	69	690
	12 × 12	11½ × 11½	87	870		8½ × 17	8½ 16¾	87	870
	13 × 13	13 × 13	124	1240		10 × 18	10 17¾	112	1120
	17 × 17	16¾ × 16¾	171	1710		12 × 16	11½ 15½	120	1200
	18 × 18	17¾ 17¾	232	2320		13 × 17	12¾ 16¾	134	1340
	21 × 21	21 × 21	269	2690		13 × 21	12¾ 21	173	1730
	24 × 24	23 × 23	385	3850		16 × 20	15¼ 19½	208	2080
	24 × 24	25 × 25	420	4200		17 × 21	16¾ 21	223	2230
						20 × 24	19½ 23½	320	3200
ROUND	8½	8½	39	390	**ROUND**	27	31	551	5510
	10	11¾	75	750		30	34¼	683	6830
	13	12¾	91	1092		33	37½	829	8300
	18	20½	240	2400		36	41	990	9900
	20	22¾	298	3000					
	24	27¼	433	4330					

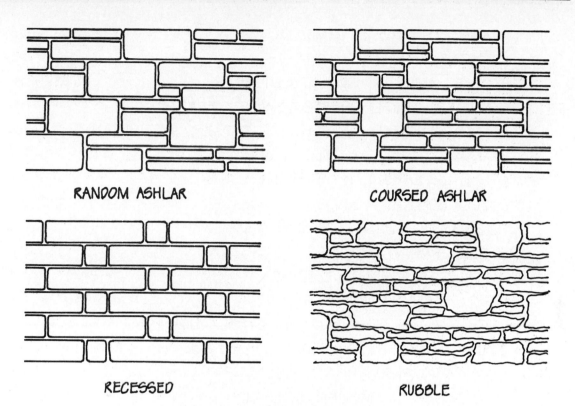

RANDOM ASHLAR   COURSED ASHLAR

RECESSED   RUBBLE

INDIANA LIMESTONE LINTELS
ALLOWABLE UNIFORM LOAD IN POUNDS-INCH WIDTH OF LINTEL

SPAN FEET	HEIGHT OF BEAM OR LINTEL IN INCHES												
	4	6	8	10	12	14	16	18	20	22	24	26	28
3	63	149	272	433	631	865	1140	1450	1790	2170	2590	3050	3550
4	40	101	190	307	452	625	825	1050	1310	1590	1900	2240	2610
5	24	70	138	228	340	474	631	810	1010	1230	1480	1750	2040
6	13	4	100	171	261	370	497	642	806	988	1190	1410	1650
7		29	71	128	202	291	396	517	654	806	975	1160	1360
8		14	47	94	154	228	316	418	534	664	808	966	1140
9			27	64	114	176	251	338	437	549	673	809	958
10			9	39	80	132	196	270	356	452	560	679	809
11				16	50	93	147	211	285	369	463	568	682
12					23	59	104	159	223	296	379	470	571
13						27	65	112	167	231	303	384	474
14							30	69	117	172	235	307	386

MODULUS OF RUPTURE = 1000 PSI
STONE DENSITY = 144 LB./CU.FT.
LINTEL WIDTH = 1 INCH WIDE
FACTOR OF SAFETY = 8
MAX. BENDING STRENGTH = 125 PSI

$$F = \frac{4}{3}\frac{H^2}{L}(125) - \frac{H(L)}{12}$$

F = ALLOWABLE UNIFORM LOAD INCH WIDTH
H = LINTEL HEIGHT IN INCHES
L = CLEAR SPAN IN INCHES

INDIANA LIMESTONE INSTITUTE

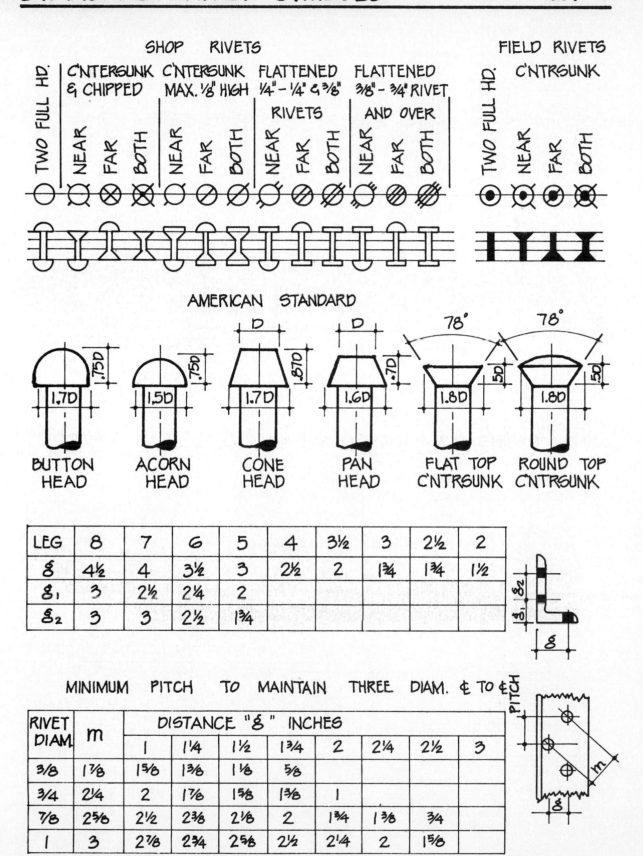

SHOP RIVETS

TWO FULL HD.	C'NTERSUNK & CHIPPED			C'NTERSUNK MAX. ⅛" HIGH			FLATTENED ¼" - ¼" & ⅜" RIVETS			FLATTENED ⅜" - ¾" RIVET AND OVER		
	NEAR	FAR	BOTH	NEAR	FAR	BOTH	NEAR	FAR	BOTH	NEAR	FAR	BOTH

FIELD RIVETS

TWO FULL HD.	C'NTRSUNK		
	NEAR	FAR	BOTH

AMERICAN STANDARD

- BUTTON HEAD — 1.7D, .75D
- ACORN HEAD — 1.5D, .75D
- CONE HEAD — 1.7D, .81D
- PAN HEAD — 1.6D, .7D
- FLAT TOP C'NTRSUNK — 1.8D, 78°, .5D
- ROUND TOP C'NTRSUNK — 1.8D, 78°, .5D

LEG	8	7	6	5	4	3½	3	2½	2
g	4½	4	3½	3	2½	2	1¾	1¾	1½
g_1	3	2½	2¼	2					
g_2	3	3	2½	1¾					

MINIMUM PITCH TO MAINTAIN THREE DIAM. ₵ TO ₵

RIVET DIAM.	m	DISTANCE "g" INCHES							
		1	1¼	1½	1¾	2	2¼	2½	3
3/8	1⅞	1⅝	1⅜	1⅛	⅝				
3/4	2¼	2	1⅞	1⅝	1⅜	1			
7/8	2⅝	2½	2⅜	2⅛	2	1¾	1⅜	¾	
1	3	2⅞	2¾	2⅝	2½	2¼	2	1⅝	

117

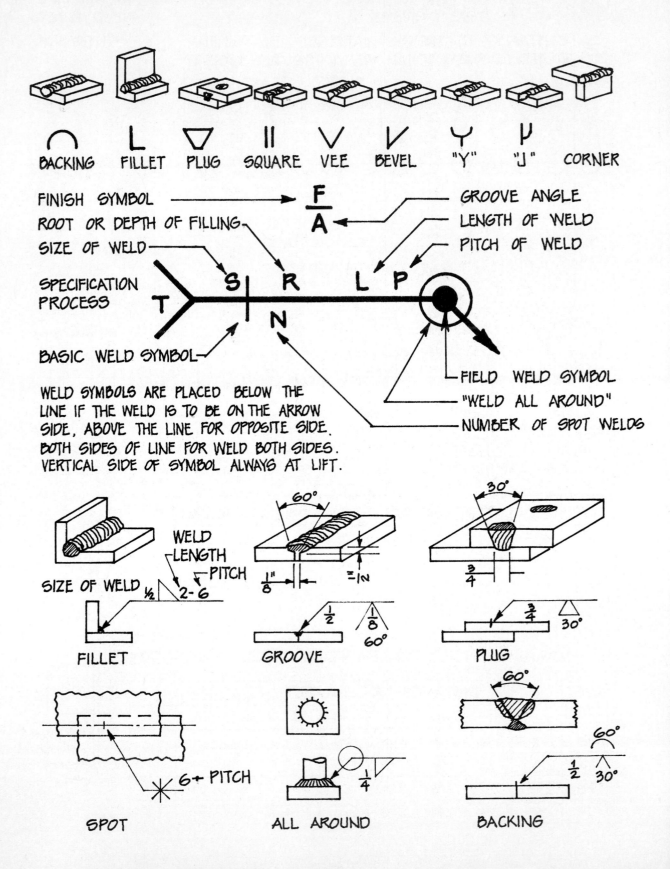

BACKING   FILLET   PLUG   SQUARE   VEE   BEVEL   "Y"   "J"   CORNER

FINISH SYMBOL ——————→

$\dfrac{F}{A}$

ROOT OR DEPTH OF FILLING

SIZE OF WELD

SPECIFICATION
PROCESS

T   S   R   L   P   N

GROOVE ANGLE

LENGTH OF WELD

PITCH OF WELD

BASIC WELD SYMBOL

FIELD WELD SYMBOL

"WELD ALL AROUND"

NUMBER OF SPOT WELDS

WELD SYMBOLS ARE PLACED BELOW THE
LINE IF THE WELD IS TO BE ON THE ARROW
SIDE, ABOVE THE LINE FOR OPPOSITE SIDE.
BOTH SIDES OF LINE FOR WELD BOTH SIDES.
VERTICAL SIDE OF SYMBOL ALWAYS AT LIFT.

WELD
LENGTH
PITCH

SIZE OF WELD $\frac{1}{2}$ 2-6

FILLET

60° $\frac{1}{8}''$ $\frac{1}{2}$

$\frac{1}{2}$ $\frac{1}{8}$ 60°

GROOVE

30° $\frac{3}{4}$

$\frac{3}{4}$ 30°

PLUG

6+ PITCH

SPOT

$\frac{1}{4}$

ALL AROUND

60°

$\frac{1}{2}$ 60°   30°

BACKING

118

SQUARE AND ROUND STEEL BARS
WEIGHT AND AREA

SIZE INCHES	WEIGHT LB. PER FOOT ■	●	AREA SQUARE INCHES ◩	◎	SIZE INCHES	WEIGHT LB. PER FOOT ■	●	AREA SQUARE INCHES ◩	◎
0					3	30.60	24.03	9.000	7.069
1/16	.013	.010	.0039	.0031	1/16	31.89	25.05	9.379	7.366
1/8	.053	.042	.0156	.0123	1/8	33.20	26.08	9.766	7.670
3/16	.120	.094	.0352	.0276	3/16	34.54	27.13	10.160	7.980
1/4	.213	.167	.0625	.0491	1/4	35.91	28.21	10.563	8.296
5/16	.332	.261	.0977	.0767	5/16	37.31	29.30	10.973	8.618
3/8	.478	.376	.1406	.1105	3/8	38.75	30.42	11.391	8.946
7/16	.651	.511	.1914	.1503	7/16	40.18	31.55	11.816	9.281
1/2	.850	.668	.2500	.1963	1/2	41.65	32.71	12.250	9.621
9/16	1.076	.845	.3164	.2485	9/16	43.15	33.89	12.691	9.968
5/8	1.328	1.043	.3906	.3068	5/8	44.68	35.09	13.141	10.321
11/16	1.607	1.262	.4727	.3712	11/16	45.23	36.31	13.598	10.680
3/4	1.913	1.502	.5625	.4418	3/4	47.81	37.55	14.063	11.045
13/16	2.245	1.768	.6602	.5185	13/16	49.42	38.81	14.535	11.416
7/8	2.603	2.044	.7656	.6013	7/8	51.05	40.10	15.016	11.793
15/16	2.988	2.347	.8789	.6903	15/16	52.71	41.40	15.504	12.177
1	3.400	2.670	1.0000	.7854	4	54.40	42.73	16.000	12.566
1/16	3.838	3.015	1.1289	.8866	1/16	55.11	44.07	16.504	12.962
1/8	4.303	3.380	1.2656	.9940	1/8	57.85	45.44	17.016	13.364
3/16	4.795	3.766	1.4102	1.1075	3/16	59.62	46.83	17.535	13.772
1/4	5.313	4.172	1.5625	1.2272	1/4	61.41	48.23	18.063	14.186
5/16	5.857	4.600	1.7227	1.3530	5/16	63.23	49.66	18.598	14.607
3/8	6.428	5.049	1.8906	1.4849	3/8	65.08	51.11	19.141	15.033
7/16	7.026	5.518	2.0664	1.6230	7/16	66.95	52.58	19.691	15.466
1/2	7.650	6.008	2.2500	1.7671	1/2	68.85	54.07	20.250	15.904
9/16	8.301	6.519	2.4414	1.9175	9/16	70.78	55.59	20.816	16.349
5/8	8.978	7.051	2.6406	2.0739	5/8	72.73	57.12	21.391	16.800
11/16	9.682	7.604	2.8477	2.2365	11/16	74.71	58.67	21.973	17.257
3/4	10.413	8.178	3.0625	2.4053	3/4	76.71	60.25	22.563	17.721
13/16	11.170	8.773	3.2852	2.5802	13/16	78.74	61.85	23.160	18.190
7/8	11.953	9.388	3.5156	2.7612	7/8	80.80	63.46	23.766	18.655
15/16	12.763	10.024	3.7539	2.9483	15/16	82.89	65.10	24.379	19.147
2	13.600	10.681	4.0000	3.1416	5	85.00	66.76	25.000	19.635
1/16	14.463	11.359	4.2539	3.3410	1/16	87.14	68.44	25.629	20.129
1/8	15.353	12.058	4.5156	3.5466	1/8	89.30	70.14	26.266	20.629
3/16	16.270	12.778	4.7852	3.7583	3/16	91.49	71.86	26.910	21.135
1/4	17.213	13.519	5.0625	3.9761	1/4	93.71	73.60	27.563	21.648
5/16	18.182	14.280	5.3477	4.2000	5/16	95.96	75.36	28.223	22.166
3/8	19.178	15.062	5.6406	4.4301	3/8	98.23	77.15	28.891	22.691
7/16	20.201	15.866	5.9414	4.6664	7/16	100.53	78.95	29.566	23.221
1/2	21.250	16.690	6.2500	4.9087	1/2	102.85	80.78	30.250	23.758
9/16	22.326	17.534	6.5664	5.1572	9/16	105.20	82.62	30.941	24.301
5/8	23.428	18.400	6.8906	5.4119	5/8	107.58	84.49	31.641	24.850
11/16	24.557	19.287	7.2227	5.6727	11/16	109.98	86.38	32.348	25.406
3/4	25.713	20.195	7.5625	5.9396	3/4	112.41	88.29	33.063	25.967
13/16	26.895	21.123	7.9102	6.2126	13/16	114.87	90.22	33.785	26.535
7/8	28.103	22.072	8.2656	6.4918	7/8	117.35	92.17	34.516	27.109
15/16	29.338	23.042	8.6289	6.7771	15/16	119.86	94.14	35.254	27.688
3	30.600	24.033	9.0000	7.0686	6	122.40	96.13	36.000	28.274

SQUARE AND ROUND STEEL BARS
WEIGHT AND AREA

SIZE INCHES	WEIGHT LB. PER FOOT ■	WEIGHT LB. PER FOOT ●	AREA SQUARE INCHES ◪	AREA SQUARE INCHES ◯	SIZE INCHES	WEIGHT LB. PER FOOT ■	WEIGHT LB. PER FOOT ●	AREA SQUARE INCHES ◪	AREA SQUARE INCHES ◯
6	122.40	96.13	36.000	28.274	9	275.40	216.30	81.000	63.617
1/16	124.96	98.15	36.754	28.866	1/16	279.24	219.31	82.129	64.504
1/8	127.55	100.18	37.516	29.465	1/8	283.10	222.35	83.266	65.397
3/16	130.17	102.23	38.285	30.069	3/16	286.99	225.41	84.410	66.296
1/4	132.81	104.31	39.063	30.680	1/4	290.91	228.48	85.563	67.201
5/16	135.48	106.41	39.848	31.296	5/16	294.85	231.58	86.723	68.112
3/8	138.18	108.53	40.641	31.919	3/8	298.83	234.70	87.891	69.029
7/16	140.90	110.66	41.441	32.548	7/16	302.83	237.84	89.066	69.953
1/2	143.65	112.82	42.250	33.183	1/2	306.85	241.00	90.250	70.882
9/16	145.43	115.00	43.065	33.824	9/16	310.90	244.18	91.441	71.818
5/8	149.23	117.20	43.891	34.472	5/8	314.98	247.38	92.641	72.760
11/16	152.05	119.43	44.723	35.125	11/16	319.08	250.61	93.848	73.708
3/4	154.91	121.67	45.563	35.785	3/4	323.21	253.85	95.063	74.662
13/16	157.79	123.98	45.410	36.450	13/16	327.37	257.12	96.285	75.622
7/8	160.70	126.22	47.265	37.122	7/8	331.55	260.40	97.516	76.587
15/16	163.64	128.52	48.129	37.800	15/16	335.76	263.71	98.754	77.561
7	166.60	130.85	49.000	38.485	10	340.00	267.04	100.000	78.540
1/16	169.59	133.19	49.879	39.175	1/16	344.26	270.38	101.254	79.525
1/8	172.60	135.56	50.766	39.871	1/8	348.55	273.75	102.516	80.516
3/16	175.64	137.95	51.660	40.574	3/16	352.87	277.14	103.785	81.513
1/4	178.71	140.36	52.563	41.282	1/4	357.21	280.55	105.063	82.516
5/16	181.81	142.79	53.473	41.997	5/16	361.58	283.99	106.348	83.525
3/8	184.93	145.24	54.391	42.718	3/8	365.98	287.44	107.641	84.541
7/16	188.07	147.71	55.316	43.445	7/16	370.40	290.91	108.941	85.553
1/2	191.25	150.21	56.250	44.179	1/2	374.85	294.41	110.250	86.590
9/16	194.45	152.72	57.191	44.918	9/16	379.33	297.92	111.566	87.624
5/8	197.68	155.26	58.141	45.664	5/8	383.83	301.46	112.891	88.664
11/16	200.93	157.81	59.098	46.415	11/16	388.36	305.02	114.223	89.710
3/4	204.21	160.39	60.063	47.173	3/4	392.91	308.59	115.563	90.763
13/16	207.52	162.99	61.035	47.937	13/16	397.49	312.19	116.910	91.821
7/8	210.85	165.60	62.016	48.707	7/8	402.10	315.81	118.266	92.884
15/16	214.21	168.24	63.004	49.483	15/16	406.74	319.45	119.629	93.957
8	217.60	170.90	64.000	50.265	11	411.40	323.11	121.000	95.033
1/16	221.01	173.58	65.004	51.054	1/16	416.89	326.80	122.379	96.116
1/8	224.45	176.29	66.016	51.849	1/8	420.80	330.50	123.766	97.205
3/16	227.92	179.01	67.035	52.649	3/16	425.54	334.22	125.160	98.301
1/4	231.41	181.75	68.063	53.456	1/4	430.31	337.97	126.563	99.402
5/16	234.93	184.52	69.098	54.269	5/16	435.11	341.73	127.973	100.510
3/8	238.48	187.30	70.141	55.088	3/8	439.93	345.52	129.391	101.623
7/16	242.05	190.11	71.191	55.914	7/16	444.78	349.33	130.816	102.743
1/2	245.65	192.98	72.250	56.745	1/2	449.65	353.16	132.250	103.869
9/16	249.28	195.78	73.316	57.583	9/16	454.55	357.00	133.691	105.001
5/8	252.93	198.65	74.391	58.426	5/8	459.48	360.87	135.141	106.139
11/16	256.61	201.54	75.473	59.276	11/16	464.43	364.76	136.598	107.284
3/4	260.31	204.45	76.563	60.132	3/4	469.41	368.68	138.063	108.434
13/16	264.04	207.38	77.660	60.994	13/16	474.42	372.61	139.535	109.591
7/8	267.80	210.33	78.766	61.863	7/8	479.45	376.56	141.016	110.754
15/16	271.59	213.31	79.879	62.737	15/16	484.51	380.54	142.504	111.923
9	275.40	216.30	81.000	63.617	12	489.60	384.53	144.000	113.098

THE FOLLOWING TABLES ARE ABBREV-
-IATED FROM "1978 STRUCTURAL SHAPES",
BETHLEHEM STEEL CORP. AND COMPLIES WITH ASTM.
A6-77b. FOR DESIGN DATA OR OTHER SIZES REFER
TO THE DOCUMENT NOTED ABOVE. INFORMATION
INDICATED BELOW EFFECTIVE SEPT. 1, 1978.

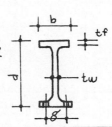

SECTION NUMBER	WEIGHT PER FOOT POUNDS	DEPTH OF SECTION d	FLANGE		WEB THICKN'S t_w	USUAL FLANGE GAUGE g	AREA OF SECTION (IN.²)
			WIDTH b	THICKN'S t_f			
W36	300	36 ¾	16 ⅝	1 ¹¹/₁₆	15/16	5 ½	88.3
W36	210	36 ¾	12 ⅛	1 ⅜	13/16	5 ½	61.8
W33	241	34 ⅛	15 ⅞	1 ⅜	13/16	5 ½	70.9
W33	152	33 ½	11 ⅝	1 1/16	⅝	5 ½	44.7
W30	211	31	15 ⅛	1 5/16	¾	5 ½	62.0
W30	132	30 ¼	10 ½	1	⅝	5 ½	38.9
W27	178	27 ¾	14 ⅛	1 3/16	¾	5 ½	52.3
W27	114	27 ¼	10 ⅛	15/16	9/16	5 ½	33.5
W24	162	25	13	1 ¼	11/16	5 ½	47.7
W24	94	24 ¼	9 ⅛	⅞	½	5 ½	27.7
W21	147	22	12 ½	1 ⅛	¾	5 ½	43.2
W21	93	21 ⅝	8 ⅜	15/16	9/16	5 ½	27.3
W18	119	19	11 ¼	1 1/16	⅝	5 ½	35.1
W18	71	18 ½	7 ⅝	13/16	½	3 ½	20.8
W16	100	17	10 ⅜	1	9/16	5 ½	29.4
W16	57	16 ⅜	7 ⅛	11/16	7/16	3 ½	16.8
W14	132	14 ⅝	14 ¾	1	⅝	5 ½	38.8
W14	82	14 ¼	10 ⅛	⅞	½	5 ½	24.1
W14	38	14 ⅛	6 ¾	½	5/16	3 ½	11.2
W12	106	12 ⅞	12 ¼	1	⅝	5 ½	31.2
W12	58	12 ¼	10	⅝	⅜	5 ½	17.0
W12	22	12 ¼	4	7/16	¼	2 ¼	6.48
W10	112	11 ⅜	10 ⅜	1 ¼	¾	5 ½	32.9
W10	45	10 ⅛	8	⅝	⅜	5 ½	13.3
W10	19	10 ¼	4	⅜	¼	2 ¼	5.62
W8	67	9	8 ¼	15/16	9/16	5 ½	19.7
W8	28	8	6 ½	7/16	5/16	3 ½	8.25
W6	25	6 ⅜	6 ⅛	7/16	5/16	3 ½	7.34
W6	16	6 ¼	4	⅜	¼	2 ¼	4.74
W5	19	5 ⅛	5	7/16	¼	2 ¾	5.54
W4	13	4 ⅛	4	⅜	¼	2 ¼	3.83

Table title: **WIDE FLANGE SHAPES**

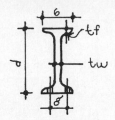
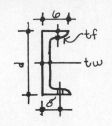

			"S" SHAPES • "I" BEAMS				
			FLANGE				
SECTION NUMBER	WEIGHT PER FOOT POUNDS	DEPTH OF SECTION d	WIDTH b	THICKN'S tf	WEB THICKN'S fw	USUAL FLANGE GAGE g	AREA OF SECTION IN².
S24	121	24 ½	8	1 1/16	13/16	4	35.6
S24	100	24	7 ¼	7/8	3/4	4	29.3
S20	86	20 ¼	7 ¼	15/16	13/16	4	28.2
S20	75	20	6 3/8	13/16	5/8	3 ½	22.0
S18	70	18	6 ¼	11/16	11/16	3 ½	20.6
S15	50	15	5 5/8	5/8	9/16	3 ½	14.7
S12	50	12	5 ½	11/16	11/16	3	14.7
S10	35	10	5	½	5/8	2 ¾	10.3
S8	23	8	4 1/8	7/16	7/16	2 ¼	6.77
S7	15.3	7	3 5/8	3/8	¼	2 ¼	4.50
S6	17.25	6	3 5/8	3/8	7/16	2	5.07
S5	10.0	5	3	5/16	3/16	—	2.94
S4	9.5	4	2 ¾	5/16	5/16	—	2.79
S3	7.5	3	2 ½	¼	3/8	—	2.21
			CHANNELS				
C15	50	15	3 ¾	5/8	11/16	2 ¼	14.7
C12	30	12	3 1/8	½	½	1 ¾	8.82
C10	30	10	3	7/16	11/16	1 ¾	8.82
C9	15	9	2 ½	7/16	5/16	1 3/8	4.41
C8	18.75	8	2 ½	3/8	½	1 ½	5.51
C7	12.25	7	2 ¼	3/8	5/16	1 ¼	3.60
C6	13.0	6	2 1/8	5/16	7/16	1 3/8	3.83
C5	9.0	5	1 7/8	5/16	5/16	1 1/8	2.64
C4	7.25	4	1 ¾	5/16	5/16	1	2.13
C3	5.0	3	1 ½	¼	¼	—	1.47
MC18	58	18	4 ¼	5/8	11/16	2 ½	17.1
MC12	50	12	4 1/8	11/16	13/16	2 ½	14.7
MC10	41.1	10	4 3/8	9/16	13/16	2 ½	12.1
MC9	25.4	9	3 ½	9/16	7/16	2	7.47
MC8	22.8	8	3 ½	½	7/16	2	6.70
MC7	22.7	7	3 5/8	½	½	2	6.67
MC6	12.0	6	2 ½	3/8	5/16	1 ½	3.53

BETHLEHEM STEEL CORP.

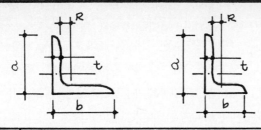

	ANGLES					
	SECTION NUMBER	SIZE a × b	LEG THICKN'S t	WEIGHT PER FOOT POUNDS	RADIUS AT INTERSECT. R	AREA OF SECTION IN²
EQUAL LEGS	L8	8 × 6	1⅛	56.9	⅝	16.7
	L6	6 × 6	1	37.4	½	11.0
	L5	5 × 5	⅞	27.2	½	7.98
	L4	4 × 4	¾	18.5	⅜	5.44
	L3½	3½ × 3½	⅜	8.5	⅜	2.48
	L3	3 × 3	½	9.4	5/16	2.75
	L2½	2½ × 2½	½	7.7	¼	2.25
	L2	2 × 2	⅜	4.7	9/32	1.36
	L1½	1½ × 1½	¼	2.34	3/16	0.69
	L1	1 × 1	¼	1.49	⅛	0.44
UNEQUAL LEGS	L9	9 × 4	⅝	26.3	½	7.73
	L8	8 × 6	1	44.2	½	13.0
	L8	8 × 4	1	37.4	½	11.0
	L7	7 × 4	¾	26.2	½	7.69
	L6	6 × 4	¾	23.6	½	6.94
	L6	6 × 3½	⅜	11.7	½	3.42
	L5	5 × 3½	¾	19.8	7/16	5.81
	L5	5 × 3	½	12.8	⅜	3.75
	L4	4 × 3½	½	11.9	⅜	3.50
	L4	4 × 3	½	11.1	⅜	3.25
	L3½	3½ × 3	⅜	7.9	⅜	2.30
	L3½	3½ × 2½	⅜	7.2	5/16	2.11
	L3	3 × 2½	⅜	6.6	5/16	1.92
	L3	3 × 2	⅜	5.9	5/16	1.73
	L2½	2½ × 2	⅜	5.3	¼	1.55
	L2½	2½ × 1½	5/16	3.92	3/16	1.15
	L2	2 × 1½	¼	2.77	3/16	0.81
	L2	2 × 1¼	⅛	1.44	3/16	0.42
	L1¾	1¾ × 1¼	¼	2.34	3/16	0.69
	L1¾	1¾ × 1¼	⅛	1.23	3/16	0.36

BETHLEHEM STEEL CORP.

CHARTS GIVEN BELOW CONSIDER ONLY THE NORMAL USE OF A SINGLE SYSTEM AND DO NOT CONSIDER EXTREME POSSIBILITIES. CHARTS SHOULD BE USED FOR PRELIMINARY DESIGN ONLY. IF GREATER THAN NORMAL LOADS ARE ANTICIPATED, OR WIDER THAN NORMAL SPACING, USE UPPER PORTIONS OF CHART. USE LOWER PORTION FOR LIGHT LOADS. FOR CANTILEVERS USE THREE TIMES THE CANTILEVER LENGTH TO DETERMINE THICKNESS OR DEPTH.

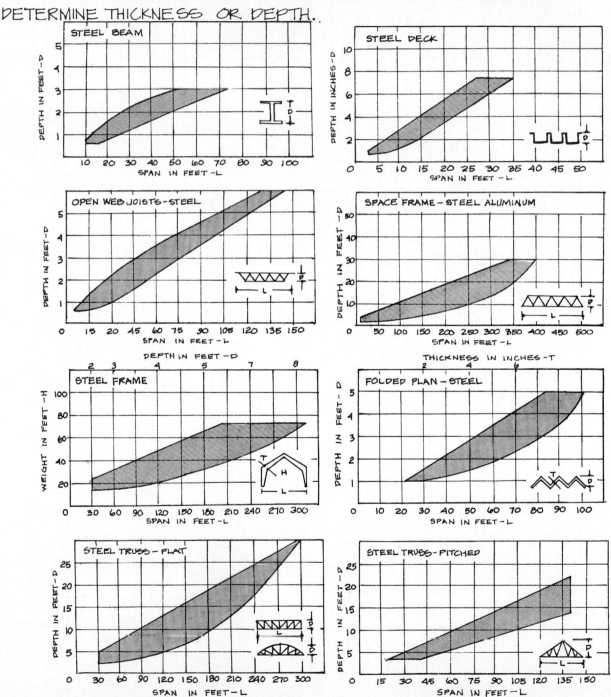

SERNOLL DIVISION: BAWDEN BROS. INC.

CHARTS BELOW ASSUME AN UNSUPPORTED HEIGHT FROM 1 TO 50 FEET AND PRIMARILY SUPPORT ONLY A ROOF OR ONE-STORY LOAD **OR** ARE STRUCTURAL SUPPORTS WHICH HAVE A NORMAL ONE-STORY HEIGHT AND MUST SUPPORT FROM 1 TO 50 STORIES. NORMAL UNSUPPORTED STORY HEIGHT IS ASSUMED 8 TO 12 FEET. MIDDLE RANGE OF CHART SHOULD BE USED FOR NORMAL LOADING, UPPER PORTIONS FOR HEAVY LOADS, AND LOWER PORTION FOR LIGHT LOADING. USE FOR PRELIMINARY DESIGN ONLY.

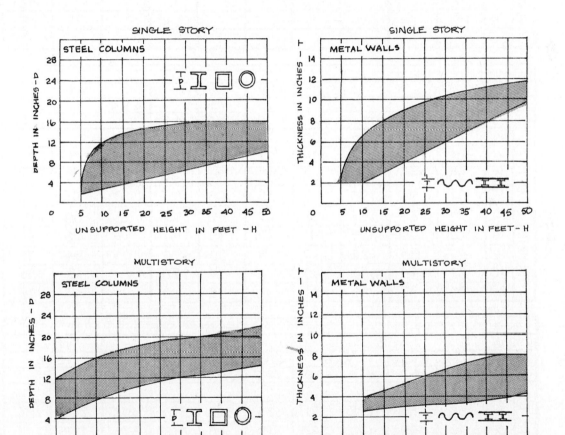

SERNOLL DIVISION : BAWDEN BROS. INC.

DESIG.	S3		S4		S5		S6		M4	M5
D x W	3 x 2⅜		4 x 2⅝		5 x 3		6 x 3⅜		4 x 4	5 x 5
WT./FT.	5.7	7.5	7.7	9.5	10.0	14.75	12.5	17.25	13.0	18.9
COLUMN LENGTH, FT. 3	28	36	39	48	52	76	67	92	74	111
6	13	17	22	26	34	47	47	61	60	96
8		10	12	15	20	27	30	37	48	85
10					13	17	17	24	35	71
12									24	56
14									18	42
16										32
18										25
20										

DESIG.	M6		M8		W4	W5		W6		
D x W	6 x 6		8 x 8		4 x 4	5 x 5		6 x 4	6 x 6	
WT./FT.	20.0	22.5	32.6	34.3	13.0	16.0	18.5	12.0	20.0	25.0
COLUMN LENGTH, FT. 3	119	134	198	208	74	94	109	92	120	150
6	107	120	185	195	62	83	97	75	109	137
8	98	109	175	184	51	74	86	44	100	126
10	87	96	164	172	39	64	75	31	91	114
12	74	82	151	158	27	52	62	21	80	101
14	61	66	137	143	20	39	47	16	68	86
16	47	50	122	127	15	30	36		54	70
18	37	40	106	109		24	28		43	55
20	30	32	89	91		19	23		35	45

DESIG.	W8				W10				W12	
D x W	8 x 5¼	8 x 6½	8 x 8		10 x 8	10 x 10			12 x 8	
WT./FT.	17.0	28.0	35.0	48.0	39.0	54.0	72.0	100.0	40.0	50.0
COLUMN LENGTH, FT. 3	100	168								
6	88	155	201	276	224	319	426	592	229	286
8	78	144	191	263	213	308	412	573	217	271
10	66	132	180	249	200	296	396	551	204	254
12	53	118	168	233	186	283	378	528	189	236
14	39	103	155	215	170	268	359	503	172	216
16	30	86	141	196	154	253	339	476	155	195
18	24	69	125	176	136	236	317	446	136	171
20	19	56	109	154	95	219	294	416	115	146

CONCENTRIC AXIAL LOADS IN KIPS. $F_y = 36$ KSI.

ADAPTED FROM AMERICAN INSTITUTE OF STEEL CONSTRUCTION INC.

DESIG.	W12						W14			
D×W	12×10	12×12					14×8	14×10	14×12	14×14½
WT./FT.	58.0	79.0	92.0	106.0	133.0	190.0	48.0	68.0	84.0	111.0
COLUMN LENGTH, FT.										
6	343	473	553	637	799	1144	273	400	503	675
8	331	460	538	620	779	1117	258	385	489	662
10	317	446	522	602	757	1086	242	369	475	647
12	302	431	505	583	732	1053	224	351	458	631
14	286	415	486	561	706	1017	204	332	441	614
16	269	398	466	539	679	979	182	311	422	596
18	251	379	445	514	649	939	159	289	402	576
20	231	360	422	489	618	896	133	266	381	556
24	189	317	374	433	550	803	93	214	335	512

DESIG.	W14									
D×W	14×16									
WT./FT.	150.0	167.0	184.0	202.0	228.0	264.0	320.0	398.0	500.0	665.0
COLUMN LENGTH, FT.										
6	914	1017	1121	1232	1392	1611	1954			
8	897	999	1102	1210	1368	1583	1921			
10	879	979	1080	1186	1342	1553	1885			
12	860	958	1056	1161	1313	1520	1845	2304	2905	3892
14	839	935	1031	1133	1282	1486	1804	2255	2845	3817
16	816	910	1004	1104	1250	1448	1759	2202	2781	3737
18	793	884	976	1073	1215	1409	1712	2146	2714	3652
20	768	857	946	1040	1179	1368	1662	2087	2642	3563
24	686	766	882	970	1101	1278	1555	1960	2490	3372

	DOUBLE EQUAL LEG ANGLES X–X AXIS					DOUBLE EQUAL LEG ANGLES Y–Y AXIS				
SIZE	3×3	4×4	5×5	6×6	8×8	3×3	4×4	5×5	6×6	8×8
THICK.	3/8	1/2	5/8	3/4	7/8	3/8	1/2	5/8	3/4	7/8
WT./FT.	14.4	25.6	40.0	57.4	90.0	14.4	25.6	40.0	57.4	90.0
COLUMN LENGTH, FT.										
2	85					88				
4	76	144				83				
6	71	131	217			77	144	232		
8	65	116	200	306		70	136	222		
10	59	99	181	285	489	66	127	211	318	520
12	52	89	160	262		62	116	200	304	
14	44	59	136	236	439	58	105	187	290	
16		45		209		54	93	173	275	490
18				179	382		79	158	258	

CONCENTRIC AXIAL LOADS IN KIPS. F_y = 36 KSI.

ADAPTED FROM AMERICAN INSTITUTE OF STEEL CONSTRUCTION INC.

ROUND PIPE COLUMNS

DESIG.	STANDARD STEEL					EXTRA STRONG			DBL. X-STRONG	
NOM. DIA.	3	4	5	6	8	4	6	10	6	8
WT./FT.	7.58	10.79	14.62	18.97	28.55	14.98	28.57	54.74	53.16	72.42
COLUMN LENGTH, FT. 6	38	59	83	110	171	81	166	332	306	431
8	34	54	78	106	166	75	159	325	292	417
10	28	49	73	101	161	67	151	318	275	403
12	22	43	68	95	155	59	142	309	257	387
14		36	61	89	149	49	132	301	237	369
16		29	55	82	142	39	122	291	216	351
18			47	75	135		111	281	193	331
20			39	67	127		99	271	168	310
24					111			248		119

SQUARE STRUCTURAL TUBING

SIZE	4 x 4		5 x 5		6 x 6		7 x 7		8 x 8	10 x 10
WALL	5/16	1/2	5/16	1/2	5/16	1/2	5/16	1/2	1/2	1/2
WT./FT.	14.52	20.88	18.77	27.68	23.02	34.48	26.99	40.55	47.35	60.95
COLUMN LENGTH, FT. 6	79	111	107	156	134	199	160	239	283	370
8	72	101	101	147	129	191	155	231	275	363
10	65	86	94	136	123	181	149	222	267	355
12	57	75	87	124	116	170	143	212	257	347
14	47	60	79	111	109	159	137	201	247	338
16			70	97	101	146	129	190	237	328
18			61	82	93	133	122	178	225	318
20					84	118	114	165	213	307
24							96	136	187	284

RECTANGULAR STRUCTURAL TUBING

SIZE	3 x 2	4 x 2	4 x 3	5 x 3	6 x 3	6 x 4	7 x 5	8 x 4	8 x 6	10 x 6
WALL	1/4	1/4	1/4	1/4	1/4	5/16	5/16	3/8	3/8	3/8
WT./FT.	7.10	8.80	10.50	12.02	16.65	18.77	23.02	27.04	31.73	36.83
COLUMN LENGTH, FT. 3	48	60	77	89	102	143				
6	31	41	65	75	86	128	165	185	234	272
8	19	25	54	63	74	116	155	169	223	260
10			42	50	59	103	143	150	210	246
12			29		43	88	130	129	196	231
14						71	116	105	182	214
16							101		165	197
18									148	177
20									130	157

CONCENTRIC AXIAL LOADS IN KIPS. $F_y = 36$ KSI, EXCEPT RECTANGULAR TUBE $F_y = 46$ KSI.

ADAPTED FROM AMERICAN INSTITUTE OF STEEL CONSTRUCTION INC.

LIGHT GAGE ECONOMY DECK : TOTAL LOAD PSF

TYPE	SPAN	GAGE	2-0	2-6	3-0	3-6	4-0	4-6	5-0	5-6	6-0	6-6
		26	200	128	89	63	45	34				
		24	276	177	123	89	62	46	36	29		
		26	200	128	89	65	50	40	32			
		24	276	177	123	90	69	55	44	37	31	
		26	350	160	111	82	63	49	40	33	28	
		24	346	221	154	113	86	68	55	46	38	30

24 GA. M = .083

NARROW RIB DECK, TYPE NR : TOTAL LOAD PSF

TYPE	SPAN	GAGE	4-0	4-6	5-0	5-6	6-0	6-6	7-0	7-6	8-0	8-6
		22	74	58	47							
		20	90	72	58	48	40					
		18	121	95	77	64	54	46				
		22	80	64	51	42						
		20	96	76	62	51	43					
		18	124	98	79	66	55	47	40			
		22	100	79	64	53	45					
		20	120	95	77	64	53	46				
		18	155	122	99	82	69	59	51	44		

20 GA. M = .151   2.18 PSF

INTERMEDIATE RIB DECK, TYPE IR : TOTAL LOAD PSF

TYPE	SPAN	GAGE	4-0	4-6	5-0	5-6	6-0	6-6	7-0	7-6	8-0	8-6
		22	86	68	55	45						
		20	106	83	68	56	47	40				
		18	141	112	90	75	63	54	46			
		22	93	74	60	49	41					
		20	112	88	82	59	50	42				
		18	145	114	93	76	64	55	47	41		
		22	116	92	74	62	52	44				
		20	140	110	89	74	62	53	46	40		
		18	181	143	116	96	80	68	59	51	45	40

20 GA. M = .169   2.16 PSF

WIDE RIB DECK, TYPE WR : TOTAL LOAD PSF

TYPE	SPAN	GAGE	5-0	5-6	6-0	6-6	7-0	7-6	8-0	8-6	9-0	9-6
		22	89	70	56	46						
		20	112	87	69	56	47	40				
		18	154	118	94	76	63	53	45			
		22	98	81	68	58	50	43				
		20	125	103	87	74	64	56	49	43		
		18	165	136	115	98	84	73	64	57	51	45
		22	122	101	85	70	58	49	42			
		20	156	129	108	87	72	60	52	45		
		18	207	171	143	120	98	81	69	59	51	45

20. GA. M = .246   2.16 PSF

LOADS IN SHADED PORTIONS GOVERNED BY LIVE LOAD DEFLECTION TO $\frac{1}{240}$ × SPAN.

WHEELING CORRUGATING COMPANY
STEEL DECK INSTITUTE

ALLOWABLE AXIAL LOAD (LB.) INTERIOR STUD WALL, NO WIND

	8-0	9-0	10-0	11-0	12-0	14-0	16-0	18-0	20-0
2½ × 16	4977	4295	3548	2932	2464	1810	1386		
3⅝ × 16	6414	6098	5744	5352	4924	3955	3033	2396	1941
4 × 16	7091	6804	6482	6127	5739	4860	3859	3049	2470
6 × 16	7232	7126	7007	6876	6733	6408	6034	5610	5135
8 × 16	7960	7902	7839	7748	7690	7515	7313	7084	6828

MAXIMUM ALLOWABLE LOAD (LB.) EXTERIOR WALL, 15 # WIND

	8-0		9-0		10-0		11-0		12-0		14-0		16-0		18-0		20-0
	16	24	16	24	16	24	16	24	16	24	16	24	16	24	16	24	12
2½ × 16	4206	3585	3198	2617	2381	1853	1774	1294	1327	887	736	358	380	50			
3⅝ × 16	6414	6414	6098	5490	5277	4539	4416	3675	3693	2923	2393	1744	1518	950	950	445	838
4 × 16	7091	7091	6804	6600	6403	5627	5505	4696	4659	3849	3226	2468	2140	1465	1394	794	1211
6 × 16	7232	7232	7126	7126	7007	7007	6876	6876	6733	6733	6372	5546	5235	4322	4159	3227	3760
8 × 16	7960	7960	7902	7902	7839	7839	7768	7768	7690	7690	7515	7515	7313	7123	7066	6114	6757

MAXIMUM ALLOWABLE LOAD (LB.) EXTERIOR WALL, 20 # WIND

	8-0		9-0		10-0		11-0		12-0		14-0		16-0		18-0		20-0
	16	24	16	24	16	24	16	24	16	24	16	24	16	24	16	24	12
2½ × 16	3779	3061	2798	2128	2018	1408	1443	889	1025	516	476	40	152				
3⅝ × 16	6414	5920	5711	4882	4771	3908	3906	3047	3147	2314	1946	1198	1127	471	602		567
4 × 16	7091	7009	6804	5976	5872	4952	4950	4003	4102	3163	2704	1829	1675	896	981	288	889
6 × 16	7232	7232	7126	7126	7007	7007	6876	6733	6733	6167	5809	4812	4610	3535	3519	2436	3219
8 × 16	7960	7960	7902	7902	7839	7839	7768	7768	7690	7690	7515	7457	7313	6380	6420	5255	6155

MAXIMUM ALLOWABLE LOAD (LB.) EXTERIOR WALL, 30 # WIND

	8-0		9-0		10-0		11-0		12-0		14-0		16-0		18-0		20-0
	16	24	16	24	16	24	16	24	16	24	16	24	16	24	16	24	12
2½ × 16	3061	2180	2128	1306	1408	661	899	210	516								
3⅝ × 16	5920	4947	4882	3830	3908	2835	3047	1990	2314	1293	1198	281	471				
4 × 16	7009	6033	5976	4876	4952	3792	4003	2830	3163	2008	1829	758	896		288		349
6 × 16	7232	7232	7126	7126	7007	6582	6823	5827	6167	5047	4812	3528	3535	2191	2436	1102	2309
8 × 16	7960	7960	7902	7902	7839	7839	7768	7768	7690	7558	7457	6333	6380	5024	5255	3733	5092

MAXIMUM ALLOWABLE LOAD (LB.) EXTERIOR WALL, 40 # WIND

	8-0		9-0		10-0		11-0		12-0		14-0		16-0		18-0		20-0
	16	24	16	24	16	24	16	24	16	24	16	24	16	24	16	24	12
2½ × 16	2454	1436	1562	614	894	32	422		88								
3⅝ × 16	8256	4087	4161	2924	3171	1923	2320	1097	1612	432	567						
4 × 16	6346	5153	5225	3914	4156	2796	3197	1834	2369	1032	1092		238				
6 × 16	7232	7232	7126	6613	6861	5779	6149	4909	5407	4039	3934	2411	2612	1046	1518		1542
8 × 16	7960	7960	7902	7901	7839	7839	7768	7409	7690	6735	6698	5284	5406	3799	4216	2394	4158

15 # SQ. FT WIND LOAD (75 MPH WIND)
20 # SQ. FT WIND LOAD (85 MPH WIND)
30 # SQ. FT WIND LOAD (105 MPH WIND)
40 # SQ. FT WIND LOAD (125 MPH WIND)

12, 14, 16 AND 18 GA. AVAILABLE
4 × 16 = 4" DEEP PUNCHED "CEE" STUD FABRICATED FROM 16 GA STEEL WITH 1⅝" FLANGE.

CONDENSED FROM WHEELING CORRUGATING CO.

LB/SQ FT TOTAL LOADS, SINGLE SPAN CONDITION

SPACING	UNIT	8-0	9-0	10-0	11-0	12-0	13-0	14-0	15-0	16-0	17-0	18-0	19-0	20-0	21-0	22-0
12" O.C.	6 × 14	383	303	245	203	170	145	125	109	95	85	75	68	61	55	50
	6 × 16	312	246	199	165	138	118	101	88	78	69	61	55	49	45	41
	6 × 18	166	131	106	88	74	63	54	47	41	36	32	29			
	7¼ × 14	511	404	327	270	227	194	167	145	128	113	101	91	82	74	68
	7¼ × 16	415	328	265	219	184	157	135	118	104	92	82	74	66	60	55
	7¼ × 18	224	177	143	118	99	85	73	64	56	51	46	41	37	32	30
	8 × 14	589	466	377	312	262	223	192	168	147	131	116	104	94	86	78
	8 × 16	478	377	306	253	212	181	156	136	119	106	94	85	76	69	63
	8 × 18	257	203	165	136	114	97	84	73	64	57	51	46	41	35	34
16" O.C.	6 × 14	287	227	184	152	127	109	94	81	71	63	56	51	46	41	38
	6 × 16	234	184	149	123	103	88	76	66	58	51	46	41	37	33	31
	6 × 18	125	98	80	66	55	47	40	35	31						
	7¼ × 14	383	303	245	203	170	145	125	109	96	85	76	68	60	56	51
	7¼ × 16	311	246	199	164	138	118	102	88	78	69	61	55	50	49	41
	7¼ × 18	168	132	107	89	75	63	55	48	42	37	33	30			
	8 × 14	442	349	283	234	196	167	144	126	111	98	87	78	71	64	58
	8 × 16	358	283	229	190	139	136	117	102	90	79	71	64	57	52	47
	8 × 18	193	153	124	102	86	73	63	55	48	43	38	34	31		
24" O.C.	6 × 14	191	151	122	101	85	72	62	54	47	42	37	34	30		
	6 × 16	156	123	99	82	69	59	50	44	39	31	30				
	6 × 18	83	65	53	44	37	31									
	7¼ × 14	256	202	164	135	114	97	83	73	64	57	50	45	41	37	34
	7¼ × 16	207	164	133	110	92	79	68	59	52	46	41	37	33	30	
	7¼ × 18	112	88	72	59	50	42	36	32							
	8 × 14	295	233	189	156	131	112	96	84	74	65	58	52	47	43	39
	8 × 16	239	189	153	126	106	90	78	68	60	53	47	42	38	35	32
	8 × 18	129	102	82	68	97	49	42	37	32						

LB/SQ FT TOTAL LOADS, TWO EQUAL SPANS   **CANTILEVERED**

SPACING	UNIT	8-0	9-0	10-0	11-0	12-0	13-0	14-0	15-0	16-0	3-0	4-0	5-0	6-0
12" O.C.	6 × 14	383	303	245	203	170	145	125	109	95	500	300	200	130
	6 × 16	312	246	199	165	138	118	101	88	78	400	250	160	110
	6 × 18	166	131	106	88	74	63	54	47	41	240	170	90	52
	7¼ × 14	511	404	327	270	227	194	167	145	126	725	420	215	140
	7¼ × 16	415	328	265	219	184	157	135	118	104	580	340	175	120
	7¼ × 18	224	177	143	118	99	85	73	64	56	315	221	141	82
	8 × 14	389	466	377	312	262	223	192	168	147	800	500	275	160
	8 × 16	478	377	306	253	212	181	156	136	119	700	400	225	130
	8 × 18	257	203	165	136	114	97	84	73	64	400	250	150	100
16" O.C.	6 × 14	287	227	184	152	121	109	94	81	71	373	225	130	98
	6 × 16	234	184	149	123	103	88	76	66	58	300	188	120	83
	6 × 18	125	98	80	66	55	47	40	35	31	180	127	67	39
	7¼ × 14	383	303	245	303	170	145	125	109	96	543	313	161	105
	7¼ × 16	311	246	199	164	138	118	102	88	78	435	255	131	90
	7¼ × 18	168	132	107	89	75	63	55	48	42	236	164	105	61
	8 × 14	442	349	283	234	196	167	144	126	111	600	375	206	120
	8 × 16	356	283	229	190	136	136	117	102	90	525	300	168	97
	8 × 18	193	153	124	102	86	73	63	55	48	300	187	112	73
24" O.C.	6 × 14	191	151	122	101	85	72	62	54	47	250	150	100	65
	6 × 16	156	123	99	82	69	59	50	44	39	200	125	80	55
	6 × 18	83	65	53	44	37	31				120	85	45	
	7¼ × 14	256	202	164	135	114	97	83	73	64	362	210	107	70
	7¼ × 16	207	164	139	110	92	72	68	59	52	290	170	87	60
	7¼ × 18	112	88	72	59	50	42	36	32		157	110	70	41
	8 × 14	295	233	189	156	131	112	96	34	74	400	250	137	80
	8 × 16	239	189	153	126	106	90	78	68	60	350	200	112	65
	8 × 18	129	102	82	68	57	49	42	37	32	200	125	75	50

6 X 14 = 6" DEEP "CEE" JOIST FABRICATED FROM 14 GA. STEEL, 1⅝" WIDE FLANGE.

CONDENSED FROM INLAND STEEL CO., "INRYCO."

J SERIES

JOIST DESIG.	LB. LIN. FT.	DEPTH (IN.)	MAX. END REACTION	10	15	20	25	30	35	40	45	50
10J2	4.2	10	1900	400	207	117						
12J4	6.0	12	2500		333	225						
12J6	8.1	12	3000		400	300						
14J4	6.4	14	2800		373	265	170					
14J6	8.4	14	3400		453	340	245					
16J4	6.6	16	3000			288	185	128				
18J5	7.9	18	3500			350	259	180	132			
18J7	10.2	18	4200			420	336	261	192			
20J5	8.1	20	3800			380	283	196	144	110		
20J7	10.6	20	4300			430	344	283	208	159		
22J6	9.6	22	4200				336	248	182	140		
24J7	11.1	24	4700				376	313	250	192	151	

H SERIES

JOIST DESIG.	LB. LIN. FT.	DEPTH (IN.)	MAX. END REACTION	10	15	20	25	30	35	40	45	50
10H2	4.2	10	2200	440								
10H4	6.1	10	2800	560	373 / 299	247 / 126						
12H4	6.2	12	3200		427	300 / 186						
12H6	8.2	12	3900		520	390 / 268						
14H4	6.3	14	3500		467	350 / 258	226 / 132					
14H6	8.6	14	4200		560	420 / 374	327 / 191					
16H5	7.8	16	4300			430 / 413	308 / 211	214 / 122				
16H7	10.3	16	4900			490	392 / 295	306 / 171				
18H6	9.2	18	4800			480	384 / 325	284 / 188	208 / 118			
18H8	11.6	18	5400			540	432	360 / 251	294 / 158			
20H6	9.6	20	5100			510	408 / 405	301 / 234	221 / 147	169 / 98		
20H8	12.2	20	5600			560	448	373 / 313	320 / 197	251 / 132		
22H7	10.7	22	5600				448	373 / 332	286 / 209	219 / 140		
24H7	11.5	24	5800				464	387	313 / 251	240 / 168	190 / 118	

LJ SERIES

JOIST DESIG.	LB. LIN. FT.	DEPTH (IN.)	MAX. END REACTION	CLEAR OPENING OR NET SPAN IN FEET													
				25	30	35	40	45	50	55	60	65	70	75	80	85	90
18LJ07	19	18	7610	593 554	415 324	307 206											
20LJ07	20	20	8262		557 510	385 293	296 185										
24LJ07	20	24	8214			449 432	360 291	285 206									
28LJ09	24	28	10229			456 400	376 289	312 215									
32LJ10	27	32	10653						416 379	353 286	300 221						
36LJ11	28	36	11100						373 327	320 256	278 204						
40LJ12	30	40	12181									371 317	323 254	284 207	251 171		
44LJ13	35	44	13517											348 284	306 239	271 199	
48LJ14	36	48	14618													306 259	291 218

LH SERIES

JOIST. DESIG.	LB. LIN. FT.	DEPTH (IN.)	MAX END REACTION	CLEAR OPENING OR NET SPAN IN FEET													
				25	30	35	40	45	50	55	60	65	70	75	80	85	90
18LH05	17	18	8775	684 509	508 298	375 189											
20LH04	16	20	7366	574 545	467 319	353 203	275 137										
24LH06	19	24	10161		555 382	437 258	348 182										
28LH08	21	28	11250					456 293	371 214	308 161							
32LH09	24	32	12814						498 341	418 257	356 198						
32LH10	26	36	13090								443 267	357 210	311 169				
36LH11	28	36	14272								451 296	389 233	339 187				
40LH12	32	40	15957									486 329	424 264	373 215	330 177		
44LH13	35	44	17569											454 289	404 239	361 199	
48LH14	36	48	19395													434 239	390 218

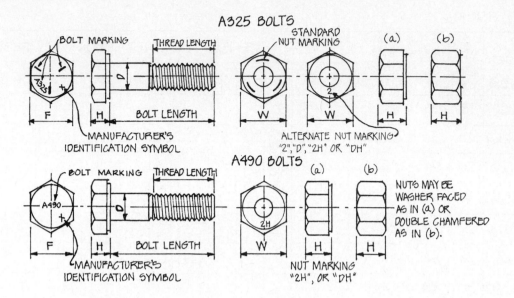

A325 BOLTS

A490 BOLTS

	BOLT DIMENSIONS, IN INCHES			NUT DIMENSIONS, IN INCHES	
NOMINAL BOLT SIZE, D	HEAVY HEX STRUCTURAL BOLTS			HEAVY HEX NUTS	
	WIDTH ACROSS FLATS, F	HEIGHT, H	THREAD LENGTH	WIDTH ACROSS FLATS, W	HEIGHT, H
1/2	7/8	5/16	1	7/8	31/64
5/8	1 1/16	25/64	1 1/4	1 1/16	39/64
3/4	1 1/4	15/32	1 3/8	1 1/4	47/64
7/8	1 7/16	35/64	1 1/2	1 7/16	55/64
1	1 5/8	39/64	1 3/4	1 5/8	63/64
1 1/8	1 13/16	11/16	2	1 13/16	1 7/64
1 1/4	2	25/32	2	2	1 7/32
1 3/8	2 3/16	27/32	2 1/4	2 3/16	1 11/32
1 1/2	2 3/8	15/16	2 1/4	2 3/8	1 15/32

MECHANICAL FINISHES

ALUMINUM ASSOC.		NAAMM	ALCOA	KAISER	OLIN	REYNOLDS
AS FABRICATED						
M-10	UNSPECIFIED	NA-O	AS FAB	NF	NF	XXOX
M-12	NONSPECULAR					
BUFFED						
M-21	SMOOTH SPECULAR	NA-2	A-1	M-2	M-2	XX2X
M-22	SPECULAR		A-2			
DIRECTIONAL TEXTURED						
M-31	FINE SATIN	NA-1		M-1	M-1	
M-32	MEDIUM SATIN	NA-5	C-1	M-5	M-5	XX5X
M-33	COARSE SATIN	NA-3				
M-34	HAND RUBBED	NA-6	C-2	M-6	M-6	
M-35	BRUSHED	NA-7	K6C3	M-7	M-7	
NONDIRECTIONAL TEXTURE						
M-42	FINE MATTE	NA-11	G-2	M-11	M-11	
M-43	MEDIUM MATTE	NA-10	G-3	M-10	M-10	XX4X
M-44	COARSE MATTE	NA-9	G-4	M-9	M-9	
M-45	FINE SHOT BLAST		H-1			
M-46	MEDIUM SHOT BLAST	NA-12	H-2	M-12	M-12	

CHEMICAL FINISHES

ALUMINUM ASSOC.		NAAMM	ALCOA	KAISER	OLIN	REYNOLDS
NONETCHED: CLEANED						
C-11	DEGREASED	NO DESIGNATIONS				
C-12	CHEMICALLY CLEANED					
ETCHED						
C-22	MEDIUM MATTE	NA-CE	R-1	C-1	C-1	XX6X
BRIGHTENED						
C-31	HIGHLY SPECULAR	NA-CB	R-5			XXIX
C-32	DIFFUSE BRIGHT		R1-R5			

EXAMPLE 1

WANTED: MATTE ANODIZED OVER ETCH WITH DURABLE CLEAR ANODIC COAT.

AA-C22A41 REPRESENTS

C22-CHEMICAL ETCH – MED MATTE

A-41-ANODIC COATING CLEAR

.07 THICK OR MORE

EXAMPLE 2

WANTED: ANODIZED SMOOTH FINISH WITH INTEGRAL COLOR.

AA-M21C22A42 REPRESENTS

M21-MECHANICAL SMOOTH BUFF

C22-CHEMICAL MED. MATTE

A42-ANODIC COLOR FILM

.07 MIL OR MORE

NATIONAL ASSOCIATION OF ARCHITECTURAL METAL MANUFACTURERS.

ANODIC COATINGS

ARCHITECTURAL, CLASS I   NAAMM ALCOA KAISER OLIN REYNOLDS

(THICKNESS 0.7 MILS OR MORE)

A-41 CLEAR, NATURAL

A-42 INTEGRAL COLOR   NA-2A   215   A-2   A-2

DURANODIC KALCOLOR   REYNOCOLOR
100 & 300   4000 & 5000

A-43 IMPREGNATED COLOR   2030-4005

A-4X OTHER AS SPECIFIED   GOLD 4010

ARCHITECTURAL, CLASS II

(0.4 TO 0.7 MILL THICKNESS)

A-31 CLEAR, NATURAL   NA-1A   204   A-1   A-1

A-32 INTEGRAL COLOR

A-33 IMPREGNATED COLOR

A-3X OTHER AS SPECIFIED

PROTECTIVE, DECORATIVE

(THICKNESS LESS THAN 0.4 MIL)

A-21 CLEAR, NATURAL   200
                           201
                           203

A-22 INTEGRAL COLOR

A-13 ABRASION RESISTANT   225
                           725

A-11 PREPARATION FOR OTHER COATINGS

    CLASS I: GENERALLY REQUIRES 15% SULFURIC ACID AT 70° ± 2°F, 12 AMP / SQ. FT. FOR 60 MINUTES.

    CLASS II: GENERALLY REQUIRES 15% SULFURIC ACID AT 70° ± 2°F, 12 AMP/ SQ. FT. FOR 30 MINUTES.

    CLASS III (DECORATIVE): SAME AS ABOVE EXCEPT TIME AS SPECIFIED.

    A-11: 0.1 MIL THICK SAME AS ABOVE, EXCEPT 10 MINUTES ONLY.

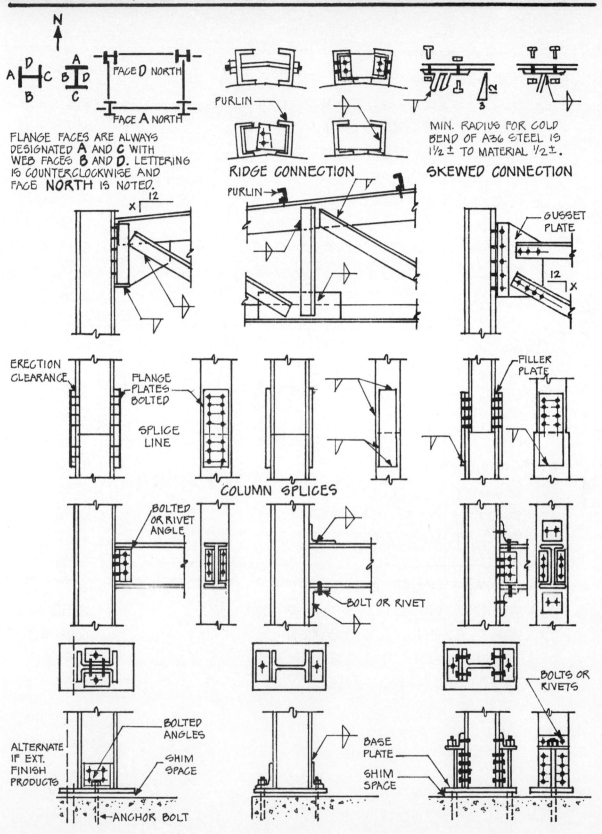

FLANGE FACES ARE ALWAYS
DESIGNATED **A** AND **C** WITH
WEB FACES **B** AND **D**. LETTERING
IS COUNTERCLOCKWISE AND
FACE **NORTH** IS NOTED.

FACE **D** NORTH

FACE **A** NORTH

PURLIN

RIDGE CONNECTION

PURLIN

MIN. RADIUS FOR COLD
BEND OF A36 STEEL IS
1½± TO MATERIAL ½±.

SKEWED CONNECTION

GUSSET PLATE

ERECTION CLEARANCE

FLANGE PLATES BOLTED

SPLICE LINE

FILLER PLATE

COLUMN SPLICES

BOLTED OR RIVET ANGLE

BOLT OR RIVET

ALTERNATE IF EXT. FINISH PRODUCTS

BOLTED ANGLES

SHIM SPACE

ANCHOR BOLT

BASE PLATE

SHIM SPACE

BOLTS OR RIVETS

COLUMN BASES

WOOD AND PLASTICS　　DIVISION 6

LUMBER SIZES AND PROPERTIES 6.1

NOMINAL SIZE (IN.) b X d	ACTUAL SIZE (IN.) b X d	AREA (IN.²)	MOMENT OF INERTIA (IN⁴)	SECTION MODULUS (IN³)	BOARD MEASURE PER LIN. FOOT	WEIGHT PER LIN. FT. AT 40LB FT³
1 X 2	3/4 x 1½	1.325	0.250	0.72	1/8	.36
1 X 3	3/4 x 2½	1.875	0.977	0.781	1/4	.52
1 X 4	3/4 x 3½	2.625	2.680	1.531	1/3	.73
1 X 6	3/4 x 5½	4.125	10.398	3.781	1/2	1.14
1 X 8	3/4 x 7¼	5.438	23.817	6.570	2/3	1.51
1 X 10	3/4 x 9¼	6.938	49.466	10.695	5/6	1.93
1 X 12	3/4 x 11¼	8.438	88.989	15.820	1	2.34
2 X 2	1½ x 1½	2.250	0.422	0.562	1/3	.73
2 X 3	1½ x 2½	3.750	1.953	1.563	1/2	1.04
2 X 4	1½ x 3½	5.250	5.359	3.063	2/3	1.46
2 X 6	1½ x 5½	8.250	20.797	7.563	1	2.29
2 X 8	1½ x 7¼	10.875	47.635	13.141	1 1/3	3.02
2 X 10	1½ x 9¼	13.875	98.932	21.391	1 1/4	3.85
2 X 12	1½ x 11¼	16.875	177.979	31.641	2	4.69
2 X 14	1½ x 13¼	19.875	290.775	43.891	2 1/3	5.52
3 X 3	2½ x 2½	6.250	3.250	2.600	3/4	1.98
3 X 4	2½ x 3½	8.750	8.932	5.104	1	2.43
3 X 6	2½ x 5½	13.750	34.661	12.604	1 1/2	3.82
3 X 8	2½ x 7¼	18.125	79.391	21.901	2	5.04
3 X 10	2½ x 9¼	23.125	164.886	35.651	2 1/2	6.42
3 X 12	2½ x 11¼	28.125	296.631	52.734	3	7.81
3 X 14	2½ x 13¼	33.125	484.625	73.151	3 1/2	9.20
3 X 16	2½ x 15¼	38.125	738.870	96.901	4	10.59
4 X 4	3½ x 3½	12.250	12.505	7.146	1 1/3	3.40
4 X 5	3½ x 4½	15.750	26.580	11.811	1 5/6	4.46
4 X 6	3½ x 5½	19.250	48.526	17.646	2	5.35
4 X 8	3½ x 7¼	25.375	111.148	30.661	2 2/3	7.05
4 X 10	3½ x 9¼	32.375	230.840	49.911	3 1/3	8.93
4 X 12	3½ x 11¼	39.375	415.283	73.828	4	10.94
4 X 14	3½ x 13½	47.250	717.609	106.313	4 2/3	13.13
4 X 16	3½ x 15½	54.250	1086.130	140.146	5 1/3	15.07
6 X 6	5½ x 5½	30.250	76.255	27.729	3	8.40
6 X 8	5½ x 7½	41.250	193.359	51.563	4	11.46
6 X 10	5½ x 9½	52.250	392.963	82.729	5	14.51
6 X 12	5½ x 11½	63.250	697.068	121.229	6	17.57
6 X 14	5½ x 13½	74.250	1127.672	167.063	7	20.63
6 X 16	5½ x 15½	65.250	1706.776	220.229	8	23.69
6 X 18	5½ x 17½	96.250	2456.380	280.729	9	26.74
6 X 20	5½ x 19½	107.250	3398.484	348.563	10	29.79
6 X 22	5½ x 21½	118.250	4555.086	423.729	11	32.85
6 X 24	5½ x 23½	129.250	5948.191	506.229	12	35.90

FOR SIZES AND PROPERTIES OF HEAVY TIMBER (8 X 8 AND LARGER) REFER TO PLATES 6.5 AND 6.6

LUMBER BOARD MEASURE CONTENTS 6.2

MEMBER SIZE	LENGTH IN FEET								
	8	10	12	14	16	18	20	22	24
1 X 2	1⅓	1⅔	2	2⅓	2⅔	3	3⅓	3⅔	4
1 X 3	2	2½	3	3½	4	4½	5	5½	6
1 X 4	2⅔	3⅓	4	4⅔	5⅓	6	6⅔	7⅓	8
1 X 6	4	5	6	7	8	9	10	11	12
1 X 8	5⅓	6⅔	8	9⅓	10⅔	12	13⅓	14⅔	16
1 X 10	6⅔	8⅓	10	11⅔	13⅓	15	16⅔	18⅓	20
1 X 12	8	10	12	14	16	18	20	22	24
1 X 14	9⅓	11⅔	14	16⅓	18⅔	21	23⅓	25⅔	28
1 X 16	10⅔	13⅓	16	18⅔	21⅓	24	26⅔	29⅓	32
2 X 4	5⅓	6⅔	8	9⅓	10⅔	12	13⅓	14⅔	16
2 X 6	8	10	12	14	16	18	20	22	24
2 X 8	10⅔	13⅓	16	18⅔	21⅓	24	26⅔	29⅓	32
2 X 10	13⅓	16⅔	20	23⅓	26⅔	30	33⅓	36⅔	40
2 X 12	16	20	24	28	32	36	40	44	48
2 X 14	18⅔	23⅓	28	32⅔	37⅓	42	46⅔	51⅓	56
2 X 16	21⅓	26⅔	32	37⅓	42⅔	48	53⅓	58⅔	64
3 X 4	8	10	12	14	16	18	20	22	24
3 X 6	12	15	18	21	24	27	30	33	36
3 X 8	16	20	24	28	32	36	40	44	48
3 X 10	20	25	30	35	40	45	50	55	60
3 X 12	24	30	36	42	48	54	60	66	72
3 X 14	28	35	42	49	56	63	70	77	84
3 X 16	32	40	48	56	64	72	80	88	96
4 X 4	10⅔	13⅓	16	18⅔	21⅓	24	26⅔	29⅓	32
4 X 6	16	20	24	28	32	36	40	44	48
4 X 8	21⅓	26⅔	32	37⅓	42⅔	48	53⅓	58⅔	64
4 X 10	26⅔	33⅓	40	46⅔	53⅓	60	66⅔	73⅓	80
4 X 12	32	40	48	56	64	72	80	88	96
4 X 14	37⅓	46⅔	56	65⅓	74⅔	84	93⅓	102⅔	112
4 X 16	42⅔	53⅓	64	74⅔	85⅓	96	106⅔	117⅓	128

ONE BOARD FOOT IS 12" X 12" X 1" NOMINAL. FOR LARGER SIZES THAN GIVEN ABOVE, ADD PROPER COMBINATIONS FOR TOTALS.

WEIGHTS AND SPECIFIC GRAVITIES
OF
COMMERCIAL LUMBER SPECIES

SPECIES	SPECIFIC GRAVITY		WEIGHT, PCF	
	BASED ON OVEN-DRY WEIGHT AND VOLUME AT 12% MC[a]	BASED ON OVEN-DRY WEIGHT AND VOLUME WHEN GREEN[b]	BASED ON WEIGHT AND VOLUME AT 12% MC	BASED ON WEIGHT AND VOLUME AT 20% MC
SOFTWOODS				
CEDAR				
INCENSE	0.37	0.35	25.9	27.0
NORTHERN WHITE	0.30	0.29	21.0	22.5
WESTERN	0.35	0.33	24.5	25.5
WESTERN RED	0.35	0.33	24.5	25.5
CYPRESS, SOUTHERN	0.46	0.43	32.1	33.7
DOUGLAS FIR	0.48	0.45	33.5	35.2
DOUGLAS FIR, SOUTH	0.46	0.43	32.1	33.7
DOUGLAS FIR, LARCH	0.48	0.45	33.5	35.2
FIR				
BALSAM	0.36	0.34	25.2	26.2
SUBALPINE	0.33	0.31	23.1	24.0
HEMLOCK				
EASTERN-TAMARACK	0.45	0.40	30.0	31.4
MOUNTAIN	0.45	0.42	31.4	33.0
WEST COAST	0.45	0.42	29.3	30.7
HEM-FIR	0.42	0.39	26.6	27.7
LARCH	0.52	0.48	36.3	37.4
PINE				
EASTERN WHITE	0.37	0.35	25.9	27.0
IDAHO WHITE (WESTERN)	0.39	0.37	27.2	28.4
LODGEPOLE	0.42	0.39	29.3	30.7
NORTHERN (JACK)	0.43	0.40	30.0	31.4
PONDEROSA-SUGAR	0.41	0.39	29.3	30.7
SOUTHERN	0.52	0.48	36.3	37.4
REDWOOD	0.38	0.36	26.6	27.7
SPRUCE				
EASTERN	0.40	0.38	28.0	29.2
ENGELMANN	0.34	0.32	23.8	24.7
SITKA	0.40	0.38	28.0	29.2
HARDWOODS				
ASH				
COMMERCIAL WHITE	0.59	0.54	41.2	42.7
BLACK	0.48	0.45	33.5	35.2
BEECH	0.63	0.57	44.0	44.9
BIRCH				
SWEET	0.66	0.60	46.1	47.2
YELLOW	0.60	0.55	41.9	41.2
COTTONWOOD, EASTERN	0.39	0.37	27.2	28.4
ELM				
AMERICAN	0.50	0.46	34.9	35.9
ROCK[c]	0.63	0.57	44.0	44.9

SPECIES	SPECIFIC GRAVITY		WEIGHT, PCF	
	BASED ON OVEN-DRY WEIGHT AND VOLUME AT 12% MC[a]	BASED ON OVEN-DRY WEIGHT AND VOLUME WHEN GREEN[b]	BASED ON WEIGHT AND VOLUME AT 12% MC	BASED ON WEIGHT AND VOLUME AT 20% MC
ELM (CONTINUED)				
SLIPPERY	0.53	0.49	37.0	38.2
HICKORY				
PECAN	0.68	0.61	47.3	48.7
SHAGBARK	0.71	0.64	49.6	50.9
MAPLE				
BLACK	0.57	0.52	39.8	40.4
SUGAR	0.63	0.57	44.0	44.9
OAK				
RED	0.63	0.57	44.0	44.9
WHITE	0.66	0.69	41.9	47.2
SWEETGUM	0.50	0.46	34.9	35.9
TUPELO				
BLACK	0.51	0.47	35.6	36.7
WATER	0.50	0.46	34.9	35.9
YELLOW-POPLAR	0.43	0.40	30.0	31.4

NOMINAL SIZE (IN.) b x d	ACTUAL SIZE (IN.) b x d	AREA (IN.²)	MOMENT OF INERTIA (IN.⁴)	SECTION MODULUS (IN.³)	BOARD MEASURE PER LIN. FOOT	WEIGHT PER LIN. FOOT AT 40 lb./ft³
8 x 8	7½ x 7½	56.250	263.67	70.31	5⅓	15.62
8 x 10	7½ x 9½	71.250	535.85	112.81	6⅔	19.79
8 x 12	7½ x 11½	86.250	950.54	165.31	8	23.96
8 x 14	7½ x 13½	101.250	1,537.73	227.81	9⅓	28.13
8 x 16	7½ x 15½	116.250	2,327.42	300.31	10⅔	32.29
8 x 18	7½ x 17½	131.250	3,349.61	382.81	12	36.46
8 x 20	7½ x 19½	146.250	4,634.29	475.31	13⅓	40.63
8 x 22	7½ x 21½	161.250	6,211.48	577.81	14⅔	44.79
8 x 24	7½ x 23½	176.250	8,111.17	690.31	16	48.96
10 x 8	9½ x 7½	71.250	333.98	89.06	6⅔	19.79
10 x 10	9½ x 9½	90.250	678.76	142.90	8⅓	25.07
10 x 12	9½ x 11½	109.250	1,204.03	209.40	10⅓	30.35
10 x 14	9½ x 13½	128.250	1,947.80	288.56	11⅔	35.63
10 x 16	9½ x 15½	147.250	2,948.07	380.40	13⅓	40.90
10 x 18	9½ x 17½	166.250	4,242.84	484.90	15	46.18
10 x 20	9½ x 19½	185.250	5,870.11	602.03	16⅔	51.46
10 x 22	9½ x 21½	204.250	7,867.88	731.90	18⅓	56.74
10 x 24	9½ x 23½	223.250	10,274.15	874.40	20	62.01
12 x 8	11½ x 7½	86.250	404.29	107.81	6	23.96
12 x 10	11½ x 9½	109.250	821.65	172.98	10	30.35
12 x 12	11½ x 11½	132.250	1,457.51	253.48	12	36.74
12 x 14	11½ x 13½	155.250	2,357.86	349.31	14	43.13
12 x 16	11½ x 15½	178.250	3,568.71	460.48	16	49.51
12 x 18	11½ x 17½	201.250	5,136.07	586.98	18	55.90
12 x 20	11½ x 19½	224.250	7,105.92	728.81	20	62.29
12 x 22	11½ x 21½	247.250	9,524.27	885.98	22	68.68
12 x 24	11½ x 23½	270.250	12,437.13	1,058.48	24	75.07
14 x 10	13½ x 9½	128.250	964.55	203.06	11⅔	35.63
14 x 12	13½ x 11½	155.250	1,710.98	297.56	14	43.13
14 x 16	13½ x 15½	209.250	4,189.36	540.56	18⅔	58.13
14 x 18	13½ x 17½	236.250	6,029.30	689.06	21	65.63
14 x 20	13½ x 19½	263.250	8,431.73	855.56	23⅓	73.13
14 x 22	13½ x 21½	290.250	11,180.67	1,040.06	25⅔	80.63
14 x 24	13½ x 23½	317.250	14,600.11	1,242.56	28	88.13

AMERICAN INSTITUTE OF TIMBER CONSTRUCTION.

HEAVY TIMBER SIZES AND PROPERTIES   6.6

NOMINAL SIZE (IN.) b x d	ACTUAL SIZE (IN.) b x d	AREA (IN.²)	MOMENT OF INERTIA (IN.⁴)	SECTION MODULUS (IN.³)	BOARD MEASURE PER LIN. FOOT	WEIGHT PER LIN. FOOT AT 40 lb/ft³
16 x 12	15½ x 11½	178.250	1946.46	341.64	16	49.51
16 x 14	15½ x 13½	209.250	3,177.98	470.81	18⅔	58.13
16 x 16	15½ x 15½	240.250	4,810.00	620.65	21⅓	66.74
16 x 18	15½ x 17½	271.250	6,922.52	791.15	24	75.34
16 x 20	15½ x 19½	302.250	9,577.31	982.31	26⅔	83.96
16 x 22	15½ x 21½	333.250	12,837.07	1,194.15	29⅓	92.60
16 x 24	15½ x 23½	364.250	16,763.09	1,426.65	32	101.18
18 x 12	17½ x 11½	201.250	2,217.94	385.73	18	55.90
18 x 14	17½ x 13½	236.250	3,588.05	531.56	21	65.62
18 x 16	17½ x 15½	271.250	5,430.65	700.73	24	75.35
18 x 18	17½ x 17½	306.250	7,815.75	893.23	27	85.07
18 x 20	17½ x 19½	341.250	10,813.36	1,109.06	30	94.72
18 x 22	17½ x 21½	376.250	14,493.46	1,348.23	33	104.51
18 x 24	17½ x 23½	411.250	18,926.07	1,610.73	36	114.24
20 x 14	19½ x 13½	263.250	3,998.11	592.31	23⅓	73.13
20 x 16	19½ x 15½	302.250	6,051.30	780.81	26⅔	83.96
20 x 18	19½ x 17½	341.250	8,798.98	995.31	30	94.79
20 x 20	19½ x 19½	380.250	12,049.17	1,235.81	33⅓	105.63
20 x 22	19½ x 21½	419.250	16,149.86	1,502.31	36⅔	116.46
20 x 24	19½ x 23½	458.250	21,089.05	1,794.81	40	127.29
22 x 14	21½ x 13½	290.250	4,408.17	653.06	25⅔	80.63
22 x 16	21½ x 15½	333.250	6,671.94	860.90	29⅓	92.57
22 x 18	21½ x 17½	376.250	9,602.21	1,097.40	33	104.51
22 x 20	21½ x 19½	419.250	13,284.98	1,362.56	36⅔	116.46
22 x 22	21½ x 21½	462.250	17,806.25	1,656.40	40⅓	128.40
22 x 24	21½ x 23½	505.250	23,252.02	1,978.90	44	140.35
24 x 16	23½ x 15½	364.250	7,292.59	940.98	32	101.18
24 x 18	23½ x 17½	411.250	10,495.44	1,199.48	36	114.24
24 x 20	23½ x 19½	458.250	14,520.80	1,489.31	40	127.29
24 x 22	23½ x 21½	505.250	19,462.65	1,810.48	44	140.35
24 x 24	23½ x 23½	552.250	25,415.00	2,162.98	48	153.40

SIZES AND PROPERTIES FOR FRAMING LUMBER SMALLER THAN 8x8 ARE GIVEN ON PLATE 6.1.

AMERICAN INSTITUTE OF TIMBER CONSTRUCTION.

CHARTS GIVEN BELOW CONSIDER ONLY THE NORMAL USE OF A SINGLE SYSTEM
AND DO NOT CONSIDER EXTREME POSSIBILITIES. CHARTS SHOULD BE USED
FOR PRELIMINARY DESIGN ONLY. IF GREATER THAN NORMAL LOADS ARE
ANTICIPATED, OR WIDER THAN NORMAL SPACING, USE UPPER PORTION
OF CHART. USE LOWER PORTION FOR LIGHT LOADS. FOR CANTILEVERS USE
THREE TIMES CANTILEVER LENGTH TO DETERMINE THICKNESS OR
DEPTH.

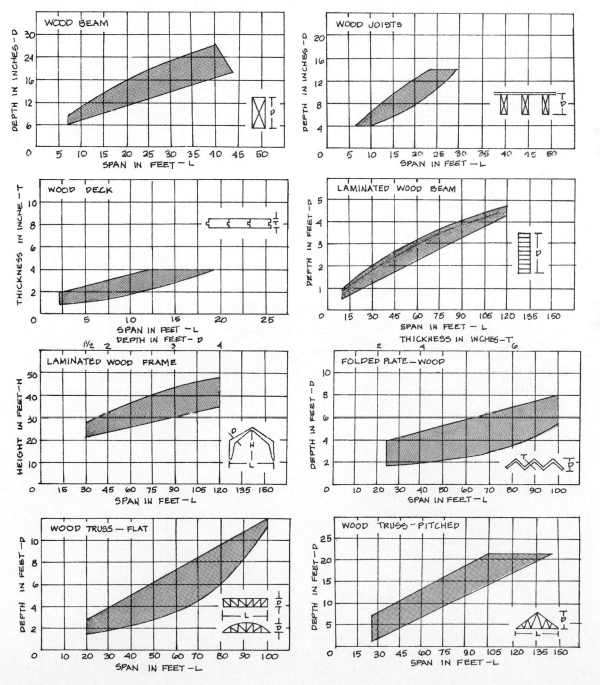

SERNOLL DIVISION: BAWDEN BROS. INC.

CHARTS GIVEN BELOW ASSUME AN UNSUPPORTED HEIGHT FROM
1 TO 50 FEET AND PRIMARILY ONLY A ROOF OR ONE-STORY LOAD
OR ARE STRUCTURAL SUPPORTS WHICH HAVE A NORMAL ONE STORY
HEIGHT AND MUST SUPPORT FROM 1 TO 50 STORIES. NORMAL UNSUPPORTED
STORY HEIGHT IS ASSUMED 8 TO 12 FEET. MIDDLE RANGE OF CHART
SHOULD BE USED FOR NORMAL LOADING, UPPER PORTION FOR HEAVY
LOADS, AND LOWER PORTION FOR LIGHT LOADING. USE FOR
PRELIMINARY DESIGN ONLY.

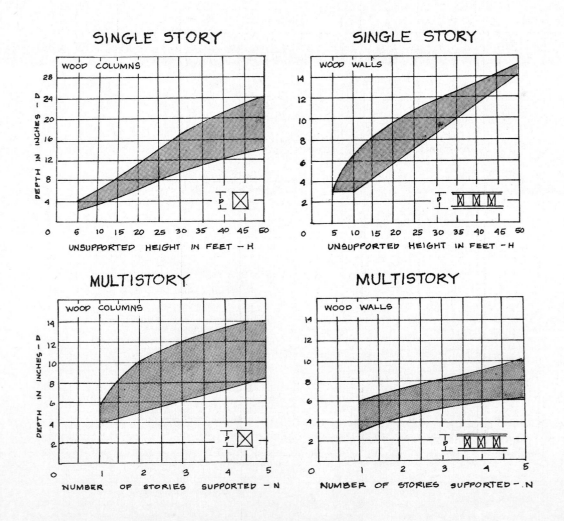

SERNOLL DIVISION: BAWDEN BROS. INC.

DOUGLAS FIR JOIST AND BEAMS (1500 f)

NOM. SIZE	TOTAL LOAD IN POUNDS, – SPAN IN FEET										
	3-0	4-0	5-0	6-0	8-0	10-0	12-0	14-0	16-0	18-0	20-0
2x4	1120	888	71	592	444						
3x4	1910	1440	1150	957	718						
2x6	2080	1870	1640	1370	1020	819	632				
3x6	3360	3020	2650	2210	1650	1320	1100				
4x6	4640	4170	3650	3050	2280	1830	1520				
2x8	3340	2840	2600	2460	1910	1220	1270	1090	952		
3x8	5400	4580	4200	3980	3080	2460	2050	1760	1540		
4x8	7460	6330	5800	5490	4250	3400	2830	2430	2120		
2x10		4090	3620	3360	3080	2450	2040	1750	1530	1360	1220
4x10		9120	8060	7490	6820	5450	4540	3890	3410	3030	2730
6x10		13800	12200	11400	10300	8270	6890	5910	5170	4600	4140
2x12		5740	4850	4390	3930	3580	2980	2560	2240	1990	1790
4x12		12800	10800	9800	8770	7990	6660	5710	4990	4440	3990
2x14			6380	5620	4880	4530	4110	3530	3090	2740	2470
4x14			14200	12500	10900	10100	9180	7870	6880	6120	5500

TOTAL LOADS IN POUNDS, INCLUDING WEIGHT OF BEAM, AT A DEFLECTION OF 1/360 OF THE SPAN. MODULUS OF ELASTICITY AT 1,760,000. f = ALLOWABLE FIBER STRESS. MAX. MOISTURE CONTENT = 19%.

DOUGLAS FIR JOISTS AND BEAMS (1750 f)

NOM. SIZE	TOTAL LOAD IN POUNDS, – SPAN IN FEET										
	3-0	4-0	5-0	6-0	8-0	10-0	12-0	14-0	16-0	18-0	20-0
2x4											
3x4											
2x6	2080	1870	1760	1590	1190	955	796				
3x6	3360	3020	2840	2570	1930	1540	1290				
4x6	4640	4170	3930	3550	2660	2130	1780				
2x5	3340	2840	2600	2460	2220	1780	1480	1270	1110		
3x8	5400	4580	4200	3980	3590	2870	2390	2050	1790		
4x8	7460	6330	5800	5490	4960	3970	3300	2830	2480		
2x10		4090	3620	3360	3080	2850	2380	2040	1780	1580	1430
4x10		9120	8060	7490	6870	6360	5300	4540	3970	3530	3180
6x10		13800	12200	11400	10400	9650	8040	6890	6030	5360	4820
2x12		5740	4850	4390	3930	3700	3480	2990	2610	2320	2090
4x12		12800	10800	9800	8770	8250	7770	6660	5850	5180	4660
2x14			6380	5620	4880	4530	4320	4110	3600	3200	2880
4x14			14200	12500	10900	10100	9640	9180	8030	7140	6420

DOUGLAS FIR (1200 C)

NOM. SIZE	TOTAL LOAD IN POUNDS – UNSUPPORTED LENGTH IN FEET										
	3-0	4-0	5-0	6-0	8-0	10-0	12-0	14-0	16-0	18-0	20-0
2×4	6340	3560	2280	1580							
3×4	11400	11400	9620	6680	3760	2400					
4×4	15900	15800	13100	15800	9890	6330	4400	3230			
3×6	17300	17300	14600	10100	5700	3650					
4×6	23900	23900	23900	23900	15000	9610	6670	4900			
6×6			36300	36300	36300	33600	23300	17100	13100	10400	8390
4×8	32600	32600	32600	32600	20500	13100	9100	6650			
6×8			49600	49500	49600	45800	31800	23300	17900	14100	11400
8×8					67500	67500	67500	59200	45300	35900	29000
4×10	41300	41300	41300	41300	25900	16600	11500	8470			
6×10			62700	62700	62700	58000	40200	29600	22600	17900	14500
8×10					85500	85500	85500	75000	57400	45400	36700
10×10						108000	108000	108000	108000	92200	74700
8×12					104000	104000	104000	90800	69500	54900	44500
10×12						131000	131000	131000	131000	112000	90400
12×12							159000	159000	159000	159000	159000

TOTAL LOADS IN POUNDS, CONCENTRICALLY LOADED MODULUS OF ELASTICITY E = 1,760,000 LBS. SQ. IN. SLENDERNESS RATIO l/d = 50.

DOUGLAS FIR (1500 C)

NOM. SIZE	TOTAL LOAD IN POUNDS, UNSUPPORTED LENGTH IN FEET										
	3-0	4-0	5-0	6-0	8-0	10-0	12-0	14-0	16-0	18-0	20-0
2×4	6340	3560	2280	1580							
3×4	14300	14300	9620	6680	3760	2400					
4×4	19700	19700	19700	17600	9890	6330	4400	3230			
3×6	21700	21700	14600	10100	5700	3650					
4×6	23900	29900	29900	26700	15000	9610	6670	4940			
6×6			45400	45400	45400	33600	23300	17100	13100	10400	8390
4×8	40800	40800	40800	36400	20500	13100	9100	6680			
6×8			61900	61900	61900	45800	31800	23300	17900	14100	11400
8×8					84400	84400	80600	59200	45300	35800	29000
4×10	51700	51700	51700	46100	25900	16600	11500	8470			
6×10			78400	78400	78400	58000	40200	29600	22600	17900	14500
8×10						107000	102000	75000	57400	45400	36700
10×10						135000	135000	135000	117000	92200	74700
8×12					129000	129000	124000	90800	69500	54900	44500
10×12						164000	164000	164000	141000	112000	90400
12×12							198000	198000	198000	198000	160000

NOMINAL SIZE	IN. O.C.	SELECT	CONSTRUC-TION	STANDARD	UTILITY	SELECT	CONSTRUC-TION	STANDARD	UTILITY
FLOOR JOIST									
30-LB. LIVE LOAD					**40-LB. LIVE LOAD**			
2 x 6	12	11-4	11-4	11-4	8-4	10-6	10-6	10-6	7-4
	16	10-4	10-4	10-4	7-2	9-8	9-8	9-8	6-4
	24	9-0	9-0	9-0	5-10	8-4	8-4	8-2	5-2
2 x 8	12	15-4	15-4	15-4	13-4	14-4	14-4	14-4	12-0
	16	14-0	14-0	14-0	11-6	13-0	13-0	13-0	10-4
	24	12-4	12-4	12-4	9-6	11-6	11-6	11-0	8-4
2 x 10	12	18-4	18-4	18-4	17-10	17-4	17-4	17-4	16-2
	16	17-0	17-0	17-0	15-6	16-2	16-2	16-2	14-0
	24	15-6	15-6	15-6	12-10	14-6	14-6	14-0	11-4
2 x 12	12	21-2	21-2	21-2	21-2	20-0	20-0	20-0	19-6
	16	19-8	19-8	19-8	18-8	18-8	18-8	18-8	16-8
	24	17-10	17-10	17-10	15-6	16-10	16-10	16-10	14-8
CEILING JOIST									
NO ATTIC STORAGE					**LIMITED ATTIC STORAGE**			
2 x 4	12	11-10	11-8	8-10	6-2	9-4	8-2	6-4	4-4
	16	10-10	10-0	7-8	5-4	8-0	7-2	5-6	3-10
	24	9-4	8-2	6-4	4-4	6-8	5-10	4-6	3-2
2 x 6	12	17-2	17-2	17-2	14-8	14-4	14-4	14-4	9-6
	16	16-0	16-0	16-0	11-8	13-0	13-0	12-10	8-4
	24	14-4	14-4	14-4	9-6	11-4	11-4	10-6	6-8
2 x 8	12	21-8	21-8	21-8	21-8	18-4	18-4	18-4	15-4
	16	20-2	20-2	20-2	18-10	17-0	17-0	17-0	13-4
	24	18-4	18-4	18-4	15-4	15-4	15-4	14-4	10-10
2 x 10	12	24-0	24-0	24-0	24-0	21-10	21-10	21-10	20-8
	16	24-0	24-0	24-0	24-0	20-4	20-4	20-4	18-0
	24	21-10	21-10	21-10	20-8	18-4	18-4	18-0	14-8

WESTERN PINE ASSOCIATION

NOMINAL SIZE	IN. O.C.	SELECT	CONSTRUC-TION	STANDARD	UTILITY	SELECT	CONSTRUC-TION	STANDARD	UTILITY
ROOF JOIST, 3:12 OR LESS									
		NONSUPPORTING CEILING				SUPPORTING CEILING			
2 x 6	12	14 - 4	14 - 4	14 - 4	9 - 6	13 - 8	13 - 8	13 - 8	8 - 10
	16	13 - 0	13 - 0	12 - 10	8 - 4	12 - 4	12 - 4	11 - 10	7 - 8
	24	11 - 4	11 - 4	10 - 6	6 - 8	10 - 10	10 - 8	9 - 8	6 - 2
2 x 8	12	18 - 4	18 - 4	18 - 4	15 - 4	17 - 8	17 - 8	17 - 8	14 - 2
	16	17 - 0	17 - 0	17 - 0	13 - 4	16 - 4	16 - 4	16 - 2	12 - 4
	24	15 - 4	15 - 4	14 - 4	10 - 10	14 - 6	14 - 6	13 - 2	10 - 0
2 x 10	12	21 - 10	21 - 10	21 - 10	20 - 8	21 - 0	21 - 0	21 - 0	19 - 0
	16	20 - 4	20 - 4	20 - 4	18 - 0	19 - 6	19 - 6	19 - 6	16 - 8
	24	18 - 4	18 - 4	18 - 0	14 - 8	17 - 8	17 - 8	16 - 8	13 - 6
2 x 12	12	24 - 0	24 - 0	24 - 0	24 - 0	24 - 0	24 - 0	24 - 0	23 - 0
	16	23 - 6	23 - 6	23 - 6	21 - 10	22 - 6	22 - 6	22 - 6	20 - 0
	24	21 - 2	21 - 2	21 - 2	19 - 6	20 - 4	20 - 4	20 - 2	16 - 4
ROOF RAFTERS, OVER 3:12									
		LIGHT ROOFING				HEAVY ROOFING			
2 x 4	12	10 - 10	9 - 6	7 - 4	5 - 2	9 - 4	8 - 2	6 - 4	4 - 4
	16	10 - 0	8 - 4	6 - 4	4 - 6	8 - 0	7 - 2	5 - 6	3 - 10
	24	7 - 4	6 - 10	5 - 2	3 - 8	6 - 8	5 - 10	4 - 6	3 - 2
2 x 6	12	16 - 10	16 - 10	16 - 10	11 - 2	15 - 6	15 - 6	14 - 10	9 - 6
	16	15 - 8	15 - 8	15 - 0	9 - 8	14 - 4	14 - 0	12 - 10	8 - 4
	24	13 - 10	13 - 6	12 - 2	7 - 8	12 - 6	11 - 6	10 - 6	6 - 8
2 x 8	12	21 - 2	21 - 2	21 - 2	18 - 0	19 - 8	19 - 8	19 - 8	15 - 4
	16	19 - 10	19 - 10	19 - 0	15 - 8	18 - 4	18 - 4	17 - 6	13 - 4
	24	17 - 10	17 - 10	16 - 8	12 - 8	16 - 6	15 - 8	14 - 4	10 - 10
2 x 10	12	24 - 0	24 - 0	24 - 0	24 - 0	23 - 6	23 - 6	23 - 6	20 - 8
	16	23 - 8	23 - 8	23 - 8	21 - 0	21 - 10	21 - 10	21 - 10	18 - 0
	24	21 - 4	21 - 4	21 - 0	17 - 2	19 - 8	19 - 8	18 - 0	14 - 8

HOW TO READ THE BASIC GRADE—TRADEMARKS OF THE AMERICAN PLYWOOD ASSOCIATION

PRODUCT STANDARD 1-74 IS A PERFORMANCE STANDARD FOR CLEAR UNDERSTANDING BETWEEN BUYER AND SELLER. TO IDENTIFY PLYWOOD MANUFACTURED BY ASSOCIATION MEMBER MILLS UNDER THE REQUIREMENTS OF PRODUCT STANDARD PS 1-74, FOUR TYPES OF GRADE—TRADEMARKS AND ONE TYPICAL EDGE MARK ARE USED TO ILLUSTRATE THE PLYWOOD'S TYPE, GRADE, GROUP, CLASS AND IDENTIFICATION INDEX. HERE IS HOW THEY LOOK TOGETHER WITH NOTATIONS ON WHAT EACH ELEMENT MEANS.

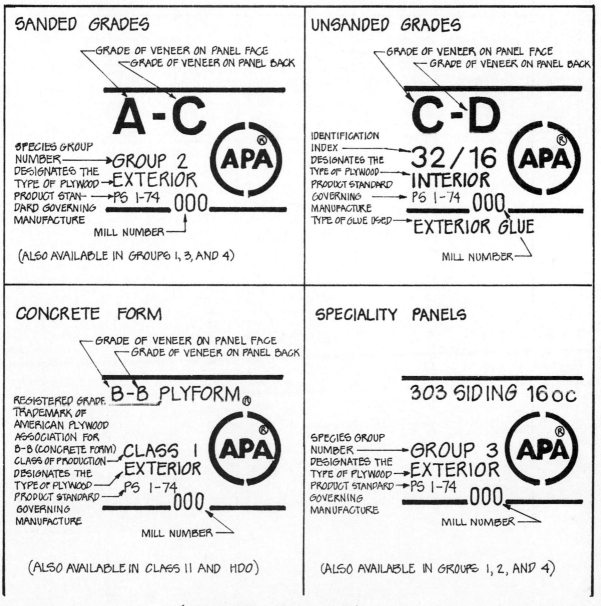

SANDED GRADES

GRADE OF VENEER ON PANEL FACE
GRADE OF VENEER ON PANEL BACK

A-C (APA)

SPECIES GROUP NUMBER → GROUP 2
DESIGNATES THE TYPE OF PLYWOOD → EXTERIOR
PRODUCT STANDARD GOVERNING MANUFACTURE → PS 1-74 000

MILL NUMBER

(ALSO AVAILABLE IN GROUPS 1, 3, AND 4)

UNSANDED GRADES

GRADE OF VENEER ON PANEL FACE
GRADE OF VENEER ON PANEL BACK

C-D (APA)

IDENTIFICATION INDEX → 32/16
DESIGNATES THE TYPE OF PLYWOOD → INTERIOR
PRODUCT STANDARD GOVERNING MANUFACTURE → PS 1-74 000
TYPE OF GLUE USED → EXTERIOR GLUE

MILL NUMBER

CONCRETE FORM

GRADE OF VENEER ON PANEL FACE
GRADE OF VENEER ON PANEL BACK

B-B PLYFORM® (APA)

REGISTERED GRADE TRADEMARK OF AMERICAN PLYWOOD ASSOCIATION FOR B-B (CONCRETE FORM)
CLASS OF PRODUCTION → CLASS 1
DESIGNATES THE TYPE OF PLYWOOD → EXTERIOR
PRODUCT STANDARD GOVERNING MANUFACTURE → PS 1-74 000

MILL NUMBER

(ALSO AVAILABLE IN CLASS II AND HDO)

SPECIALITY PANELS

303 SIDING 16 oc (APA)

SPECIES GROUP NUMBER → GROUP 3
DESIGNATES THE TYPE OF PLYWOOD → EXTERIOR
PRODUCT STANDARD GOVERNING MANUFACTURE → PS 1-74 000

MILL NUMBER

(ALSO AVAILABLE IN GROUPS 1, 2, AND 4)

(CONTINUED NEXT PAGE)

AMERICAN PLYWOOD ASSOCIATION

(CONTINUED FROM PRECEDING PAGE)

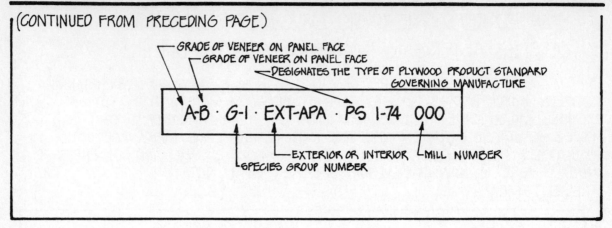

INTERIOR TYPE	USE THESE SYMBOLS WHEN YOU SPECIFY PLYWOOD	DESCRIPTION AND MOST COMMON USES	TYPICAL GRADE TRADEMARKS (2)	VENEER GRADE FACE	BACK	INNER PLYS	MOST COMMON THICKNESS (3) (INCH) 1/4	5/16	3/8	1/2	5/8	3/4	1
	N-N, NA, N-B, N-D INT-DFPA	NATURAL FINISH CABINET QUALITY. ONE OR BOTH SIDES, SELECT ALL HEARTWOOD OR ALL SAPWOOD VENEER. FOR FURNITURE HAVING A NATURAL FINISH, CABINET DOORS, BUILT-INS. USE N-D FOR NATURAL FINISH PANELING. SPECIAL ORDER ITEMS.	N-N·G1·INT-DFPA-PS 1-66 / N-A·G-2·INT DFPA-PS 1-66	N	N,A B OR D	C OR D	●					●	
	A-A INT-DFPA	FOR INTERIOR APPLICATIONS WHERE BOTH SIDES WILL BE ON VIEW. BUILT-INS, CABINETS, FURNITURE AND PARTITIONS. FACE IS SMOOTH AND SUITABLE FOR PAINTING	A-A·G-3·INT-DFPA PS 1-66	A	A	D	●		●	●	●	●	●
	A-B INT-DFPA	FOR USES SIMILAR TO INTERIOR A-A BUT WHERE APPEARANCE OF ONE SIDE IS LESS IMPORTANT AND TWO SMOOTH SOLID SURFACES ARE NECESSARY.	A-B·G-4·INT-DFPA PS 1-66	A	B	D	●		●	●	●	●	●
	A-D INT-DFPA	FOR INTERIOR USES WHERE THE APPEARANCE OF ONLY ONE SIDE IS IMPORTANT. PANELING, BUILT-INS, SHELVING, PARTITIONS AND FLOW-RACKS.	A-D GROUP 1 INTERIOR (DFPA)	A	D	D	●		●	●	●	●	●
	B-B INT-DFPA	INTERIOR UTILITY PANEL USED WHERE TWO SMOOTH SIDES ARE DESIRED. PERMITS CIRCULAR PLUGS. PAINTABLE.	B-B·G-3·INT-DFPA PS 1-66	B	B	D	●		●	●	●	●	●
	B-D INT-DFPA	INTERIOR UTILITY PANEL FOR USE WHERE ONE SMOOTH SIDE IS REQUIRED. GOOD FOR BACKING, SIDES OR BUILT-INS. INDUSTRY: SHELVING, SLIP-SHEETS, SEPARATOR BOARDS AND BINS.	B-D GROUP 3 INTERIOR (DFPA)	B	D	D	●		●	●	●	●	●
	DECORATIVE PANELS	ROUGH-SAWN, BRUSHED, GROOVED OR STRIATED FACES. GOOD FOR INTERIOR ACCENT WALLS, BUILT-INS, COUNTER FACING, DISPLAYS AND EXHIBITS.		B OR BTR.	D	D		●	●	●			
	PLYRON INT-DFPA	HARDBOARD FACE ON BOTH SIDES. FOR COUNTER TOPS, SHELVING, CABINET DOORS, FLOORING. HARDBOARD FACES MAY BE TEMPERED, UNTEMPERED, SMOOTH OR SCREENED.	PLYRON-INT-DFPA			C & D				●	●	●	

NOTES:

(1) SANDED BOTH SIDES EXCEPT WHERE DECORATIVE OR OTHER SURFACES SPECIFIED.

(2) AVAILABLE IN GROUP 1, 2, 3 OR 4 UNLESS OTHERWISE SPECIFIED.

(3) STANDARD 4 X 8 PANEL SIZES, OTHER SIZES AVAILABLE.

(4) ALSO AVAILABLE IN STRUCTURAL I (FACE, BACK AND INNER PLYS LIMITED TO GROUP 1 SPECIES).

EXTERIOR TYPE

USE THESE SYMBOLS WHEN YOU SPECIFY PLYWOOD	DESCRIPTION AND MOST COMMON USES	TYPICAL GRADE-TRADEMARKS (2)	VENEER GRADE FACE	BACK	INNER PLYS	1/4	5/16	3/8	1/2	5/8	3/4	1
A-A EXT-DFPA (4)	USE WHERE THE APPEARANCE OF BOTH SIDES IS IMPORTANT. FENCES, BUILT-INS, SIGNS, BOATS, CABINETS, COMMERCIAL REFRIGERATORS, SHIPPING CONTAINERS, TOTE BOXES, TANKS AND DUCTS.	A-A·G-4 EXT-DFPA·PS 1-66	A	A	C	•		•	•	•	•	•
A-B EXT-DFPA (4)	FOR USE SIMILAR TO A-A EXT PANELS BUT WHERE THE APPEARANCE OF ONE SIDE IS LESS IMPORTANT.	A-B·G-1·EXT-DFPA PS 1-66	A	B	C	•		•	•	•	•	•
A-C EXT-DFPA (4)	EXTERIOR USE WHERE THE APPEARANCE OF ONLY ONE SIDE IS IMPORTANT. SIDINGS, SOFFITS, FENCES STRUCTURAL USES, BOXCAR AND TRUCK LINING AND FARM BUILDINGS. TANKS, TRAYS, COMMERCIAL REFRIGERATORS.	A-C (DFPA) GROUP 2 EXTERIOR	A	C	C	•		•	•	•	•	
B-C EXT-DFPA(4)	AN OUTDOOR UTILITY PANEL FOR FARM SERVICE AND WORK BUILDINGS, BOX CAR AND TRUCK LININGS, CONTAINERS, TANKS, AGRICULTURAL EQUIPMENT.	B-C (DFPA) GROUP 3 EXTERIOR	B	C	C	•		•	•	•	•	
B-B EXT-DFPA(4)	AN OUTDOOR UTILITY PANEL WITH SOLID, PAINT-ABLE FACES FOR USES WHERE HIGHER QUALITY IS NOT NECESSARY.	B-B·G-1·EXT-DFPA PS 1-66	B	B	C	•		•	•	•	•	
HDO EXT-DFPA (4)	EXTERIOR TYPE HIGH DENSITY OVERLAY PLYWOOD WITH HARD, SEMI-OPAQUE RESIN FIBER OVERLAY. ABRASION RESISTANT. PAINTING NOT ORDINARILY REQUIRED. FOR CONCRETE FORMS, SIGNS, ACID TANKS, CABINETS, COUNTER TOPS.	HDO·G-1·EXT-DFPA PS 1-66	A OR B	A OR B	C PLUGGED			•	•	•	•	
MDO EXT-DFPA(4)	EXTERIOR TYPE MEDIUM DENSITY OVERLAY WITH SMOOTH, OPAQUE RESIN-FIBER OVERLAY HEAT FUSED TO ONE OR BOTH FACES. IDEAL BASE FOR PAINT. HIGHLY RECOMMENDED FOR SIDING AND OTHER OUTDOOR APPLICATIONS. ALSO GOOD FOR BUILT-INS, SIGNS AND DISPLAYS.	MDO·G-2·EXT-DFPA PS 1-66	B	B OR C	C			•	•	•	•	
303 SPECIAL SIDING EXT-DFPA	GRADE DESIGNATION COVERS PROPRIETARY PLY-WOOD PRODUCTS FOR EXTERIOR SIDING, FENCING, ETC., WITH SPECIAL SURFACE TREATMENT SUCH AS V-GROOVE, CHANNEL GROOVE, STRAITED, BRUSHED AND ROUGH SAWN.	303 SIDING 16 QC. (DFPA) GROUP 4 EXTERIOR	B OR BTR.	C	C			•	•	•		
T1-11 EXT-DFPA	EXTERIOR TYPE, SANDED OR UNSANDED, SHIP-LAPPED EDGES WITH PARALLEL GROOVES 1/4" DEEP, 3/8" WIDE. GROOVES ARE 2" OR 4" O.C. AVAIL-ABLE IN 8' AND 10' LENGTHS AND MD OVERLAY. FOR SIDING AND ACCENT PANELING.	T1-11 (DFPA) GROUP 1 EXTERIOR	C OR BTR.	C	C					•		
PLYRON EXT-DFPA	EXTERIOR PANEL SURFACED BOTH SIDES WITH HARD-BOARD FOR USE IN EXTERIOR APPLICATIONS. FACES ARE TEMPERED, SMOOTH OR SCREENED.	PLYRON-EXT-DFPA			C				•	•	•	
MARINE EXT-DFPA	EXTERIOR TYPE PLYWOOD MADE ONLY WITH DOUG-LAS FIR OR WESTERN LARCH. SPECIAL SOLID JOINTED CORE CONSTRUCTION. SUBJECT TO SPEC-IAL LIMITATIONS ON CORE GAPS AND NUMBER OF FACE REPAIRS. IDEAL FOR BOAT HULLS. ALSO AVAILABLE WITH OVERLAID FACES.	MARINE·A-A·EXT-DFPA·PS 1-66	A OR B	A OR B	B	•		•	•	•	•	•
SPECIAL EXTERIOR	PREMIUM EXTERIOR PANEL SIMILAR TO MARINE GRADE BUT PERMITS ANY SPECIES COVERED UNDER PS 1-66.		A OR B	A OR B	B	•		•	•	•	•	•

NOTES: (1) SANDED BOTH SIDES EXCEPT WHERE DECORATIVE OR OTHER SURFACES SPECIFIED.

(2) AVAILABLE IN GROUP 1, 2, 3, OR 4 UNLESS OTHERWISE INDICATED.

(3) STANDARD 4 x 8 PANEL SIZES, OTHER SIZES AVAILABLE.

(4) ALSO AVAILABLE IN STRUCTURAL I (FACE, BACK AND INNER PLYS LIMITED TO GROUP 1 SPECIES).

AMERICAN PLYWOOD ASSOCIATION

ALLOWABLE CLEAR SPANS FOR PLYWOOD GLUED FLOORS

	JOIST SIZE	D. FIR LARCH 1	D. FIR LARCH 2	D. FIR SO. 1	D. FIR SO. 2	HEM. FIR 1	HEM. FIR 2	SO. PINE 1	SO. PINE 2	SO. PINE 3	KD. SO. PINE 1
5/8 PLYWOOD JOIST @ 16"	2 x 6	11-2	10-6	10-5	10-1	10-3	9-4	11-2	9-6	7-11	11-4
	2 x 8	14-5	13-10	13-6	13-2	13-7	10-4	14-5	12-7	10-5	14-8
	2 x 10	18-2	17-7	16-11	16-7	17-3	15-8	18-2	16-0	13-3	18-5
	2 x 12	21-10	21-5	20-4	19-11	20-9	19-1	21-10	19-6	16-2	22-2
3/4 PLYWOOD JOIST @ 16"	2 x 6	11-5	10-6	10-8	10-1	10-3	9-4	11-5	9-6	7-11	11-7
	2 x 8	14-8	13-10	13-9	13-4	13-7	12-4	14-8	12-7	10-5	14-10
	2 x 10	18-4	17-7	17-2	16-10	17-4	15-8	18-4	16-0	13-3	18-8
	2 x 12	22-1	21-5	20-7	20-2	21-0	19-1	22-1	19-6	16-2	22-5
3/4 PLYWOOD JOIST @ 24"	2 x 6	9-5	8-7	9-1	8-3	8-5	7-7	9-5	7-9	6-5	9-9
	2 x 8	12-5	11-3	12-0	10-11	11-1	10-0	12-5	10-3	8-6	12-11
	2 x 10	15-10	14-5	15-4	13-10	14-2	12-10	15-10	13-1	10-10	16-6
	2 x 12	19-3	17-6	18-5	16-11	17-2	15-7	19-3	15-11	13-2	20-0

THE **APA** GLUED FLOOR SYSTEM FUSES FLOOR AND JOIST INTO INTEGRAL T-BEAM UNITS, INCREASING FLOOR STIFFNESS FROM 10 TO 90 PERCENT. NAIL EDGES AND INTERMEDIATE SUPPORTS AT 12" O.C. WITH 6D DEFORMED SHANK NAILS OR 8D COMMON. USE T&G EDGE PLYWOOD OR SOLID BLOCK EDGES. GLUE TOP OF JOIST, BLOCKING AND T&G PANEL EDGES. TABLE ABOVE BASED ON 40 LB. SQ. FT. LIVE LOAD, DEFLECTION 1/360 SPAN, SINGLE FLOOR CONSTRUCTION.

PLYWOOD RECOMMENDED FOR UNIFORM HEAVY LOADS

UNIFORM LIVE LOAD (psf)	CENTER TO CENTER OF 2-INCH WIDTH SUPPORTS				
	12	**16**	**20**	**24**	**32**
50	32/16	32/16	42/20	48/24	2:4:1
100	32/16	32/16	42/20	48/24	2:4:1
150	32/16	32/16	42/20	48/24	2:4:1
200	32/16	42/20	42/20	2:4:1	1 3/8
250	32/16	42/20	48/24	2:4:1	1 1/2
300	32/16	48/24	2:4:1	1 3/8	1 5/8
350	42/20	48/24	2:4:1	1 3/8	2
400	42/20	2:4:1	2:4:1	1 3/8	2
450	42/20	2:4:1	2:4:1	1 1/2	2 1/4
500	42/24	2:4:1	2:4:1	1 1/2	2 1/4

BLOCKING REQUIRED UNDER ALL PLYWOOD PANEL EDGES.

AMERICAN PLYWOOD ASSOCIATION

MAXIMUM ALLOWABLE UNIFORM LIVE LOADS
5 psf DEAD LOAD OF PLYWOOD AND ROOFING

PANEL IDENT. INDEX	PLYWOOD THICKNESS (IN.)	MAX. SPAN (IN.)	UNSUPPORTED MAX. EDGE	ALLOWABLE LIVE LOAD (psf) SPACING OF SUPPORTS CENTER TO CENTER									
				12	16	20	24	30	32	36	42	48	60
12/0	5/16	12	12	150									
16/0	5/16 3/8	16	16	160	75								
20/0	5/16 3/8	20	20	190	105	65							
24/0	3/8	24	20	250	140	95	50						
	1/2		24										
32/16	1/2 5/8	32	28	385	215	150	95	50	40				
42/20	5/8 3/4 7/8	42	32		330	230	145	90	75	50	35		
48/24	3/4 7/8	48	36			300	190	120	105	65	45	35	
48/24F							225	125	105	75	55	40	
2:4:1	1 1/8	72	48				390	245	215	135	100	75	45
1 1/2" GP. 1 & 2	1 1/8	72	48				305	195	170	105	75	55	35
1 1/4" GP. 3 & 4	1 1/4	72	48				355	225	195	215	90	65	40

UNIFORM LOAD DEFLECTION LIMIT: 1/180TH SPAN UNDER LIVE LOAD PLUS DEAD LOAD, 1/240TH UNDER LIVE LOAD ONLY. PLYWOOD CONTINUOUS OVER TWO OR MORE SPANS, GRAIN OF FACE PLIES ALONG SUPPORTS. USE 6D NAILS FOR 1/2" OR THINNER, AND 8D FOR 1" OR THINNER. USE 10D FOR THICKER THAN 1". SPACE NAILS 6" O.C. AT PANEL EDGES AND 12" O.C. AT INTERIOR SUPPORTS, EXCEPT WHERE SPANS ARE 48" OR MORE NAIL 6" O.C. ALL POINTS.

PLYWOOD DECK CONNECTIONS TO METAL FRAMING

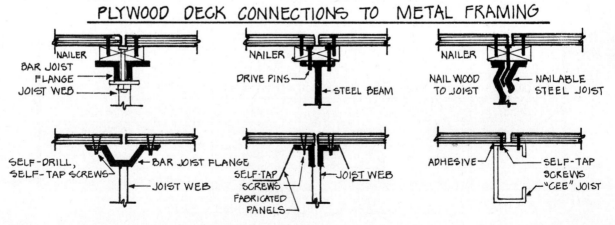

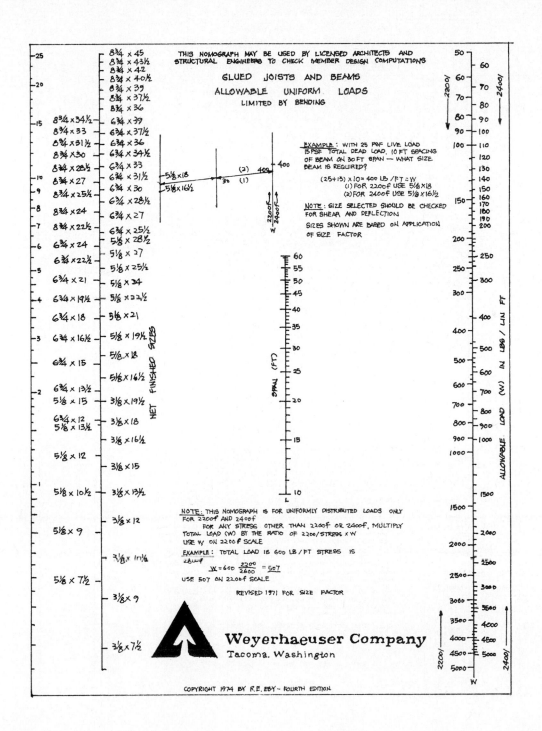

THIS NOMOGRAPH MAY BE USED BY LICENSED ARCHITECTS AND
STRUCTURAL ENGINEERS TO CHECK MEMBER DESIGN COMPUTATIONS

GLUED JOISTS AND BEAMS
ALLOWABLE UNIFORM LOADS
LIMITED BY BENDING

EXAMPLE: WITH 25 PSF LIVE LOAD
15 PSF TOTAL DEAD LOAD, 10 FT SPACING
OF BEAM ON 30 FT SPAN — WHAT SIZE
BEAM IS REQUIRED?

(25+15) x 10 = 400 LB /FT = W
(1) FOR 2200f USE 5⅛ X18
(2) FOR 2400f USE 5⅛ x16½

NOTE: SIZE SELECTED SHOULD BE CHECKED
FOR SHEAR AND DEFLECTION

SIZES SHOWN ARE BASED ON APPLICATION
OF SIZE FACTOR

NOTE: THIS NOMOGRAPH IS FOR UNIFORMLY DISTRIBUTED LOADS ONLY
FOR 2200f AND 2400f
FOR ANY STRESS OTHER THAN 2200f OR 2400f, MULTIPLY
TOTAL LOAD (W) BY THE RATIO OF 2200/STRESS x W
USE W ON 2200f SCALE
EXAMPLE: TOTAL LOAD IS 600 LB/FT STRESS IS
2600f
$W = 600 \frac{2200}{2600} = 507$
USE 507 ON 2200f SCALE

REVISED 1971 FOR SIZE FACTOR

Weyerhaeuser Company
Tacoma, Washington

WEYERHAEUSER CO.

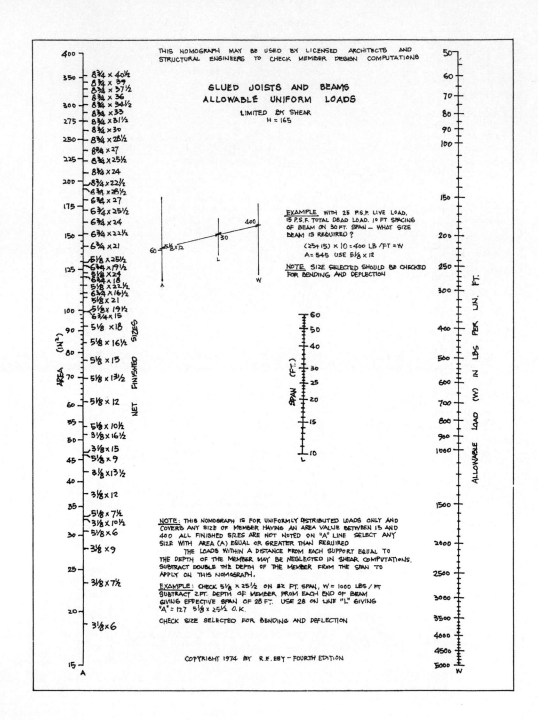

THIS NOMOGRAPH MAY BE USED BY LICENSED ARCHITECTS AND STRUCTURAL ENGINEERS TO CHECK MEMBER DESIGN COMPUTATIONS

GLUED JOISTS AND BEAMS
ALLOWABLE UNIFORM LOADS
LIMITED BY SHEAR
H = 165

EXAMPLE WITH 25 P.S.F. LIVE LOAD, 15 P.S.F. TOTAL DEAD LOAD, 10 FT SPACING OF BEAM ON 30 FT. SPAN — WHAT SIZE BEAM IS REQUIRED ?

$(25+15) \times 10 = 400$ LB /FT = W
A = 545 USE $5\frac{1}{8} \times 12$

NOTE SIZE SELECTED SHOULD BE CHECKED FOR BENDING AND DEFLECTION

NOTE: THIS NOMOGRAPH IS FOR UNIFORMLY DISTRIBUTED LOADS ONLY AND COVERS ANY SIZE OF MEMBER HAVING AN AREA VALUE BETWEEN 15 AND 400. ALL FINISHED SIZES ARE NOT NOTED ON "A" LINE. SELECT ANY SIZE WITH AREA (A) EQUAL OR GREATER THAN REQUIRED

THE LOADS WITHIN A DISTANCE FROM EACH SUPPORT EQUAL TO THE DEPTH OF THE MEMBER MAY BE NEGLECTED IN SHEAR COMPUTATIONS. SUBTRACT DOUBLE THE DEPTH OF THE MEMBER FROM THE SPAN TO APPLY ON THIS NOMOGRAPH.

EXAMPLE: CHECK $5\frac{1}{8} \times 25\frac{1}{2}$ ON 32 FT. SPAN, W = 1000 LBS / FT SUBTRACT 2 FT. DEPTH OF MEMBER FROM EACH END OF BEAM GIVING EFFECTIVE SPAN OF 28 FT. USE 28 ON LINE "L" GIVING "A" = 127 $5\frac{1}{8} \times 25\frac{1}{2}$ O.K.

CHECK SIZE SELECTED FOR BENDING AND DEFLECTION

WEYERHAEUSER CO.

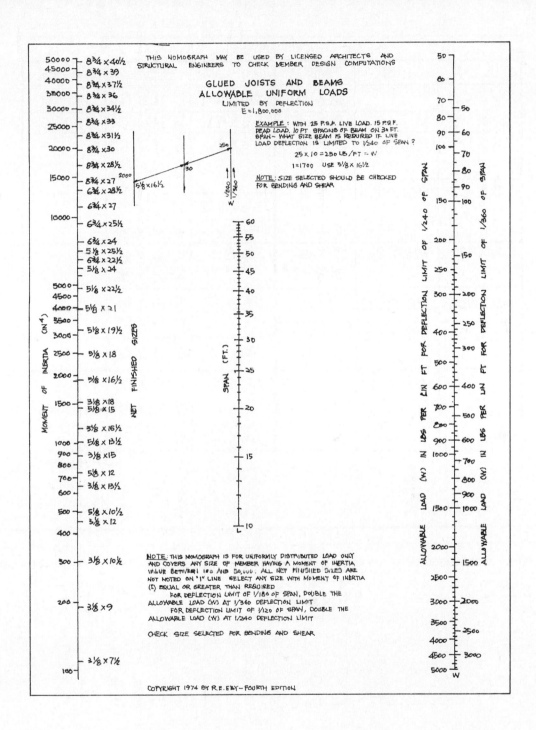

THIS NOMOGRAPH MAY BE USED BY LICENSED ARCHITECTS AND STRUCTURAL ENGINEERS TO CHECK MEMBER DESIGN COMPUTATIONS

GLUED JOISTS AND BEAMS
ALLOWABLE UNIFORM LOADS
LIMITED BY DEFLECTION
E = 1,800,000

EXAMPLE : WITH 25 P.S.F. LIVE LOAD, 15 P.S.F. DEAD LOAD, 10 FT. SPACING OF BEAM ON 30 FT. SPAN ~ WHAT SIZE BEAM IS REQUIRED IF LIVE LOAD DEFLECTION IS LIMITED TO 1/240 OF SPAN?

$$25 \times 10 = 250 \ LB/FT = W$$

$$I = 1700 \quad USE \ 5\tfrac{1}{8} \times 16\tfrac{1}{2}$$

NOTE : SIZE SELECTED SHOULD BE CHECKED FOR BENDING AND SHEAR

NOTE : THIS NOMOGRAPH IS FOR UNIFORMLY DISTRIBUTED LOAD ONLY AND COVERS ANY SIZE OF MEMBER HAVING A MOMENT OF INERTIA VALUE BETWEEN 100 AND 50,000. ALL NET FINISHED SIZES ARE NOT NOTED ON "I" LINE. SELECT ANY SIZE WITH MOMENT OF INERTIA (I) EQUAL OR GREATER THAN REQUIRED.
   FOR DEFLECTION LIMIT OF 1/180 OF SPAN, DOUBLE THE ALLOWABLE LOAD (W) AT 1/360 DEFLECTION LIMIT.
   FOR DEFLECTION LIMIT OF 1/120 OF SPAN, DOUBLE THE ALLOWABLE LOAD (W) AT 1/240 DEFLECTION LIMIT

CHECK SIZE SELECTED FOR BENDING AND SHEAR

COPYRIGHT 1974 BY R.E. ELY — FOURTH EDITION

WEYERHAEUSER CO.

SIZE COMPARISON CHART					
GLU.-LAM.	STEEL	TIMBER	GLU.-LAM.	STEEL	TIMBER
3⅛ X 6		3 X 8	5⅛ X 12	M 12 X 11.8	6 X 14
3⅛ X 7½	M 7 X 5.5	3 X 10	5⅛ X 13½	M 14 X 17.2	6 X 16
3⅛ X 9	M 8 X 6.5	3 X 12 4 X 10	5⅛ X 15	W 12 X 16.5 W 12 X 19 C 12 X 20.7	
3⅛ X 10½	MC 10 X 8.4	3 X 14 4 X 12 6 X 10	5⅛ X 16½	W 12 X 22	
			5⅛ X 18	W 14 X 22	
3⅛ X 12	M 10 X 9	3 X 16 4 X 14	5⅛ X 21	W 16 X 26 W 14 X 30	
3⅛ X 13½	MC 12 X 10.6	6 X 12	5⅛ X 24	W 16 X 31 W 14 X 34	
3⅛ X 15	M 12 X 11.8	4 X 16 6 X 14	6¾ X 24	W 18 X 40	
3⅛ X 16½	W 12 X 14		6¾ X 28½	W 18 X 50 W 21 X 49	
5⅛ X 9	MC 10 X 8.4	6 X 10			
5⅛ X 10½	MC 12 X 10.6	6 X 12	6¾ X 31½	W 24 X 55	

SPAN	SPACING	ROOF BEAMS TOTAL LOAD			FLOOR BEAMS TOTAL LOAD
		40 PSF	45 PSF	50 PSF	50 PSF
8'	4'	3⅛x6	3⅛x6	3⅛x6	3⅛x6
	6'	3⅛x6	3⅛x6	3⅛x6	3⅛x6
	8'	3⅛x6	3⅛x6	3⅛x6	3⅛x7½
10'	4'	3⅛x6	3⅛x6	3⅛x6	3⅛x7½
	6'	3⅛x6	3⅛x6	3⅛x6	3⅛x7½
	8'	3⅛x7½	3⅛x7½	3⅛x7½	3⅛x9
	10'	3⅛x7½	3⅛x7½	3⅛x7½	3⅛x9
12'	4'	3⅛x6	3⅛x7½	3⅛x7½	3⅛x7½
	6'	3⅛x7½	3⅛x7½	3⅛x7½	3⅛x9
	8'	3⅛x9	3⅛x9 / 5⅛x7½	3⅛x9 / 5⅛x7½	3⅛x10½
	10'	3⅛x9 / 5⅛x7½	3⅛x9 / 5⅛x7½	3⅛x9 / 5⅛x7½	3⅛x10½
	12'	3⅛x9 / 5⅛x7½	3⅛x9 / 5⅛x7½	3⅛x10½ / 5⅛x9	3⅛x12 / 5⅛x9
	14'	3⅛x10½/5⅛x9	3⅛x10½/ 5⅛x9	3⅛x12 / 5⅛x9	3⅛x13½/5⅛x12
14'	4'	3⅛x7½/	3⅛x7½/	3⅛x7½/	3⅛x9
	6'	3⅛x9 / 5⅛x7½	3⅛x9 / 5⅛x7½	3⅛x9 / 5⅛x7½	3⅛x10½
	8'	3⅛x9 / 5⅛x7½	3⅛x9 / 5⅛x9	3⅛x10½/5⅛x9	3⅛x12/5⅛x10½
	10'	3⅛x10½/5⅛x9	3⅛x10½/ 5⅛x9	3⅛x10½/ 5⅛x9	3⅛x12 / 5⅛x10½
	12'	3⅛x10½/5⅛x9	3⅛x10½/ 5⅛x9	3⅛x12 / 5⅛x9	3⅛x13½/5⅛x10½
	14'	3⅛x12 /5⅛x9	3⅛x12 / 5⅛x9	3⅛x12 / 5⅛x10½	3⅛x13½/5⅛x12
16'	4'	3⅛x9 / 5⅛x7½	3⅛x9 / 5⅛x7½	3⅛x9 / 5⅛x7½	3⅛x10½
	6'	3⅛x9 / 5⅛x9	3⅛x10½/ 5⅛x9	3⅛x10½/ 5⅛x9	3⅛x12/5⅛x10½
	8'	3⅛x10½/5⅛x9	3⅛x10½/ 5⅛x9	3⅛x12 / 5⅛x9	3⅛x13½/5⅛x10½
	10'	3⅛x12 / 5⅛x9	3⅛x12 / 5⅛x9	3⅛x12 / 5⅛x10½	3⅛x13½/5⅛x12
	12'	3⅛x12 / 5⅛x10½	3⅛x12 / 5⅛x10½	3⅛x13 / 5⅛x10½	3⅛x15/5⅛x12
	14'	3⅛x13½/5⅛x10½	3⅛x13½/ 5⅛x10½	3⅛x15 / 5⅛x12	3⅛x15 /5⅛x13½
18'	4'	3⅛x9 / 5⅛x7½	3⅛x10½/ 5⅛x7½	3⅛x10½/ 5⅛x9	3⅛x12 / 5⅛x10½
	6'	3⅛x10½/ 5⅛x9	3⅛x10½/ 5⅛x9	3⅛x12 /5⅛x10½	3⅛x13½/5⅛x12
	8'	3⅛x12 / 5⅛x10½	3⅛x12 / 5⅛x10½	3⅛x12/5⅛x10½	3⅛x15 / 5⅛x12
	10'	3⅛x12 / 5⅛x10½	3⅛x13½/ 5⅛x10½	3⅛x13 / 5⅛x12	3⅛x15/5⅛x13½
	12'	3⅛x13 / 5⅛x12	3⅛x13½/ 5⅛x12	3⅛x15 / 5⅛x12	3⅛x16½/5⅛x13½
	14'	3⅛x15/5⅛x12	3⅛x15 / 5⅛x12	3⅛x16 / 5⅛x13½	5⅛x15 / 6¾x13½
	16'	3⅛x15/ 5⅛x12	3⅛x16½/ 5⅛x12	5⅛x13½/ 6¾x12	5⅛x15 /6¾x13½

WEYERHAEUSER CO.

LAMINATED TIMBER TABLES 6.24

SPAN	SPACING	ROOF BEAMS TOTAL LOAD			FLOOR BEAMS TOTAL LOAD
		40 PSF	45 PSF	50 PSF	50 PSF
20'	4'	3⅛x10 / 5⅛x9	3⅛x10½ / 5⅛x9	3⅛x10½ / 5⅛x9	3⅛x13½ / 5⅛x10½
	6'	3⅛x12 / 5⅛x10½	3⅛x12 / 5⅛x10½	3⅛x12 / 5⅛x10½	3⅛x15 / 5⅛x12
	8'	3⅛x13½ / 5⅛x10½	3⅛x13 / 5⅛x12	3⅛x13½ / 5⅛x12	3⅛x16½ / 5⅛x13½
	10'	3⅛x13½ / 5⅛x12	3⅛x15 / 5⅛x12	3⅛x15 / 5⅛x13½	5⅛x15 / 6¾x13½
	12'	3⅛x15 / 5⅛x12	3⅛x16½ / 5⅛x13½	3⅛x16½ / 5⅛x13½	5⅛x15 / 6¾x15
	14'	3⅛x16 / 5⅛x13½	3⅛x16½ / 5⅛x13½	5⅛x13½ / 6¾x13½	5⅛x16½ / 6¾x16½
	16'	5⅛x13½ / 6¾x12	5⅛x15 / 6¾x13½	5⅛x15 / 6¾x13½	5⅛x18 / 6¾x16½
22'	4'	3⅛x12 / 5⅛x10½	3⅛x12 / 5⅛x10½	3⅛x12 / 5⅛x10½	3⅛x13½ / 5⅛x12
	6'	3⅛x13½ / 5⅛x10½	3⅛x13½ / 5⅛x12	3⅛x13½ / 5⅛x12	3⅛x16½ / 5⅛x13½
	8'	3⅛x13½ / 5⅛x12	3⅛x15 / 5⅛x12	3⅛x15 / 5⅛x13½	5⅛x15 / 6¾x13½
	10'	3⅛x15 / 5⅛x13½	3⅛x16½ / 5⅛x13½	3⅛x16½ / 5⅛x13½	5⅛x16½ / 6¾x15
	12'	3⅛x16½ / 5⅛x13½	5⅛x15 / 6¾x13½	5⅛x15 / 6¾x13½	5⅛x16½ / 6¾x16½
	14'	5⅛x15 / 6¾x13½	5⅛x15 / 6¾x13½	5⅛x15 / 6¾x15	5⅛x18 / 6¾x16½
	16'	5⅛x15 / 6¾x13½	5⅛x16½ / 6¾x15	5⅛x16½ / 6¾x15	5⅛x19½ / 6¾x18
24'	4'	3⅛x12 / 5⅛x10½	3⅛x13½ / 5⅛x10½	3⅛x13½ / 5⅛x12	3⅛x15 / 5⅛x13½
	6'	3⅛x13½ / 5⅛x12	3⅛x15 / 5⅛x12	3⅛x15 / 5⅛x13½	5⅛x15 / 6¾x13½
	8'	3⅛x15 / 5⅛x13½	3⅛x16½ / 5⅛x13½	3⅛x16½ / 5⅛x13½	5⅛x16½ / 6¾x15
	10'	3⅛x16½ / 5⅛x13½	5⅛x15 / 6¾x13½	5⅛x15 / 6¾x13½	5⅛x18 / 6¾x16½
	12'	5⅛x15 / 6¾x13½	5⅛x15 / 6¾x13½	5⅛x16½ / 6¾x15	5⅛x18 / 6¾x16½
	14'	5⅛x15 / 6¾x15	5⅛x16½ / 6¾x15	5⅛x16½ / 6¾x15	5⅛x19½ / 6¾x18
	16'	5⅛x16½ / 6¾x15	5⅛x16½ / 6¾x15	5⅛x18 / 6¾x16½	5⅛x21 / 6¾x19½
26'	4'	3⅛x13½ / 5⅛x12	3⅛x13½ / 5⅛x12	3⅛x15 / 5⅛x12	3⅛x16½ / 5⅛x13½
	6'	3⅛x15 / 5⅛x13½	3⅛x16½ / 5⅛x13½	3⅛x16½ / 5⅛x13½	5⅛x16½ / 6¾x15
	8'	3⅛x16½ / 5⅛x13½	3⅛x16½ / 5⅛x15	5⅛x15 / 6¾x13½	5⅛x18 / 6¾x16½
	10'	5⅛x15 / 6¾x13½	5⅛x16½ / 6¾x15	5⅛x16½ / 6¾x15	5⅛x19½ / 6¾x18
	12'	5⅛x16½ / 6¾x15	5⅛x16½ / 6¾x15	5⅛x18 / 6¾x16½	5⅛x19½ / 6¾x18
	14'	5⅛x16½ / 6¾x15	5⅛x18 / 6¾x16½	5⅛x18 / 6¾x16½	5⅛x21 / 6¾x19½
	16'	5⅛x18 / 6¾x16½	5⅛x18 / 6¾x16½	5⅛x19½ / 6¾x18	5⅛x22½ / 6¾x19½
28'	4'	3⅛x15 / 5⅛x12	3⅛x15 / 5⅛x12	3⅛x15 / 5⅛x13½	5⅛x15 / 5⅛x15
	6'	3⅛x16½ / 5⅛x13½	3⅛x16½ / 5⅛x15	5⅛x15 / 6¾x13½	5⅛x18 / 6¾x16½
	8'	5⅛x15 / 6¾x13½	5⅛x16½ / 6¾x15	5⅛x16½ / 6¾x15	5⅛x19½ / 6¾x18
	10'	5⅛x16½ / 6¾x15	5⅛x16½ / 6¾x15	5⅛x18 / 6¾x16½	5⅛x21 / 6¾x18
	12'	5⅛x18 / 6¾x16½	5⅛x18 / 6¾x16½	5⅛x18 / 6¾x16½	5⅛x21 / 6¾x19½
	14'	5⅛x18 / 6¾x16½	5⅛x19½ / 6¾x18	5⅛x19½ / 6¾x18	5⅛x22½ / 6¾x21
	16'	5⅛x19½ / 6¾x18	5⅛x19½ / 6¾x18	5⅛x21 / 6¾x18	5⅛x24 / 6¾x22½

SPAN	SPACING	ROOF BEAMS TOTAL LOAD			FLOOR BEAMS TOTAL LOAD
		40 PSF	45 PSF	50 PSF	50 PSF
30'	4'	3⅛x15 /5⅛x13½	3⅛x16½/5⅛x13½	3⅛x16½ /5⅛x13½	5⅛x16½ /6¾x15
	6'	5⅛x15 /6¾x13½	5⅛x15 /6¾x13½	5⅛x16½/6¾x15	5⅛x18 /6¾x16½
	8'	5⅛x16½/6¾x15	5⅛x16½/6¾x15	5⅛x18 /6¾x16½	5⅛x21 /6¾x18
	10'	5⅛x18 /6¾x16½	5⅛x18 /6¾x16½	5⅛x19½/6¾x16½	5⅛x22½/6¾x19½
	12'	5⅛x18 /6¾x16½	5⅛x19½/6¾x18	5⅛x19½/6¾x18	5⅛x22½/6¾x21
	14'	5⅛x19½/6¾x18	5⅛x19½/6¾x18	5⅛x21 /6¾x19½	5⅛x24 /6¾x22½
	16'	5⅛x21 /6¾x18	5⅛x21 /6¾x19½	5⅛x22½/6¾x19½	5⅛x25½/6¾x24
	18'	5⅛x21 /6¾x19½	5⅛x22½/6¾x19½	5⅛x24 /6¾x21	5⅛x27 /6¾x24
	20'	5⅛x22½/6¾x19½	5⅛x24 /6¾x21	5⅛x25½/6¾x22½	5⅛x27 /6¾x25½
32'	4'	3⅛x16½/5⅛x13½	3⅛x16½/5⅛x15	5⅛x15 /6¾x13½	5⅛x18 /6¾x16½
	6'	5⅛x16½/6¾x15	5⅛x16½/6¾x15	5⅛x16½/6¾x15	5⅛x19½/6¾x19½
	8'	5⅛x18/6¾x16½	5⅛x18/6¾x16½	5⅛x18/6¾x16	5⅛x21/6¾x21
	10'	5⅛x18/6¾x16½	5⅛x19½/6¾x18	5⅛x19½/6¾x18	5⅛x24/6¾x22½
	12'	5⅛x19½/6¾x18	5⅛x21/6¾x19½	5⅛x21/6¾x19½	5⅛x24/6¾x24
	14'	5⅛x21/6¾x19½	5⅛x21/6¾x19½	5⅛x22½/6¾x21	5⅛x25½/8¾x22½
	16'	5⅛x21/6¾x19½	5⅛x22½/6¾x21	5⅛x24/6¾x21	6¾x25½/8¾x24
	18'	5⅛x22½/6¾x21	5⅛x24/6¾x21	5⅛x24/6¾x22½	6¾x25½/8¾x25½
	20'	5⅛x24/6¾x21	5⅛x25½/6¾x22½	5⅛x25½/6¾x22½	6¾x27/8¾x25½
34'	4'	3⅛x16½/5⅛x15	5⅛x15/6¾x13½	5⅛x16½/6¾x15	5⅛x18/6¾x16½
	6'	5⅛x16½/6¾x15	5⅛x18/6¾x16½	5⅛x18/6¾x16½	5⅛x21/6¾x19½
	8'	5⅛x18/6¾x16½	5⅛x19½/6¾x18	5⅛x19½/6¾x18	5⅛x22½/6¾x21
	10'	5⅛x19½/6¾x18	5⅛x21/6¾x19½	5⅛x21/6¾x19½	5⅛x24/6¾x22½
	12'	5⅛x21/6¾x19½	5⅛x21/6¾x19½	5⅛x22½/6¾x21	5⅛x25½/6¾x24
	14'	5⅛x22½/6¾x19½	5⅛x22½/6¾x21	5⅛x24/6¾x21	6¾x25½/8¾x22½
	16'	5⅛x22½/6¾x21	5⅛x24/6¾x22½	5⅛x27/6¾x22½	6¾x27/8¾x24
	18'	5⅛x24/6¾x22½	5⅛x25½/6¾x22½	6¾x24/8¾x21	6¾x27/8¾x25½
	20'	5⅛x25½/6¾x22½	6¾x24/6¾x24	6¾x25½/8¾x22½	6¾x28½/8¾x25½
36'	4'	5⅛x15/6¾x13½	5⅛x16½/6¾x15	5⅛x16½/6¾x15	5⅛x19½/6¾x18
	6'	5⅛x18/6¾x16½	5⅛x18/6¾x16½	5⅛x19½/6¾x16½	5⅛x22½/6¾x19½
	8'	5⅛x19½/6¾x18	5⅛x19½/6¾x18	5⅛x21/6¾x18	5⅛x24/6¾x22½
	10'	5⅛x21/6¾x19½	5⅛x21/6¾x19½	5⅛x22½/6¾x19½	5⅛x25½/6¾x24
	12'	5⅛x22½/6¾x19½	5⅛x22½/6¾x21	5⅛x24/6¾x21	6¾x25½/8¾x24
	14'	5⅛x22½/6¾x21	5⅛x24/6¾x22½	5⅛x25½/6¾x21	6¾x27/8¾x24

WEYERHAEUSER CO.

LAMINATED TIMBER TABLES 6.26

SPAN	SPACING	ROOF BEAMS TOTAL LOAD			FLOOR BEAMS TOTAL LOAD
		40 PSF	45 PSF	50 PSF	50 PSF
36'	16'	5⅛ x 24 / 6¾ x 22½	5⅛ x 25½ / 6¾ x 22½	6¾ x 24 / 8¾ x 22½	6¾ x 27 / 8¾ x 25½
	18'	5⅛ x 25½ / 6¾ x 22½	6¾ x 24 / 8¾ x 22½	6¾ x 25½ / 8¾ x 22½	6¾ x 28½ / 8¾ x 27
	20'	5⅛ x 25½ / 6¾ x 24	6¾ x 25½ / 8¾ x 22½	6¾ x 27 / 8¾ x 24	6¾ x 30 / 8¾ x 27
38'	4'	5⅛ x 16½ / 6¾ x 15	5⅛ x 16½ / 6¾ x 15	5⅛ x 18 / 6¾ x 16½	5⅛ x 21 / 6¾ x 18
	6'	5⅛ x 18 / 6¾ x 16½	5⅛ x 19½ / 6¾ x 18	5⅛ x 19½ / 6¾ x 18	5⅛ x 22½ / 6¾ x 21
	8'	5⅛ x 21 / 6¾ x 18	5⅛ x 21 / 6¾ x 19½	5⅛ x 22½ / 6¾ x 19½	5⅛ x 25½ / 6¾ x 22½
	10'	5⅛ x 22½ / 6¾ x 19½	5⅛ x 22½ / 6¾ x 21	5⅛ x 24 / 6¾ x 21	6¾ x 25½ / 8¾ x 24½
	12'	5⅛ x 24 / 6¾ x 21	5⅛ x 24 / 6¾ x 22½	5⅛ x 25½ / 6¾ x 22½	6¾ x 27 / 8¾ x 24
	14'	5⅛ x 24 / 6¾ x 22½	5⅛ x 25½ / 6¾ x 24	6¾ x 24 / 8¾ x 22½	6¾ x 28½ / 8¾ x 25½
	16'	5⅛ x 25½ / 6¾ x 24	6¾ x 24 / 8¾ x 22½	6¾ x 25½ / 8¾ x 22½	6¾ x 28½ / 8¾ x 27
	18'	6¾ x 24 / 8¾ x 22½	6¾ x 25½ / 8¾ x 22½	6¾ x 27 / 8¾ x 24	6¾ x 30 / 8¾ x 28½
	20'	6¾ x 25½ / 8¾ x 22½	6¾ x 27 / 8¾ x 24	6¾ x 28½ / 8¾ x 25½	6¾ x 31½ / 8¾ x 28½
40'	4'	5⅛ x 16½ / 6¾ x 16½	5⅛ x 18 / 6¾ x 16½	5⅛ x 18 / 6¾ x 16½	5⅛ x 21 / 6¾ x 19½
	6'	5⅛ x 19½ / 6¾ x 18	5⅛ x 21 / 6¾ x 18	5⅛ x 21 / 6¾ x 19½	5⅛ x 24 / 6¾ x 22½
	8'	5⅛ x 21 / 6¾ x 19½	5⅛ x 22½ / 6¾ x 21	5⅛ x 22½ / 6¾ x 21	6¾ x 24 / 8¾ x 22½
	10'	5⅛ x 22½ / 6¾ x 21	5⅛ x 24 / 6¾ x 22½	5⅛ x 25½ / 6¾ x 22½	6¾ x 27 / 8¾ x 24
	12'	5⅛ x 24 / 6¾ x 22½	5⅛ x 25½ / 6¾ x 24	6¾ x 24 / 8¾ x 22½	6¾ x 28½ / 8¾ x 25½
	14'	5⅛ x 25½ / 6¾ x 24	6¾ x 24 / 8¾ x 22½	6¾ x 25½ / 8¾ x 24	6¾ x 30 / 8¾ x 27
	16'	6¾ x 24 / 8¾ x 22½	6¾ x 25½ / 8¾ x 24	6¾ x 27 / 8¾ x 24	6¾ x 31½ / 8¾ x 28½
	18'	6¾ x 25½ / 8¾ x 24	6¾ x 27 / 8¾ x 24	6¾ x 28½ / 8¾ x 25½	6¾ x 31½ / 8¾ x 30
	20'	6¾ x 27 / 8¾ x 24	6¾ x 28½ / 8¾ x 25½	6¾ x 30 / 8¾ x 25½	6¾ x 33 / 8¾ x 30
42'	4'	5⅛ x 18 / 6¾ x 16½	5⅛ x 18 / 6¾ x 16½	5⅛ x 19½ / 6¾ x 18	5⅛ x 22½ / 6¾ x 21
	6'	5⅛ x 21 / 6¾ x 18	5⅛ x 21 / 6¾ x 19½	5⅛ x 22½ / 6¾ x 19½	5⅛ x 25½ / 6¾ x 24
	8'	5⅛ x 22½ / 6¾ x 21	5⅛ x 24 / 6¾ x 21	5⅛ x 24 / 6¾ x 22½	6¾ x 25½ / 8¾ x 24
	10'	5⅛ x 24 / 6¾ x 22½	5⅛ x 25½ / 6¾ x 22½	5⅛ x 25½ / 6¾ x 24	6¾ x 27 / 8¾ x 25½
	12'	5⅛ x 25½ / 6¾ x 24	6¾ x 24 / 8¾ x 22½	6¾ x 25½ / 8¾ x 22½	6¾ x 30 / 8¾ x 27
	14'	6¾ x 24 / 8¾ x 22½	6¾ x 25½ / 8¾ x 24	6¾ x 27 / 8¾ x 24	6¾ x 31½ / 8¾ x 28½
	16'	6¾ x 25½ / 8¾ x 24	6¾ x 27 / 8¾ x 24	6¾ x 28½ / 8¾ x 25½	6¾ x 33 / 8¾ x 30
	18'	6¾ x 27 / 8¾ x 24	6¾ x 28½ / 8¾ x 25½	6¾ x 30 / 8¾ x 27	6¾ x 33 / 8¾ x 31½
	20'	6¾ x 28½ / 8¾ x 25½	6¾ x 30 / 8¾ x 27	6¾ x 31½ / 8¾ x 28½	6¾ x 34½ / 8¾ x 31½
44'	4'	5⅛ x 19½ / 6¾ x 16½	5⅛ x 19½ / 6¾ x 18	5⅛ x 19½ / 6¾ x 18	5⅛ x 24 / 6¾ x 21
	6'	5⅛ x 21 / 6¾ x 19½	5⅛ x 22½ / 6¾ x 19½	5⅛ x 22½ / 6¾ x 21	6¾ x 24 / 8¾ x 22½
	8'	5⅛ x 24 / 6¾ x 21	5⅛ x 24 / 6¾ x 22½	5⅛ x 25½ / 6¾ x 22½	6¾ x 27 / 8¾ x 25½

WEYERHAEUSER CO.

SPAN	SPACING	ROOF BEAMS TOTAL LOAD			FLOOR BEAMS TOTAL LOAD
		40 PSF	45 PSF	50 PSF	50 PSF
44'	10'	5⅛ x 25½ / 6¾ x 22½	6¾ x 24 / 8¾ x 22½	6¾ x 25½ / 8¾ x 22½	6¾ x 28 / 8¾ x 27
	12'	6¾ x 24 / 8¾ x 22½	6¾ x 25½ / 8¾ x 24	6¾ x 25½ / 8¾ x 24	6¾ x 31½ / 8¾ x 28½
	14'	6¾ x 25½ / 8¾ x 24	6¾ x 27 / 8¾ x 24	6¾ x 28½ / 8¾ x 25½	6¾ x 33 / 8¾ x 30
	16'	6¾ x 27 / 8¾ x 25½	6¾ x 28½ / 8¾ x 25½	6¾ x 30 / 8¾ x 27	6¾ x 33 / 8¾ x 31½
	18'	6¾ x 28½ / 8¾ x 25½	6¾ x 30 / 8¾ x 27	6¾ x 31½ / 8¾ x 28½	6¾ x 34½ / 8¾ x 31½
	20'	6¾ x 30 / 8¾ x 27	6¾ x 30 / 8¾ x 27	6¾ x 33 / 8¾ x 30	6¾ x 36 / 8¾ x 33
46'	4'	5⅛ x 19½ / 6¾ x 18	5⅛ x 21 / 6¾ x 18	5⅛ x 21 / 6¾ x 19½	5⅛ x 24 / 6¾ x 22½
	6'	5⅛ x 22½ / 6¾ x 21	5⅛ x 22½ / 6¾ x 21	5⅛ x 24 / 6¾ x 22½	6¾ x 26½ / 8¾ x 24
	8'	5⅛ x 24 / 6¾ x 22½	5⅛ x 25½ / 6¾ x 24	6¾ x 24 / 8¾ x 22½	6¾ x 28½ / 8¾ x 25½
	10'	6¾ x 24 / 8¾ x 22½	6¾ x 25½ / 8¾ x 22½	6¾ x 25½ / 8¾ x 24	6¾ x 30 / 8¾ x 28½
	12'	6¾ x 25½ / 8¾ x 24	6¾ x 27 / 8¾ x 24	6¾ x 27 / 8¾ x 25½	6¾ x 31½ / 8¾ x 30
	14'	6¾ x 27 / 8¾ x 25½	6¾ x 28½ / 8¾ x 25½	6¾ x 28½ / 8¾ x 27	6¾ x 33 / 8¾ x 31½
	16'	6¾ x 28½ / 8¾ x 25½	6¾ x 28½ / 8¾ x 27	6¾ x 30 / 8¾ x 28½	6¾ x 36 / 8¾ x 33
	18'	6¾ x 28½ / 8¾ x 27	6¾ x 30 / 8¾ x 28½	6¾ x 33 / 8¾ x 28½	6¾ x 36 / 8¾ x 33
	20'	6¾ x 30 / 8¾ x 28½	6¾ x 31½ / 8¾ x 28½	6¾ x 34½ / 8¾ x 30	8¾ x 34½ / 10¾ x 33
48'	4'	5⅛ x 21 / 6¾ x 19½	5⅛ x 21 / 6¾ x 19½	5⅛ x 22½ / 6¾ x 19½	5⅛ x 25½ / 6¾ x 24
	6'	5⅛ x 24 / 6¾ x 21	5⅛ x 24 / 6¾ x 22½	5⅛ x 25½ / 6¾ x 22½	6¾ x 27 / 8¾ x 24
	8'	5⅛ x 25½ / 6¾ x 24	6¾ x 24 / 8¾ x 22½	6¾ x 25½ / 8¾ x 22½	6¾ x 30 / 8¾ x 27
	10'	6¾ x 25½ / 8¾ x 22½	6¾ x 25½ / 8¾ x 24	6¾ x 27 / 8¾ x 25½	6¾ x 31½ / 8¾ x 28½
	12'	6¾ x 27 / 8¾ x 24	6¾ x 28½ / 8¾ x 25½	6¾ x 28½ / 8¾ x 27	6¾ x 33 / 8¾ x 31½
	14'	6¾ x 28½ / 8¾ x 25½	6¾ x 30 / 8¾ x 27	6¾ x 30 / 8¾ x 28½	6¾ x 34½ / 8¾ x 33
	16'	6¾ x 30 / 8¾ x 27	6¾ x 30 / 8¾ x 28½	6¾ x 31½ / 8¾ x 28½	6¾ x 37½ / 8¾ x 34½
	18'	6¾ x 30 / 8¾ x 28½	6¾ x 31½ / 8¾ x 28½	6¾ x 34½ / 8¾ x 30	8¾ x 34½ / 10¾ x 33
	20'	6¾ x 31½ / 8¾ x 28½	6¾ x 33 / 8¾ x 30	6¾ x 36 / 8¾ x 31½	8¾ x 36 / 10¾ x 34½
50'	4'	5⅛ x 21 / 6¾ x 19½	5⅛ x 22½ / 6¾ x 21	5⅛ x 22½ / 6¾ x 21	6¾ x 24 / 8¾ x 22½
	6'	5⅛ x 24 / 6¾ x 22½	5⅛ x 25½ / 6¾ x 22½	5⅛ x 25½ / 6¾ x 24	6¾ x 28½ / 8¾ x 25½
	8'	6¾ x 24 / 8¾ x 22½	6¾ x 25½ / 8¾ x 24	6¾ x 27 / 8¾ x 24	6¾ x 30 / 8¾ x 28½
	10'	6¾ x 25½ / 8¾ x 24	6¾ x 27 / 8¾ x 25½	6¾ x 28½ / 8¾ x 25½	6¾ x 33 / 8¾ x 30
	12'	6¾ x 28½ / 8¾ x 25½	6¾ x 28½ / 8¾ x 27	6¾ x 30 / 8¾ x 27	6¾ x 34½ / 8¾ x 31½
	14'	6¾ x 28½ / 8¾ x 27	6¾ x 30 / 8¾ x 28½	6¾ x 31½ / 8¾ x 28½	6¾ x 36 / 8¾ x 33
	16'	6¾ x 30 / 8¾ x 28½	6¾ x 31½ / 8¾ x 28½	6¾ x 33 / 8¾ x 30	8¾ x 34½ / 10¾ x 33
	18'	6¾ x 31½ / 8¾ x 28½	6¾ x 34½ / 8¾ x 30	6¾ x 36 / 8¾ x 31½	8¾ x 36 / 10¾ x 34½
	20'	6¾ x 33 / 8¾ x 30	6¾ x 36 / 8¾ x 31½	8¾ x 33 / 10¾ x 30	8¾ x 37½ / 10¾ x 34½

WEYERHAEUSER CO.

CANTILEVER BEAMS

MAIN SUPPORT SPACING②, ft.	DEAD LOAD③ psf	LIVE LOAD psf	TWO-SPAN SYSTEM④		THREE-SPAN SYSTEM⑤	
			SUSPENDED BEAM	CANTILEVER'D BEAM	SUSPENDED BEAM	CANTILEVER'D BEAMS
32	10	12	5⅛ × 15	5⅛ × 16½	5⅛ × 10½	5⅛ × 16½
		20	5⅛ × 16½	5⅛ × 19½	5⅛ × 10½	5⅛ × 19½
		30	5⅛ × 19½	5⅛ × 25½	5⅛ × 12½	5⅛ × 24
	12	12	5⅛ × 15	5⅛ × 16½	5⅛ × 10½	5⅛ × 16½
		20	5⅛ × 18	5⅛ × 21	5⅛ × 12	5⅛ × 21
		30	5⅛ × 21	5⅛ × 27	5⅛ × 12	5⅛ × 24
	15	20	5⅛ × 19½	5⅛ × 22½	5⅛ × 12	5⅛ × 21
		30	5⅛ × 21	5⅛ × 28½	5⅛ × 13½	5⅛ × 25½
36	10	12	5⅛ × 16½	5⅛ × 18	5⅛ × 10½	5⅛ × 18
		20	5⅛ × 19½	5⅛ × 22½	5⅛ × 12	5⅛ × 22½
		30	5⅛ × 22½	5⅛ × 28½	5⅛ × 13½	5⅛ × 27
	12	12	5⅛ × 16½	5⅛ × 19½	5⅛ × 12	5⅛ × 19½
		20	5⅛ × 19½	5⅛ × 24	5⅛ × 12	5⅛ × 24
		30	5⅛ × 22½	5⅛ × 30	5⅛ × 13½	5⅛ × 27
	15	20	5⅛ × 21	5⅛ × 25½	5⅛ × 13½	5⅛ × 24
		30	5⅛ × 24	5⅛ × 33	5⅛ × 15	5⅛ × 28½
40	10	12	5⅛ × 18	5⅛ × 21	5⅛ × 12	5⅛ × 21
		20	5⅛ × 21	5⅛ × 25½	5⅛ × 13½	5⅛ × 25½
		30	5⅛ × 25½	5⅛ × 31½	5⅛ × 15	5⅛ × 30
	12	12	5⅛ × 18	5⅛ × 21	5⅛ × 12	5⅛ × 21
		20	5⅛ × 22½	5⅛ × 25½	5⅛ × 13½	5⅛ × 25½
		30	5⅛ × 25½	5⅛ × 33	5⅛ × 15	5⅛ × 30
	15	20	5⅛ × 24	5⅛ × 28½	5⅛ × 15	5⅛ × 27
		30	5⅛ × 27	5⅛ × 36	5⅛ × 16½	5⅛ × 31½
44	10	12	5⅛ × 19½	5⅛ × 22½	5⅛ × 12	5⅛ × 22½
		20	5⅛ × 24	5⅛ × 28½	5⅛ × 15	5⅛ × 28½
		30	5⅛ × 27	5⅛ × 34½	5⅛ × 16½	5⅛ × 33
	12	12	5⅛ × 21	5⅛ × 22½	5⅛ × 13½	5⅛ × 24
		20	5⅛ × 24	5⅛ × 28½	5⅛ × 15	5⅛ × 28½
		30	5⅛ × 28½	5⅛ × 36	5⅛ × 18	5⅛ × 33
	15	20	5⅛ × 25½	5⅛ × 31½	5⅛ × 16½	5⅛ × 30
		30	5⅛ × 30	6¾ × 30	5⅛ × 18	5⅛ × 34½
48	10	12	5⅛ × 21	5⅛ × 24	5⅛ × 13½	5⅛ × 24
		20	5⅛ × 25½	5⅛ × 30	5⅛ × 16½	5⅛ × 30
		30	5⅛ × 30	5⅛ × 37½	5⅛ × 18	5⅛ × 36
	12	12	5⅛ × 22½	5⅛ × 25½	5⅛ × 13½	5⅛ × 25½
		20	5⅛ × 27	5⅛ × 31½	5⅛ × 16½	5⅛ × 31½
		30	5⅛ × 31½	6¾ × 31½	5⅛ × 19½	5⅛ × 36
	15	20	5⅛ × 28½	5⅛ × 34½	5⅛ × 18	5⅛ × 33
		30	5⅛ × 33	6¾ × 33	5⅛ × 19½	5⅛ × 37½

AMERICAN INSTITUTE OF TIMBER CONSTRUCTION.

CANTILEVER BEAMS

MAIN [2] SUPPORT SPACING, (FT.)	DEAD LOAD [3], PSF	LIVE LOAD, PSF	TWO-SPAN SYSTEM [4] SUSPENDED BEAM	CANTILEVERED BEAM	THREE SPAN SYSTEM [5] SUSPENDED BEAM	CANTILEVERED BEAM
52	10	12	5⅛ x 24	5⅛ x 27	5⅛ x 15	5⅛ x 27
		20	5⅛ x 28½	6¾ x 28½	5⅛ x 18	6¾ x 28½
		30	5⅛ x 33	6¾ x 33	5⅛ x 19½	6¾ x 34½
	12	12	5⅛ x 24	5⅛ x 27	5⅛ x 15	5⅛ x 27
		20	5⅛ x 30	6¾ x 30	5⅛ x 18	6¾ x 30
		30	5⅛ x 33	6¾ x 34½	5⅛ x 21	6¾ x 34½
	15	20	5⅛ x 31½	6¾ x 30	5⅛ x 19½	6¾ x 31½
		30	5⅛ x 34½	6¾ x 36	5⅛ x 21	6¾ x 36
56	10	12	5⅛ x 25½	5⅛ x 28½	5⅛ x 15	5⅛ x 28½
		20	5⅛ x 31½	5⅛ x 36	5⅛ x 19½	6¾ x 31½
		30	5⅛ x 36	6¾ x 36	5⅛ x 22½	6¾ x 36
	12	12	5⅛ x 27	5⅛ x 30	5⅛ x 16½	5⅛ x 30
		20	5⅛ x 31½	6¾ x 31½	5⅛ x 19½	6¾ x 31½
		30	5⅛ x 36	6¾ x 37	5⅛ x 22½	6¾ x 37½
	15	20	5⅛ x 33	6¾ x 33	5⅛ x 21	6¾ x 33
		30	5⅛ x 37½	6¾ x 39	5⅛ x 34	6¾ x 39
60	10	12	5⅛ x 27	5⅛ x 31½	5⅛ x 16½	5⅛ x 31½
		20	5⅛ x 33	6¾ x 33	5⅛ x 21	6¾ x 33
		30	5⅛ x 37½	6¾ x 39	5⅛ x 24	6¾ x 39
	12	12	5⅛ x 28½	5⅛ x 31½	5⅛ x 18	5⅛ x 31½
		20	5⅛ x 34½	6¾ x 34½	5⅛ x 21	6¾ x 34½
		30	6¾ x 34½	8¾ x 34½	5⅛ x 24	8¾ x 34½
	15	20	5⅛ x 36	6¾ x 36	5⅛ x 22½	6¾ x 36
		30	6¾ x 36	8¾ x 36	5⅛ x 25½	8¾ x 36
64	10	12	5⅛ x 28½	5⅛ x 33	5⅛ x 18	5⅛ x 33
		20	5⅛ x 36	6¾ x 36	5⅛ x 21	6¾ x 36
		30	6¾ x 36	8¾ x 36	5⅛ x 25½	8¾ x 36
	12	12	5⅛ x 30	5⅛ x 34½	5⅛ x 19½	5⅛ x 34½
		20	5⅛ x 36	6¾ x 36	5⅛ x 22½	6¾ x 36
		30	6¾ x 36	8¾ x 37½	5⅛ x 25½	8¾ x 37½
	15	20	6¾ x 33	6¾ x 37½	5⅛ x 24	6¾ x 39
		30	6¾ x 37½	8¾ x 39	5⅛ x 27	8¾ x 39

THIS BEAM DESIGN TABLE APPLIES FOR STRAIGHT, CANTILEVERED, LAMINATED TIMBER BEAMS. MEMBER SIZES ARE GOVERNED BY EITHER BENDING OR SHEAR. WHERE BUILDING CODE DEFLECTION REQUIREMENTS APPLY, THE MEMBER SIZES MUST BE CHECKED. A MINIMUM ROOF SLOPE OF ¼ IN. PER FOOT SHOULD BE PROVIDED TO MINIMIZE WATER PONDING.

SPECIFICATIONS AND ALLOWABLE STRESSES:

BEAM SPACING: 20'-0"
BENDING STRESS, $F = 2400$ PSI
SHEAR STRESS, $F_v = 165$ PSI
COMPRESSION PERPENDICULAR TO GRAIN STRESS, $F_{c\perp} = 385$ PSI
MODULUS OF ELASTICITY, $E = 1,800,000$; PSI
DURATION OF LOAD FACTOR: 1.25 FOR 12 PSF LIVE LOADS; AND 1.15 FOR 20 AND 30 PSF LIVE LOADS

MEMBER SIZES ARE CHECKED FOR FULL UNBALANCED LIVE LOADING.
[1] MAIN SUPPORTS ARE COLUMNS OR BEARING WALLS. TABLE IS BASED ON EQUAL SPACING OF MAIN SUPPORTS.
[2] DOES NOT INCLUDE WEIGHT OF GLULAM.

AMERICAN INSTITUTE OF TIMBER CONSTRUCTION

ARCH TABLES

LOADING	ROOF PITCH	WALL HT. (FT.)	30' SPAN WIDTH	30' SPAN BASE	30' SPAN LOWER TANG.	30' SPAN UPPER TANG.	30' SPAN CROWN	35' SPAN WIDTH	35' SPAN BASE	35' SPAN LOWER TANG.	35' SPAN UPPER TANG.	35' SPAN CROWN	40' SPAN WIDTH	40' SPAN BASE	40' SPAN LOWER TANG.	40' SPAN UPPER TANG.	40' SPAN CROWN
VERTICAL DEAD + LIVE LOAD = 400#/FT. 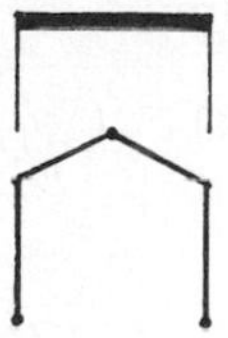	3/12	10	3 1/8	8 1/4	12	10 3/4	7 1/2	3 1/8	10 1/2	13 1/4	12	7 1/2	3 1/8	13 1/4	14 1/2	13 1/4	7 1/2
		12	5 1/8	7 1/2	11	10 3/4	7 1/2	5 1/8	7 1/2	12	12	7 1/2	5 1/8	7 1/2	13 1/4	13	7 1/2
		14	5 1/8	7 1/2	12	12	7 1/2	5 1/8	7 1/2	13 1/2	13 1/4	7 1/2	5 1/8	7 1/2	14 3/4	14 1/2	7 1/2
		16	5 1/8	7 1/2	13 1/4	13	7 1/2	5 1/8	7 1/2	14 3/4	14 1/2	7 1/2	5 1/8	7 1/2	16	16	7 1/2
		18	5 1/8	7 1/2	14 1/4	14 1/4	7 1/2	5 1/8	7 1/2	16	15 3/4	7 1/2	5 1/8	7 1/2	17 1/2	17 1/4	7 1/2
	4/12	10	3 1/8	7 1/2	11 3/4	12 3/4	7 1/2	5 1/8	9 3/4	13 1/2	12 3/4	7 1/2	3 1/8	12	15 1/4	12 3/4	7 1/2
		12	5 1/8	7 1/2	10 3/4	10 3/4	7 1/2	5 1/8	7 1/2	11 3/4	11 3/4	7 1/2	5 1/8	7 1/2	12 3/4	12 1/2	7 1/2
		14	5 1/8	7 1/2	12	12	7 1/2	5 1/8	7 1/2	13 1/4	13	7 1/2	5 1/8	7 1/2	14 1/4	14 1/4	7 1/2
		16	5 1/8	7 1/2	13 1/4	13	7 1/2	5 1/8	7 1/2	14 1/2	14 1/2	7 1/2	5 1/8	7 1/2	15 3/4	15 1/2	7 1/2
		18	5 1/8	7 1/2	14 1/4	14	7 1/2	5 1/8	7 1/2	15 3/4	15 1/2	7 1/2	5 1/8	7 1/2	17	17	7 1/2
	6/12	12	5 1/8	7 1/2	10 1/2	10 1/2	7 1/2	5 1/8	7 1/2	11 1/2	11 1/4	7 1/2	5 1/8	7 1/2	12 1/4	11 1/2	7 1/2
		14	5 1/8	7 1/2	11 3/4	11 3/4	7 1/2	5 1/8	7 1/2	12 3/4	12 3/4	7 1/2	5 1/8	7 1/2	13 3/4	13 1/4	7 1/2
		16	5 1/8	7 1/2	13	12 3/4	7 1/2	5 1/8	7 1/2	14	14	7 1/2	5 1/8	7 1/2	15	15	7 1/2
		18	5 1/8	7 1/2	14	14	7 1/2	5 1/8	7 1/2	15 1/4	15 1/4	7 1/2	5 1/8	7 1/2	16 1/2	16 1/4	7 1/2
	8/12	12	5 1/8	7 1/2	10 1/4	10	7 1/2	5 1/8	7 1/2	11	10 1/2	7 1/2	5 1/8	7 1/2	12	10 1/4	7 1/2
		14	5 1/8	7 1/2	11 1/2	11 1/4	7 1/2	5 1/8	7 1/2	12 1/4	12	7 1/2	5 1/8	7 1/2	13 1/2	11 3/4	7 1/2
		16	5 1/8	7 1/2	12 3/4	12 1/2	7 1/2	5 1/8	7 1/2	13 1/2	13 1/2	7 1/2	5 1/8	7 1/2	14 3/4	13 1/2	7 1/2
		18	5 1/8	7 1/2	13 3/4	13 1/2	7 1/2	5 1/8	7 1/2	14 3/4	14 3/4	7 1/2	5 1/8	7 1/2	16	15	7 1/2
VERTICAL DEAD + LIVE LOAD = 600#/FT. 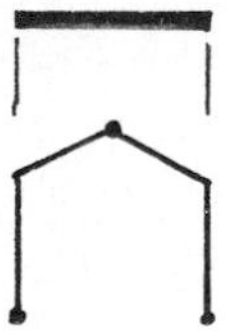	3/12	10	3 1/8	12	14 1/2	12 3/4	7 1/2	5 1/8	9 3/4	12	12 3/4	7 1/2	5 1/8	12 1/4	14	13 3/4	12 1/4
		12	5 1/8	7 1/2	12	12	7 1/2	5 1/8	8 1/2	13 1/2	13	7 1/2	5 1/8	10 3/4	15	13 1/2	7 1/2
		14	5 1/8	7 1/2	13 1/2	13 1/4	7 1/2	5 1/8	7 3/4	15 1/2	14 1/4	7 1/2	5 1/8	9 3/4	17 1/2	14 1/2	7 1/2
		16	5 1/8	7 1/2	14 3/4	14 3/4	7 1/2	5 1/8	7 1/2	17 1/4	15 1/4	7 1/2	5 1/8	8 3/4	19 1/4	15 3/4	7 1/2
		18	5 1/8	7 1/2	16	16	7 1/2	5 1/8	7 1/2	18 3/4	16 1/4	7 1/2	5 1/8	8	21 1/4	16 3/4	7 1/2
	4/12	10	3 1/8	11	15	15 1/2	7 1/2	5 1/8	9	10 1/4	15 1/2	7 1/2	5 1/8	11	11 1/4	15 1/2	12
		12	5 1/8	7 1/2	12	12	7 1/2	5 1/8	8	13 3/4	12 1/4	7 1/2	5 1/8	9 3/4	15 1/4	12 3/4	7 1/2
		14	5 1/8	7 1/2	13 1/2	13 3/4	7 1/2	5 1/8	7 1/2	15 1/2	13 3/4	7 1/2	5 1/8	9	17 1/2	13 3/4	7 1/2
		16	5 1/8	7 1/2	14 3/4	14 1/4	7 1/2	5 1/8	7 1/2	17	15	7 1/2	5 1/8	8 1/4	19 1/4	15 1/4	7 1/2
		18	5 1/8	7 1/2	16	16	7 1/2	5 1/8	7 1/2	18 1/2	16 1/4	7 1/2	5 1/8	7 1/2	21	16 1/2	7 1/2
	6/12	12	5 1/8	7 1/2	12	11 1/4	7 1/2	5 1/8	7 1/2	13 3/4	11 1/4	7 1/2	5 1/8	8 1/2	15 1/4	11	7 1/2
		14	5 1/8	7 1/2	13 1/2	12 3/4	7 1/2	5 1/8	7 1/2	15 1/2	12 1/2	7 1/2	5 1/8	7 3/4	17 1/4	12 1/2	7 1/2
		16	5 1/8	7 1/2	14 3/4	14	7 1/2	5 1/8	7 1/2	17	14	7 1/2	5 1/8	7 1/2	19	14	7 1/2
		18	5 1/8	7 1/2	16	15 1/4	7 1/2	5 1/8	7 1/2	18 1/4	15 1/2	7 1/2	5 1/8	7 1/2	20 1/2	15 1/4	7 1/2
	8/12	12	5 1/8	7 1/2	12	10 1/2	7 1/2	5 1/8	7 1/2	13 1/2	10 1/4	7 1/2	5 1/8	7 1/2	15 1/4	11	7 1/2
		14	5 1/8	7 1/2	13 1/4	12 1/4	7 1/2	5 1/8	7 1/2	15 1/4	11 1/2	7 1/2	5 1/8	7 1/2	17	11 3/4	7 1/2
		16	5 1/8	7 1/2	14 1/2	13 1/2	7 1/2	5 1/8	7 1/2	16 1/2	13 1/4	7 1/2	5 1/8	7 1/2	18 1/2	12 3/4	7 1/2
		18	5 1/8	7 1/2	15 3/4	14 3/4	7 1/2	5 1/8	7 1/2	18	14 1/4	7 1/2	5 1/8	7 1/2	20 1/4	13 3/4	7 1/2
VERTICAL DEAD + LIVE LOAD = 800#/FT. 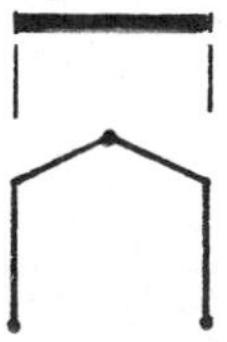	3/12	10	5 1/8	10	12 1/4	12 1/4	12 1/4	5 1/8	13	13 3/4	13 3/4	12 1/4	5 1/8	16	16	14 1/2	12 1/4
		12	5 1/8	8 3/4	13 3/4	12	7 1/2	5 1/8	11 1/4	15 3/4	12 1/2	7 1/2	5 1/8	14	17 1/4	13 1/4	7 1/2
		14	5 1/8	7 3/4	15 3/4	12 3/4	7 1/2	5 1/8	10	18 1/4	13 1/4	7 1/2	5 1/8	12 3/4	20 1/2	13 3/4	7 1/2
		16	5 1/8	7 1/2	17 1/2	13 3/4	7 1/2	5 1/8	9 1/4	20 1/4	14	7 1/2	5 1/8	11 1/2	22 3/4	14 1/2	7 1/2
		18	5 1/8	7 1/2	19 1/4	14 1/4	7 1/2	5 1/8	8 1/4	22 1/4	14 3/4	7 1/2	5 1/8	10 1/2	25	15 1/4	7 1/2
	4/12	10	5 1/8	9 1/4	9 3/4	18 1/2	12	5 1/8	11 3/4	11 3/4	18 1/2	12	5 1/8	14 1/2	14 1/2	18 1/2	12
		12	5 1/8	8	14	11 1/2	7 1/2	5 1/8	10 1/2	16	11 3/4	7 1/2	5 1/8	12 3/4	17 3/4	13	7 1/2
		14	5 1/8	7 1/2	16	12 1/2	7 1/2	5 1/8	9 1/2	18 1/4	12 3/4	7 1/2	5 1/8	11 3/4	20 1/2	13 1/2	7 1/2
		16	5 1/8	7 1/2	17 1/2	13 1/2	7 1/2	5 1/8	8 1/2	20 1/4	13 3/4	7 1/2	5 1/8	10 3/4	22 3/4	13 3/4	7 1/2
		18	5 1/8	7 1/2	19	14 1/2	7 1/2	5 1/8	7 3/4	22	14 3/4	7 1/2	5 1/8	9 3/4	25	14 1/2	7 1/2
	6/12	12	5 1/8	7 1/2	14 1/4	10 3/4	7 1/2	5 1/8	9	16 1/4	10 1/2	7 1/2	5 1/8	11	18	12 1/2	7 1/2
		14	5 1/8	7 1/2	16	11 3/4	7 1/2	5 1/8	8 1/4	18 1/4	11 3/4	7 1/2	5 1/8	10	20 1/4	13 1/4	7 1/2
		16	5 1/8	7 1/2	17 1/2	13	7 1/2	5 1/8	7 1/2	20	13	7 1/2	5 1/8	9 1/4	22 1/2	13 3/4	7 1/2
		18	5 1/8	7 1/2	19	14	7 1/2	5 1/8	7 1/2	21 3/4	14	7 1/2	5 1/8	8 3/4	24 1/2	14 1/4	7 1/2
	8/12	12	5 1/8	7 1/2	14 1/4	9 3/4	7 1/2	5 1/8	8	16	10 3/4	7 1/2	5 1/8	9 1/2	17 3/4	12 1/2	8
		14	5 1/8	7 1/2	15 3/4	11 1/4	7 1/2	5 1/8	7 1/2	18	11 1/2	7 1/2	5 1/8	9	20	13 1/2	7 1/2
		16	5 1/8	7 1/2	17 1/4	12 1/2	7 1/2	5 1/8	7 1/2	19 3/4	12	7 1/2	5 1/8	8 1/4	22	14	7 1/2
		18	5 1/8	7 1/2	18 3/4	13 1/2	7 1/2	5 1/8	7 1/2	21 1/2	13	7 1/2	5 1/8	7 3/4	24	14 1/2	7 1/2

LAMINATED TIMBER TABLES 6.31

ARCH TABLES

LOADING	ROOF PITCH	WALL HT. (FT.)	30' SPAN					35' SPAN					40' SPAN				
			WIDTH	BASE	LOWER TANG.	UPPER TANG.	CROWN	WIDTH	BASE	LOWER TANG.	UPPER TANG.	CROWN	WIDTH	BASE	LOWER TANG.	UPPER TANG.	CROWN
VERTICAL DEAD + LIVE LOAD = 1000#/FT.	3/12	10	5 1/8	12 1/2	12 1/2	18 1/2	12 1/4	5 1/8	16	16	18 1/2	12 1/4	5 1/8	19 3/4	19 3/4	18 1/2	12 1/4
		12	5 1/8	10 3/4	15 1/2	11 1/4	7 1/2	5 1/8	13 3/4	17 1/2	13	7 1/2	5 1/8	17 1/2	19	16	12 1/4
		14	5 1/8	9 1/2	18	11 3/4	7 1/2	5 1/8	12 1/2	20 1/2	12 3/4	7 1/2	5 1/8	15 3/4	23	15 3/4	12 1/4
		16	5 1/8	8 3/4	20	12 1/4	7 1/2	5 1/8	11 1/4	23	12 3/4	7 1/2	6 3/4	11	20 1/2	17 1/4	12 1/4
		18	5 1/8	8	22	12 3/4	7 1/2	5 1/8	10 1/4	25 1/4	13 1/4	7 1/2	6 3/4	10	22 1/4	18 1/2	12 1/4
	4/12	10	5 1/8	11 1/2	11 1/2	23	12	5 1/8	14 1/2	14 1/2	23	12	5 1/8	17 3/4	17 3/4	23	12
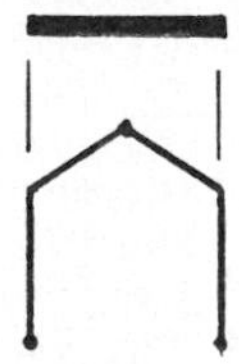		12	5 1/8	10	15 3/4	11	7 1/2	5 1/8	12 3/4	18	13	7 1/2	5 1/8	16	19 3/4	15 3/4	12
		14	5 1/8	9	18	11 3/4	7 1/2	5 1/8	11 1/2	20 3/4	12 3/4	7 1/2	5 1/8	14 1/2	23 1/4	15 1/2	12
		16	5 1/8	8 1/4	20	12 1/4	7 1/2	5 1/8	10 1/2	23	12 1/2	7 1/2	6 3/4	10 1/4	20 1/2	16 3/4	12
		18	5 1/8	7 1/2	21 3/4	13 1/4	7 1/2	5 1/8	9 3/4	25 1/4	13	7 1/2	6 3/4	9 1/2	22	18 1/4	12
	6/12	12	5 1/8	8 3/4	16 1/4	10	7 1/2	5 1/8	11	18 1/4	11 3/4	7 1/2	5 1/8	13 3/4	20 1/2	14 1/4	11 1/4
		14	5 1/8	8	18	11 1/4	7 1/2	5 1/8	10 1/4	20 3/4	12 1/4	7 1/2	5 1/8	12 1/2	23 1/4	14 1/2	11 1/4
		16	5 1/8	7 1/2	20	12	7 1/2	5 1/8	9 1/2	22 3/4	12 1/2	7 1/2	5 1/8	11 3/4	25 3/4	15	11 1/4
		18	5 1/8	7 1/2	21 3/4	12 3/4	7 1/2	5 1/8	8 3/4	25	13	7 1/2	6 3/4	8 1/4	21 3/4	17 1/4	11 1/4
	8/12	12	5 1/8	7 1/2	16	9 3/4	7 1/2	5 1/8	9 3/4	18 1/4	12	7 1/2	5 1/8	12	20 1/4	14	10 1/2
		14	5 1/8	7 1/2	18	10 1/2	7 1/2	5 1/8	9	20 1/4	12 3/4	7 1/2	5 1/8	11	22 3/4	14 3/4	10 1/2
		16	5 1/8	7 1/2	19 3/4	11 1/2	7 1/2	5 1/8	8 1/2	22 1/2	13 1/4	7 1/2	5 1/8	10 1/4	25 1/4	15 1/2	10 1/2
		18	5 1/8	7 1/2	21 1/2	12 1/4	7 1/2	5 1/8	8	24 1/2	13 1/2	7 1/2	6 3/4	7 1/2	21	17 1/2	10 1/2
VERTICAL DEAD = 240#/FT. HORIZONTAL WIND = 320#/FT.	10/12	8	5 1/8	7 1/2	7 1/2	11	7 1/2	5 1/8	7 1/2	7 1/2	12	10 1/4	5 1/8	7 1/2	8 1/4	13	12 3/4
		10	5 1/8	7 1/2	9 1/4	12 1/2	12 1/2	5 1/8	7 1/2	10	13 1/4	8	5 1/8	7 1/2	10 3/4	14 1/4	11 3/4
		12	5 1/8	7 1/2	11 1/4	13 3/4	13 3/4	5 1/8	7 1/2	12	14 3/4	7 1/2	5 1/8	7 1/2	12 3/4	15 3/4	9 3/4
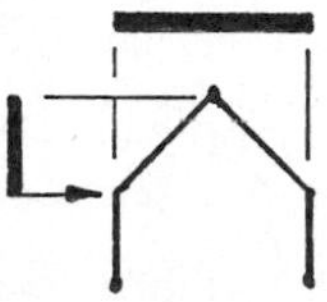	12/12	8	5 1/8	7 1/2	7 1/2	12 1/2	8 3/4	5 1/8	7 1/2	8 1/4	13 1/2	12	5 1/8	7 1/2	8 3/4	14 3/4	14 1/2
		10	5 1/8	7 1/2	9 3/4	13 3/4	9	5 1/8	7 1/2	10 1/2	15	10 1/4	5 1/8	7 1/2	11	16 1/4	13 3/4
		12	5 1/8	7 1/2	11 3/4	15 1/4	15 1/4	5 1/8	7 1/2	12 1/2	16 1/2	9	5 1/8	7 1/2	13 1/4	17 1/2	11 3/4
	14/12	8	5 1/8	7 1/2	8 3/4	13 3/4	10 1/2	5 1/8	7 1/2	9	15	13 3/4	5 1/8	7 1/2	9 1/2	16 1/4	16 1/4
		10	5 1/8	7 1/2	11 1/4	15 1/4	8 1/4	5 1/8	7 1/2	11 1/2	16 1/2	12 1/4	5 1/8	7 1/2	12 1/2	18	15 3/4
		12	5 1/8	7 1/2	13 1/4	17	17	5 1/8	7 1/2	14	18	8 1/4	5 1/8	7 1/2	14 1/2	19 1/2	14 1/4
	16/12	8	5 1/8	7 1/2	10	15	12 1/2	5 1/8	7 1/2	10 1/2	16 1/4	15 3/4	5 1/8	7 1/2	11	18	18
		10	5 1/8	7 1/2	12 1/4	16 1/2	9 1/2	5 1/8	7 1/2	13	18	14 1/2	5 1/8	7 3/4	14	19 1/2	18
		12	5 1/8	7 1/2	14 3/4	18 1/4	7 1/2	5 1/8	7 1/2	15 1/2	19 3/4	11 1/2	5 1/8	8 1/4	16 1/4	21 1/4	16 3/4
VERTICAL DEAD = 320#/FT. HORIZONTAL WIND = 320#/FT.	10/12	8	5 1/8	7 1/2	7 1/2	10 3/4	9	5 1/8	7 1/2	8 1/4	11 3/4	11 1/2	5 1/8	7 1/2	9	13	13
		10	5 1/8	7 1/2	10	12	7 1/2	5 1/8	7 1/2	10 3/4	13	10 1/2	5 1/8	7 1/2	11 1/2	14	13 1/2
		12	5 1/8	7 1/2	12	13 1/4	13 1/4	5 1/8	7 1/2	12 3/4	14 1/4	8 1/2	5 1/8	7 1/2	13 3/4	15 1/4	12 1/2
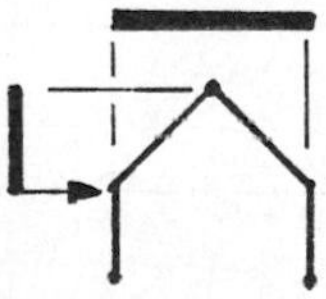	12/12	8	5 1/8	7 1/2	8 1/4	12 1/4	10 1/4	5 1/8	7 1/2	9 1/4	13 1/4	13 1/4	5 1/8	7 1/2	9 1/2	14 3/4	14 3/4
		10	5 1/8	7 1/2	10 1/2	13 1/2	9	5 1/8	7 1/2	11 1/4	14 3/4	12 1/4	5 1/8	7 1/2	12	15 3/4	15 1/4
		12	5 1/8	7 1/2	12 1/2	15	9	5 1/8	7 1/2	13 1/4	16	10 1/4	5 1/8	7 1/2	14 1/4	17 1/4	14 1/4
	14/12	8	5 1/8	7 1/2	8 3/4	13 1/2	12	5 1/8	7 1/2	9 1/4	14 3/4	14 3/4	5 1/8	7 1/2	10	16 1/2	16 1/2
		10	5 1/8	7 1/2	10 3/4	15	10 1/4	5 1/8	7 1/2	11 3/4	16 1/4	14 1/4	5 1/8	7 1/2	12 1/2	17 1/2	17 1/4
		12	5 1/8	7 1/2	12 3/4	16 1/2	8 1/4	5 1/8	7 1/2	13 3/4	17 3/4	12 1/2	5 1/8	7 1/2	14 3/4	19 1/4	16 1/2
	16/12	8	5 1/8	7 1/2	9 1/2	15	13 3/4	5 1/8	7 1/2	9 3/4	16 1/4	16 1/4	5 1/8	7 1/2	10 1/4	18 1/4	18 1/4
		10	5 1/8	7 1/2	11 3/4	16 1/2	12 1/4	5 1/8	7 1/2	12 3/4	18	16 1/4	5 1/8	7 1/2	13	19 1/4	19 1/4
		12	5 1/8	7 1/2	14 1/4	18	7 3/4	5 1/8	1 1/2	14 3/4	19 1/2	14 1/2	5 1/8	7 1/2	15 3/4	21	18 3/4
VERTICAL DEAD = 480#/FT. HORIZONTAL WIND = 320#/FT.	10/12	8	5 1/8	7 1/2	9	10 1/2	10 1/2	5 1/8	7 1/2	9 3/4	12	12	5 1/8	8	10 1/2	13 1/2	13 1/2
		10	5 1/8	7 1/2	11 1/4	11 1/2	10 1/4	5 1/8	7 1/2	12 1/4	12 1/2	12 1/2	5 1/8	7 3/4	13 1/4	14	14
		12	5 1/8	7 1/2	13 1/2	12 3/4	8 3/4	5 1/8	7 1/2	14 3/4	13 1/2	12 1/2	5 1/8	7 3/4	16	14 3/4	14 3/4
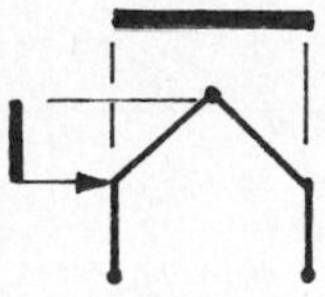	12/12	8	5 1/8	7 1/2	9 1/4	12	12	5 1/8	7 1/2	10 1/4	13 1/2	13 1/2	5 1/8	7 3/4	11	15 1/4	15 1/4
		10	5 1/8	7 1/2	11 3/4	13 1/4	11 1/2	5 1/8	7 1/2	12 3/4	14 1/4	14 1/4	5 1/8	7 3/4	13 3/4	15 3/4	15 3/4
		12	5 1/8	7 1/2	13 3/4	14 1/2	10	5 1/8	7 1/2	15	15 1/2	14	5 1/8	7 3/4	16 1/4	16 3/4	16 3/4
	14/12	8	5 1/8	7 1/2	9 3/4	13 1/4	13 1/4	5 1/8	7 1/2	10 1/2	15	15	5 1/8	7 3/4	11 1/4	17	17
		10	5 1/8	7 1/2	12	14 3/4	13	5 1/8	7 1/2	13	16	16	5 1/8	7 3/4	14	17 3/4	17 3/4
		12	5 1/8	7 1/2	14 1/4	16	11 1/2	5 1/8	7 1/2	15 1/2	17 1/2	15 1/2	5 1/8	7 3/4	16 1/2	18 3/4	18 3/4
	16/12	8	5 1/8	7 1/2	10	14 3/4	14 3/4	5 1/8	7 1/2	10 3/4	16 3/4	16 3/4	5 1/8	7 3/4	11 1/2	18 3/4	18 3/4
		10	5 1/8	7 1/2	12 1/4	16 1/4	14 1/2	5 1/8	7 1/2	13 1/4	17 3/4	17 3/4	5 1/8	7 3/4	14 1/4	19 1/2	19 1/2
		12	5 1/8	7 1/2	14 1/2	17 3/4	13 1/4	5 1/8	7 1/2	15 3/4	19 1/4	17 1/2	5 1/8	7 3/4	17	20 1/4	20 3/4

ARCH TABLES

LOADING	ROOF PITCH	WALL HT.(FT.)	50' SPAN WIDTH	50' SPAN BASE	50' SPAN LOWER TANG.	50' SPAN UPPER TANG.	50' SPAN CROWN	WALL HT.(FT.)	60' SPAN WIDTH	60' SPAN BASE	60' SPAN LOWER TANG.	60' SPAN UPPER TANG.	60' SPAN CROWN	70' SPAN WIDTH	70' SPAN BASE	70' SPAN LOWER TANG.	70' SPAN UPPER TANG.	70' SPAN CROWN
VERTICAL DEAD + LIVE LOAD = 400#/FT. 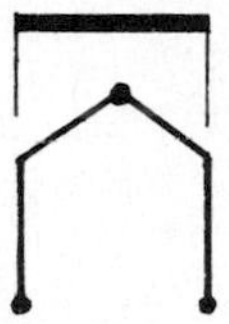	3/12	10	5⅛	11¾	14	13¾	7½	12	5⅛	14	16¼	16¾	7½	5⅛	17¾	17¾	20	7½
		12	5⅛	10½	14¾	14½	7½	14	5⅛	12¾	19½	17½	7½	5⅛	16¼	22	20¾	7½
		14	5⅛	9½	16¾	16¼	7½	16	5⅛	11¾	22	17¾	7½	5⅛	15	25	21¼	7½
		16	5⅛	8¾	18¾	17½	7½	18	5⅛	10¾	24	19¼	7½	6¾	10¾	22	21¼	7½
		18	5⅛	8	20½	19	7½	20	6¾	7¾	22	22	7½	6¾	10	23½	23¼	7½
	4/12	10	5⅛	10½	13	12¾	7½	12	5⅛	12½	16¾	15¾	7½	5⅛	15¾	18½	18¾	7¾
		12	5⅛	9½	14½	13½	7½	14	5⅛	11½	19½	16½	7½	5⅛	14½	22	19½	7½
		14	5⅛	8¾	16¾	15	7½	16	5⅛	10½	21¾	17	7½	5⅛	13½	24½	20¼	7½
		16	5⅛	8	18½	16½	7½	18	5⅛	10	23¾	17¾	7½	6¾	9¾	21½	19½	7½
		18	5⅛	7½	20¼	18	7½	20	5⅛	9¼	25½	19¼	7½	6¾	9	23	21½	7½
	6/12	12	5⅛	8	14¾	11¾	7½	12	5⅛	10¼	16¾	14¼	8¼	5⅛	12¾	18¾	16¾	10½
		14	5⅛	7½	16½	12¾	7½	14	5⅛	9½	19	15¼	7½	5⅛	12	21½	17¾	9
		16	5⅛	7½	18¼	14¼	7½	16	5⅛	9	21	16	7½	5⅛	11¼	23¾	18¾	7¾
		18	5⅛	7½	19¾	16	7½	18	5⅛	8½	23	16½	7½	6¾	8	20¾	17¼	7½
	8/12	12	5⅛	7½	14¼	11½	7½	12	5⅛	8¾	16½	13½	10	5⅛	10¾	18½	15½	12¾
		14	5⅛	7½	16	12¼	7½	14	5⅛	8¼	18½	14½	8¾	5⅛	10¼	20¾	16¾	11¼
		16	5⅛	7½	17¾	13	7½	16	5⅛	7¾	20½	15½	7½	5⅛	9½	23	17¾	9¾
		18	5⅛	7½	19¼	14	7½	18	5⅛	7½	22¼	16¼	7½	5⅛	9¼	25¼	18¾	8¾
VERTICAL DEAD + LIVE LOAD = 600#/FT. 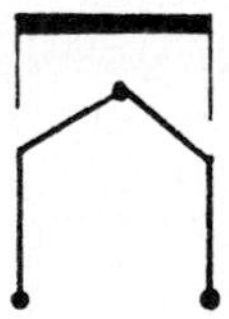	3/12	10	5⅛	17½	17½	15½	12¼	12	5⅛	20½	20½	20¼	7½	5⅛	26¼	26¼	24	12¼
		12	5⅛	15½	17½	16	7½	14	5⅛	18¾	24	21	7½	6¾	18	22	22¼	12¼
		14	5⅛	14	21	16½	7½	16	6¾	13¼	22	19	7½	6¾	17	25	23	12¼
		16	5⅛	12¾	23½	17	7½	18	6¾	12¼	24	20¼	7½	6¾	16¼	27¼	23½	12¼
		18	6¾	9	20½	20¼	7½	20	6¾	11½	25¾	21¾	7½	6¾	14½	29½	24	12¼
	4/12	10	5⅛	15½	15½	15½	12	12	5⅛	18¼	20¼	19¼	7½	5⅛	23¼	23¼	22¾	12
		12	5⅛	14	18	15¼	7½	14	5⅛	17	24¼	20	7½	6¾	16½	22	21¼	12
		14	5⅛	12¾	21	16	7½	16	6¾	12	21¾	18¼	7½	6¾	15½	24¾	21¾	12
		16	5⅛	11¾	23½	16½	7½	18	6¾	11¼	23½	18¾	7½	6¾	14½	27	22½	12
		18	5⅛	10¾	25½	16¾	7½	20	6¾	10½	25¼	20½	7½	6¾	13½	28¾	23	12
	6/12	12	5⅛	11¾	18¼	14½	7½	12	5⅛	15¼	21	17½	10¼	5⅛	18¾	23¼	20½	13¼
		14	5⅛	10¾	20¾	15¼	7½	14	5⅛	14	24	18½	8¾	6¾	13½	21¾	19¼	11¼
		16	5⅛	10	23	15¾	7½	16	6¾	10¼	21¼	17¼	7½	6¾	12¾	24	20	11¼
		18	5⅛	9½	25	16½	7½	18	6¾	9½	22¾	17¾	7½	6¾	12	26	21	11¼
	8/12	12	5⅛	10	18	14	9½	12	5⅛	13	20¾	16½	12½	5⅛	16	23¼	19	16
		14	5⅛	9¼	20¼	15	8	14	5⅛	12¼	23¼	17¾	10¾	6¾	11½	21	18	12
		16	5⅛	8¼	22¼	15¾	7½	16	6¾	8¾	20½	16½	8	6¾	10	23	19¼	10½
		18	5⅛	8¼	24¼	16¼	7½	18	6¾	8¼	22	17½	7½	6¾	10½	25	20	10½
VERTICAL DEAD + LIVE LOAD = 800#/FT. 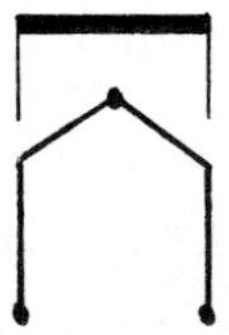	3/12	10	5⅛	22¾	22¾	18½	12¼	12	5⅛	27¼	27¼	23	12¼	6¾	26¾	23¾	24¼	12¼
		12	5⅛	20½	20½	18½	12¼	14	6¾	19¼	22½	21¼	12¼	6¾	24½	24½	25¾	12¼
		14	5⅛	18½	24½	19	12¼	16	6¾	17½	25¾	21¾	12¼	6¾	22½	28¾	26¼	12¼
		16	6¾	13	22	18¾	12¼	18	6¾	16¼	28	22¼	12¼	6¾	21	31¾	26¾	12¼
		18	6¾	12	24	20	12¼	20	6¾	15	30¼	22½	12¼	8¾	15¼	28¼	24¾	12¼
	4/12	10	5⅛	20½	20½	18½	12	12	5⅛	24¼	24¼	22	12	6¾	23½	23½	23	12
		12	5⅛	18½	20¾	17½	12	14	6¾	17¼	22¾	20¼	12	6¾	21¾	25¼	24¼	12
		14	5⅛	16¾	24¾	18¼	12	16	6¾	16	25½	21	12	6¾	20¼	28¾	25	12
		16	6¾	12	22	17¾	12	18	6¾	14¾	27¾	21½	12	6¾	19	31½	25¾	12
		18	6¾	11	23¾	19¼	12	20	6¾	13¾	29¾	22	12	6¾	17¾	33¾	26¼	12
	6/12	12	5⅛	15¼	21½	16½	11¼	12	5⅛	20	24¼	20¼	12	6¾	19	22	21	13
		14	5⅛	14¼	24½	17¼	11¼	14	6¾	14¼	22½	18¾	11¼	6¾	17¾	25¼	22	11¼
		16	6¾	10½	21½	16	11¼	16	6¾	13½	24¾	19¾	11¼	6¾	16¾	28	23	11¼
		18	6¾	9½	23	17½	11¼	18	6¾	12¾	26¾	20½	11¼	6¾	16	30½	24	11¼
	8/12	12	5⅛	13¼	21¼	16	11	12	5⅛	17	24½	19	14¾	6¾	16	22	19¼	16
		14	5⅛	12½	24	17	10½	14	6¾	12¼	22	18	10¾	6¾	15¼	24¼	20¾	14
		16	6¾	9	20¾	16	10½	16	6¾	11½	24	19	10½	6¾	14½	27	22	12¼
		18	6¾	8½	22½	16½	10½	18	6¾	11	26	20	10½	6¾	13¾	29¼	23	11

AMERICAN INSTITUTE OF TIMBER CONSTRUCTION

LAMINATED TIMBER TABLES 6.33

ARCH TABLES

LOADING	ROOF PITCH	WALL HT. FT.	50' SPAN WIDTH	50' SPAN BASE	50' SPAN LOWER TANG.	50' SPAN UPPER TANG.	50' SPAN CROWN	WALL HT. FT.	60' SPAN WIDTH	60' SPAN BASE	60' SPAN LOWER TANG.	60' SPAN UPPER TANG.	60' SPAN CROWN	70' SPAN WIDTH	70' SPAN BASE	70' SPAN LOWER TANG.	70' SPAN UPPER TANG.	70' SPAN CROWN
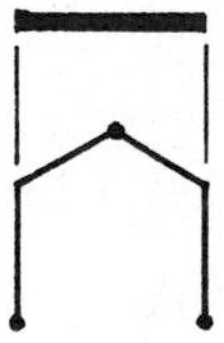	3/12	10	5 1/8	28 1/4	28 1/4	23	17	12	6 3/4	26	26	22 1/2	12 1/4	6 3/4	32 3/4	32 3/4	26 1/2	12 1/4
		12	5 1/8	25	25	22 1/4	12 1/4	14	6 3/4	23 1/2	25	23 3/4	12 1/4	6 3/4	30	30	28 1/2	12 1/4
		14	6 3/4	17 1/2	22	18 3/4	12 1/4	16	6 3/4	21 3/4	28 3/4	24 1/4	12 1/4	6 3/4	27 3/4	32 1/4	29 1/4	12 1/4
		16	6 3/4	16	24 3/4	19	12 1/4	18	6 3/4	20	31 1/2	24 3/4	12 1/4	8 3/4	20 1/4	29 3/4	26 1/2	12 1/4
		18	6 3/4	14 3/4	27	19 1/2	12 1/4	20	8 3/4	14 1/2	28	23 1/2	12 1/4	8 3/4	18 3/4	31 3/4	27	12 1/4
	4/12	10	5 1/8	25 1/4	25 1/4	23	16 3/4	12	6 3/4	23	23	21 1/2	12	6 3/4	29	29	25 1/4	12
		12	5 1/8	22 1/2	22 1/2	21 3/4	12	14	6 3/4	21 1/2	25 1/2	22 1/2	12	6 3/4	26 3/4	28	27	12
		14	6 3/4	16	22 1/4	18	12	16	6 3/4	19 3/4	28 3/4	23 1/4	12	6 3/4	25	32 1/4	27 3/4	12
		16	6 3/4	14 3/4	24 3/4	18 1/2	12	18	6 3/4	18 1/4	31 1/4	24	12	8 3/4	18 1/4	29 1/4	25 1/2	12
		18	6 3/4	13 3/4	26 3/4	19	12	20	6 3/4	17 3/4	33 3/4	24 1/4	12	8 3/4	17 1/4	31 1/4	26	12
	6/12	12	5 1/8	19	24	19	11 1/4	12	6 3/4	19	22	19 3/4	11 1/2	6 3/4	23 1/2	24 1/4	23 1/4	14 3/4
		14	6 3/4	13 1/2	22	17 1/4	11 1/4	14	6 3/4	17 3/4	25 1/4	21	11 1/4	6 3/4	22	28 1/4	24 1/2	13
		16	6 3/4	12 3/4	24 1/4	17 3/4	11 1/4	16	6 3/4	16 1/2	28	22	11 1/4	6 3/4	20 3/4	31 1/2	25 3/4	11 1/4
		18	6 3/4	11 3/4	26 1/4	18 1/2	11 1/4	18	6 3/4	15 3/4	30 1/2	22 3/4	11 1/4	8 3/4	15 1/4	28 1/4	23 3/4	11 1/4
	8/12	12	5 1/8	16 1/4	24	17 3/4	12 1/2	12	6 3/4	16 1/4	22	18 3/4	14	6 3/4	20	24 1/2	21 1/2	18
		14	6 3/4	11 3/4	21 1/2	16 3/4	10 1/2	14	6 3/4	15 1/4	24 3/4	20 1/4	12 1/4	6 3/4	18 3/4	27 3/4	23 1/4	15 3/4
		16	6 3/4	11	23 1/2	17 3/4	10 1/2	16	6 3/4	14 1/4	27 1/4	21 1/4	10 3/4	6 3/4	18	30 1/2	24 1/2	14
		18	6 3/4	10 1/2	25 1/4	18 1/2	10 1/2	18	6 3/4	13 3/4	29 1/2	22 1/4	10 1/2	6 3/4	17	33 1/4	25 3/4	12 1/2
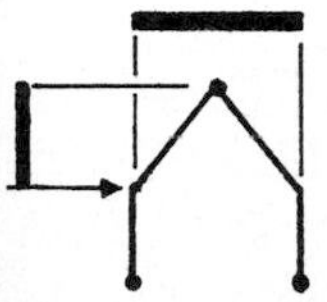	10/12	8	5 1/8	7 1/2	9 1/4	15 1/2	15 1/2											
		10	5 1/8	7 1/2	12	16 1/4	16 1/4											
		12	5 1/8	1 1/2	14 1/4	17 1/2	16											
	12/12	8	5 1/8	7 1/2	9 3/4	17 1/2	17 1/2											
		10	5 1/8	7 1/2	12 1/2	18 1/2	18 1/2											
		12	5 1/8	7 1/2	14 3/4	20	18 1/4											
	14/12	8	5 1/8	7 1/2	10 1/4	19 1/2	19 1/2											
		10	5 1/8	7 3/4	13 1/4	20 1/2	20 1/2											
		12	5 1/8	8 1/4	16	22	20 3/4											
	16/12	8	5 1/8	9	11	21 1/2	21 1/2											
		10	5 1/8	9 1/4	14 3/4	22 3/4	22 3/4											
		12	5 1/8	9 3/4	17 1/2	24	23 1/2											
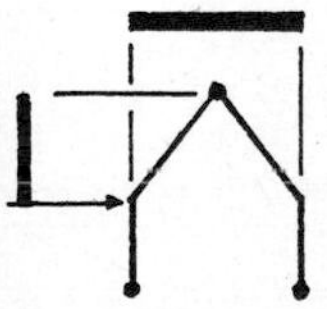	10/12	8	5 1/8	8	10	15 3/4	15 3/4											
		10	5 1/8	7 3/4	13	16 1/2	16 1/2											
		12	5 1/8	7 3/4	15 3/4	17 1/4	17 1/4											
	12/12	8	5 1/8	7 3/4	10 1/2	17 3/4	17 3/4											
		10	5 1/8	7 3/4	13 1/2	18 3/4	18 3/4											
		12	5 1/8	7 3/4	16	19 1/2	19 1/2											
	14/12	8	5 1/8	7 3/4	10 1/2	19 3/4	19 3/4											
		10	5 1/8	7 3/4	13 3/4	20 3/4	20 3/4											
		12	5 1/8	8	16 1/2	21 3/4	21 3/4											
	16/12	8	5 1/8	8 1/4	10 3/4	22	22											
		10	5 1/8	8 1/2	14	23	23											
		12	5 1/8	9	16 3/4	24 1/4	24 1/4											

1. UNIFORM LOADING
2. RADIUS OF CURVATURE AT THE HAUNCH = 9'-4".
3. ALLOWABLE STRESSES:
   BENDING STRESS, F_b = 2400 PSI (REDUCED BY SIZE FACTOR AND CURVATURE FACTOR WHEN APPLICABLE
   SHEAR STRESS, F_v = 165 PSI
   COMPRESSION PARALLEL TO GRAIN, F_c = 1500 PSI (ADJUSTED FOR L/D RATIO)
   MODULUS OF ELASTICITY, E = 1,800,000 PSI
   THESE STRESSES WERE INCREASED 15% FOR SHORT DURATION OF LOADING AND 33 1/3% FOR WIND LOADING WHEN APPLICABLE.
4. DEFLECTION LIMITS: 1/180 FOR DEAD PLUS LIVE LOAD; 1/240 FOR LIVE LOAD ONLY.
5. VERTICAL ARCH LEGS ARE LATERALLY UNSUPPORTED WITH TANGENT POINT DEPTH TO BREADTH RATIO NOT EXCEEDING 5:1. (WHEN VERTICAL ARCH LEGS ARE LATERALLY SUPPORTED, TANGENT POINT DEPTH TO BREADTH RATIO NOT EXCEEDING 6:1 MAY BE USED.)
6. DEAD LOAD EQUAL TO ONE-THIRD OF THE TOTAL VERTICAL LOAD.
7. ARCH SPACING = 20 FT.

AMERICAN INSTITUTE OF TIMBER CONSTRUCTION

STANDARD WIDTH OF GLU-LAM TIMBER								
NORMAL WIDTH (INCHES)	3	4	6	8	10	12	14	16
NET FINISH WIDTH (INCHES)	2¼	3⅛	5⅛	6¾	8¾	10¾	12¼	14¼

AITC-303-70   TOLERANCE PLUS OR MINUS 1⁄16"

ARCH SIZE TABLE

SPAN (FT.)	CENTER HEIGHT (FT.)	RADIUS (FT.)	W = TOTAL LOAD, POUND PER LINEAL FOOT			
			320	480	640	800
40-0	10-0	25-0	3⅛ X 12	3⅛ X 13½	3⅛ X 15	3⅛ X 15
50-0	12-6	31-3	3⅛ X 13½	3⅛ X 15	3⅛ X 15	3⅛ X 16½
60-0	15-0	37-6	3⅛ X 15	3⅛ X 16½	3⅛ X 16½	5⅛ X 16½
70-0	17-6	43-9	3⅛ X 16½	3⅛ X 18	5⅛ X 18	5⅛ X 19½
80-0	20-0	50-0	3⅛ X 18	5⅛ X 18	5⅛ X 19½	5⅛ X 21
90-0	22-6	56-3	5⅛ X 16½	5⅛ X 19½	5⅛ X 22½	5⅛ X 24
100-0	25-0	62-6	5⅛ X 18	5⅛ X 21	5⅛ X 24	5⅛ X 25½
110-0	27-6	68-9	5⅛ X 19½	5⅛ X 22½	5⅛ X 25½	6¾ X 25½
120-0	30-0	75-0	5⅛ X 21	5⅛ X 25½	6¾ X 25½	6¾ X 27

BASED ON 2400 F

VERTICAL REACTION $\frac{WL}{2}$; APPROX. HORIZONTAL REACTION $\frac{WL}{2}$

WEYERHAEUSER CO.

DIMENSIONS OF DOUGLAS FIR AND SOUTHERN PINE POLES

CLASS	1	2	3	4	5	6	7	9	10
MIN. TOP CIRCUM	27	25	23	21	19	17	15	15	12
LENGTH (FT.) / GND. LINE FROM BUTT	MIN. CIRCUMFERENCE 6 FEET FROM BUTT (IN.)								
20 / 4.0	31.0	29.0	27.0	25.0	23.0	21.0	19.5	17.5	14.0
25 / 5.0	33.5	31.5	29.5	27.0	25.5	23.0	21.5	19.5	15.0
30 / 5.5	36.5	34.0	32.0	29.5	27.5	25.0	23.5	20.5	
35 / 6.0	39.0	36.5	34.0	31.5	29.0	27.0	25.0		
40 / 6.0	41.0	38.5	36.0	33.5	31.0	28.5			
45 / 6.5	43.0	40.5	37.5	35.0	32.5	30.0			
50 / 7.0	45.0	42.0	39.0	36.5	34.0				
55 / 7.5	46.5	43.5	40.5	38.0					
60 / 8.0	48.0	45.0	42.0	39.0					
65 / 8.5	49.5	46.5	43.5	40.5					
70 / 9.0	51.0	48.0	45.0	41.5					
75 / 9.5	52.5	49.0	46.0						
80 / 10.0	54.0	50.5	47.0						
85 / 10.5	55.0	51.5	48.0						
90 / 11.0	56.0	53.0	49.0						
95 / 11.0	57.0	54.0							
100 / 11.0	58.5	55.0							

CLASS	H-1	H-2	H-3	H-4	H-5	H-6
MIN. TOP CIRCUM.	29	31	33	35	37	39
LENGTH (FT.) / GND. LINE FROM BUTT	MIN. CIRCUMFERENCE 6 FEET FROM BUTT (IN.)					
20 / 4.0						
25 / 5.0						
30 / 5.5						
35 / 6.0	41.5	43.5				
40 / 6.0	43.5	46.0	48.5	51.0	56.0	
45 / 6.5	45.5	48.5	51.0	53.5	56.0	58.5
50 / 7.0	47.5	50.5	53.0	55.5	58.0	61.0
55 / 7.5	49.5	52.0	55.0	58.0	60.5	63.5
60 / 8.0	51.0	54.0	57.0	59.5	62.5	65.5
65 / 8.5	52.5	55.5	58.5	61.5	64.5	67.5
70 / 9.0	54.0	57.0	60.5	63.5	66.5	69.0
75 / 9.5	55.5	59.0	62.0	65.0	68.0	71.0
80 / 10.0	57.0	60.0	63.5	66.5	69.5	72.5
85 / 10.5	58.5	61.5	65.0	68.0	71.5	74.5
90 / 11.0	59.0	63.0	66.5	69.5	73.0	76.0
95 / 11.0	61.0	64.5	67.5	71.0	74.5	77.5
100 / 11.0	62.0	65.5	69.0	72.5	76.0	79.0

WEIGHT OF INSTALLED HEAVY TIMBER DECKING
POUNDS PER SQUARE FOOT OF ROOF SURFACE

SPECIES	1½ NET 2 NOM.	2½ NET 3 NOM.	3½ NET 4 NOM.	GRADING AGENCY
CEDAR, NORTHERN WHITE	2.7	4.5	6.3	1
CEDAR, WESTERN	3.0	4.9	6.9	3, 4
CEDAR, NORTHWESTERN	2.9	4.8	6.7	2
CEDAR, COAST SPECIES	3.9	6.4	9.0	2
DOUGLAS FIR - LARCH	4.3	7.2	10.1	3, 4
DOUGLAS FIR - LARCH (NORTH)	4.4	7.3	10.3	2
DOUGLAS FIR	4.1	6.9	9.5	3
FIR, BALSAM	3.2	5.4	7.5	1
HEM - FIR	3.7	6.1	8.6	3, 4
HEM - FIR (NORTH)	3.8	6.3	8.8	2
HEMLOCK, EASTERN - TAMERACK	3.8	6.3	8.8	1
HEMLOCK, EASTERN - TAM. (NORTH)	4.0	6.7	9.4	2
HEMLOCK, MOUNTAIN	4.0	6.7	9.4	3, 4
HEMLOCK, WESTERN	4.0	6.7	9.4	3, 4
PINE, EASTERN WHITE	3.3	5.5	7.7	1
PINE, IDAHO WHITE	3.5	5.8	8.2	3
PINE, LODGEPOLE	3.7	6.1	8.6	3
PINE, NORTHERN	4.1	7.0	9.3	1
PINE, PONDEROSA	4.1	6.9	9.6	2
PINE, SUGAR	3.6	6.0	8.4	3
PINE, RED	3.7	6.1	8.6	2
PINE, SOUTHERN	4.6	7.6	10.7	5
PINE, WESTERN WHITE	3.4	5.7	8.0	2
REDWOOD, CALIFORNIA	3.7	6.1	8.6	6
SPRUCE, COAST SITKA	3.3	5.5	7.7	2
SPRUCE, EASTERN	3.6	6.0	8.4	1
SPRUCE, EASTERN BALSAM - FIR	3.4	5.7	8.0	1
SPRUCE, ENGLISHMANN	3.0	5.1	7.1	3
SPRUCE, PINE - FIR	3.5	5.9	8.0	2
SPRUCE, SITKA	3.6	6.0	8.4	4

GRADING AGENCIES

1. Ne LME	4. WCLIB
2. NLGA (CANADIAN)	5. SPIB
3. WWPA	6. RIS

ALASKA CEDAR, SITKA AND WHITE SPRUCE

ALLOWABLE UNIFORMLY DISTRIBUTED TOTAL ROOF LOAD IN PSF —LIMITED BY

SPAN ft	BENDING		DEFLECTION, E=1,320,000 psi					
	SELECT COMM. GRADE f 1.265,[a] psi	GRADE f 977.5,[a] psi	SIMPLE SPAN- END JOINTS OVER SUPPORTS			CONTROLLED RANDOM LAYUP CONTINUOUS OVER 3 OR MORE SPANS		
			$\ell/160$	$\ell/240$	$\ell/360$	$\ell/180$	$\ell/240$	$\ell/360$
10	117	90	71	54	36	108	61	54
11	97	75	54	40	27	81	61	41
12	81	63	41	31	21	62	47	31
13	69	54	33	25	17	49	37	25
14	60	46	26	20	13	40	30	20
15	52	40	21	16	11	32	24	16
16	46	36	16	13	9	27	20	14
17	41	32	15	11	8	22	17	11
18	36	28	13	10	7	19	14	10
19	33	25	11	8	6	16	12	8
20	30	25	9	7	5	14	11	7
10	207	160	168	126	84	264	191	127
11	171	132	126	95	63	191	143	96
12	144	111	98	73	49	147	111	74
13	123	95	77	58	39	116	87	58
14	106	82	62	46	31	93	70	47
15	92	71	50	38	25	76	57	38
16	81	63	41	31	21	62	47	31
17	72	56	35	26	18	52	39	26
18	64	50	29	22	15	44	33	22
19	58	45	25	19	13	37	28	19
20	52	40	21	16	11	32	24	16

THESE VALUES ARE INCREASED 15% OVER NORMAL LOAD VALUES FOR 2 MONTHS DURATION OF LOAD AS FOR SNOW.

INCENSE CEDAR

ALLOWABLE UNIFORMLY DISTRIBUTED TOTAL ROOF LOAD IN psf LIMITED BY

SPAN, ft.	BENDING		DEFLECTION,E = 990,000 psi					
	SELECT COMM. GRADE GRADE f 1,265,[a] f 977.5,[a] psi psi		SIMPLE SPAN — END JOINTS OVER SUPPORTS			CONTROLLED RANDOM LAYUP CONTINUOUS OVER 3 OR MORE SPANS		
			$\ell/180$	$\ell/240$	$\ell/360$	$\ell/180$	$\ell/240$	$\ell/360$
3 IN. (2 5/8 IN. NET THICKNESS)								
10	117	90	54	40	27	81	61	41
11	97	75	40	30	20	61	46	31
12	81	63	31	24	16	47	35	24
13	69	54	25	19	13	37	28	19
14	60	46	20	15	10	30	22	15
15	52	40	16	12	8	24	18	12
16	46	36	13	10	7	20	15	10
17	41	32	11	9	6	17	13	9
18	36	28	10	7	5	14	11	7
19	33	25	8	6	4	12	9	6
20	30	23	7	5	4	11	8	6
4 IN. (3 1/2 IN. NET THICKNESS)								
10	207	160	126	95	63	191	143	96
11	171	132	95	71	48	143	108	72
12	144	111	73	55	37	111	83	56
13	123	95	58	43	29	87	65	44
14	106	82	46	35	23	70	53	35
15	92	71	38	28	19	57	43	29
16	81	63	31	24	16	47	35	24
17	72	56	26	20	13	39	30	20
18	64	50	22	17	11	33	25	17
19	58	45	19	14	10	28	21	14
20	52	40	16	12	8	24	18	12

AMERICAN INSTITUTE OF TIMBER CONSTRUCTION.

WESTERN RED CEDAR, IDAHO WHITE, LODGEPOLE, PONDEROSA, AND SUGAR PINE

ALLOWABLE UNIFORMLY DISTRIBUTED TOTAL ROOF LOAD IN psf LIMITED BY

SPAN, ft.	BENDING		DEFLECTION, E = 1,100,000 psi					
	SELECT GRADE f 1,035[a] psi	COMM. GRADE f 805[a] psi	SIMPLE SPAN— END JOINTS OVER SUPPORTS			CONTROLLED RANDOM LAYUP CONTINUOUS OVER 3 OR MORE SPANS		
			l/180	l/240	l/360	l/180	l/240	l/360
3 IN. (2 5/8 IN. NET THICKNESS)								
10	96	74	59	45	30	90	67	45
11	79	62	45	34	23	68	51	34
12	67	52	35	26	18	52	39	26
13	57	44	27	21	14	41	31	21
14	49	38	22	17	11	33	25	17
15	43	33	18	14	9	27	20	14
16	38	29	15	11	8	22	17	11
17	33	26	12	9	6	19	14	10
18	30	23	11	8	6	16	12	8
19	27	21	9	7	5	14	10	7
20	24	19	8	6	4	12	9	6
4 IN. (3 1/2 IN. NET THICKNESS)								
10	170	132	140	105	70	212	159	106
11	140	109	105	79	53	159	120	80
12	118	92	81	61	41	123	92	62
13	101	78	64	48	32	97	73	49
14	87	68	51	39	26	78	58	39
15	76	59	42	32	21	63	47	32
16	67	52	35	26	18	52	39	28
17	59	46	29	22	15	44	33	22
18	53	41	24	18	12	37	28	19
19	47	37	21	16	11	31	24	16
20	43	33	18	14	9	27	20	14

AMERICAN INSTITUTE OF TIMBER CONSTRUCTION.

PORT ORFORD CEDAR

ALLOWABLE UNIFORMILY DISTRIBUTED TOTAL ROOF LOAD IN psf LIMITED BY

SPAN ft.	BENDING		DEFLECTION, E= 1,650,000 psi					
	SELECT COMM. GRADE f 1,265,[a] psi	GRADE f 977.5,[a] psi	SIMPLE SPAN END JOINTS OVER SUPPORTS			CONTROLLED RANDOM LAYUP CONTINUOUS OVER 3 OR MORE SPANS		
			ℓ/180	ℓ/240	ℓ/360	ℓ/180	ℓ/240	ℓ/360
3 IN. (2⅝ IN. NET THICKNESS)								
10	117	90	89	67	45	134	101	67
11	97	75	67	50	34	101	76	51
12	81	63	52	39	26	78	59	39
13	69	54	41	31	21	61	46	31
14	60	46	33	25	17	49	37	25
15	52	40	27	20	14	40	30	20
16	46	36	22	17	11	33	25	17
17	41	32	18	14	9	28	21	14
18	36	28	16	12	8	23	18	12
19	33	25	13	10	7	20	15	10
20	30	23	12	9	6	17	13	9
4 IN. (3½ IN. NET THICKNESS)								
10	207	160	210	158	105	318	238	159
11	171	132	158	119	79	239	179	120
12	144	111	122	91	61	184	138	92
13	123	95	96	72	48	145	109	73
14	106	82	77	58	39	116	87	58
15	92	71	63	47	32	94	71	47
16	81	63	52	39	26	78	59	39
17	72	56	43	32	22	65	49	33
18	64	50	36	27	18	55	41	28
19	58	45	31	23	16	47	35	24
20	52	40	27	20	14	40	30	20

AMERICAN INSTITUTE OF TIMBER CONSTRUCTION.

WHITE FIR

ALLOWABLE UNIFORMLY DISTRIBUTED TOTAL ROOF LOAD IN psf — LIMITED BY

SPAN ft.	BENDING		DEFLECTION, E = 1,210,000 psi					
	SELECT COMM. GRADE f 1,265,[a] psi	GRADE f 977.5,[a] psi	SIMPLE SPAN — END JOINTS OVER SUPPORTS			CONTROLLED RANDOM LAYUP CONTINUOUS OVER 3 OR MORE SPANS		
			ℓ/180	ℓ/240	ℓ/360	ℓ/180	ℓ/240	ℓ/360
3 IN. (2⅝ IN. NET THICKNESS)								
10	117	90	65	49	33	99	74	50
11	97	75	49	37	25	74	56	37
12	81	63	38	29	19	57	43	29
13	69	54	30	23	15	45	34	23
14	60	46	24	18	12	36	27	18
15	52	40	20	15	10	30	22	15
16	46	36	16	12	8	24	18	12
17	41	32	14	10	7	20	15	10
18	36	28	12	9	6	17	13	9
1	33	25	10	8	5	15	11	8
20	30	23	9	7	5	13	10	7
4 IN. (3½ IN. NET THICKNESS)								
10	207	160	154	116	77	233	175	117
11	171	132	116	87	58	175	132	88
12	144	111	89	67	45	135	101	68
13	123	95	70	53	35	106	80	53
14	106	82	57	43	29	85	64	43
15	92	71	46	35	23	69	52	35
16	81	63	38	29	19	57	43	29
17	72	56	32	24	16	48	36	24
18	64	50	27	20	14	40	30	20
19	58	45	23	17	12	34	26	17
20	52	40	20	15	10	30	22	15

AMERICAN INSTITUTE OF TIMBER CONSTRUCTION.

DOUGLAS FIR AND WESTERN LARCH

ALLOWABLE UNIFORMLY DISTRIBUTED TOTAL ROOF LOAD IN psf—LIMITED BY

SPAN, ft.	BENDING		DEFLECTION, E= 1,760,000 psi					
	SELECT GRADE f 1,725,[a] psi	COMM. GRADE f 1,380,[a] psi	SIMPLE SPAN— END JOINTS OVER SUPPORTS			CONTROLLED RANDOM LAYUP CONTINUOUS OVER 3 OR MORE SPANS		
			ℓ/180	ℓ/240	ℓ/360	ℓ/180	ℓ/240	ℓ/360
3 IN. (2 5/8 IN. NET THICKNESS)								
10	159	127	95	71	48	143	108	72
11	131	105	71	54	36	108	81	54
12	111	89	55	41	28	83	62	42
13	94	76	43	33	22	65	49	33
14	81	65	35	26	18	53	40	27
15	71	57	28	21	14	43	32	22
16	62	50	24	18	12	35	27	18
17	55	44	20	15	10	30	22	15
18	49	40	17	13	9	25	19	13
19	44	36	14	11	7	21	16	11
20	40	32	12	9	6	18	14	9
4 IN. (3 1/2 IN. NET THICKNESS)								
10	282	226	224	168	112	339	254	170
11	233	187	168	126	84	255	191	128
12	196	157	130	98	65	196	147	98
13	167	134	102	77	51	154	116	77
14	144	115	82	62	41	124	93	62
15	128	101	67	50	34	101	76	51
16	111	89	55	41	28	83	62	42
17	98	78	46	35	23	69	52	35
18	87	70	39	29	20	59	44	30
19	79	63	33	25	17	50	37	25
20	71	57	28	21	14	43	32	22

AMERICAN INSTITUTE OF TIMBER CONSTRUCTION.

SOUTHERN PINE

ALLOWABLE UNIFORMLY DISTRIBUTED TOTAL ROOF IN psf LIMITED BY

SPAN ft.	BENDING		DEFLECTION, E = 1,760,000 psi					
	SELECT GRADE f 1,380,[a] psi	COMM. GRADE f 1,380,[a] psi	SIMPLE SPAN— END JOINTS OVER SUPPORTS			CONTROLLED RANDOM LAYUP CONTINUOUS OVER 3 OR MORE SPANS		
			$\ell/180$	$\ell/240$	$\ell/360$	$\ell/180$	$\ell/240$	$\ell/360$
3 IN. (2⅝ IN. NET THICKNESS)								
10	127	127	95	71	48	143	108	72
11	105	105	71	54	36	108	81	54
12	89	89	55	41	28	83	62	42
13	76	76	43	33	22	65	49	33
14	65	65	35	26	18	53	40	27
15	57	57	28	21	14	43	32	22
16	50	50	24	18	12	35	27	18
17	44	44	20	15	10	30	22	15
18	40	40	17	13	9	25	19	13
19	36	36	14	11	7	21	16	11
20	32	32	12	9	6	18	14	9
4 IN. (3½ IN. NET THICKNESS)								
10	226	226	224	168	112	339	254	170
11	187	187	168	126	84	255	191	128
12	157	157	130	98	65	196	147	98
13	134	134	102	77	51	154	116	77
14	115	115	82	62	41	124	93	62
15	101	101	67	50	34	101	76	51
16	89	89	55	41	28	83	62	42
17	78	78	46	35	23	69	52	35
18	70	70	39	29	20	59	44	30
19	63	63	33	25	17	50	37	25
20	57	57	28	21	14	43	32	22

AMERICAN INSTITUTE OF TIMBER CONSTRUCTION.

WEST COAST OR WESTERN HEMLOCK

ALLOWABLE UNIFORMLY DISTRIBUTED TOTAL ROOF LOAD IN psf —LIMITED BY

SPAN ft.	BENDING		DEFLECTION, E=1,540,000 psi					
	SELECT COMM. GRADE $f1,495,^a$ psi	GRADE $f1,150,^a$ psi	SIMPLE SPANS END JOINTS OVER SUPPORTS			CONTROLLED RANDOM LAYUP CONTINUOUS OVER 3 OR MORE SPANS		
			$l/180$	$l/240$	$l/360$	$l/180$	$l/240$	$l/360$
3 IN. (2⅝ IN. NET THICKNESS)								
10	138	106	83	62	42	125	94	63
11	114	88	63	47	32	94	71	47
12	96	74	48	36	24	73	55	37
13	82	63	38	29	19	57	43	29
14	71	54	31	23	16	46	35	23
15	62	47	25	19	13	38	28	19
16	54	42	21	16	11	31	23	16
17	48	37	17	13	9	26	20	13
18	43	33	15	11	8	22	17	11
19	39	30	13	10	7	19	14	10
20	35	27	11	8	6	15	12	8
4 IN. (3½ IN. NET THICKNESS)								
10	245	188	196	147	98	297	223	149
11	202	156	147	111	74	223	167	112
12	170	131	114	85	57	172	129	86
13	145	112	90	67	45	135	102	68
14	125	96	72	54	36	106	81	54
15	109	84	58	44	29	88	66	44
16	96	74	48	36	24	73	55	37
17	85	65	40	30	20	61	46	31
18	76	58	34	26	17	51	39	26
19	68	53	29	22	15	44	33	22
20	62	47	25	19	13	38	28	19

AMERICAN INSTITUTE OF TIMBER CONSTRUCTION.

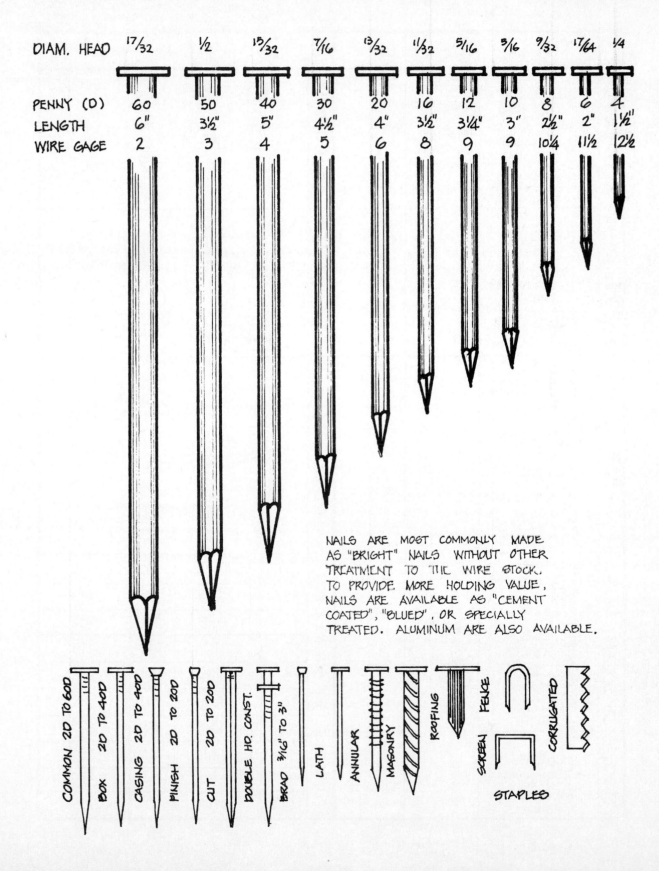

DIAM. HEAD	17/32	1/2	13/32	7/16	13/32	11/32	5/16	3/16	9/32	17/64	1/4
PENNY (D)	60	50	40	30	20	16	12	10	8	6	4
LENGTH	6"	3½"	5"	4½"	4"	3½"	3¼"	3"	2½"	2"	1½"
WIRE GAGE	2	3	4	5	6	8	9	9	10¼	11½	12½

NAILS ARE MOST COMMONLY MADE AS "BRIGHT" NAILS WITHOUT OTHER TREATMENT TO THE WIRE STOCK. TO PROVIDE MORE HOLDING VALUE, NAILS ARE AVAILABLE AS "CEMENT COATED", "BLUED", OR SPECIALLY TREATED. ALUMINUM ARE ALSO AVAILABLE.

COMMON 2D TO 60D
BOX 2D TO 40D
CASING 2D TO 40D
FINISH 2D TO 20D
CUT 2D TO 20D
DOUBLE HD. CONST.
BRAD 3/16" TO 3"
LATH
ANNULAR
MASONRY
ROOFING
SCREEN FENCE
CORRUGATED
STAPLES

	TYPE	LENGTH	GAUGE		
WOOD SCREWS	FLAT HEAD	¼ TO 1½ ⅛ INTERVALS	#0 TO #5	**NUT TYPES**	SQUARE HEXAGON CAP WING
	OVAL HEAD	⅜ TO 3 ¼ INTERVALS	#5 TO #9		
	ROUND HEAD	½ TO 3½ ⅝ TO 5	#9 AND #10 #11 TO #24		
SHEET METAL SCREWS	GIMLET	¼ TO 4	#4 TO #14	**EXPANSION SHIELDS**	MACHINE BOLTS
	BLUNT				
	THREADING				LAGS WOOD SCREW
BOLTS	MACHINE	8" TO 30"	½ TO 1½	**TOGGLE BOLTS**	SPRING WING
	CARRIAGE	8" TO 20"	¾ TO 1		TUMBLE
	FLAT HD. STOVE	3/16 TO 4	⅛ TO ½		RIVET
	RND. HD. STOVE				

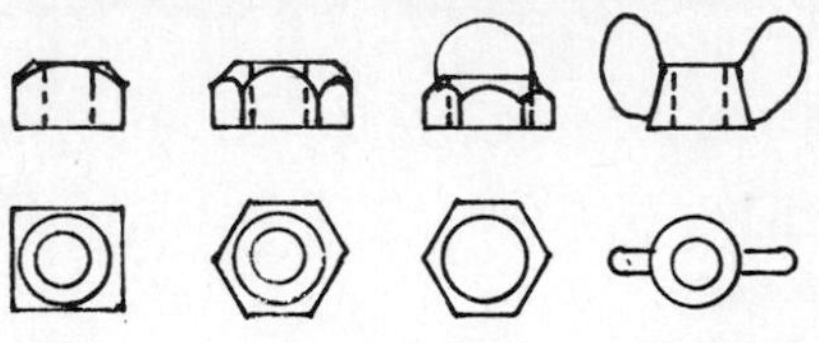

		LENGTH	GAUGE		GA.	DECIMAL	GA.	DECIMAL
LAGS	(lag screw)	1 TO 16 ½ INTERVALS TO 8-1" OVER 8"	¼ TO 1	**B & W GUAGE FOR SCREWS & BOLTS**	#2	.086	5/16"	.313
CAP SCREWS	FILLISTER	¾ X 3 TO 2 X 5			#3	.099	⅜"	.375
	HEXAGON	½ X 3½ TO 2 X 6			#4	.112	7/16"	.438
	BUTTON				#5	.125	½"	.500
					#6	.138	9/16"	.563
SET SCREWS	SQUARE HD.	½ TO 5	¼ TO 1		#8	.164	⅝"	.625
					#10	.190	¾"	.750
	HEADLESS		#4 TO ½		#12	.216	⅞"	.875
					¼"	.250	1"	1.000

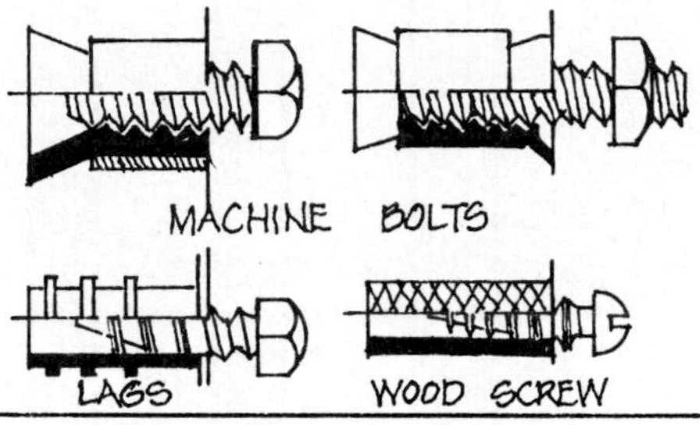

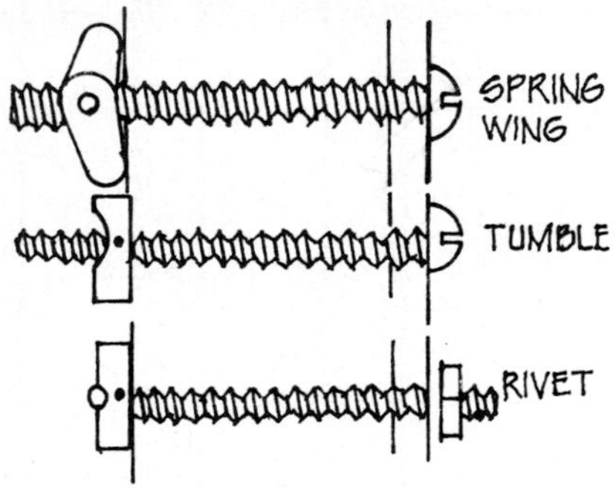

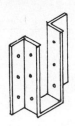 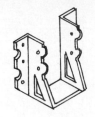 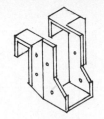 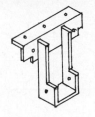

JOIST OR BEAM HANGERS

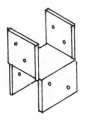 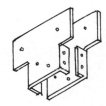 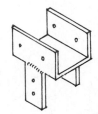 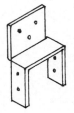 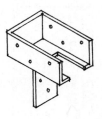

POST OR COLUMN CAPS

  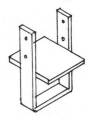 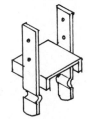 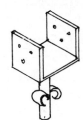

POST OR COLUMN BASES

  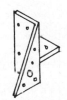  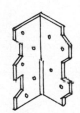 

FRAMING CLIPS

HOLD-DOWN
ANCHOR

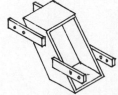 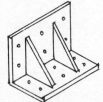   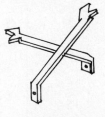

HINGE CONNECTOR   HEAVY   GLU-LAM   SPLIT-RING   BRIDGING
                ANGLE   ANCHOR

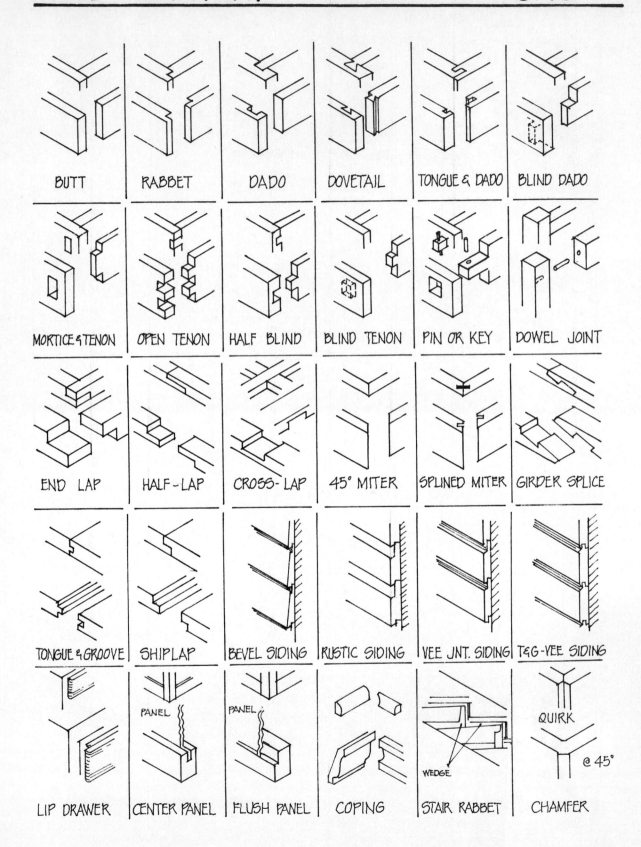

BUTT RABBET DADO DOVETAIL TONGUE & DADO BLIND DADO

MORTICE & TENON OPEN TENON HALF BLIND BLIND TENON PIN OR KEY DOWEL JOINT

END LAP HALF-LAP CROSS-LAP 45° MITER SPLINED MITER GIRDER SPLICE

TONGUE & GROOVE SHIPLAP BEVEL SIDING RUSTIC SIDING VEE JNT. SIDING T&G-VEE SIDING

LIP DRAWER CENTER PANEL FLUSH PANEL COPING STAIR RABBET CHAMFER

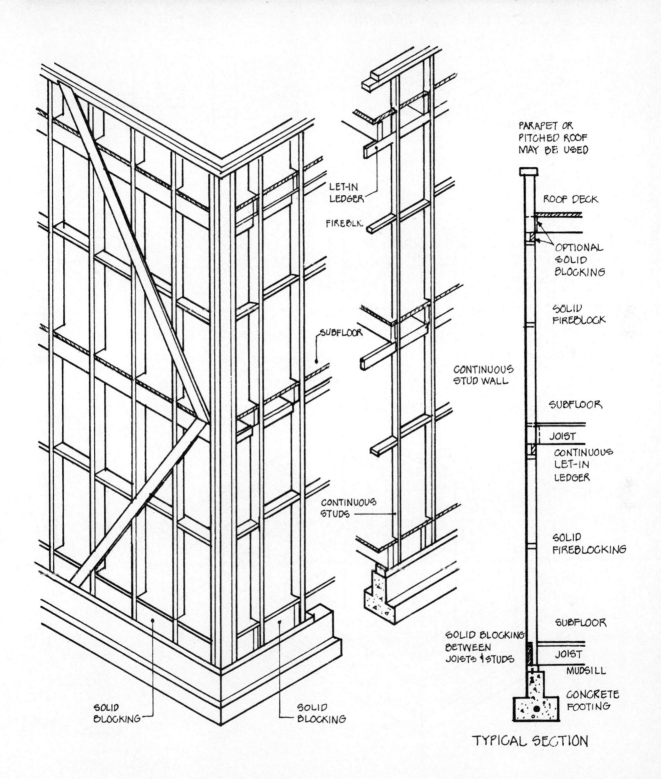

LET-IN LEDGER

FIREBLK.

SUBFLOOR

CONTINUOUS STUD WALL

CONTINUOUS STUDS

SOLID BLOCKING

SOLID BLOCKING

SOLID BLOCKING BETWEEN JOISTS & STUDS

PARAPET OR PITCHED ROOF MAY BE USED

ROOF DECK

OPTIONAL SOLID BLOCKING

SOLID FIREBLOCK

SUBFLOOR

JOIST

CONTINUOUS LET-IN LEDGER

SOLID FIREBLOCKING

SUBFLOOR

JOIST

MUDSILL

CONCRETE FOOTING

TYPICAL SECTION

WESTERN FRAME CONSTRUCTION 6.50

ALSO CALLED "PLATFORM FRAMING"

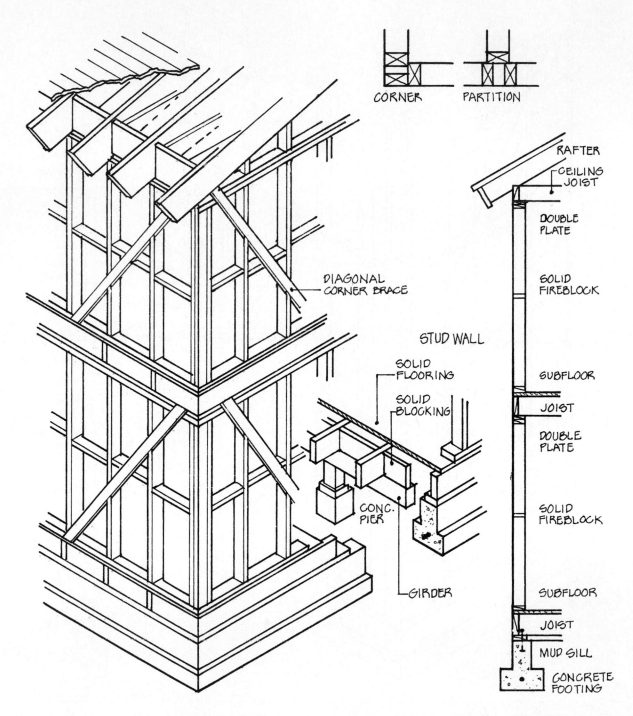

CORNER   PARTITION

DIAGONAL
CORNER BRACE

STUD WALL

SOLID
FLORING

SOLID
BLOCKING

CONC.
PIER

GIRDER

RAFTER

CEILING
JOIST

DOUBLE
PLATE

SOLID
FIREBLOCK

SUBFLOOR

JOIST

DOUBLE
PLATE

SOLID
FIREBLOCK

SUBFLOOR

JOIST

MUD SILL

CONCRETE
FOOTING

TYPICAL SECTION

COLUMN CONNECTIONS

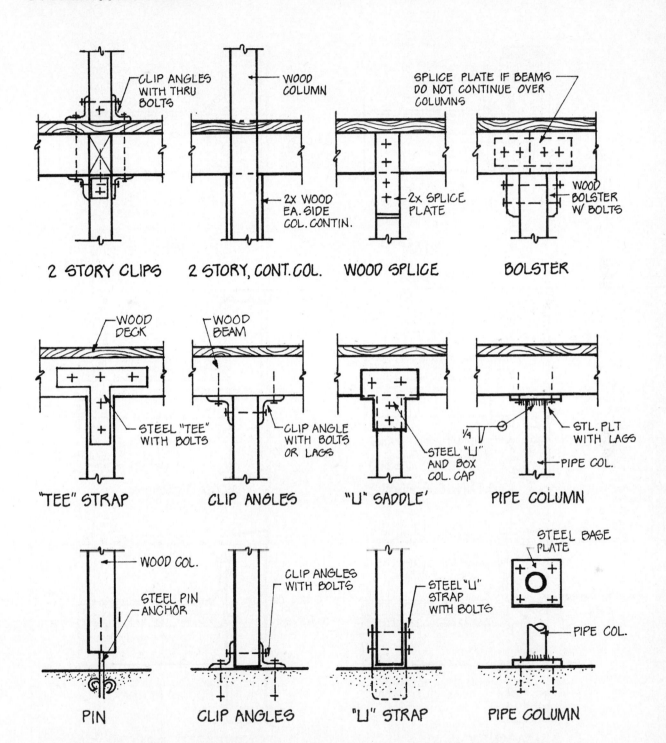

CLIP ANGLES WITH THRU BOLTS

WOOD COLUMN

SPLICE PLATE IF BEAMS DO NOT CONTINUE OVER COLUMNS

2x WOOD EA. SIDE COL. CONTIN.

2x SPLICE PLATE

WOOD BOLSTER W/ BOLTS

2 STORY CLIPS **2 STORY, CONT. COL.** **WOOD SPLICE** **BOLSTER**

WOOD DECK

WOOD BEAM

STEEL "TEE" WITH BOLTS

CLIP ANGLE WITH BOLTS OR LAGS

STEEL "U" AND BOX COL. CAP

¼

STL. PLT WITH LAGS

PIPE COL.

"TEE" STRAP **CLIP ANGLES** **"U" SADDLE'** **PIPE COLUMN**

WOOD COL.

STEEL PIN ANCHOR

CLIP ANGLES WITH BOLTS

STEEL "U" STRAP WITH BOLTS

STEEL BASE PLATE

PIPE COL.

PIN **CLIP ANGLES** **"U" STRAP** **PIPE COLUMN**

CONNECTION COLUMN-TO-BEAM AND BASE MAY BE ANY COMBINATION OF THE ABOVE. THROUGH-BOLTING IS USUALLY STRONGER THAN LAG-BOLTS BUT LARGE BEAMS MAY BE DIFFICULT TO DRILL SATISFACTORILY.

WALL TO BEAM CONNECTIONS

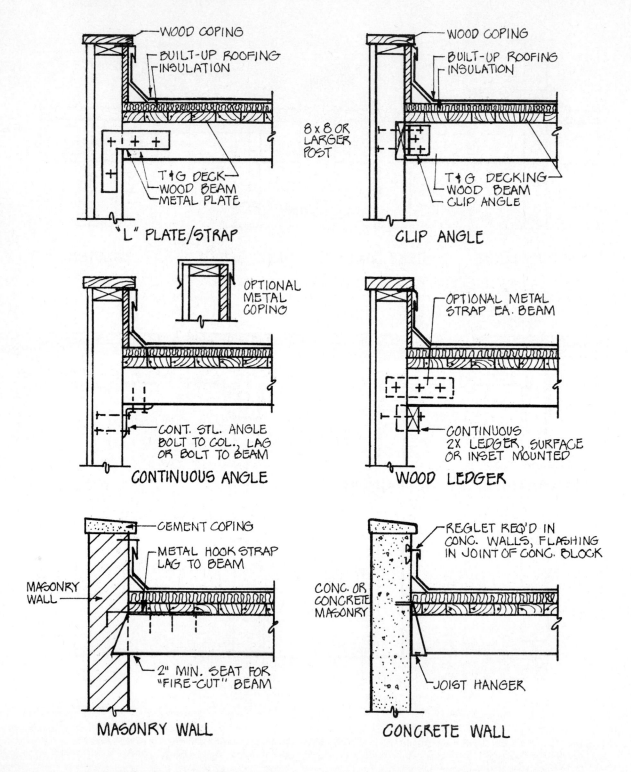

"L" PLATE/STRAP
- WOOD COPING
- BUILT-UP ROOFING
- INSULATION
- T&G DECK
- WOOD BEAM
- METAL PLATE

CLIP ANGLE
- WOOD COPING
- BUILT-UP ROOFING
- INSULATION
- 8 x 8 OR LARGER POST
- T&G DECKING
- WOOD BEAM
- CLIP ANGLE

CONTINUOUS ANGLE
- OPTIONAL METAL COPING
- CONT. STL. ANGLE BOLT TO COL., LAG OR BOLT TO BEAM

WOOD LEDGER
- OPTIONAL METAL STRAP EA. BEAM
- CONTINUOUS 2X LEDGER, SURFACE OR INSET MOUNTED

MASONRY WALL
- CEMENT COPING
- METAL HOOK STRAP LAG TO BEAM
- MASONRY WALL
- 2" MIN. SEAT FOR "FIRE-CUT" BEAM

CONCRETE WALL
- REGLET REQ'D IN CONC. WALLS, FLASHING IN JOINT OF CONC. BLOCK
- CONC. OR CONCRETE MASONRY
- JOIST HANGER

CLIP ANGLES, CONTINUOUS ANGLE, OR LEDGER METHOD MAY BE USED WITH MASONRY OR CONCRETE WALLS.

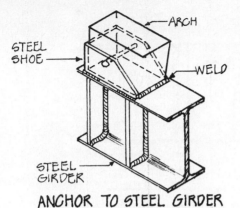

STEEL SHOE — ARCH — WELD — STEEL GIRDER

ANCHOR TO STEEL GIRDER

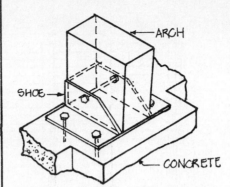

SHOE — ARCH — CONCRETE

ARCH SHOE WITH EXPOSED BOLTS

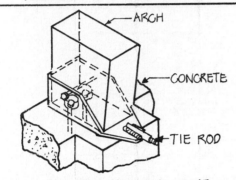

ARCH — CONCRETE — TIE ROD

TIE ROD TO ARCH SHOE

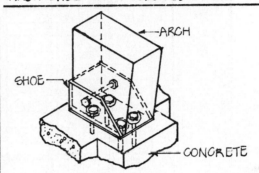

SHOE — ARCH — CONCRETE

ARCH SHOE WITH CONCEALED BOLTS

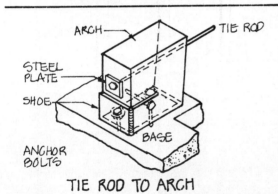

ARCH — TIE ROD — STEEL PLATE — SHOE — BASE — ANCHOR BOLTS

TIE ROD TO ARCH

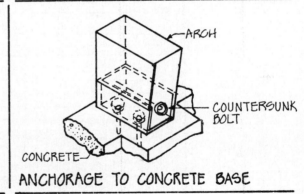

ARCH — COUNTERSUNK BOLT — CONCRETE

ANCHORAGE TO CONCRETE BASE

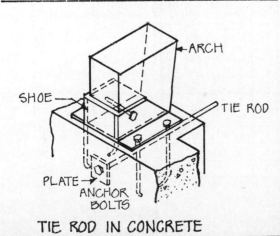

ARCH — SHOE — TIE ROD — PLATE — ANCHOR BOLTS

TIE ROD IN CONCRETE

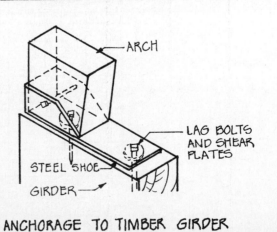

ARCH — LAG BOLTS AND SHEAR PLATES — STEEL SHOE — GIRDER

ANCHORAGE TO TIMBER GIRDER

AMERICAN INSTITUTE OF TIMBER CONSTRUCTION, AITC 104-72

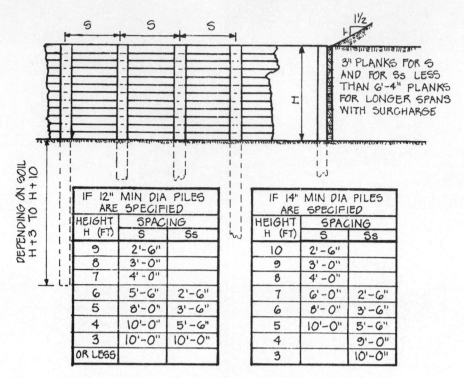

IF 12" MIN DIA PILES ARE SPECIFIED		
HEIGHT H (FT)	SPACING	
	S	Ss
9	2'-6"	
8	3'-0"	
7	4'-0"	
6	5'-6"	2'-6"
5	8'-0"	3'-6"
4	10'-0"	5'-6"
3	10'-0"	10'-0"
OR LESS		

IF 14" MIN DIA PILES ARE SPECIFIED		
HEIGHT H (FT)	SPACING	
	S	Ss
10	2'-6"	
9	3'-0"	
8	4'-0"	
7	6'-0"	2'-6"
6	8'-0"	3'-6"
5	10'-0"	5'-6"
4		9'-0"
3		10'-0"

RAILROAD-TYPE CANTILEVER WALL. NOTE: FOR WALLS WITHOUT SURCHARGE, USE SPACING IN COLUMN S; WITH SURCHARGE USE SPACING IN COLUMN Ss.

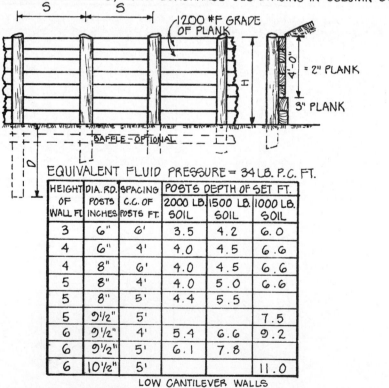

EQUIVALENT FLUID PRESSURE = 34 LB. P.C. FT.

HEIGHT OF WALL FT	DIA. RD. POSTS INCHES	SPACING C.C. OF POSTS FT.	POSTS DEPTH OF SET FT.		
			2000 LB. SOIL	1500 LB. SOIL	1000 LB. SOIL
3	6"	6'	3.5	4.2	6.0
4	6"	4'	4.0	4.5	6.6
4	8"	6'	4.0	4.5	6.6
5	8"	4'	4.0	5.0	6.6
5	8"	5'	4.4	5.5	
5	9½"	5'			7.5
6	9½"	4'	5.4	6.6	9.2
6	9½"	5'	6.1	7.8	
6	10½"	5'			11.0

LOW CANTILEVER WALLS

THERMAL AND MOISTURE PROTECTION   DIVISION 7

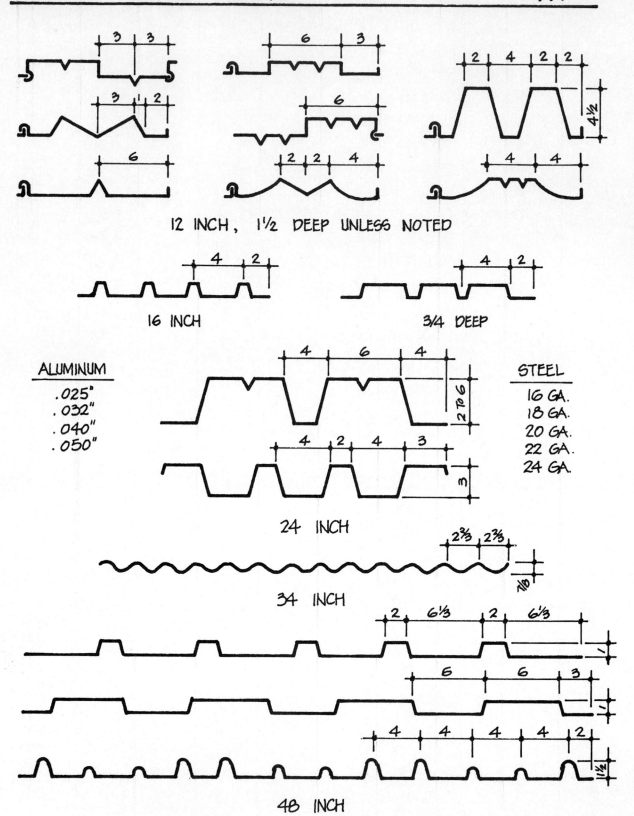

12 INCH, 1½ DEEP UNLESS NOTED

16 INCH   3/4 DEEP

ALUMINUM

.025"
.032"
.040"
.050"

STEEL

16 GA.
18 GA.
20 GA.
22 GA.
24 GA.

24 INCH

34 INCH

48 INCH

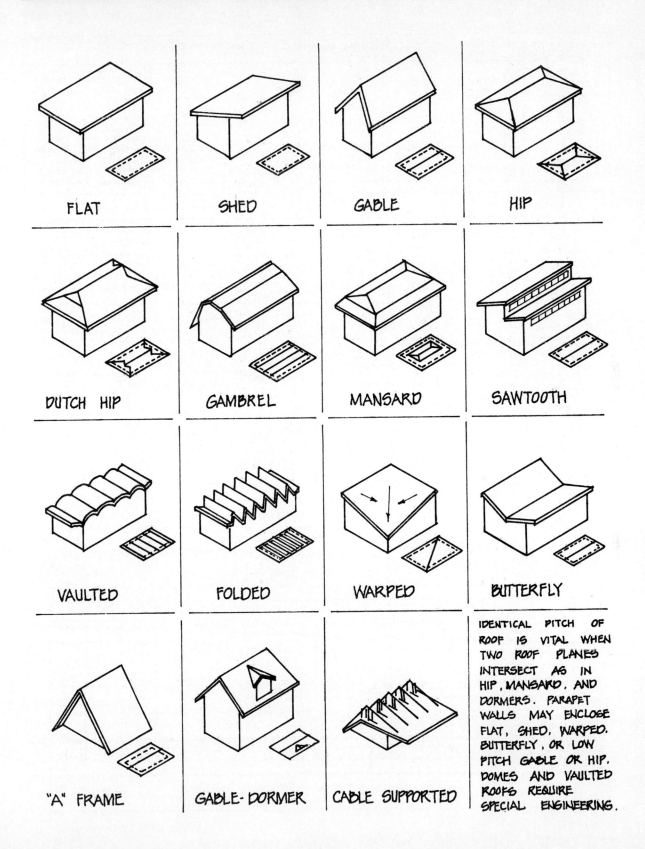

FLAT   SHED   GABLE   HIP

DUTCH HIP   GAMBREL   MANSARD   SAWTOOTH

VAULTED   FOLDED   WARPED   BUTTERFLY

"A" FRAME   GABLE-DORMER   CABLE SUPPORTED

IDENTICAL PITCH OF ROOF IS VITAL WHEN TWO ROOF PLANES INTERSECT AS IN HIP, MANSARD, AND DORMERS. PARAPET WALLS MAY ENCLOSE FLAT, SHED, WARPED, BUTTERFLY, OR LOW PITCH GABLE OR HIP. DOMES AND VAULTED ROOFS REQUIRE SPECIAL ENGINEERING.

GRADE	SIZE	PER SQUARE		DESCRIPTION
		NO.	WEIGHT	
NO. 1 BLUE LABEL	24" (ROYALS) 18" (PERFECTIONS) 16" (XXXXX)	4 BDLS. 4 BDLS. 4 BDLS.	192 LBS. 158 LBS. 144 LBS.	THE PREMIUM GRADE OF SHINGLES FOR ROOF AND SIDEWALLS. THESE SHINGLES ARE 100% HEARTWOOD. 100% CLEAR AND 100% EDGE - GRAIN.
NO. 2 RED LABEL	24" (ROYALS) 18" (PERFECTIONS) 16" (XXXXX)	4 BDLS. 4 BDLS. 4 BDLS.	192 LBS. 158 LBS. 144 LBS.	A GOOD GRADE FOR MOST APPLICATIONS. NOT LESS THAN 10" CLEAR ON 16" SHINGLES. 11" CLEAR ON 18" SHINGLES AND 16" CLEAR ON 24" SHINGLES. FLAT GRAIN AND LIMITED SAPWOOD ARE PERMITTED
NO. 3 BLACK LABEL	24" (ROYALS) 18" (PERFECTIONS) 16" (XXXXX)	4 BDLS 4 BDLS. 4 BDLS.	192 LBS. 158 LBS. 144 LBS.	A UTILITY GRADE FOR ECONOMY APPLICATIONS AND SECONDARY BUILDINGS. GUARANTEED 6" CLEAR ON 16" AND 18" SHINGLES, 10" CLEAR ON 24" SHINGLES.
NO. 4 UNDER COURSING	18" (PERFECTIONS) 16" (XXXXX)	2 BDLS. 2 BDLS.	60 LBS. 60 LBS.	A LOW GRADE FOR UNDERCOURSING ON DOUBLE - COURSED SIDEWALL APPLICATION.
NO. 1 OR NO. 2 REBUTTED- REJOINTED	18" (PERFECTIONS) 16" (XXXXX)	1 CARTON 1 CARTON	60 LBS. 60 LBS.	SAME SPECIFICATIONS AS NO. 1 AND NO. 2 GRADES ABOVE BUT MACHINE TRIMMED FOR EXACTLY PARALLEL EDGES WITH BUTTS SAWN AT PRECISE RIGHT ANGLES. USED FOR SIDEWALL APPLICATION WHERE TIGHTLY FITTING JOINTS BETWEEN SHINGLES ARE DESIRED. ALSO AVAILABLE WITH SMOOTH SANDED FACE.
NO. 1 MACHINE GROOVED	18" (PERFECTIONS) 16" (XXXXX)	1 CARTON 1 CARTON	60 LBS. 60 LBS.	SAME SPECIFICATIONS AS NO. 1 AND NO. 2 GRADES ABOVE. THESE SHINGLES ARE USED AT MAXIMUM WEATHER EXPOSURES AND ARE ALWAYS APPLIED AT THE OUTER COURSE OF DOUBLE - COURSED SIDEWALLS.
NO. 1 OR NO. 2 DIMENSION	24" (ROYALS) 18" (PERFECTIONS) 16" (XXXXX)	4 BDLS 4 BDLS. 4 BDLS.	192 LBS. 158 LBS. 144 LBS.	SAME SPECIFICATIONS AS NO. 1 AND NO. 2 GRADES ABOVE. EXCEPT THEY ARE CUT TO SPECIFIC UNIFORM WIDTHS AND MAY HAVE BUTTS TRIMMED TO SPECIAL SHAPES.

* NEARLY ALL MANUFACTURES PACK 4 BUNDLES TO COVER 100 SQ. FT. WHEN USED FOR MAXIMUM EXPOSURE FOR ROOF CONSTRUCTION; REBUTTED-AND-JOINTED AND MACHINE GROOVED SHINGLES TYPICALLY ARE PACKED ONE CARTON TO COVER 100 SQ. FT. WHEN USED AT MAXIMUM EXPOSURE FOR DOUBLE COURSE SIDEWALL.

LENGTH AND THICKNESS	APPROXIMATE COVERAGE (SQ. FT.) OF FOUR BUNDLES OR ONE CARTON													
	3½"	4"	5"	5½"	6"	7"	7½"	8"	8½"	9"	10"	11"	11½"	12"
RANDOM - WIDTH & DIMENSION 16" X 5/2"	70	80	100	110	120	140	150*	160	170	180	200	220	230	240**
18" X 5/2-1/4"	—	72½	90½	100	109	127	136	145½	154½*	163½	181½	200	209	218
24" X 4/2"	—	—	—	—	80	93	100	106½	113	120	133	140½	153*	160
REBUTTED - AND- REJOINTED 16"	—	—	—	—	50	59	63*	67	72	76	84	93	—	100**
18"	—	—	—	—	43	50	54	57	61*	64	72	79	—	86
MACHINE- GROOVED 16"	(NORMALLY APPLIED AT MAXIMUM EXPOSURE)													100**
18"	(NORMALLY APPLIED AT MAXIMUM EXPOSURE)													

RED CEDAR SHINGLE AND HANDSPLIT SHAKE BUREAU

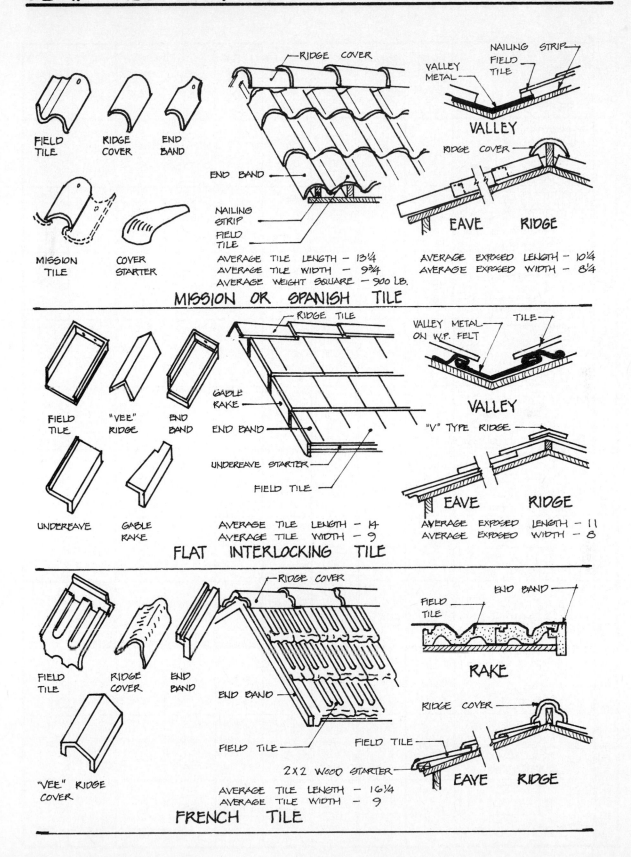

FIELD TILE **RIDGE COVER** **END BAND**

MISSION TILE **COVER STARTER**

RIDGE COVER

END BAND

NAILING STRIP
FIELD TILE

VALLEY METAL
VALLEY

NAILING STRIP
FIELD TILE

RIDGE COVER
EAVE   RIDGE

AVERAGE TILE LENGTH – 13¼
AVERAGE TILE WIDTH – 9¾
AVERAGE WEIGHT SQUARE – 900 LB.

AVERAGE EXPOSED LENGTH – 10¼
AVERAGE EXPOSED WIDTH – 8¼

MISSION OR SPANISH TILE

FIELD TILE **"VEE" RIDGE** **END BAND**

UNDEREAVE **GABLE RAKE**

RIDGE TILE

GABLE RAKE
END BAND
UNDEREAVE STARTER
FIELD TILE

VALLEY METAL ON W.P. FELT
TILE
VALLEY

"V" TYPE RIDGE
EAVE   RIDGE

AVERAGE TILE LENGTH – 14
AVERAGE TILE WIDTH – 9

AVERAGE EXPOSED LENGTH – 11
AVERAGE EXPOSED WIDTH – 8

FLAT INTERLOCKING TILE

FIELD TILE **RIDGE COVER** **END BAND**

"VEE" RIDGE COVER

RIDGE COVER

END BAND
FIELD TILE
FIELD TILE
2 X 2 WOOD STARTER

END BAND
FIELD TILE
RAKE

RIDGE COVER
EAVE   RIDGE

AVERAGE TILE LENGTH – 16¼
AVERAGE TILE WIDTH – 9

FRENCH TILE

TYPE	PRODUCT	SHIP WT. SQ. (LB)	PKG. PER SQ.	LENGTH	WIDTH	UNITS PER SQ.	SIDE LAP	TOP LAP	HEAD LAP	EXPOSURE
ROLL ROOFING	SATURATED FELT	15	1/4	144'	36"		4" TO 6"	2"		34"
		30	1/2	72'	36"		4" TO 6"	2"		34"
	SMOOTH	65	1	36'	36"		6"	2"		34"
		55	1	36'	36"		6"	2"		34"
		45	1	36'	36"		6"	2"		34"
	MINERAL SURFACE	90	1	36'	36"	1.0	6"	2"		34"
		90				1.075	6"	3"		33"
		90				1.15	6"	4"		32"
	PATTERN EDGE	105	1	42'	36"			2"		16"
		105	1	48'	32"			2"		14"
	19" SELVAGE EDGE	110 TO 120	2	36'	36"			19"	2"	17"
STRIP SHINGLE	SQUARE BUTT	235	3	36"	12"	80		7"	2"	5"
	HEXAGONAL BUTT	195	2	36"	11 1/3"	86		2"	2"	5"
INDIVIDUAL	LOCK	145	2	16"	16"	80	2 1/2"			
	STAPLE	145	2	16"	16"	80	2 1/2"			
GIANT INDIVIDUAL	AMERICAN	330	4	16"	12"	226		11"	6"	5"
	DUTCH LAP	165	2	16"	12"	113	3"	2"		10"

U.S. BUREAU OF STANDARDS HAS REPORTED THE
AVERAGE YEARS OF SERVICE FOR ALL TYPES OF
ASPHALT SHINGLES AS INDICATED ABOVE. THE
AVERAGES ARE COMPOSITE FOR ALL TYPES OF
ASPHALT SHINGLES. IT CAN BE SAFELY ASSUMED
THAT HEAVIER WEIGHTS AND MULTIPLE LAYERING
WILL GIVE ADDITIONAL LIFE, WHILE THINNER OR
LIGHTER SHINGLES WILL GIVE A SHORTER LIFE.

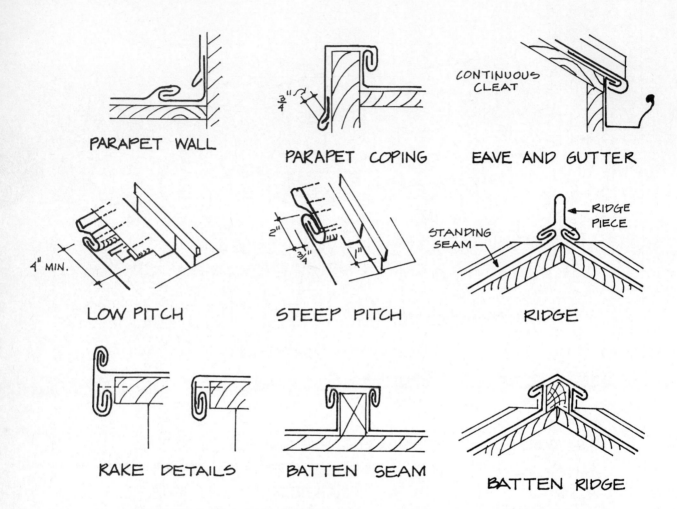

PARAPET WALL   PARAPET COPING   EAVE AND GUTTER

LOW PITCH   STEEP PITCH   RIDGE

RAKE DETAILS   BATTEN SEAM   BATTEN RIDGE

GAUGE AND PAN WIDTHS FOR STANDING SEAM ROOFS

WIDTH OF SHEET	WIDTH OF PAN (INCHES)			RECOMMENDED GAUGES		
	SEAM HT. 7/8 IN.	SEAM HT. 1 IN.	SEAM HT. 1¼ IN.	GALV. STL. GA.	COPPER OZ.	TERNE POUNDS
20	17 ¼	16 ¾	16 ¼	26	16	40
22	19 ¼	18 ¾	18 ¼	26	16	40
24	21 ¼	20 ¾	20 ¼	26	16	40
26	23 ¼	22 ¾	22 ¼	24	20	40
28	25 ¼	24 ¾	24 ¼	24	20	40

SMACNA ARCHITECTURAL MANUAL

GALV. STEEL			COPPER			ALUM.		STAINLESS		ZINC		LEAD	
GA.	THICK.	lb. sq. ft.	OZ	THICK.	lb. sq. ft.	THICK.	lb. sq. ft.	THICK.	lb. sq. ft.	THICK.	lb. sq. ft.	THICK.	lb. sq. ft.
10	.1345	5.78	96	.1250	6.00	.1250	1.76	.1250	5.75			.1250	8.00
11	.1196	5.16	88	.1190	5.50								
12	.1046	4.53	72	.0972	4.50	.1019	1.44	.1094	4.59				
13	.0897	3.91	64	.0897	4.00	.0907	1.28					.0957	6.00
14	.0747	3.28	56	.0735	3.50	.0781	1.10	.0781	3.28	.0700	2.62		
15	.0657	2.97	48	.0647	3.00	.0641	0.91					.0625	4.00
16	.0598	2.66	44	.0593	2.75								
17	.0538	2.40	40	.0539	2.50			.0563	2.37	.0500	1.87		
18	.0478	2.16	36	.0483	2.25	.0469	0.66					.0468	3.00
19	.0418	1.90						.0438	1.84				
20	.0359	1.65	28	.0377	1.75	.0359	0.51	.0375	1.58	.0360	1.35		
21	.0329	1.53	24	.0323	1.50	.0320	0.45			.0320	1.20		
22	.0299	1.41				.0313	0.44	.0313	1.31			.0312	2.00
23	.0269	1.28	20	.0270	1.25								
24	.0239	1.16	18	.0243	1.13			.0250	1.05	.0240	0.90	.0234	1.50
25	.0209	1.03	13	.0202	0.94	.0201	0.28	.0219	0.92	.0200	0.75		
26	.0179	0.91	13	.0175	0.82	.0179	0.25	.0172	0.72	.0186	0.67		
27	.0164	0.84	12	.0162	0.75								
28	.0149	0.78	11	.0148	0.68	.0142	0.20	.0156	0.66	.0140	0.52	.0156	1.00
29	.0135	0.72	10	.0135	0.63								
30	.0120	0.66	9	.0121	0.56	.0100	0.14	.0125	0.53	.0120	0.45	.0117	0.75

SEMICIRCULAR GUTTERS

GUTTER DIAM IN INCHES	MAXIMUM SQUARE FOOT PROJECTED ROOF AREA			
	1/16 IN. SLOPE	1/8 IN. SLOPE	1/4 IN. SLOPE	1 IN. SLOPE
3	170	240	340	480
4	360	510	720	1,020
5	625	280	1250	1,770
6	960	1360	1920	2,770
7	1380	1950	2760	3,900
8	1990	2800	3980	5,600
9	2835	4200	5840	8,400
10	3600	5100	7200	10,000

DEPTH OF GUTTER SHOULD BE APPROXIMATELY 2/3 THE WIDTH. SQUARE GUTTERS SHOULD BE SIZED AS THOUGH SEMICIRCULAR.

DOWNSPOUTS AND HORIZONTAL DRAINS

NOMINAL SIZE (IN.)	DOWNSPOUTS MAX. ROOF AREA (SQ. FT.)	HORIZONTAL STORM DRAINS MAX ROOF AREA		
		1/8 IN. SLOPE	1/4 IN. SLOPE	1/2 IN. SLOPE
2	720			
2½	1,300			
3	2,200	822	1,160	1,644
4	4,600	1,880	2,650	3,760
5	8,650	3,340	4,720	6,680
6	13,500	5,350	7,550	10,700
8	29,000	11,500	16,300	23,000
10		20,700	29,200	41,400
12		33,300	47,000	66,600
15		59,500	84,000	119,000

DOWNSPOUT SIZES ARE FOR ROUND SECTION. IF SQUARE OR RECTANGULAR SHAPE IS USED DOWNSPOUT SHOULD BE SIZE OF INSCRIBED CIRCLE.

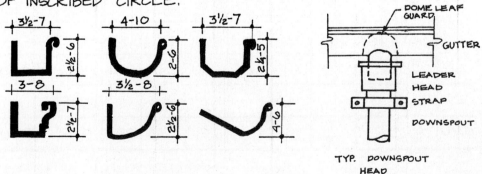

TYP. DOWNSPOUT HEAD

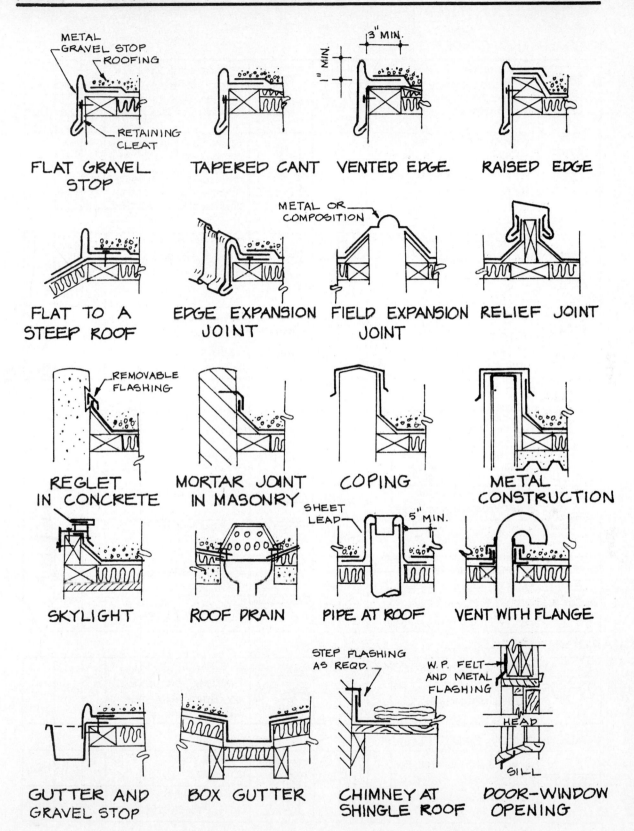

FLAT GRAVEL STOP   TAPERED CANT   VENTED EDGE   RAISED EDGE

FLAT TO A STEEP ROOF   EDGE EXPANSION JOINT   FIELD EXPANSION JOINT   RELIEF JOINT

REGLET IN CONCRETE   MORTAR JOINT IN MASONRY   COPING   METAL CONSTRUCTION

SKYLIGHT   ROOF DRAIN   PIPE AT ROOF   VENT WITH FLANGE

GUTTER AND GRAVEL STOP   BOX GUTTER   CHIMNEY AT SHINGLE ROOF   DOOR-WINDOW OPENING

BEAMS AND GIRDERS

	Description	Thk	Rating	Agency		Description	Thk	Rating	Agency
	VERMICULITE TYPE MK DIRECT TO STEEL COMPACT BM, STRESSED TO 24,000 PSI	½"	4 HR	UL		VERMICULITE TYPE MK DIRECT TO STEEL COMP. BM, SHEAR CONNECTORS WELDED TO BM.	¾"	2 HR	UL
		½"	3 HR	UL			¾"	3 HR	UL
		½"	2 HR	UL					
	VERMICULITE PLASTER ON 3.4 METAL LATH, SUPPORTED ON WIRE OR METAL HANGERS	⅞"	4 HR	UL		VERMICULITE PLASTER ON METAL LATH, 2½" AIR SPACE	1"	4 HR	UL
						VERMIC. PLAST. PLUS ½" VERMIC. ACOUST. PLAST. ON METAL LATH, 2½" AIR SPACE	⅝"	4 HR	UL

COLUMNS

	Description	Thk	Rating	Agency		Description	Thk	Rating	Agency
	VERMICULITE TYPE MK. DIRECT TO STEEL FOLLOWING CONTOUR	1½"	4 HR	UL		VERMICULITE TYPE MK DIRECT TO STEEL, ⅞" RIGID NONCOMBUSTABLE PANELS ONE SIDE COL.	1½"	4 HR	UL
		1⅞"	3 HR	UL			1⅛"	3 HR	UL
		1½"	2 HR	UL			¾"	2 HR	UL
	VERMICULITE PLASTER ON SELF-FURRING METAL LATH WRAPPED ON COL.	1¾"	4 HR	UL		PLASTER OVER TWO LAYERS, ½" GYP. BD. AND STUCCO MSH.	1½"	4 HR	NBS
							1"	3 HR	
		1⅜"	3 HR	UL		PLASTER OVER ONE LAYER ⅜" PERF GYP. LATH.	1"	2 HR	

FLOORS

	Description	Thk	Rating	Agency		Description	Thk	Rating	Agency
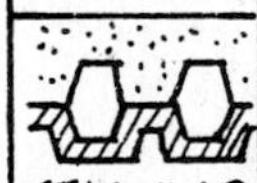 3" DEEP	2½" REG. CONC. FILL, ⅝" PLAST. UNDER CELLS, ¾" BETWEEN CELLS.		3 HR	UL	3" DEEP 	2½" REG. CONC. FILL, ¹³⁄₁₆" FIREP'FG. SIDES AND TOP FLUTED SECTION.		3 HR	UL
CELLULAR	2½ REG. CONC. FILL, ⅜" PLAST. UNDER CELLS, ½" BETWEEN CELLS.		2 HR	UL		2½" REG. CONC. FILL, FIREPFG. CELLS AND FLAT PLATES.	⅜"	2 HR	UL
1½" DEEP 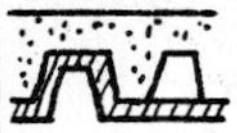	2½" REG. CONC. FILL, FIREP'FG. FOLLOW CONTOUR	⅞"	3 HR	UL	1½" DEEP 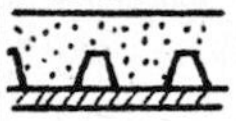	2½" REG. CONC. FILL	¾"	3 HR	UL
	2½" REG. CONC. FILL FIREPFG. FOLLOW CONTOUR	⅜"	2 HR	UL	CELLULAR	2½" REG. CONC. FILL	⅜"	2 HR	UL
	3¼" REG. CONC. FILL FLUTES FILLED WITH FIREP'FG. PLUS ½" BELOW.		4 HR	UL	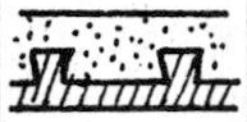	2½" REG. CONC. FILL FIREP'FG. FILL ALL GROOVES SOLIDLY PLUS COVER BELOW.	¾"	3 HR	UL

ROOF DECKS

	Description	Thk	Rating	Agency		Description	Thk	Rating	Agency
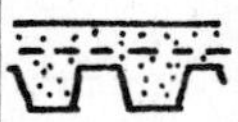	2½" VERMICULITE CONC. FILL, WIRE MESH OVER STEEL DECKING.		2 HR	UL		2" VERMICULITE FILL, TYPE MK OR VERMIC. ACOUSTIC PLASTER FIREPROOFING.	⅞"	2 HR	UL

WALLS AND PARTITIONS

	Description	Rating	Agency		Description	Thk	Rating	Agency
	LT. WT. 8x8x16 CONC. BLK. CORE FILLED SOLID, REG. OR VERMIC. CONC.	4 HR	UL		VERMIC. PLAST, ½" GYP. BD. NO STUDS, 2½" THICK	1"	2 HR	NBS
					VERMIC. PLAST, METAL LATH, STL. STUDS, 2½" THK		2 HR	NBS

VERMICULITE INSTITUTE

FLAME-SPREAD INFORMATION   7.12

THE FIRE-RETARDANCE OF BUILDING MATERIALS IS JUDGED BY FLAME-SPREAD RATINGS.
THIS RATE IS DETERMINED IN ACCORDANCE WITH TEST PROCEDURES **ASTM** E84,
UL 723, AND **NFPA** 255 TUNNEL TESTS IN WHICH THE MATERIAL IS PLACED IN A
25-FOOT-LONG TUNNEL AND A 4-FOOT GAS FLAME AT ONE END. FLAME SPREAD
IS THE DISTANCE/TIME RELATIONSHIP WITH THE PERFORMANCE OF CEMENT AS-
BESTOS BOARD AS ZERO AND RED OAK WOOD AT 100. TEST PERIODS VARY FROM
10 MINUTE TO 30 MINUTE DURATION DEPENDING UPON THE USE AS STRUCTURAL
OR FINISH MATERIAL. MATERIALS ARE CLASSIFIED AS INDICATED BELOW.

CLASS I OR A: 0-25 FLAME SPREAD
CLASS II OR B: 26-75 FLAME SPREAD
CLASS III OR C: 76-200 FLAME SPREAD

FLAME SPREAD OF SOME TYPICAL BUILDING MATERIALS IS GIVEN BELOW.

MATERIAL	FLAME SPREAD	MATERIAL	FLAME SPREAD
ACOUSTIC CEILING BRD.	00 - 25	WOOD: YELLOW BIRCH	105 - 110
MINERAL ACOUSTIC PANELS	0 - 25	WESTERN CEDAR	73
VINYL FLOOR COVERING	26 - 75	COTTONWOOD	115
SHEET RUBBER FLR. COVER	26 - 75	CYPRESS	145 - 150
CARPET	0 - 75	DOUGLAS FIR	70 - 100
FIBERGLASS BATT INSUL.	0 - 25	RED GUM	140 - 155
CEMENT-WOOD PANELS	15 - 20	HEMLOCK	60 - 75
LAM. PLASTIC ON UNTREATED PARTICLE BOARD	95 - 105	HARD MAPLE	104
LAM. PLASTIC ON TREATED PARTICLE BOARD	5 - 10	RED OR WHITE OAK	100
VINYL-FACE GYPSUM PANEL	0 - 25	WESTERN WHITE PINE	75
WOOD FACE PLY-VENEER PANEL	76 - 200	PONDEROSA PINE	105 - 230
VINYL WALL COVERING	5 - 25	POPLAR	170 - 185
FIRE-RETARDANT PAINT ON DOUGLAS FIR	0 - 25	REDWOOD	70
ACOUSTIC BOARD	10 - 15	SPRUCE	65 - 100
		WALNUT	130 - 140

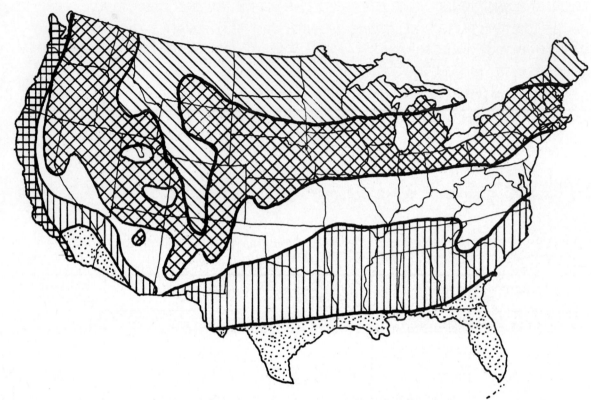

RECOMMENDED "R" VALUES FOR HOMES

	CEILING	WALL	FLOOR		CEILING	WALL	FLOOR
(diagonal hatch)	38	19	22	(vertical lines)	26	19	13
(cross hatch)	33	19	22	(dotted)	26	13	11
(blank)	30	19	19	(grid)	19	11	11

ABOVE RECOMMENDED INSULATION "R" VALUES REQUIRED IN
VARIOUS CLIMATE ZONES TO OPTIMIZE ENERGY UTILIZATION
IN HOMES. "R" VALUES OF VARIOUS MATERIALS OR COMBINATIONS
ARE INDICATED BY MANUFACTURERS OF INSULATING MATERIALS.

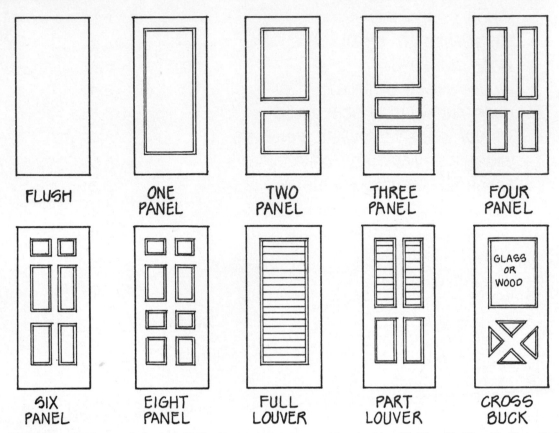

FLUSH · ONE PANEL · TWO PANEL · THREE PANEL · FOUR PANEL

SIX PANEL · EIGHT PANEL · FULL LOUVER · PART LOUVER · CROSS BUCK

GLASS OR WOOD

DOORS COMMONLY AVAILABLE 2'-0" x 6'-8", 2'-4" x 6'-8", 2'-6" x 6'-8", 2'-8" x 6'-8", 3'-0" x 6'-8", 3'-0" x 7'-0". STILES = 5½"; TOP RAIL = 5½"; BOTTOM RAIL = 9¾"; LOCK RAIL = 8"; MULLION = 5⅜", OTHER RAILS = 5⅜". INTERIOR DOORS USUALLY 1⅜" THICK; EXTERIOR DOORS 1¾" THICK.

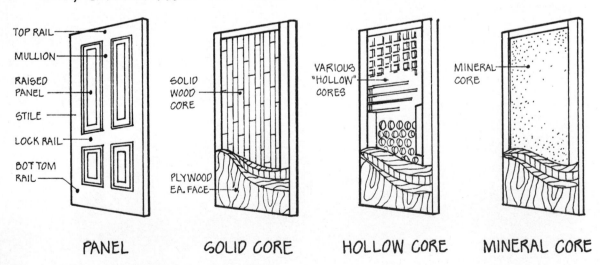

TOP RAIL — MULLION — RAISED PANEL — STILE — LOCK RAIL — BOTTOM RAIL

SOLID WOOD CORE — PLYWOOD EA. FACE

VARIOUS "HOLLOW" CORES

MINERAL CORE

PANEL · SOLID CORE · HOLLOW CORE · MINERAL CORE

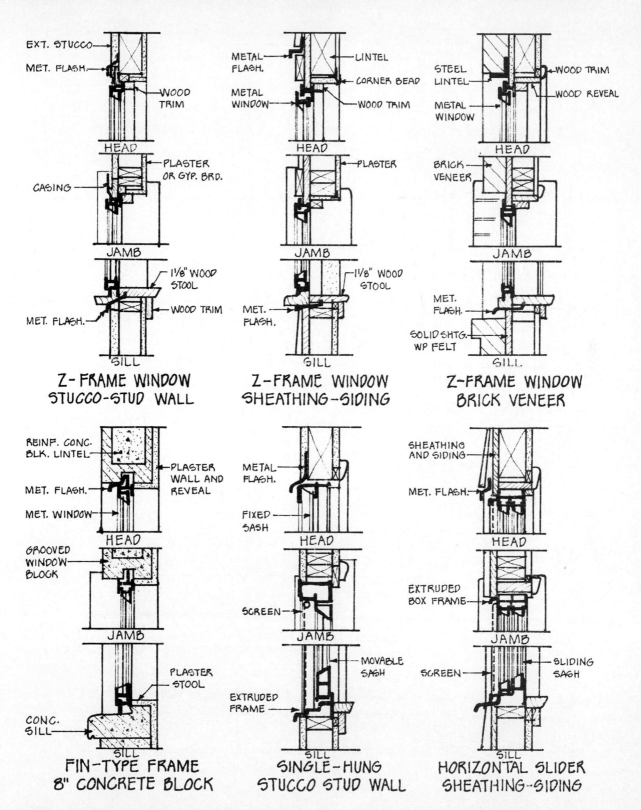

Z-FRAME WINDOW STUCCO-STUD WALL

EXT. STUCCO
MET. FLASH.
WOOD TRIM
HEAD
CASING
PLASTER OR GYP. BRD.
JAMB
1⅛" WOOD STOOL
WOOD TRIM
MET. FLASH.
SILL

Z-FRAME WINDOW SHEATHING-SIDING

METAL FLASH.
METAL WINDOW
LINTEL
CORNER BEAD
WOOD TRIM
HEAD
PLASTER
JAMB
1⅛" WOOD STOOL
MET. FLASH.
SILL

Z-FRAME WINDOW BRICK VENEER

STEEL LINTEL
METAL WINDOW
WOOD TRIM
WOOD REVEAL
HEAD
BRICK VENEER
JAMB
MET. FLASH.
SOLID SHTG. WP FELT
SILL

FIN-TYPE FRAME 8" CONCRETE BLOCK

REINF. CONC. BLK. LINTEL
MET. FLASH.
MET. WINDOW
PLASTER WALL AND REVEAL
HEAD
GROOVED WINDOW BLOCK
JAMB
PLASTER STOOL
CONC. SILL
SILL

SINGLE-HUNG STUCCO STUD WALL

METAL FLASH.
FIXED SASH
HEAD
SCREEN
JAMB
MOVABLE SASH
EXTRUDED FRAME
SILL

HORIZONTAL SLIDER SHEATHING-SIDING

SHEATHING AND SIDING
MET. FLASH.
HEAD
EXTRUDED BOX FRAME
JAMB
SCREEN
SLIDING SASH
SILL

METAL WINDOW SECTIONS VARY WITH MANUFACTURER. Z-SECTIONS MOSTLY USED FOR STEEL WHILE EXTRUDED BOX SECTIONS USED FOR ALUMINUM.

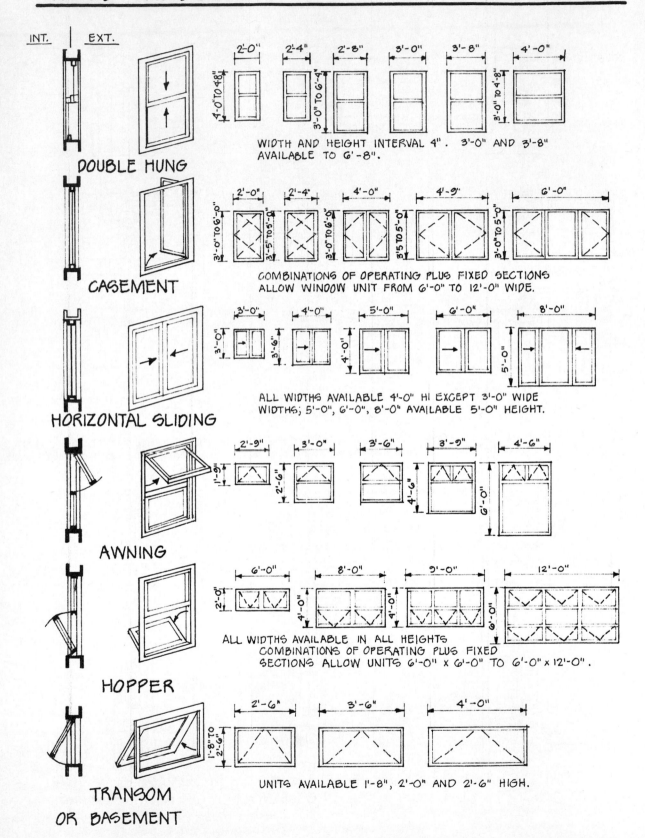

INT. | EXT.

DOUBLE HUNG

WIDTH AND HEIGHT INTERVAL 4". 3'-0" AND 3'-8"
AVAILABLE TO 6'-8".

CASEMENT

COMBINATIONS OF OPERATING PLUS FIXED SECTIONS
ALLOW WINDOW UNIT FROM 6'-0" TO 12'-0" WIDE.

HORIZONTAL SLIDING

ALL WIDTHS AVAILABLE 4'-0" HI EXCEPT 3'-0" WIDE
WIDTHS; 5'-0", 6'-0", 8'-0" AVAILABLE 5'-0" HEIGHT.

AWNING

HOPPER

ALL WIDTHS AVAILABLE IN ALL HEIGHTS
COMBINATIONS OF OPERATING PLUS FIXED
SECTIONS ALLOW UNITS 6'-0" x 6'-0" TO 6'-0" x 12'-0".

TRANSOM
OR BASEMENT

UNITS AVAILABLE 1'-8", 2'-0" AND 2'-6" HIGH.

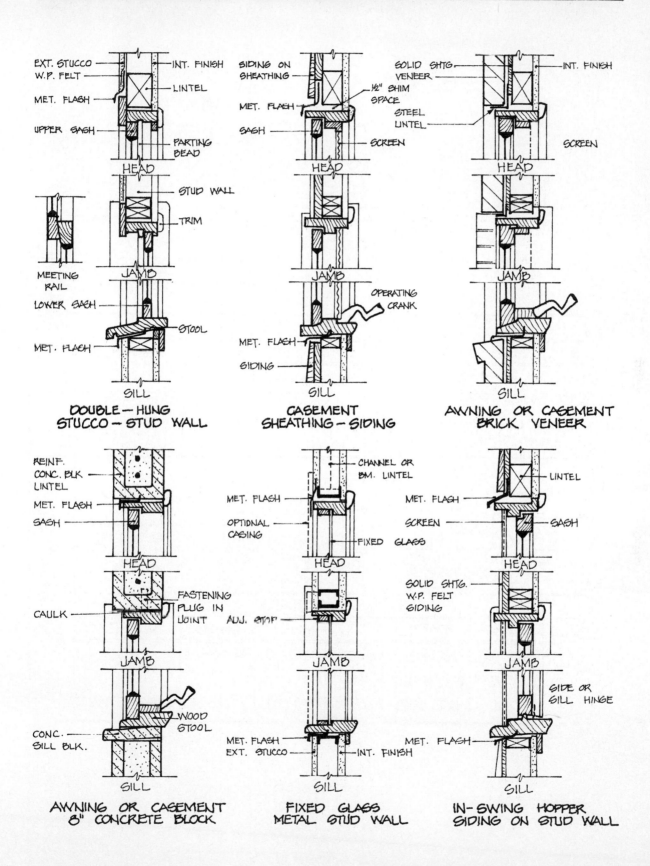

EXT. STUCCO
W.P. FELT
MET. FLASH
UPPER SASH
INT. FINISH
LINTEL
PARTING BEAD
HEAD

MEETING RAIL
LOWER SASH
MET. FLASH
STUD WALL
TRIM
JAMB
STOOL
SILL

**DOUBLE-HUNG
STUCCO-STUD WALL**

SIDING ON SHEATHING
MET. FLASH
SASH
½" SHIM SPACE
STEEL LINTEL
SCREEN
HEAD

JAMB

OPERATING CRANK
MET. FLASH
SIDING
SILL

**CASEMENT
SHEATHING-SIDING**

SOLID SHTG.
VENEER
INT. FINISH
SCREEN
HEAD

JAMB

SILL

**AWNING OR CASEMENT
BRICK VENEER**

REINF. CONC. BLK LINTEL
MET. FLASH
SASH
HEAD

CAULK
FASTENING PLUG IN JOINT
JAMB

CONC. SILL BLK.
WOOD STOOL
SILL

**AWNING OR CASEMENT
8" CONCRETE BLOCK**

CHANNEL OR BM. LINTEL
MET. FLASH
OPTIONAL CASING
FIXED GLASS
HEAD

ADJ. STOP
JAMB

MET. FLASH
EXT. STUCCO
INT. FINISH
SILL

**FIXED GLASS
METAL STUD WALL**

LINTEL
MET. FLASH
SCREEN
SASH
HEAD

SOLID SHTG.
W.P. FELT
SIDING
JAMB

SIDE OR SILL HINGE
MET. FLASH
SILL

**IN-SWING HOPPER
SIDING ON STUD WALL**

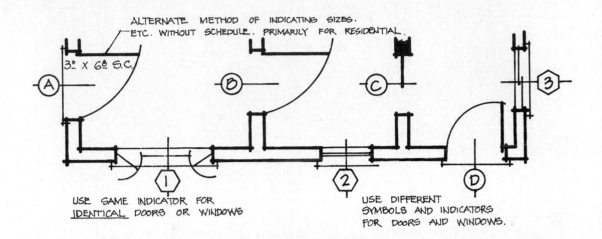

ALTERNATE METHOD OF INDICATING SIZES.
ETC. WITHOUT SCHEDULE. PRIMARILY FOR RESIDENTIAL.

3° X 6° S.C.

(A) (B) (C) (3)

(1) (2) (D)

USE SAME INDICATOR FOR
IDENTICAL DOORS OR WINDOWS

USE DIFFERENT
SYMBOLS AND INDICATORS
FOR DOORS AND WINDOWS.

DOOR SCHEDULE

SYM.	SIZE	TYPE	MATL.	MFGR.	HWDR.	REMARKS
A	3° x 6° x 1¾	SOLID CORE	MAHOG.	GENERAL	A	STAIN AND LACQUER
B	2° x 6° x 1⅜	HOLLOW CORE	BIRCH	RODDIS	C	ENAMEL
C	2⁶ x 6° x 1⅜	POCKET	BIRCH	RODDIS	MFGR.	ENAMEL
D	2° x 6° x 1¾	GLASS PAN.	DOUG. FIR	SUPERIOR	B	DSB GLASS PAN.

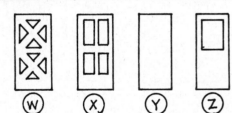

(W) (X) (Y) (Z)

ELEVATION APPEARANCE OF DOORS
(AND WINDOWS) IS OFTEN SHOWN
WITH THE SCHEDULES IF DIFFICULT
TO DESCRIBE. MULTIPLE INDICATORS
(M) (N) MAY ALSO BE USED IF **TYPE**
IS THE SAME. BUT SIZES DIFFERENT.

WINDOW SCHEDULE

SYM.	SIZE	TYPE	MATL.	MFGR.	GLASS	REMARKS
1	5" x 4°	CASEMENT	WOOD	ANDERSON	¼ BRONZE	
2	2⁶ x 4°	DBL. HUNG	WOOD	ANDERSON	D.S. "B"	
3	2" x 1"	HORIZ. SLIDE	ALUM.	REYNOLDS	⅛" OBSCURE	ANODIZE BRONZE

SYMBOL	GENERAL DESCRIPTION	METAL FINISH APPLIED TO	RESTRICTIONS
USP	PRIMED FOR PAINTING	IRON AND STEEL	
US1B	BRIGHT JAPAN (BLACK)	IRON AND STEEL	
US1D	DEAD BLACK	IRON, STEEL, BRASS	
US2C	CADMIUM PLATED	IRON AND STEEL	
US2G	ZINC COATED	IRON AND STEEL	
US2H	HOT-DIP ZINC COATED	IRON AND STEEL	
US3	BRIGHT BRASS	IRON, STEEL, WROUGHT BRASS, CAST BRASS	BRIGHT OR POLISHED SURFACES
US4	DULL BRASS	IRON, STEEL, WROUGHT BRASS, CAST BRASS	
US5	DULL BRASS, OXIDIZED AND RELIEVED	IRON, STEEL, WROUGHT BRASS, CAST BRASS	LIMITED TO ORNAMENTAL DESIGNS, PLAIN HARDWARE TO MATCH US4
US9	BRIGHT BRONZE	IRON, STEEL, WROUGHT BRONZE, CAST BRONZE	LIMITED TO BRIGHT OR POLISHED SURFACES
US10	DULL BRONZE	IRON, STEEL, WROUGHT BRONZE, CAST BRONZE	
US11	DULL BRONZE, OXIDIZED AND RELIEVED	IRON, STEEL, WROUGHT BRONZE, CAST BRONZE	LIMITED TO ORNAMENTAL DESIGNS, PLAIN HARDWARE TO MATCH US10
US14	NICKEL PLATED	IRON, STEEL, BRASS AND BRONZE	LIMITED TO BRIGHT OR POLISHED SURFACES
US15	NICKEL PLATED, DULL	IRON, STEEL, BRASS AND BRONZE	LIMITED TO PLAIN SURFACES
US19	SANDED, DULL BLACK	IRON, STEEL, BRASS AND BRONZE	
US25	WHITE BRONZE	CAST AND WROUGHT WHITE BRONZE	LIMITED TO WHITE BRONZE COMPOSITIONS AND TO WROUGHT BRONZE KICK PLATES, PUSH PLATES, BUTTS, POLISHED SURFACES.

SYMBOL	GENERAL DESCRIPTION	METAL FINISH APPLIED TO	RESTRICTIONS
US26	CHROMIUM PLATED	NICKEL COATINGS	LIMITED TO BRIGHT OR POLISHED SURFACES
US26D	CHROMIUM PLATED, DULL	NICKEL COATINGS	LIMITED TO PLAIN SURFACES
US27	SATIN ALUMINUM, LACQUER	ALUMINUM	
US28	SATIN ALUMINUM, ANODIZED	ALUMINUM	
US32	STAINLESS STEEL	STAINLESS STEEL	

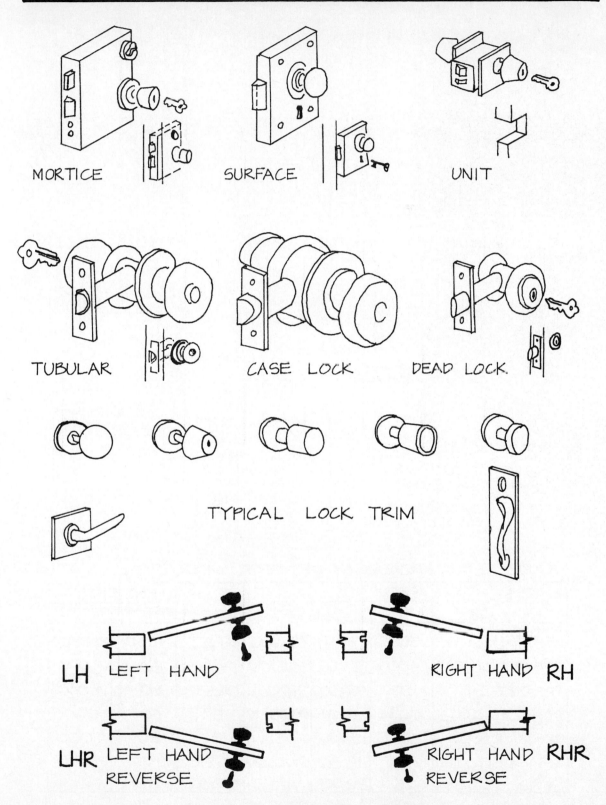

MORTICE   SURFACE   UNIT

TUBULAR   CASE LOCK   DEAD LOCK.

TYPICAL LOCK TRIM

LH   LEFT HAND   RIGHT HAND   RH

LHR   LEFT HAND REVERSE   RIGHT HAND RHR REVERSE

HAND OF DOORS

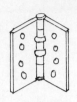
5 KNUCKLE PLAIN

5 KNUCKLE BALL BEARING

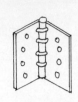
5 KNUCKLE HOSPITAL B-B

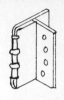
5 KNUCKLE 4 B-B

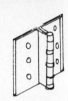
HALF SURFACE HOSPITAL

FULL SURFACE B-B

NORMAL CABINET

NARROW LEAF CABINET

SURFACE CABINET

SPRING HINGE

OFFSET CABINET

CONCEALED

STRAP HINGE

TEE STRAP

B-B TEE HEAVY DUTY

OLIVE KNUCKLE

OVERLAY CABINET

INSET CABINET

CABINET PIVOT

CHECKING FLOOR

PLAIN

BUTTON

BALL
HOSPITAL

STEEPLE
SET SCREW

HINGE PIN TERMINALS

EXPECTED FREQUENCY OF DOOR OPERATION

TYPE BUILDING	FREQUENCY		TYPE BUILDING	FREQUENCY	
	DAILY	YEARLY		DAILY	YEARLY
DEPT. STR. ENT.	5000	1,500,000	SCHOOL TOILET	1250	225,000
OFFICE BLDG. ENT.	4000	1,200,000	SCHOOL CORRIDOR	80	15,000
THEATRE ENT.	1000	450,000	STORE TOILET.	60	13,000
SCHOOL ENT.	1250	225,000	DWELLING ENT.	40	15,000
BANK ENT.	500	150,000	DWELLING TOILET	25	9,000
OFFICE BLDG TOIL.	400	118,000	DWELLING CORR.	10	3,600
OFFICE CORRIDOR	75	22,000	DWELLING CLOSET	6	2,200

TYPE	THICKNESS		MAX. AVAILABLE SIZE		APPOX. WEIGHT		VISIBLE TRANS.	AVE. REFLEC.	SOLAR TRANS.	REL. HEAT GAIN
	INCH.	MM.			lb/sq.ft.	kg/m²	%	%	%	
SHEET SS	.085	2.2	40 x	50	1.22	6	91	8	86	220
DS	.115	2.9	60 x	80	1.64	8	90		86	215
3/16	.182	4.6	84 x	120	2.50	12	90		83	
CLEAR (FLOAT)	1/8	3.2	74 x	120	1.64	8	90		84	215
	3/16	4.8	110 x	120	2.45	12	89		80	209
	1/4	6.4	130 x	204	3.27	16	88		77	200
HEAVY DUTY	3/8	9.5	120 x	240	4.90	24	87		73	195
	1/2	13.0	120 x	300	6.54	32	86		70	190
	3/4	19.0	180 x	300	9.81	48	83		63	180
HEAT ABSORB.	1/8	3.2	74 x	120	1.64	8	83	7	63	179
	3/16	4.8	110 x	120	2.45	12	79		55	161
	1/4	6.4	120 x	192	3.27	16	75		47	155
GRAY	1/4	6.4	120 x	192	3.27	16	42	5	47	150
	3/8	9.5	122 x	264	4.91	24	29		33	130
	1/2	13.0	120 x	300	6.55	32	20	4	24	115
BRONZE	1/4	6.4	124 x	204	3.27	16	51	6	46	168
	3/8	9.5	122 x	264	4.91	24	35	5	31	156
	1/2	13.0	120 x	300	6.55	32	27		22	130

WIND LOAD CHART

CHART APPLIES TO RATIOS OF WIDTH TO LENGTH FROM 2:10 TO 10:10.

CHART ASSUMES GLASS IS SUPPORTED ON ALL FOUR EDGES; DEFLECTION LIMITED TO 1/175 OF SPAN DESIGN LOAD.

MAXIMUM WINDOW GLASS AREAS SHALL BE ADJUSTED FOR RELATIVE RESISTANCE TO WIND LOADS FOR GLASS TYPES AS FOLLOWS.

HEAT STRENGTHENED: 2 TIMES AREA
FULLY TEMPERED: 4 TIMES AREA
LAMINATED: 60% OF AREA SHOWN
WIRE GLASS: 50% OF AREA SHOWN
SEALED INSULATING: 1½ TIMES AREA.

DESIGN WIND PRESSURE VALUES DERIVED FROM FOLLOWING FORMULA:

$V \times 0.00256 \times$ SHAPE FACTOR OF 1.3 $\times$ GUST FACTOR VARYING FROM 1.3 AT 30 FT. TO 1.14 AT 500 FT. $\times$ HEIGHT FACTOR USING SEVENTH-ROOT RULE.

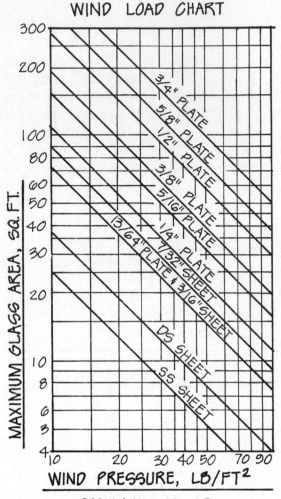

WIND LOAD CHART

DESIGN FACTOR = 2.5

REQUIRED NOMINAL THICKNESS OF REGULAR PLATE SHEET GLASS BASED ON MINIMUM THICKNESS ALLOWED IN FEDERAL SPECIFICATION DD-G-451a.

DESIGN WIND LOADS

| HEIGHT ZONE (FEET) | DESIGN WIND PRESSURE (LBS./SQ. FT.) | | | | (1) (2) |
	AREA 1 (LOW) UNDER 67 MPH	AREA 2 (MED. LOW) 67 TO 80 MPH	AREA 3 (MEDIUM) 80 TO 90 MPH	AREA 4 (MED. HIGH) 90 TO 100 MPH	AREA 5 (HIGH) (3) OVER 100 MPH
UNDER 20	15	20	25	35	45
20 TO 30	20	25	30	40	50
30 TO 50	20	25	35	40	55
50 TO 100	20	30	35	45	60
100 TO 200	20	30	40	50	65
200 TO 300	25	30	40	50	65
300 TO 500 (4)	25	30	40	50	65

U.S. DEPARTMENT OF HOUSING AND URBAN DEVELOPMENT FEDERAL HOUSING ADMINISTRATION

PREFABRICATED STUDS

STUD SIZE	OVERALL PARTITION THICKNESS		STUD SPACING			
			24	19	16	12
INCHES	METAL LATH	GYPSUM LATH	MAXIMUM HEIGHT			
1⅝ – 1⅞	3⅛ – 3⅜	3⅝ – 3⅞	7–0	8–0	9–0	10–0
2	3½	4	8–0	9–0	10–0	14–0
2½	4	4½	9–0	14–0	15–0	18–0
3¼	4¾	5¼	13–0	18–0	21–0	22–0
4	5½	6	16–0	20–0	22–0	25–0
6	7½	8	20–0	24–0	26–0	29–0

GYPSUM LATH IS ⅜ CLIP-ON AND ½ PLASTER, REQUIRING 1 INCH GROUND THICKNESS EACH SIDE.

NAILABLE STUDS

			24	19	16	12
2	3½	3¾	8–0	9–0	10–0	14–0
2½	4	4¼	9–0	14–0	15–0	18–0
3¼	4¾	5	13–0	18–0	20–0	21–0
3⅝	5⅛	5⅜	15–0	19–0	21–0	23–0
4	5½	5¾	16–0	20–0	22–0	24–0
6	7½	7¾	20–0	24–0	26–0	28–0

DIMENSION FOR GYPSUM LATH IS ⅜ WITH ½ PLASTER. WHEN USED IN EXTERIOR CONSTRUCTION, REDUCE HEIGHT 33½% FOR 15 PSF WIND LOAD. IF LIGHTWEIGHT AGGREGATE PLASTER IS USED, REDUCE HEIGHT 15%.

DOUBLE CHANNEL STUDS

SPACE BETWEEN ¾ C STUDS			24	19	16	12
½	3½	4	9–0	12–0	13–0	14–0
¾	3¾	4¼	12–0	14–0	15–0	17–0
1½	4½	5	14–0	16–0	17–0	20–0
2	5	5½	16–0	18–0	20–0	23–0
2½	5½	6	18–0	21–0	23–0	26–0
3¼	6¼	6¾	21–0	24–0	26–0	30–0
4	7	7½	23–0	26–0	29–0	33–0
6	9	9½	29–0	33–0	36–0	41–0

GYPSUM LATH IS ⅜ CLIP-ON AND ½ PLASTER, REQUIRING 1 INCH GROUND THICKNESS EACH SIDE. DOUBLE CHANNEL CONSTRUCTION REQUIRES ¾ CHANNEL HORIZONTAL STIFFENERS AT 4–6 MAX.

FOR PARTITION LENGTH EXCEEDING 1½ TIMES HEIGHT, REDUCE HEIGHT BY 20%. THICKNESS OF PARTITIONS IS INDICATED WITH FLAT LATH AND ¾ PLASTER. WITH ⅜ RIB LATH AND PLASTER, PARTITION IS ½ GREATER THAN SHOWN.

TYPES OF LATH: MAXIMUM SUPPORT SPACING

TYPE OF LATH	MIN. WEIGHT(PSY) GUAGE AND MESH SIZE	VERTICAL WOOD	VERTICAL METAL SOLID PLASTER PART'N.	VERTICAL METAL OTHER	HORIZONTAL WOOD OR CONCRETE	HORIZONTAL METAL
EXPANDED METAL LATH	2.5	16	16	12		
	3.4	16	16	16	16	13½
FLAT RIB EXPANDED METAL LATH	2.75	16	16	16	12	12
	3.4	19	24	19	19	19
3/8 RIB EXPANDED METAL LATH	3.4	24	24	24	24	24
	4.0	24	24	24	24	24
WIRE FABRIC LATH WELDED WOVEN WIRE FABRIC (STUCCO MESH)	1.4 lb. 16 GA. 2x2	16	16	16	16	16
	1.4 lb. 18 GA. 1x1	16				
	1.4 lb. 17 GA. 1½ HEX.	16				
	1.4 lb. 18 GA. 1 HEX.	16				
3/8 GYPSUM LATH PERFORATED		16		16	16	16
3/8 GYPSUM LATH PLAIN		16		16	16	16
LARGE SIZE		16		16	16	16
1/2 GYPSUM LATH PERFORATED		16		16	16	16
1/2 GYPSUM LATH PLAIN		24	NO SUPPORT	24	24	16
LARGE SIZE		24	ERECT. VERT.	24	24	16
5/8 GYPSUM LATH LARGE SIZE		24	NO SUPPORT ERECT. VERT.	24	24	16

METAL LATH AND WIRE FABRIC USED AS REINFORCEMENT FOR EXTERIOR PLASTER SHALL BE FURRED OUT AT LEAST 1/4". SELF-FURRING LATH MEETS REQUIREMENTS. FURRING NOT REQUIRED ON STEEL SUPPORTS WITH FLANGE WIDTH 1" OR LESS. LINE-WIRE OR OTHER BACKING REQUIRED ON OPEN WOOD FRAME CONSTRUCTION EXCEPT UNDER METAL LATH AND PAPER BACKED WIRE FABRIC. 3/8 AND 1/2 GYPSUM LATH INSTALLED WITH SCREWS OR ON NAILABLE METAL STUDS MAY HAVE SPAN INCREASED TO 24".

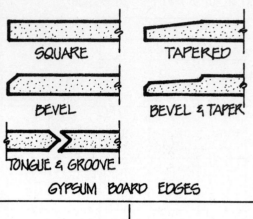

GYPSUM BOARD EDGES

SQUARE TAPERED

BEVEL BEVEL & TAPER

TONGUE & GROOVE

TYPES OF GYPSUM BOARD

REGULAR: ¼, ⅜, ½, ⅝ TAPERED EDGE OR SQUARE
6'-16', SINGLE OR DOUBLE LAYER USE.
FIRE RATED: ½, ⅜, TAPERED OR BEVEL EDGE,
6'-16', SPECIAL FIRE-RESISTANCE CORE.
INSULATION: ⅜, ½, ⅝, ALUMINUM FOIL BACK.
6'-16', RATED INSULATION .25 TO .32
BACKER BOARD: ⅜, ½, ⅝, 2' × 4' SQ. EDGE
2' T&G, 4' T&G, 8' TO 12' BASE LAYER FOR
DOUBLE LAYER INSTALLATION.
MOISTURE RESISTANCE: ½, ⅝, TAPERED EDGE
6' TO 16', NONABSORBENT FOR BATH OR TILE.
VINYL SURFACE: ½, ⅝, SQ. EDGE VINYL FACE

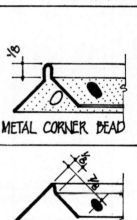

METAL CORNER BEAD

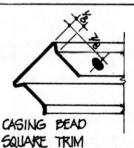

CASING BEAD
SQUARE TRIM

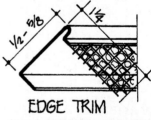

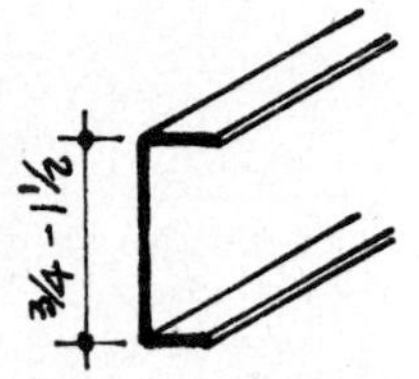

EDGE TRIM

METAL LATH BEAD

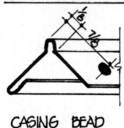

CASING BEAD
ANGLE TRIM

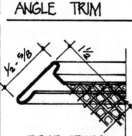

EDGE TRIM

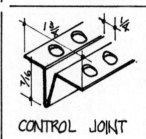

CONTROL JOINT

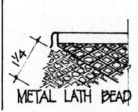

REVEAL TRIM

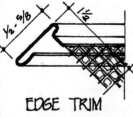

VINYL

FURRING CHANNEL

BULLNOSE TRIM

VINYL

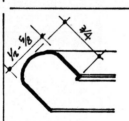
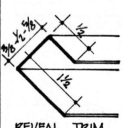
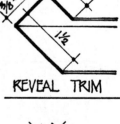

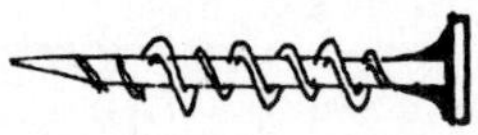

GYPSUM TO STL. FRAME
TYPE S BUGLE HEAD
⅞ TO 2¼

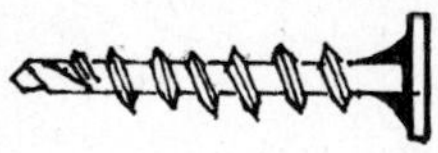

GYPSUM TO 12 GA
TYPE S12 BUGLE HD.
1 TO 1⅞

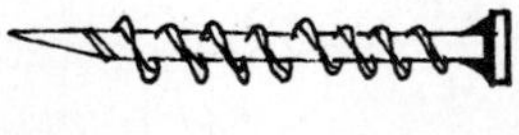

WOOD TRIM TO STEEL
TYPE S TRIM HEAD
1⅝ TO 2¼

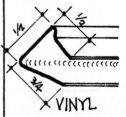
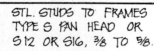

STL. STUDS TO FRAMES
TYPE S PAN HEAD OR
S12 OR S16, ⅜ TO ⅝.

TRIM AND ACCESSORIES
TYPE S18 OVAL HEAD
⅞ TO 1¼.

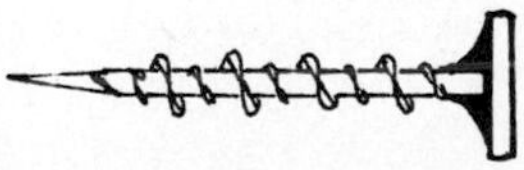

GYPSUM TO WOOD FRAME
TYPE W BUGLE HEAD
1¼.

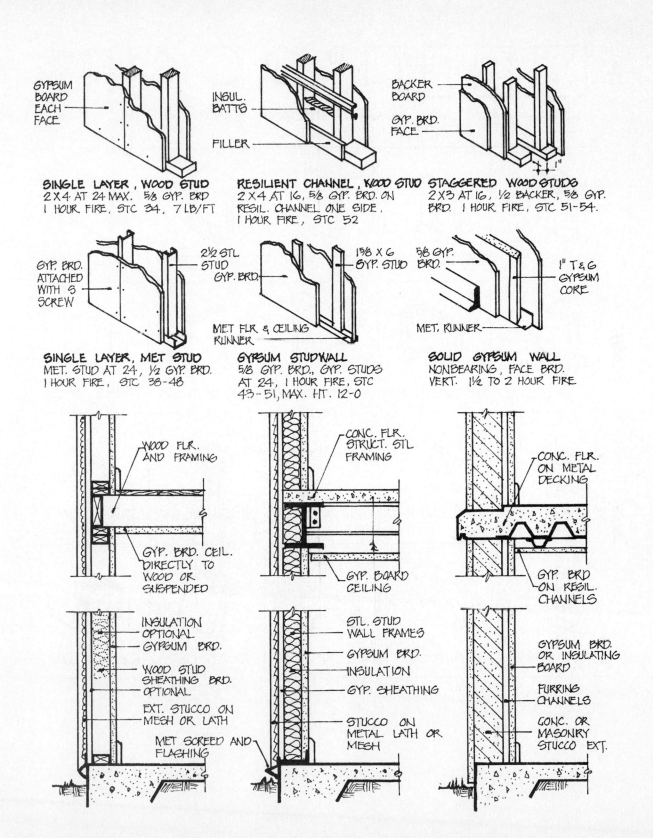

SINGLE LAYER, WOOD STUD
2 X 4 AT 24 MAX. 5/8 GYP. BRD
1 HOUR FIRE, STC 34, 7 LB/FT

GYPSUM BOARD EACH FACE

RESILIENT CHANNEL, WOOD STUD
2 X 4 AT 16, 5/8 GYP. BRD. ON RESIL. CHANNEL ONE SIDE, 1 HOUR FIRE, STC 52

INSUL. BATTS
FILLER

STAGGERED WOOD STUDS
2 X 3 AT 16, 1/2 BACKER, 5/8 GYP. BRD. 1 HOUR FIRE, STC 51-54.

BACKER BOARD
GYP. BRD. FACE
1"

SINGLE LAYER, MET STUD
MET. STUD AT 24, 1/2 GYP. BRD. 1 HOUR FIRE, STC 38-48

GYP. BRD. ATTACHED WITH S SCREW
2 1/2 STL STUD

GYPSUM STUDWALL
5/8 GYP. BRD., GYP. STUDS AT 24, 1 HOUR FIRE, STC 43-51, MAX. HT. 12-0

GYP. BRD.
1 5/8 X 6 GYP. STUD
MET FLR & CEILING RUNNER

SOLID GYPSUM WALL
NONBEARING, FACE BRD. VERT. 1 1/2 TO 2 HOUR FIRE

5/8 GYP. BRD.
1" T & G GYPSUM CORE
MET. RUNNER

WOOD FLR. AND FRAMING
GYP. BRD. CEIL. DIRECTLY TO WOOD OR SUSPENDED

CONC. FLR. STRUCT. STL FRAMING
GYP. BOARD CEILING

CONC. FLR. ON METAL DECKING
GYP. BRD ON RESIL. CHANNELS

INSULATION OPTIONAL
GYPSUM BRD.
WOOD STUD
SHEATHING BRD. OPTIONAL
EXT. STUCCO ON MESH OR LATH
MET SCREED AND FLASHING

STL. STUD WALL FRAMES
GYPSUM BRD.
INSULATION
GYP. SHEATHING
STUCCO ON METAL LATH OR MESH

GYPSUM BRD. OR INSULATING BOARD
FURRING CHANNELS
CONC. OR MASONRY STUCCO EXT.

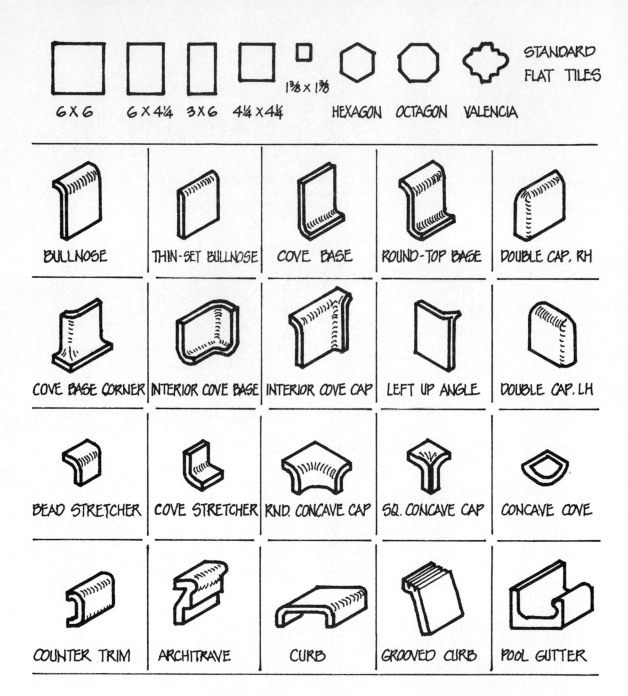

STANDARD FLAT TILES

6 X 6   6 X 4¼   3 X 6   4¼ X 4¼   1⅜ X 1⅜   HEXAGON   OCTAGON   VALENCIA

BULLNOSE	THIN-SET BULLNOSE	COVE BASE	ROUND-TOP BASE	DOUBLE CAP, RH
COVE BASE CORNER	INTERIOR COVE BASE	INTERIOR COVE CAP	LEFT UP ANGLE	DOUBLE CAP, LH
BEAD STRETCHER	COVE STRETCHER	RND. CONCAVE CAP	SQ. CONCAVE CAP	CONCAVE COVE
COUNTER TRIM	ARCHITRAVE	CURB	GROOVED CURB	POOL GUTTER

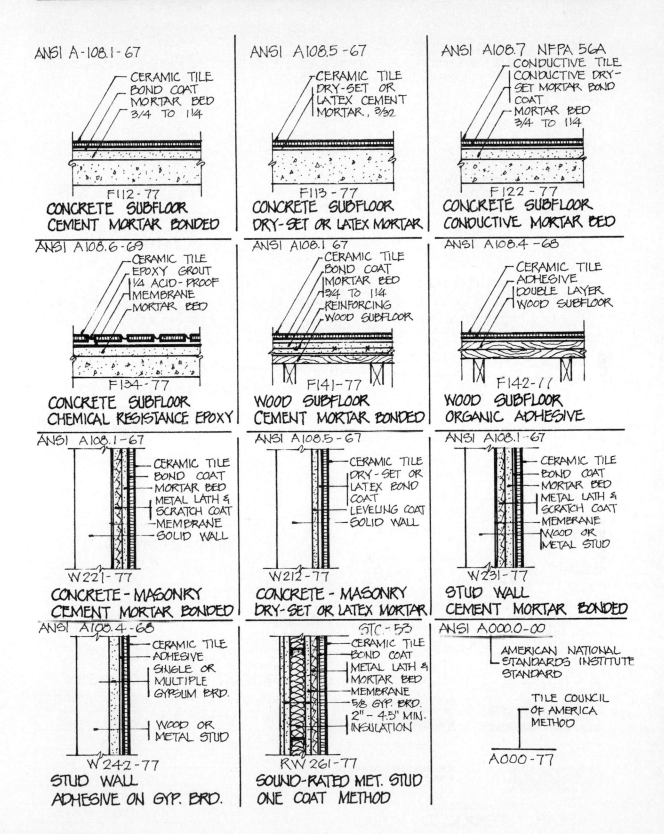

ANSI A-108.1-67
- CERAMIC TILE
- BOND COAT
- MORTAR BED
- 3/4 TO 1¼

F112-77

CONCRETE SUBFLOOR
CEMENT MORTAR BONDED

ANSI A108.5-67
- CERAMIC TILE
- DRY-SET OR LATEX CEMENT MORTAR, 3/32

F113-77

CONCRETE SUBFLOOR
DRY-SET OR LATEX MORTAR

ANSI A108.7 NFPA 56A
- CONDUCTIVE TILE
- CONDUCTIVE DRY-SET MORTAR BOND COAT
- MORTAR BED 3/4 TO 1¼

F122-77

CONCRETE SUBFLOOR
CONDUCTIVE MORTAR BED

ANSI A108.6-69
- CERAMIC TILE
- EPOXY GROUT
- ¼ ACID-PROOF
- MEMBRANE
- MORTAR BED

F134-77

CONCRETE SUBFLOOR
CHEMICAL RESISTANCE EPOXY

ANSI A108.1 67
- CERAMIC TILE
- BOND COAT
- MORTAR BED 3/4 TO 1¼
- REINFORCING
- WOOD SUBFLOOR

F141-77

WOOD SUBFLOOR
CEMENT MORTAR BONDED

ANSI A108.4-68
- CERAMIC TILE
- ADHESIVE
- DOUBLE LAYER WOOD SUBFLOOR

F142-77

WOOD SUBFLOOR
ORGANIC ADHESIVE

ANSI A108.1-67
- CERAMIC TILE
- BOND COAT
- MORTAR BED
- METAL LATH & SCRATCH COAT
- MEMBRANE
- SOLID WALL

W221-77

CONCRETE - MASONRY
CEMENT MORTAR BONDED

ANSI A108.5-67
- CERAMIC TILE
- DRY-SET OR LATEX BOND COAT
- LEVELING COAT
- SOLID WALL

W212-77

CONCRETE - MASONRY
DRY-SET OR LATEX MORTAR

ANSI A108.1-67
- CERAMIC TILE
- BOND COAT
- MORTAR BED
- METAL LATH & SCRATCH COAT
- MEMBRANE
- WOOD OR METAL STUD

W231-77

STUD WALL
CEMENT MORTAR BONDED

ANSI A108.4-68
- CERAMIC TILE
- ADHESIVE
- SINGLE OR MULTIPLE GYPSUM BRD.
- WOOD OR METAL STUD

W242-77

STUD WALL
ADHESIVE ON GYP. BRD.

STC - 53
- CERAMIC TILE
- BOND COAT
- METAL LATH & MORTAR BED
- MEMBRANE
- 5/8 GYP. BRD.
- 2" - 4.5" MIN. INSULATION

RW 261-77

SOUND-RATED MET. STUD
ONE COAT METHOD

ANSI A000.0-00
- AMERICAN NATIONAL STANDARDS INSTITUTE STANDARD
- TILE COUNCIL OF AMERICA METHOD

A000-77

TILE COUNCIL OF AMERICA

TERRAZZO IS A MIX OF CEMENT, SAND AND MARBLE CHIPS, USUALLY CAST IN PLACE AND GROUND WITH ABRASIVES TO SHOW COLORED CHIP SECTIONS AFTER THE PLASTIC MASS HAS SET. COLOR IS USUALLY INTRODUCED INTO THE CEMENT MIXTURE. EPOXY OR POLYESTER RESIN IS USED AS MATRIX FOR "THINSET" INSTALLATION.

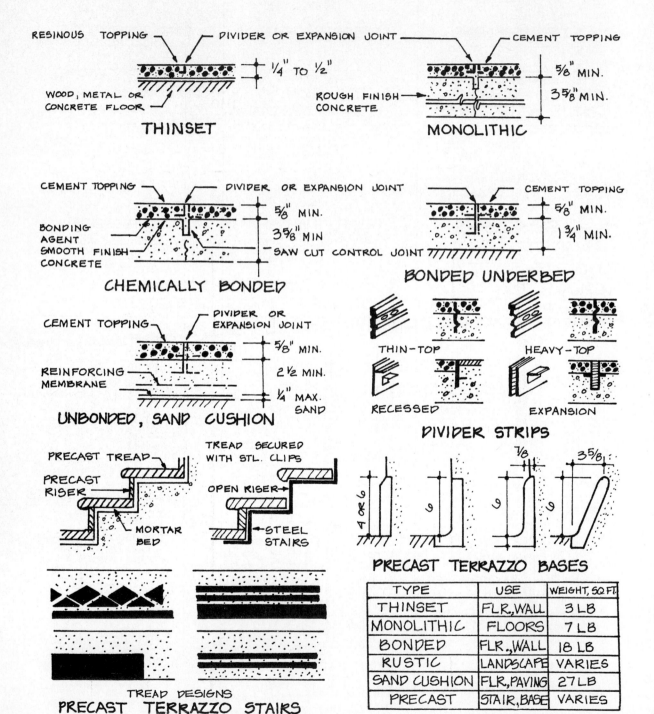

THINSET

MONOLITHIC

CHEMICALLY BONDED

BONDED UNDERBED

UNBONDED, SAND CUSHION

DIVIDER STRIPS

PRECAST TERRAZZO BASES

PRECAST TERRAZZO STAIRS

TREAD DESIGNS

TYPE	USE	WEIGHT, SQ.FT.
THINSET	FLR., WALL	3 LB
MONOLITHIC	FLOORS	7 LB
BONDED	FLR., WALL	18 LB
RUSTIC	LANDSCAPE	VARIES
SAND CUSHION	FLR, PAVING	27 LB
PRECAST	STAIR, BASE	VARIES

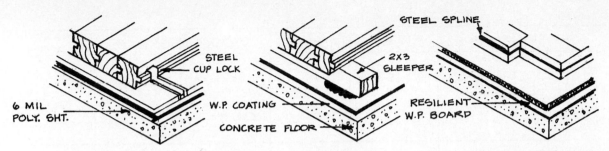

METAL BOUND LOCK   CUSHION   METAL SPLINE

PLANK OR STRIP FLOORING			
TYPE	THICKNESS AND FACE	WOOD	GRADE
METAL BOUND LOCK	33/32 X 2¼ 33/32 x 1¼ 25/32 X 2¼ 25/32 x 1¼	MAPLE, OAK NORTH PINE	2ND BETTER
CUSHION	33/32 X 1 1/32 33/32 x 1 5/16 49/32x1 5/16 25/32 X 2¼ 1½ x 1 1/32	MAPLE, OAK	2ND - 3RD INDUSTRIAL
METAL SPLINE	33/32 X 1 1/32 33/32 x 1 5/16 33/32 x 1 5/8 25/32 X 2¼ 25/32 x 1½	MAPLE	2ND BETTER
STANDARD	.080 X 2¼	HARD MAPLE	2ND BETTER GYM

PITCH "STEMS" AT CORNERS

PITCH OR CLEAR SEALER
HOT PITCH
PRIMING OIL

BEVEL CORNER   RECTANGULAR

INDUSTRIAL BLOCK FLOORING				
TYPE	SIZE	DEPTH	WOOD	TREATMENT
RECTANGULAR	3x6 3x8 4x6 4x8	2 2½ 3 4	YELLOW PINE	CREOSOTE PENTACHLOR.
BEVEL CORNER	3x6 3x8 4x6 4x8	2 2½ 3 3½ 4	YELLOW PINE MT. OAK	CREOSOTE PENTACHLOR.
GROOVED	3x6 3x8 4x6 4x8	2 2½ 3 3½ 4	YELLOW PINE MT. OAK	CREOSOTE PENTACHLOR.

INDUSTRIAL BLOCK FLOORING			
DEPTH	RECOMMENDED USE	LBS. SQ. FT.	CARTONS SQ. YD.
2	LT. MFGR., AUTOMOTIVE, STORE	.287	10.9
2½	LT. METALS, STAMPING. MFGR.	.325	8.4
3	STEEL PRODUCT, HEAVY MFGR.	.375	7.0
3½ — 4	HEAVIEST MFGR.	.425	

PATTERN	SIZE	THICKNESS	WOOD	GRADE	WEIGHT LB. 1000¢'
 STANDARD	19 × 19	5/16	CHERRY, MAPLE, OAK, CEDAR, PECAN, WALNUT, TEAK, PANGA	PREMIUM SELECT	1250
 HADDON HALL	13¼ × 13¼	5/16	TEAK, W. OAK, R. OAK, PANGA, WALNUT	SELECT BETTER	1250
 MONTICELLO	10 × 10 13¼ × 13¼	5/16	TEAK, W. OAK, R. OAK, PANGA, WALNUT	SELECT BETTER	1250
 CANTERBURY	13¼ × 13¼	5/16	TEAK, W. OAK, R. OAK, PANGA, WALNUT	SELECT BETTER	1250
 SAXONY	19 × 19	5/16	TEAK, W. OAK, R. OAK, PANGA, WALNUT	SELECT BETTER	1250
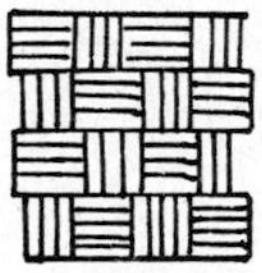 BASKETWEAVE	15½ × 19	5/16	TEAK, W. OAK, R. OAK, PANGA, WALNUT	SELECT BETTER	1250
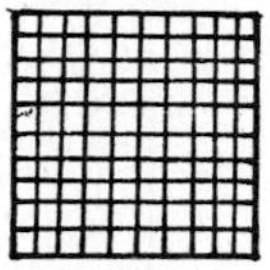 DOMINO	18 × 18 19 × 19	5/16	TEAK, W. OAK, R. OAK, PANGA, WALNUT	PREMIUM	1250
 HERRINGBONE	14⅛ × 18⅛	5/16	TEAK, W. OAK, R. OAK, PANGA, WALNUT	SELECT BETTER	1250
INDIVIDUAL PLANK	3" TO 8"	¾	TEAK, W. OAK, R. OAK	SELECT	2700
LAMINATED BLOCKS	6¾ × 6¾ 9 × 9	½	OAK, PECAN	SELECT	

TYPE	FED.SPEC	SIZE	THICKNESS	USE	BASE	
ASPHALT TILE GREASEPROOF	SS-T-312 SS-T-307	9 x 9	1/8	BOS		A-B-C-D-E GRADES
ASBESTOS VINYL TILE	SS-T-312	9x9, 12x12	1/16, 3/32, 1/8	BOS	2½, 4, 6	
SOLID VINYL TILE CONDUCTIVE	SS-T-312-IV NFPA #56	9x9, 12x12 18x18 12x12	1/16, .080" 3/32, 1/8 1/8	BOS BOS		4x36 PLANK 3x9 BRICK 4½x9 BRICK
VINYL SHEET CONDUCTIVE	L-F- 001641 L-F-475A NFPA #56	6-0, 9-0 12-0 6-0	.065, .070 .080, .095, .100, .160, .095	BOS BOS	2½, 4 AT .08	
RUBBER TILE	SS-T-312	9x9, 12x12, 36 x 36	1/8, 5/16, 1/4	BOS	1½, 2½, 4, 6	
SHEET RUBBER	ZZ-F-46la	36	.093 (3/32), 1/8, 3/16	BOS		
CORK	LLL-T-00431	12 x12, 6x36	.126	S		PREFINISHED OR JOB FIN.
CORK CARPET		2 METER (78")	3/16, 1/4	S		
LINOLEUM TILE	LLL-F-471b	9x9, 12x12	.090	S		PRINTED PATTERN
LINOLEUM SHEET	LLL-F-1238a	2 METERS 6-0, 12-0	.080, .090 1/8	S		PRINTED PATTERN
PLASTIC	SS-T-312 L-F-475 NFPA #56	24x24, 36x24 24x12, 62x4 ROLLS 49'x4'	.080, .100, 1/8, .200			PVC TYPE HEAT-WELD SEAMLESS

B = BELOW GRADE, O = ON GRADE, S = SUSPENDED

COLOR	APPROX. PERCENT OF REFLECTION
WHITE, DULL OR FLAT	75 – 85
WHITE, GLOSS	85 – 90
LIGHT TINTS	
CREAM OR EGGSHELL	79
IVORY	75
PALE PINK AND PALE YELLOW	75 – 80
LIGHT GREEN, LIGHT BLUE, LIGHT ORCHID	70 – 75
SOFT PINK, LIGHT PEACH	69
LIGHT BEIGE, PALE GREY	70
MEDIUM TONES	
APRICOT	56 – 62
PINK	64
TAN, YELLOW GOLD	55
LIGHT GREYS	35 – 50
MEDIUM TOURQUOISE	44
MEDIUM LIGHT BLUE	42
YELLOW GREEN	45
OLD GOLD, PUMPKIN	34
ROSE	29
DEEP TONES	
COCOA BROWN, MAUVE	24
MEDIUM GREEN, MEDIUM BLUE	21
	20
UNSUITABLE DARK COLORS	
DARK BROWN, DARK GREY	10 – 15
OLIVE GREEN	12
DARK BLUE, BLUE GREEN	5 – 10
FOREST GREEN	7
NATURAL WOOD TONES	
BIRCH AND BEECH	35 – 50
LIGHT MAPLE	25 – 35
LIGHT OAK	25 – 35
DARK OAK, CHERRY	10 – 15
REDWOOD	10 – 15
BLACK WALNUT, MAHOGANY	5 – 15

RECOMMENDED CEILING VALUES SHOULD BE IN THE RANGE OF 60-90%. FLOOR REFLECTION VALUES SHOULD BE IN THE RANGE OF 15-35%. OVERALL REFLECTION VALUES OF A ROOM SHOULD BE IN THE 35-60% RANGE.

SOUND ABSORPTION COEFFICIENTS (CYCLES PER SECOND)

MATERIAL	125	250	500	1000	2000	4000
AIR, SABINS PER 1000 CU. FT.					2.3	7.2
BRICK, UNGLAZED	.03	.03	.03	.04	.05	.07
BRICK, UNGLAZED, PAINTED	.01	.01	.02	.02	.02	.03
CARPET, HEAVY, ON CONCRETE	.02	.06	.14	.37	.60	.65
CARPET, ON 40-OZ. FELT OR FOAM	.08	.24	.57	.69	.71	.73
CARPET, LATEX BACK ON 40-OZ. PAD	.08	.27	.39	.34	.48	.63
CONCRETE BLOCK, UNPAINTED	.36	.44	.31	.29	.39	.25
CONCRETE BLOCK, PAINTED	.10	.05	.06	.07	.09	.08
DRAPES, 10 OZ., HUNG STRAIGHT	.03	.04	.11	.17	.24	.35
DRAPES, 10 OZ., HUNG HALF AREA	.07	.31	.49	.75	.70	.60
DRAPES, 18 OZ., DRAPED HALF AREA	.14	.35	.55	.72	.70	.65
FLOORS, CONCRETE OR TERRAZZO	.01	.01	.015	.02	.02	.02
FLOORS, RESILIENT ON CONCRETE	.02	.02	.03	.03	.03	.02
FLOORS, WOOD	.15	.11	.10	.07	.06	.07
FLOORS, WOOD PARQUET ON CONCRETE	.04	.04	.07	.06	.06	.07
GLASS, HEAVY PLATE	.18	.06	.04	.03	.02	.02
GLASS, SHEET WINDOW GLASS	.35	.25	.18	.12	.07	.04
GYPSUM BOARD ON 2x4 AT 16"O.C.	.29	.10	.05	.04	.07	.09
MARBLE OR GLAZED TILE	.01	.01	.01	.01	.02	.02
PLASTER, SMOOTH ON SOLID BACK	.013	.015	.02	.03	.04	.05
PLASTER, ON LATH, ROUGH FINISH	.02	.03	.04	.05	.04	.03
PLASTER, ON LATH, SMOOTH FINISH	.02	.02	.03	.04	.04	.03
PLYWOOD PANELS, 3/8" THICK	.28	.22	.17	.09	.10	.11
WATER SURFACES, SWIMMING POOL	.008	.008	.013	.015	.020	.025

ONE UNIT OF ABSORPTION (SABIN) IS EQUAL TO 1 SQUARE FOOT OF TOTALLY ABSORBENT SURFACE. ABSORBENT COEFFICIENT MEASURES THE PERCENTAGE OF INCIDENT SOUND ENERGY ABSORBED BY A MATERIAL. COEFFICIENTS THEORETICALLY VARY FROM 0 TO 1.0. A PERFECT ABSORPTIVE MATERIAL WOULD HAVE AN A=1. A PERFECT REFLECTIVE MATERIAL WOULD HAVE AN A=0.

ACCOUSTIC MATERIALS ASSOCIATION, BULLETIN XXVIII

THE INTENT OF A ROOM FINISH SCHEDULE ON WORKING DRAWINGS IS TO INDICATE THE MAJOR MATERIALS THAT WILL BE REQUIRED TO FINISH THE FLOORS, WALLS, AND CEILINGS. THE TWO SCHEDULES SHOWN HERE ARE DIFFERENT IN THAT THE FIRST INDICATES THE MATERIALS IN UPPERCASE BY NAME FOR EACH SURFACE. THIS REQUIRES LETTERING THE WORDS IN EACH SPACE BUT ALLOWS FOR MORE COMPLETE DESCRIPTION. THE SECOND CASE IS MOST OFTEN USED WHEN MATERIALS ARE MORE GENERAL AND MAY BE ACCOMPANIED BY A MATERIAL DESCRIPTION LIST.

ROOM	FLOOR	BASE	WALLS NORTH	EAST	SOUTH	WEST	CEILING MAT'L.	HT.	REMARKS
ENTRY	SLATE	WOOD	PLAST.	PLAST.	PLAST.	PLAST.	PLAST.	8-0	WALLPAPER WALLS
LIVING RM.	CARPET	WOOD	PLAST.	PLAST.	PLAST.	BRICK	ACOUST.	8-0	PLAST. PAINTED
DINING RM.	CARPET	WOOD	PLAST.	PLAST.	PLAST.	PLAST.	ACOUST.	8-0	PLAST. PAINTED
KITCHEN	VINYL	VINYL	PLAST.	PLAST.	PLAST.	PLAST.	ACOUST.	8-0	PLAST. ENAMEL
MASTER BDRM.	CARPET	WOOD	PLAST.	PLAST.	PLAST.	WOOD	ACOUST.	8-0	HD'WD. WALL PANEL.
BDRM. #2	CARPET	WOOD	PLAST.	PLAST.	PLAST.	PLAST.	ACOUST.	8-0	WALLPAPER NORTH
BDRM. #3	CARPET	WOOD	PLAST.	PLAST.	PLAST.	PLAST.	ACOUST.	8-0	WALLPAPER EAST
BATH #1	CER.TILE	TILE	TILE	TILE	TILE	TILE	PLAST.	8-0	PLAST. ENAMEL
BATH #2	VINYL	VINYL	PLAST.	PLAST.	PLAST.	PLAST.	PLAST.	8-0	PLAST. ENAMEL
HALL	CARPET	WOOD	PLAST.	PLAST.	WOOD	PLAST.	ACOUST.	7-6	

NO.	ROOM	FLOOR: CONCRETE	WOOD	ASPHALT/VINYL	CERAMIC TILE	BASE: WOOD	RUBBER/VINYL	CERAMIC TILE	WALLS: PLASTER, PAINTED	GYPBD., PAINTED	WOOD PANEL	CERAMIC TILE	MASONRY	CEILING: PLASTER, PAINTED	GYPBD., PAINTED	ACOUSTIC TILE	WOOD PANEL	EXPOSED FRAME	NOTES
101	LOBBY	●				●			●					●					STAIN CONC. FLR.
102	RECEPTION		●			●				●	●					●			
103	CONFERENCE		●			●							●			●			
104	OFFICE		●			●				●	●					●	●		VERT. WALL PANEL ON WALLS
105	OFFICE		●			●				●						●			
106	TOILET				●			●				●	●			●			TILE 6° HIGH
107	CORRIDOR			●			●			●								●	CEIL. HT. 12° ±

SPECIALTIES   DIVISION 10

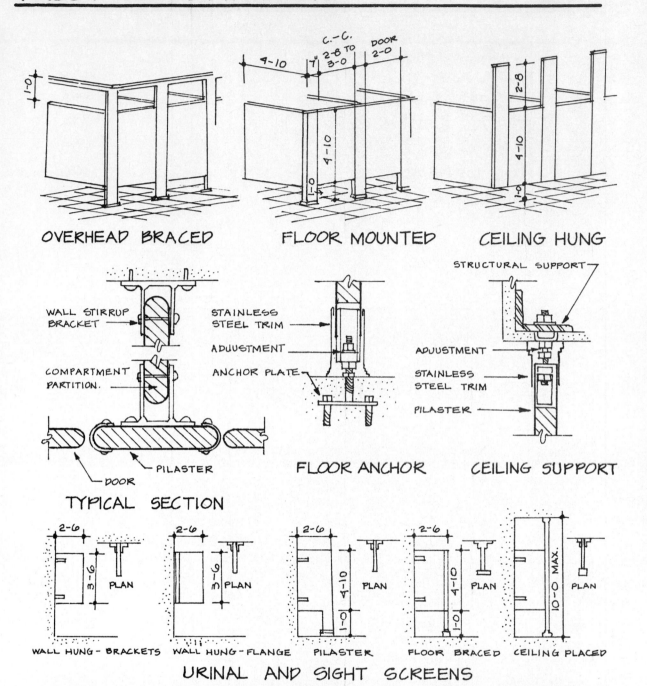

OVERHEAD BRACED   FLOOR MOUNTED   CEILING HUNG

WALL STIRRUP BRACKET

STAINLESS STEEL TRIM

ADJUSTMENT

STRUCTURAL SUPPORT

COMPARTMENT PARTITION.

ANCHOR PLATE

ADJUSTMENT

STAINLESS STEEL TRIM

PILASTER

PILASTER

DOOR

FLOOR ANCHOR   CEILING SUPPORT

TYPICAL SECTION

WALL HUNG - BRACKETS   WALL HUNG - FLANGE   PILASTER   FLOOR BRACED   CEILING PLACED

URINAL AND SIGHT SCREENS

COMPARTMENTS MAY BE STEEL OR LAMINATED PLASTIC. STEEL COMPARTMENTS ARE FABRICATED WITH 20 GA. FACINGS ON PARTITIONS, 16 GA. ON PILASTERS, AND 22 GA. ON DOORS. FITTINGS ARE STAINLESS STEEL, ANODIZED ALUMINUM, OR PLATED BRASS. FINISHES ARE AVAILABLE IN MANY COLORS IN ENAMEL OR PORCELAINIZED COATINGS. LAMINATED PLASTIC COMPARTMENTS ARE SIMILAR IN DESIGN AND IN CONSTRUCTION EXCEPT PLASTIC IS THE COVER SURFACE OVER STEEL CORE. STEEL PARTITIONS ARE NORMALLY 1¼" THICK, DOORS 1" THICK. PLASTIC PARTITIONS ARE NORMALLY 1" THICK WITH 1" DOORS. CHECK REQUIREMENTS WITH MANUFACTURER.

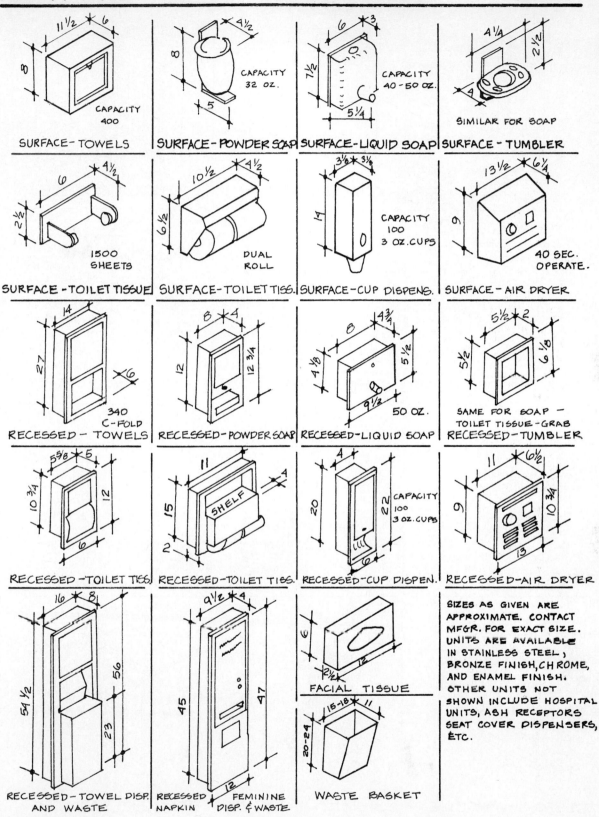

11½ 6
8
CAPACITY 400
SURFACE-TOWELS

4½
8
CAPACITY 32 OZ.
5
SURFACE-POWDER SOAP

6 3
7½
CAPACITY 40-50 OZ.
5¼
SURFACE-LIQUID SOAP

4¼
2½
SIMILAR FOR SOAP
SURFACE - TUMBLER

4½
6
2½
1500 SHEETS
SURFACE -TOILET TISSUE

10½ 4½
6½
DUAL ROLL
SURFACE-TOILET TISS.

3½ 3½
11
CAPACITY 100 3 OZ. CUPS
SURFACE-CUP DISPENS.

13½ 6¼
9
40 SEC. OPERATE.
SURFACE – AIR DRYER

14
27
6
340 C-FOLD
RECESSED - TOWELS

8 4
12
12¾
RECESSED-POWDER SOAP

4¾
8
4⅛
5½
9½
50 OZ.
RECESSED-LIQUID SOAP

5½ 2
5½
6⅛
SAME FOR SOAP - TOILET TISSUE-GRAB
RECESSED-TUMBLER

5⅝ 5
10¾
12
6
RECESSED -TOILET TISS.

11
4
15
SHELF
2
RECESSED-TOILET TISS.

4
20
22
CAPACITY 100 3 OZ. CUPS
RECESSED-CUP DISPEN.

11 6½
9
10¾
13
RECESSED-AIR DRYER

16 8
54½
56
23
RECESSED-TOWEL DISP. AND WASTE

9½ 4
45
47
12
RECESSED NAPKIN   FEMININE DISP. & WASTE

6
12
2½
FACIAL TISSUE

15-18 11
20-24
WASTE BASKET

SIZES AS GIVEN ARE APPROXIMATE. CONTACT MFGR. FOR EXACT SIZE. UNITS ARE AVAILABLE IN STAINLESS STEEL, BRONZE FINISH, CHROME, AND ENAMEL FINISH. OTHER UNITS NOT SHOWN INCLUDE HOSPITAL UNITS, ASH RECEPTORS SEAT COVER DISPENSERS, ETC.

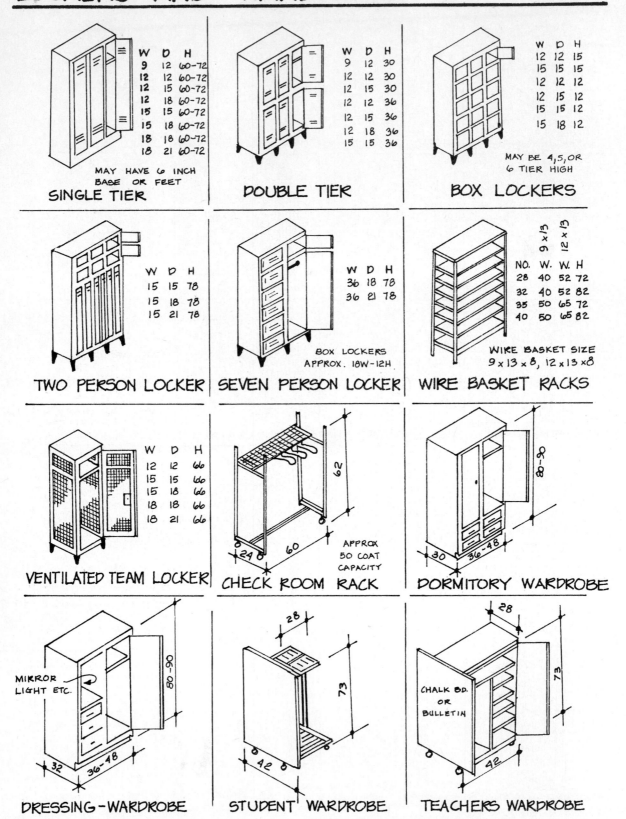

SINGLE TIER

W	D	H
9	12	60-72
12	12	60-72
12	15	60-72
12	18	60-72
15	15	60-72
15	18	60-72
18	18	60-72
18	21	60-72

MAY HAVE 6 INCH BASE OR FEET

DOUBLE TIER

W	D	H
9	12	30
12	12	30
12	15	30
12	12	36
12	15	36
12	18	36
15	15	36

BOX LOCKERS

W	D	H
12	12	15
15	15	15
12	12	12
12	15	12
15	15	12
15	18	12

MAY BE 4,5,OR 6 TIER HIGH

TWO PERSON LOCKER

W	D	H
15	15	78
15	18	78
15	21	78

SEVEN PERSON LOCKER

W	D	H
36	18	78
36	21	78

BOX LOCKERS APPROX. 18W-12H

WIRE BASKET RACKS

9 x 13   12 x 13

NO.	W.	W.	H
28	40	52	72
32	40	52	82
35	50	65	72
40	50	65	82

WIRE BASKET SIZE 9 x 13 x 8, 12 x 13 x 8

VENTILATED TEAM LOCKER

W	D	H
12	12	66
15	15	66
15	18	66
18	18	66
18	21	66

CHECK ROOM RACK

62   24   60   APPROX 50 COAT CAPACITY

DORMITORY WARDROBE

80-90   30   36-48

DRESSING-WARDROBE

MIRROR LIGHT ETC.   80-90   32   36-48

STUDENT WARDROBE

28   73   42

TEACHERS WARDROBE

28   73   CHALK BD. OR BULLETIN   42

#17 U.S. POSTAL PUBLICATION EFFECTIVE 5-1-75

VERTICAL MAILBOXES

- MINIMUM INSIDE DIMENSIONS, 5" WIDE 6" DEEP, 15" HIGH.
- MAXIMUM NUMBER OF BOXES WHICH MAY BE INSTALLED UNDER ONE POST OFFICE KEY IS 7. MINIMUM IS 3.
- LOCKS MUST BE 5 PIN CYLINDER WITH 1000 POSSIBLE KEY CHANGES. NO MASTER KEYS ALLOWED.
- NO MORE THAN TWO ROWS OF BOXES.
- MASTER LOCK NO MORE THAN 58" ABOVE FINISH FLOOR AND NO LOWER THAN 30".

HORIZONTAL MAILBOXES

- MINIMUM INSIDE DIMENSIONS, 5" HIGH 6" WIDE, 15" DEEP.
- MAXIMUM NUMBER OF BOXES IN ONE GROUP 35, 7 UNITS HIGH BY 5 WIDE.
- LOCKS MUST BE 5 PIN CYLINDER WITH 1000 POSSIBLE KEY CHANGES. NO MASTER KEYS ALLOWED.
- MAXIMUM HEIGHT FROM FINISH FLOOR TO TOPMOST TENANT LOCK 67". HEIGHT FROM FINISH FLOOR TO BOTTOM OF THE LOWEST TIER OF BOXES NOT LESS THAN 28".

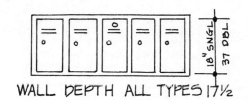

WALL DEPTH ALL TYPES 17½   18" SNGL 37 DBL

FRONT·LOADING VERTICAL

SINGLE ROW	DOUBLE ROW	LAYOUT PER ROW	R.O. OPEN'G	WIDTH O. ALL
3	6	3	17½	19
4	8	4	23	24½
5	10	5	28½	30
6	12	6	35	36
7	14	7	39½	42
8	16	4-4	48	49
9	18	5-4	53½	55
10	20	5-5	59	60
13	26	7-6	75½	77
15	30	5-5-5	89	90

FRONT·LOADING HORIZONTAL

TOTAL UNITS	USUABLE UNITS	LAYOUT W×H	R.O. WIDTH	R.O. HEIGHT
15	14	3-5	20	28
18	17	3-6	20	33
20	19	4-5	26½	28
21	20	3-7	20	39
24	23	4-6	26½	33
25	24	5-5	33	28
28	27	4-7	26½	39
30	29	5-6	33	33
35	34	5-7	33	39

ROUGH OPENINGS VARY SLIGHTLY. CHECK FOR EXACT SIZES WITH MANUFACTURER. "MAGAZINE RACK" COMPARTMENTS ILLEGAL UNDER NEW REQUIRMENTS.

US MAIL

COLLECTION BOX
FRAME: 20" H BY 17" WIDE
COMPARTMENT: 16" × 13" × 15" D.
R.O. OPENING: 18½" × 15½" × 16" D.

A WIDE VARIETY OF TENANT DIRECTORIES, CALL SYSTEMS, INTERCOM SYSTEMS IS AVAILABLE. FOR "NEIGHBORHOOD" MAIL DELIVERY THERE ARE 12 OR 16 BOX FREE-STANDING PEDESTAL REAR-LOADING UNITS AVAILABLE ALSO.

CONE TAPERED ALUMINUM POLE

EXPOS. HT.	TOTAL HT.	DIAM. BUTT	DIAM. TOP	TAPER LENGTH	STRAIGHT LENGTH	BALL DIAM.	SLEEVE DIAM.	FLAG SIZE
20-0	23-0	5	3	11-0	12-0	5	10	4x6
25-0	28-0	5½	3½	11-0	17-0	6	10	4x6
30-0	33-0	6	3½	13-9	19-3	6	10	5x8
35-0	38-6	7	3½	19-3	19-3	8	10	5x8
40-0	44-0	8	3½	25-9	19-3	8	12	6x10
45-0	49-6	8	3½	24-9	24-9	8	12	6x10
50-0	55-0	10	4	33-0	22-0	10	15	8x12
60-0	65-0	12	4	49-0	16-0	12	15	10x15
70-0	77-0	12	4	49-0	28-0	12	15	10x15
80-0	88-0	12	4	49-0	39-0	12	15	15x25

ALUMINUM ALLOY 6063-TG.

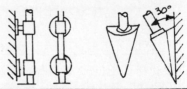

TAPERED ALUMINUM VERTICAL MOUNT

LENGTH FT.	DIAM. BUTT	DIAM. TOP	TAPER LENGTH	STRAIGHT LENGTH	BALL DIAM.
15-0	4	2⅜	9-0	6-0	4
20-0	4½	2⅞	9-0	11-0	5
23-0	5	3¼	9-8	13-4	5
28-0	5½	3½	11-0	17-0	6
33-0	6	3½	13-9	19-3	6
38-6	7	3½	19-3	19-3	6

ENTASIS TAPER STAINLESS STEEL POLE

EXPOS. HT.	TOTAL HT.	DIAM BUTT	DIAM TOP	TAPER LENGTH	STRAIGHT LENGTH	BALL DIAM.	SET DEPTH	FLAG SIZE
20-0	22-0	4	2	13-0	9-0	4	2-0	3x5
25-0	27-6	4½	2½	17-0	10-6	5	2-6	5x8
30-0	33-0	5½	3	20-0	13-0	6	3-0	5x8
35-0	38-6	5½	3	23-0	15-6	6	3-6	5x8
40-0	44-0	6⅝	3½	25-0	19-0	6	4-0	6x10
50-0	55-0	8⅝	3½	35-0	20-0	8	5-0	8x12
60-0	66-0	8⅝	3½	40-0	26-0	8	6-0	10x15
70-0	77-0	10¾	4	45-0	32-0	10	7-0	10x15
80-0	88-0	12¾	4	50-0	38-0	12	8-0	10x15
90-0	99-0	14	4	60-0	39-0	14	9-0	15x25

STAINLESS STEEL ALLOY 304

TAPERED ALUMINUM OUTRIGGER

LENGTH FT.	DIAM. BUTT	DIAM. TOP	TAPER LENGTH	STRAIGHT LENGTH	BALL DIAM.
8-0	3½	2⅜	6-0	2-0	4
10-0	3½	2⅜	6-0	4-0	4
15-0	4	2⅜	9-0	6-0	4
18-0	4½	2⅞	9-0	9-0	5
20-0	4½	2⅞	9-0	11-0	5
23-0	5	3¼	9-4	13-8	6

FLAG SIZES: 8-0, 3x5; 10 TO 15, 5x8; 18 TO 23, 6x10.

FOUNDATION DIMENSIONS

EXPOS HT.	A	B	C	D	E	F	G	H
20-0	3-0	3-6	6	18	30	24	10	14
25-0	3-0	3-6	6	18	30	24	10	14
30-0	3-0	3-6	6	18	30	24	10	14
35-0	3-6	4-0	6	18	36	30	10	14
40-0	4-0	4-6	6	18	42	36	12	16
45-0	4-6	5-0	6	24	48	42	12	16
50-0	5-0	5-8	8	24	48	42	15	18
60-0	6-0	6-10	10	24	48	42	15	24
70-0	7-0	8-0	12	24	60	48	15	24
80-0	8-0	9-0	12	24	60	48	15	24

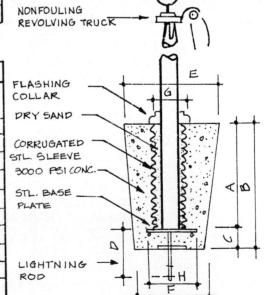

NONFOULING REVOLVING TRUCK

FLASHING COLLAR

DRY SAND

CORRUGATED STL. SLEEVE

3000 PSI CONC.

STL. BASE PLATE

LIGHTNING ROD

TELEPHONE	MAIL	FIRST AID	INFORMATION
TOILET-WOMEN	TOILET-MEN	ELEVATOR	HANDICAPPED
AIRPORT	WATER TRANSPORT	RAILROAD	GROUND TRANSPORT
CAR RENTAL	PROCESS-CHECK IN	BAGGAGE	IMMIGRATION-CUSTOMS
LOST & FOUND	CLOAK ROOM	DIRECTION	NO SMOKING
RESTAURANT	COFFEE SHOP	BAR	HOTEL-MOTEL

AMERICAN INSTITUTE OF GRAPHIC ARTS AND U.S. DEPARTMENT OF TRANSPORTATION HAVE CREATED ABOVE SIGNS TO FACILITATE PEDESTRIAN TRAFFIC RELATED TO TRANSPORTATION FACILITIES.

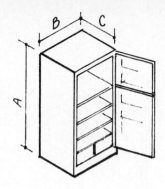

	A	B	C			A	B	C
22 FT.	66	33	32		15 FT.	65	30	31
19 FT.	66	32	29		15 FT.	59	30	31
17 FT.	66	32	29					

SINGLE DOOR REFRIGERATOR

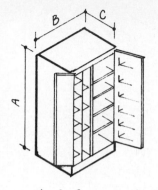

	A	B	C			A	B	C
24 FT.	66	36	33		19 FT.	66	33	29
22 FT.	66	33	32					

SIDE BY SIDE DOUBLE DOOR REFRIGERATOR

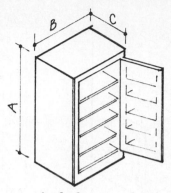

	A	B	C			A	B	C
30 FT.	72	36	34		16 FT.	66	30	32
27 FT.	69	36	32		15 FT.	66	30	31
20 FT.	66	33	31		12 FT.	57	24	31

UPRIGHT FREEZER

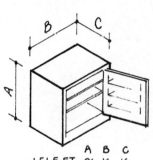

	A	B	C
1.5 1.5 FT.	26	16	16
2.5 FT.	25	17	24½
5.2 FT.	35	24	24
6.6 FT.	35	24	24½

UNDER COUNTER REFRIGERATOR

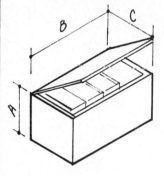

	A	B	C			A	B	C
27 FT.	29	71	36		15 FT.	29	43	36
23 FT.	29	62	36		9 FT.	28	37	35
18 FT.	29	51	36		6 FT.	28	26	35

HORIZONTAL CHEST FREEZER

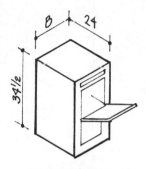

80 CUBES/HR = 2 LB.
35 LB. STORAGE
4.6 AMP. 350 WATT

DOMESTIC ICE-CUBE MAKER

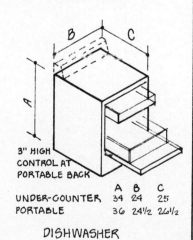

3" HIGH CONTROL AT PORTABLE BACK

	A	B	C
UNDER-COUNTER	34	24	25
PORTABLE	36	24½	26½

DISHWASHER

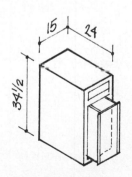

1½ BU. CAP.
35,000 BTU
GAS FIRED
6" FLUE

DOMESTIC INCINERATOR

60 GAL. CAP.
460 W. PER CYCLE

TRASH COMPACTOR

DIMENSIONS ARE TYPICAL, CHECK WITH MANUFACTURERS FOR SPECIFIC MODELS AND SIZES.

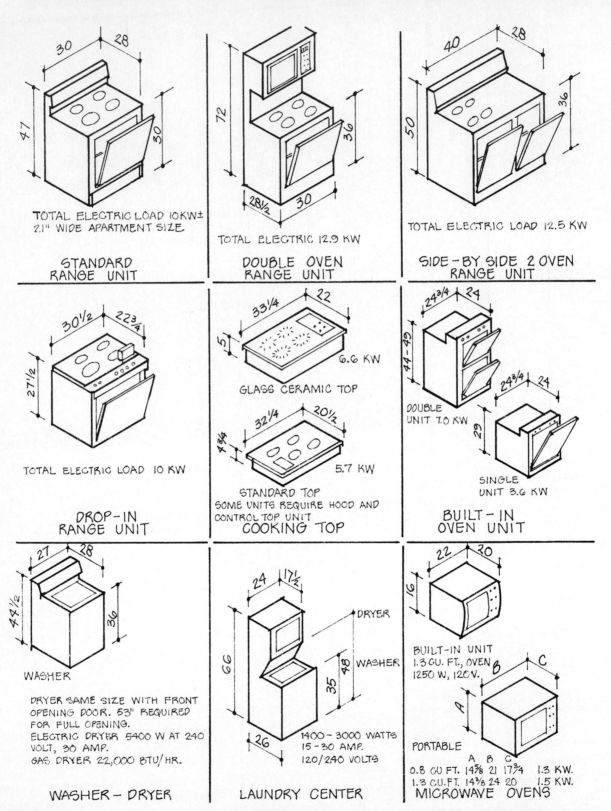

TOTAL ELECTRIC LOAD 10KW±
21" WIDE APARTMENT SIZE

**STANDARD
RANGE UNIT**

TOTAL ELECTRIC 12.9 KW

**DOUBLE OVEN
RANGE UNIT**

TOTAL ELECTRIC LOAD 12.5 KW

**SIDE-BY SIDE 2 OVEN
RANGE UNIT**

TOTAL ELECTRIC LOAD 10 KW

**DROP-IN
RANGE UNIT**

6.6 KW

GLASS CERAMIC TOP

5.7 KW

STANDARD TOP
SOME UNITS REQUIRE HOOD AND
CONTROL TOP UNIT
COOKING TOP

DOUBLE
UNIT 7.0 KW

SINGLE
UNIT 3.6 KW

**BUILT-IN
OVEN UNIT**

WASHER

DRYER SAME SIZE WITH FRONT
OPENING DOOR. 53" REQUIRED
FOR FULL OPENING.
ELECTRIC DRYER 5400 W AT 240
VOLT, 30 AMP.
GAS DRYER 22,000 BTU/HR.

WASHER - DRYER

DRYER

WASHER

1400 - 3000 WATTS
15 - 30 AMP.
120/240 VOLTS

LAUNDRY CENTER

BUILT-IN UNIT
1.3 CU. FT., OVEN
1250 W, 120 V.

PORTABLE

	A	B	C
0.8 CU FT.	14⅝	21	17¾	1.3 KW.
1.3 CU.FT.	14⅜	24	20	1.5 KW.

MICROWAVE OVENS

DIMENSIONS ARE TYPICAL. CHECK WITH MANUFACTURER FOR SPECIFIC MODELS AND SIZES.

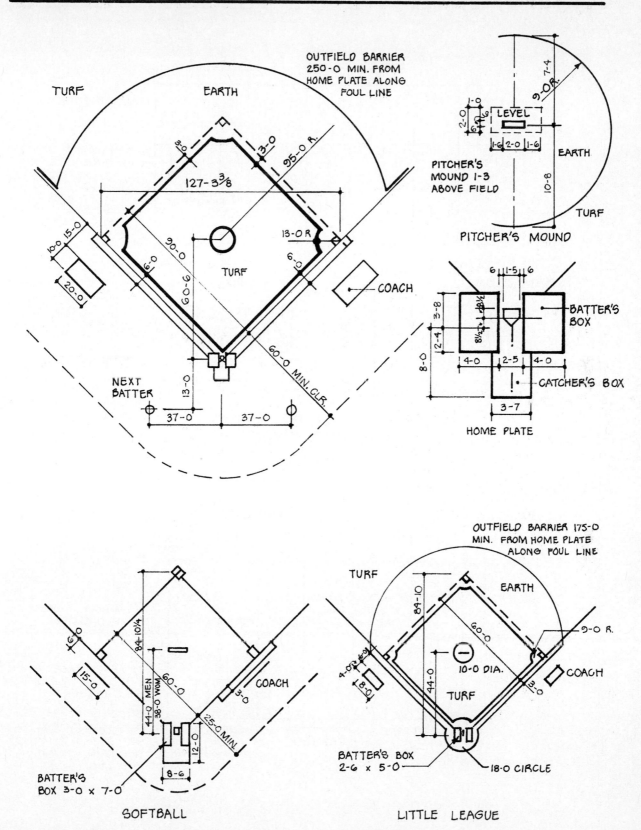

OUTFIELD BARRIER 250-0 MIN. FROM HOME PLATE ALONG FOUL LINE

TURF   EARTH

127-3⅜
95-0 R.
3-0   3-0
13-0 R
90-0
6-0
60-0
6-0
TURF
10-0 15-0
20-0
COACH
NEXT BATTER
13-0
60-0 MIN. CLR.
37-0   37-0

PITCHER'S MOUND 1-3 ABOVE FIELD

9-0 R.   7-4
1-0
2-0   6-0
LEVEL
1-6 2-0 1-6
EARTH
10-8
TURF

PITCHER'S MOUND

HOME PLATE
6 5 6
3-8
2⅛
8½
2-4
8-0
4-0   2-5   4-0
BATTER'S BOX
CATCHER'S BOX
3-7

OUTFIELD BARRIER 175-0 MIN. FROM HOME PLATE ALONG FOUL LINE

TURF   EARTH

SOFTBALL

84-10¼
3-0
15-0
60-0
44-0 MEN
38-0 WOM
COACH
3-0
25-0 MIN.
12-0
8-6
BATTER'S BOX 3-0 x 7-0

LITTLE LEAGUE

84-10
60-0
9-0 R.
4-0 6-0
44-0
10-0 DIA.
TURF
COACH
3-0
8-0
BATTER'S BOX 2-6 x 5-0
18-0 CIRCLE

243

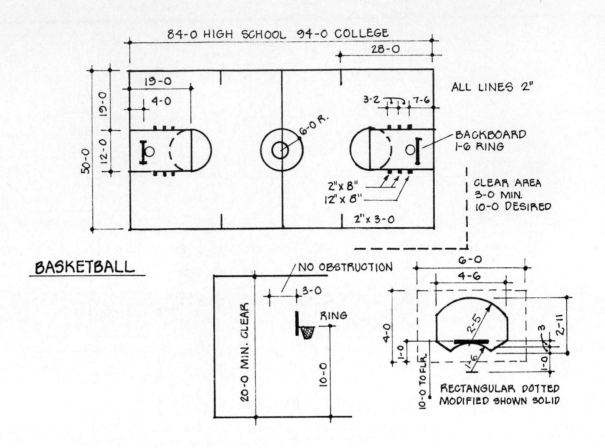

BASKETBALL

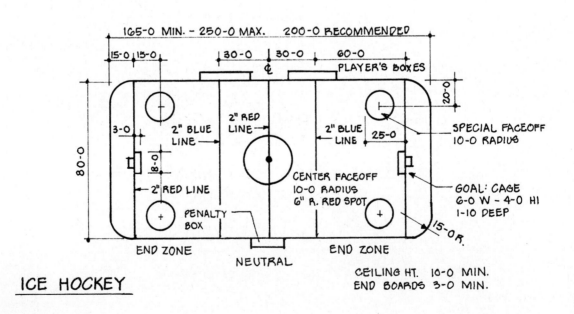

ICE HOCKEY

244

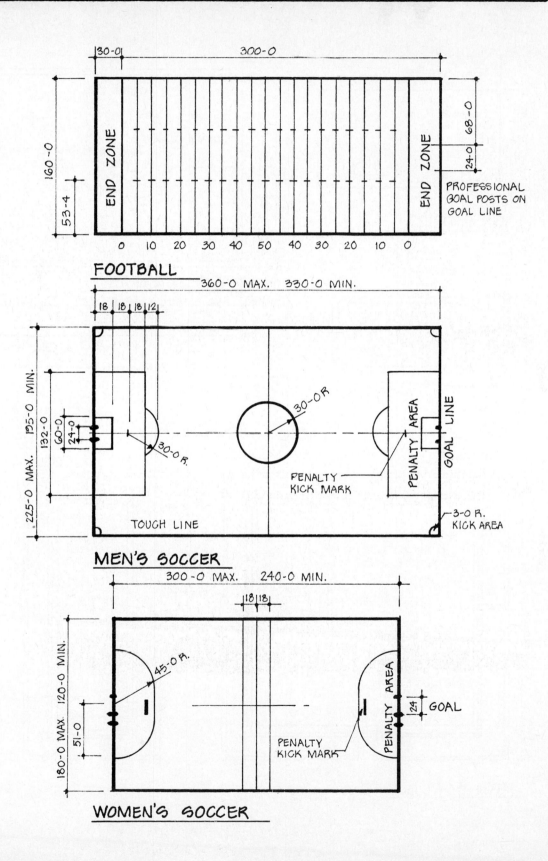

FOOTBALL

MEN'S SOCCER

WOMEN'S SOCCER

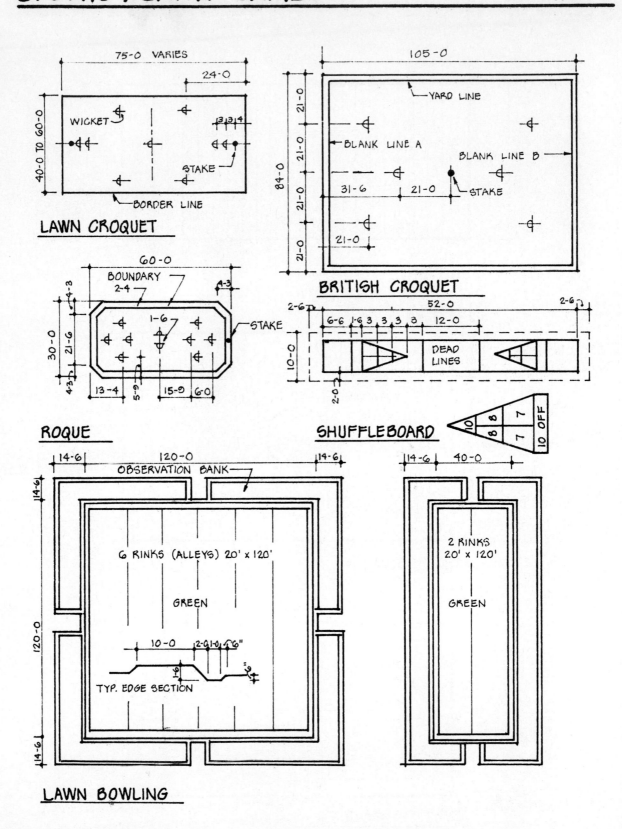

LAWN CROQUET

BRITISH CROQUET

ROQUE

SHUFFLEBOARD

LAWN BOWLING

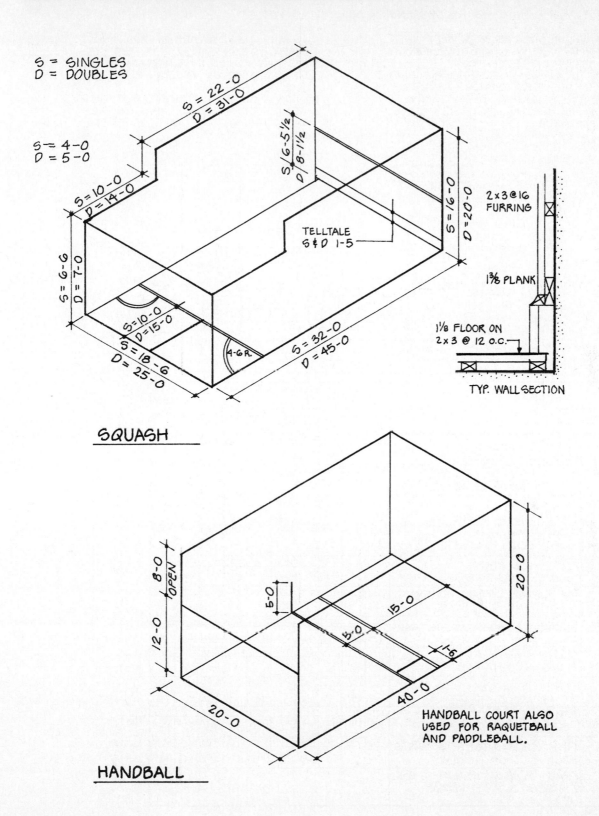

S = SINGLES
D = DOUBLES

S = 22-0
D = 31-0

S = 4-0
D = 5-0

S = 10-0
D = 14-0

S 6-5½
D 8-1½

S = 6-6
D = 7-0

S 16-0
D 20-0

TELLTALE
S & D 1-5

S = 10-0
D = 15-0

S = 32-0
D = 45-0

S = 18-6
D = 25-0

4-6 R.

2 x 3 @ 16
FURRING

1⅜ PLANK

1⅛ FLOOR ON
2 x 3 @ 12 O.C.

TYP. WALL SECTION

SQUASH

8-0
OPEN

12-0

5-0

15-0

5-0

1-6

20-0

20-0

40-0

HANDBALL COURT ALSO
USED FOR RAQUETBALL
AND PADDLEBALL.

HANDBALL

ADDITIONAL FEATURES RECOMMENDED FOR DIVING POOLS

MINIMUM SIZE: 45 BY 36 FEET
SEPARATE FROM COMPETITIVE POOL,
  BUT IN THE SAME ROOM
DEPTH: 14 TO 16 FEET TO ACCOMODATE
  THREE-METER BOARDS AND PLATFORMS
CEILING HEIGHT OF 15 FEET ABOVE
HIGHEST BOARD, OR 10 FEET ABOVE
PLATFORM.

ONE- AND THREE-METER BOARDS AND
  PLATFORMS INSTALLED TO MEET COM-
  PETITIVE REGULATIONS.(PLATFORMS MAY
  BE INSTALLED ON PILLARS HUNG FROM
  THE CEILING.)
BOARDS INSTALLED 10 FEET APART (USE
  CENTER OF BOARD TO MEASURE DIS-
  TANCE) ALONG ONE WALL, 10 FEET
  FROM SIDEWALKS.

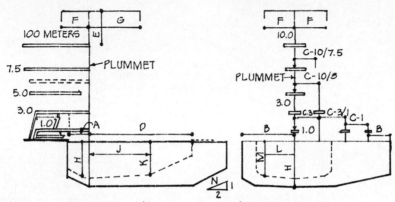

LONGITUDINAL SECTION   DIAGRAMATIC CROSS SECTION

MINIMUM STANDARD DIVING FACILITY DIMENSIONS (ADOPTION BY NCAA IN 1969)		1-METER SPRINGB'D 16' x 1'-8"		3-METER SPRINGB'D 16' x 1'-8"		INTER-MED. PLATFORM 16' x 5'		7½-METER PLATFORM 18' x 6'		10-METER PLATFORM 20' x 6'-6"	
		DIST.	DEPTH	DIST.	DEPTH	DIST.	DEPTH	DIST.	DEPTH	DIST.	DEPTH
A	FROM PLUMMET: BACK TO POOL WALL	A-1 6'	—	A-3 6'	—	A-INT 5'	--	A-7.5 5'	—	A-10 6'	—
	BACK TO PLATFORM DIRECTLY BELOW	—	--	—	—	—	—	5'	—	5'	—
B	FROM PLUMMET TO POOL WALL AT SIDE	B-1 10'		B-3 12'		B-INT 14'		B-7.5 15'		B-10 17'	
C	FROM PLUMMET TO ADJACENT PLUMMET	C-1 8'		C-3 8'	C-3/1 10'	C-INT		C-7.5	C10/7.5	C-10	C-10/3 12'
D	FROM PLUMMENT TO POOL WALL AHEAD	D-1 29'		D-3 34'		D-INT 34'		D-7.5 36'		D-10 45'	
E	ON PLUMMET, FROM BOARD TO CEILING OVERHEAD	E-1 16'		E-3 16'		E-INT 10'		E-7.5 10'6"		E-10 11'	
F E	CLEAR OVERHEAD, BEHIND AND EACH SIDE OF PLUMMET	F-1 8'	E-1 16'	F-3 8'	E-3 16'	F-INT 9'	E-INT 12'	F-7.5 9'	E-7.5 12'	F-10 16'	E-10 12'
G	CLEAR OVERHEAD, AHEAD OF PLUMMET	G-1 16'	E-1 16'	G-3 16'	E-3 16'	G-INT 16'	E-INT 12'	G-7.5 16'	E-7.5 12'	G-10 20'	E-10 12'
H	DEPTH OF WATER AT PLUMMET	H-1	12'	H-3	13'	H-INT	14'	H-7.5	15'	H-10	17'
J-K	DISTANCE, AND DEPTH OF WATER, AHEAD OF PLUMMET	J-1 20'	K-1 10'9"	J-3 20'	K-3 11'9"	J-INT 20'	K-INT 11'9"	J-7.5 26'	K-7.5 13'	J-10 40'	K-10 14'
L-M	DISTANCE, AND DEPTH OF WATER, EACH SIDE OF PLUMMET.	L-1 8	M-1 12	L-3 10	M-3 11'9"	L INT 12	M-INT 11'9"	L-7.5 13	M-7.5 11'9"	L-10 14'	M-10 14'
N	MAXIMUM RATIO, VERTICAL TO HORIZONTAL, OF SLOPE TO REDUCE DEPTH 1:2	1:2		1:2		1:2		1:2		1:2	

SPORTS, TENNIS AND BADMINTON   11.9

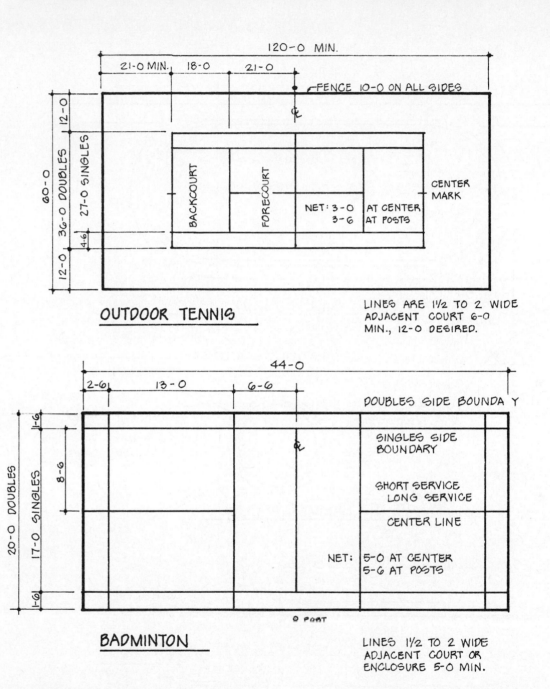

OUTDOOR TENNIS

LINES ARE 1½ TO 2 WIDE
ADJACENT COURT 6-0
MIN., 12-0 DESIRED.

BADMINTON

LINES 1½ TO 2 WIDE
ADJACENT COURT OR
ENCLOSURE 5-0 MIN.

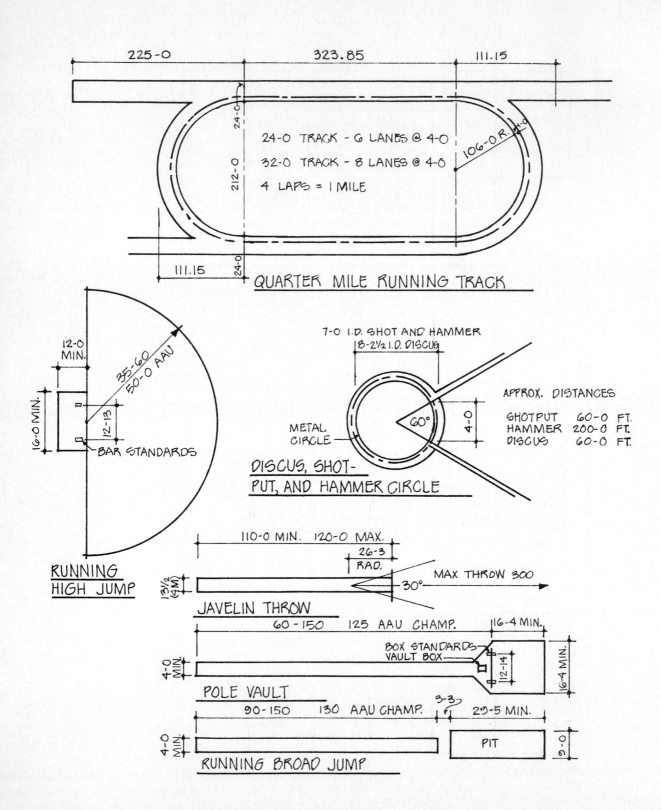

225-0   323.85   111.15

24-0 TRACK - 6 LANES @ 4-0

32-0 TRACK - 8 LANES @ 4-0

4 LAPS = 1 MILE

24-0

212-0

106-0 R.

111.15   24-0

QUARTER MILE RUNNING TRACK

12-0 MIN.

35-60
50-0 AAU

16-0 MIN.

12-13

BAR STANDARDS

RUNNING HIGH JUMP

7-0 I.D. SHOT AND HAMMER

8-2½ I.D. DISCUS

METAL CIRCLE

60°

4-0

APPROX. DISTANCES

SHOTPUT   60-0 FT.
HAMMER   200-0 FT.
DISCUS   60-0 FT.

DISCUS, SHOT-PUT, AND HAMMER CIRCLE

110-0 MIN.   120-0 MAX.

26-3 RAD.

MAX THROW 300

13½ (4M)

30°

JAVELIN THROW

60 - 150   125 AAU CHAMP.   16-4 MIN.

BOX STANDARDS
VAULT BOX

12-14

16-4 MIN.

4-0 MIN.

POLE VAULT

90-150   130 AAU CHAMP.   3-3   29-5 MIN.

4-0 MIN.

PIT

6-0

RUNNING BROAD JUMP

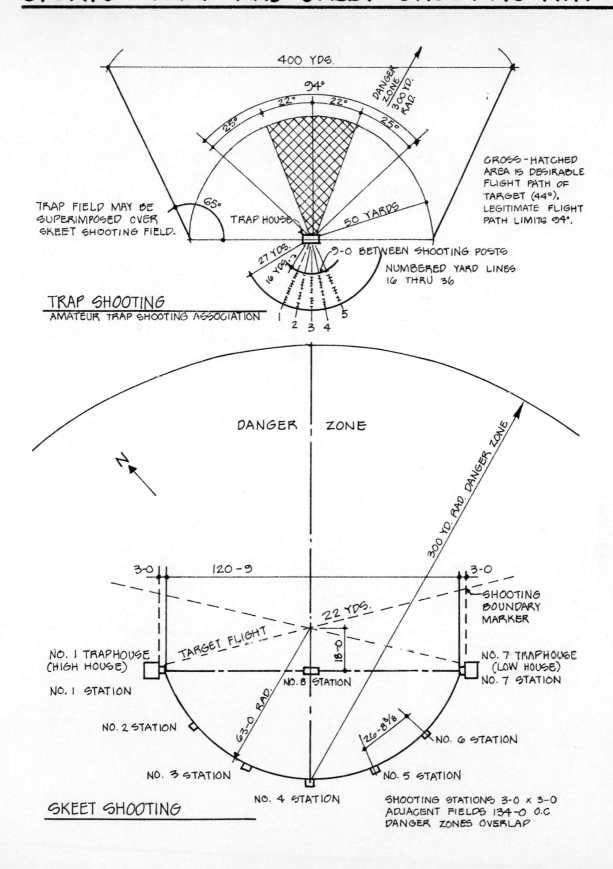

400 YDS.

94°

22° 22°

25° 25°

DANGER ZONE 300 YD. RAD.

CROSS-HATCHED AREA IS DESIRABLE FLIGHT PATH OF TARGET (44°). LEGITIMATE FLIGHT PATH LIMITS 94°.

TRAP FIELD MAY BE SUPERIMPOSED OVER SKEET SHOOTING FIELD.

65°

TRAP HOUSE

50 YARDS

27 YDS.

16 YDS.

9-0 BETWEEN SHOOTING POSTS
NUMBERED YARD LINES 16 THRU 36

TRAP SHOOTING
AMATEUR TRAP SHOOTING ASSOCIATION

1 2 3 4 5

DANGER   ZONE

N

300 YD. RAD. DANGER ZONE

3-0   120-9   3-0

SHOOTING BOUNDARY MARKER

22 YDS.

TARGET FLIGHT

18-0

NO. 1 TRAPHOUSE (HIGH HOUSE)

NO. 7 TRAPHOUSE (LOW HOUSE)

NO. 1 STATION

NO. 8 STATION

NO. 7 STATION

63-0 RAD.

NO. 2 STATION

26-8⅜

NO. 6 STATION

NO. 3 STATION

NO. 5 STATION

NO. 4 STATION

SKEET SHOOTING

SHOOTING STATIONS 3-0 x 3-0
ADJACENT FIELDS 134-0 O.C
DANGER ZONES OVERLAP

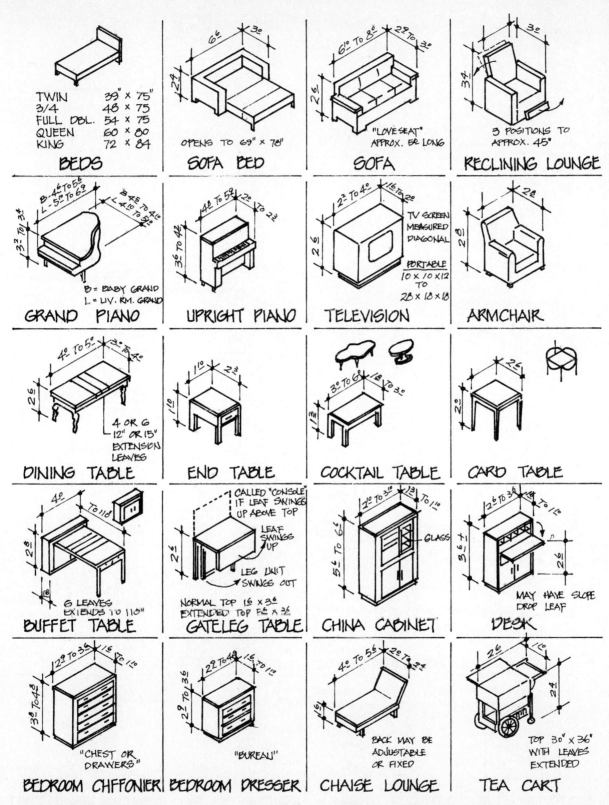

BEDS

TWIN	39" × 75"	
3/4	48 × 75	
FULL DBL.	54 × 75	
QUEEN	60 × 80	
KING	72 × 84	

SOFA BED

OPENS TO 69" × 78"

SOFA

"LOVE SEAT"
APPROX. 5' LONG

RECLINING LOUNGE

3 POSITIONS TO
APPROX. 45°

GRAND PIANO

B = BABY GRAND
L = LIV. RM. GRAND

UPRIGHT PIANO

TELEVISION

TV SCREEN
MEASURED
DIAGONAL

PORTABLE
10 × 10 × 12
TO
28 × 18 × 18

ARMCHAIR

DINING TABLE

4 OR 6
12" OR 15"
EXTENSION
LEAVES

END TABLE

COCKTAIL TABLE

CARD TABLE

BUFFET TABLE

6 LEAVES
EXTENDS TO 110"

GATELEG TABLE

CALLED "CONSOLE"
IF LEAF SWINGS
UP ABOVE TOP

LEAF
SWINGS
UP

LEG UNIT
SWINGS OUT

NORMAL TOP 16 × 36
EXTENDED TOP 55 × 36

CHINA CABINET

GLASS

DESK

MAY HAVE SLOPE
DROP LEAF

BEDROOM CHIFFONIER

"CHEST OR
DRAWERS"

BEDROOM DRESSER

"BUREAU"

CHAISE LOUNGE

BACK MAY BE
ADJUSTABLE
OR FIXED

TEA CART

TOP 30" × 36"
WITH LEAVES
EXTENDED

DIMENSIONS ARE TYPICAL, CHECK MANUFACTURER FOR SPECIFIC TYPES OR MODELS.

FOLDING STEEL

	H	W	D
JUV.	22	14	15
JR.	28	16	17
STD.	30	18	19

STACKING CHAIR — 32, 17½, 20, 10

PLASTIC STACKING — FORMED PLASTIC SEAT — 32, 21, 16

"CONTINENTAL" — PLASTIC SEAT — 30, 20, 20

ARMLESS SIDE CHAIR — 30, 21, 20

SIDE CHAIR WITH ARMS — 30, 20½, 20

ARMLESS SIDE CHAIR — 29½, 18½, 16

SECRETARIAL — 30, ADJ. 16-20, 16, 16

FULL SHELL TABLET ARM — FULL MOULD SEAT/BACK — 30-32, 19, 36, 27

EXECUTIVE SIDE CHAIR — NON-ADJ. HEIGHT, MAY BE NONSWIVEL — 30-32, 21, 24

EXECUTIVE LO-BACK — ADJUSTABLE HEIGHT — 30-36, 21, 26

EXECUTIVE HI-BACK — ADJUSTABLE HEIGHT — 42-60, 26

SCHOOL SIDE CHAIR — 30, 18, 16

MOULDED PLYWD CHAIR — 30, 20, 17

FOLDING ARM — 28-30, 22, 18

DECK CHAIR — 30, 32, 22

ADJ. DRAFTING STOOL — ADJ. BACK, 12" DIA. SEAT, ADJ. 16-24

WOOD DRAFT'G STOOL — 28-30

BOSTON ROCKER — 42, 32, 22

CAPTAIN'S CHAIR — 28, 17, 18

AUDITORIUM SEAT — 32½, 26, 19-22

THEATER LOUNGER — RECLINER BACK — 36, 29, 20-24

STADIUM SEATING — 30, 21½, 18-22

FOLDING UPHOLSTERED — STORED 40H × 4T — 31¼, 22, 22

DIMENSIONS ARE TYPICAL, CHECK WITH MANUFACTURES FOR SPECIFIC MODELS AND SIZES.

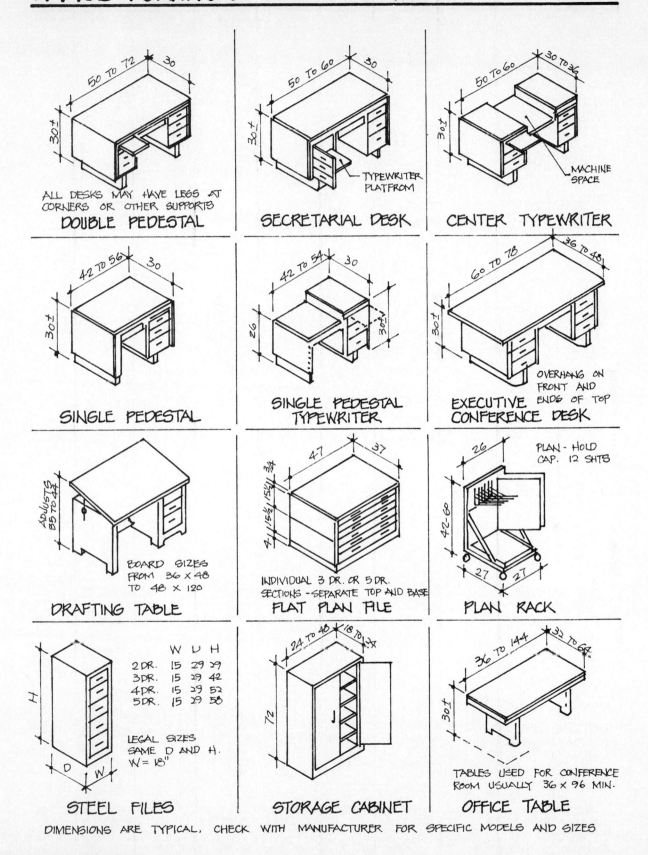

DOUBLE PEDESTAL
50 TO 72 / 30 / 30±
ALL DESKS MAY HAVE LEGS AT CORNERS OR OTHER SUPPORTS

SECRETARIAL DESK
50 TO 60 / 30 / 30±
TYPEWRITER PLATFORM

CENTER TYPEWRITER
50 TO 60 / 30 TO 36 / 30±
MACHINE SPACE

SINGLE PEDESTAL
42 TO 56 / 30 / 30±

SINGLE PEDESTAL TYPEWRITER
42 TO 54 / 30 / 26 / 30±

EXECUTIVE CONFERENCE DESK
60 TO 78 / 36 TO 48 / 30±
OVERHANG ON FRONT AND ENDS OF TOP

DRAFTING TABLE
ADJUSTS 35 TO 44
BOARD SIZES FROM 36 X 48 TO 48 X 120

FLAT PLAN FILE
47 / 37 / 3¼ / 4 / 15½ / 15¾
INDIVIDUAL 3 DR. OR 5 DR. SECTIONS - SEPARATE TOP AND BASE

PLAN RACK
26 / 42-60 / 27 / 27
PLAN - HOLD CAP. 12 SHTS

STEEL FILES

	W	D	H
2 DR.	15	29	29
3 DR.	15	29	42
4 DR.	15	29	52
5 DR.	15	29	58

LEGAL SIZES SAME D AND H. W = 18"

STORAGE CABINET
24 TO 40 / 18 TO 24 / 72

OFFICE TABLE
36 TO 144 / 33 TO 60 / 30±
TABLES USED FOR CONFERENCE ROOM USUALLY 36 x 96 MIN.

DIMENSIONS ARE TYPICAL, CHECK WITH MANUFACTURER FOR SPECIFIC MODELS AND SIZES

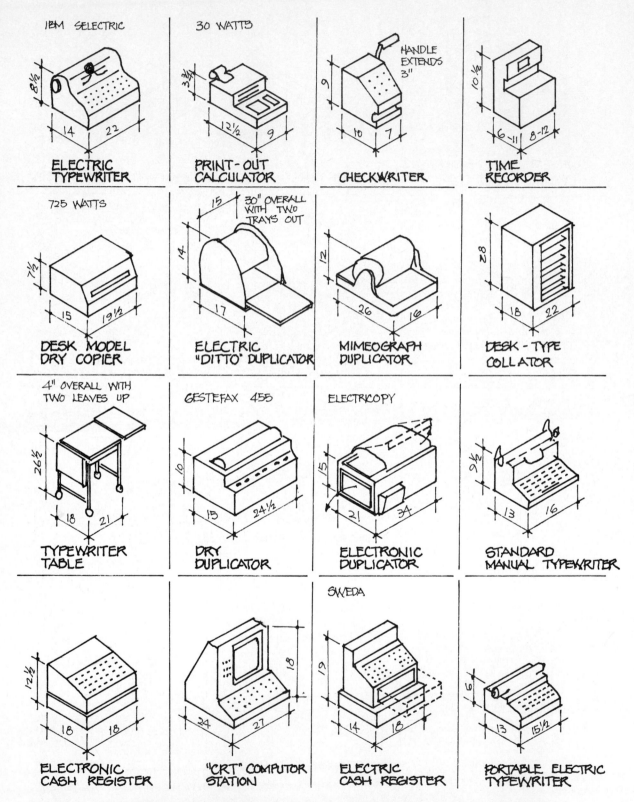

IBM SELECTRIC

ELECTRIC TYPEWRITER
8½, 14, 22

30 WATTS

PRINT-OUT CALCULATOR
3¾, 12½, 9

HANDLE EXTENDS 3"

CHECKWRITER
9, 10, 7

TIME RECORDER
10½, 6-11, 8-12

725 WATTS

DESK MODEL DRY COPIER
7½, 15, 19½

30" OVERALL WITH TWO TRAYS OUT

ELECTRIC "DITTO" DUPLICATOR
15, 14, 17

MIMEOGRAPH DUPLICATOR
12, 26, 16

DESK-TYPE COLLATOR
28, 18, 22

4" OVERALL WITH TWO LEAVES UP

TYPEWRITER TABLE
26½, 18, 21

GESTEFAX 455

DRY DUPLICATOR
10, 15, 24½

ELECTRICOPY

ELECTRONIC DUPLICATOR
15, 21, 34

STANDARD MANUAL TYPEWRITER
9½, 13, 16

ELECTRONIC CASH REGISTER
12½, 18, 18

"CRT" COMPUTOR STATION
18, 24, 27

SWEDA

ELECTRIC CASH REGISTER
19, 14, 18

PORTABLE ELECTRIC TYPEWRITER
6, 13, 15½

DIMENSIONS ARE TYPICAL, CHECK WITH MANUFACTURER FOR SPECIFIC MODELS AND SIZES.

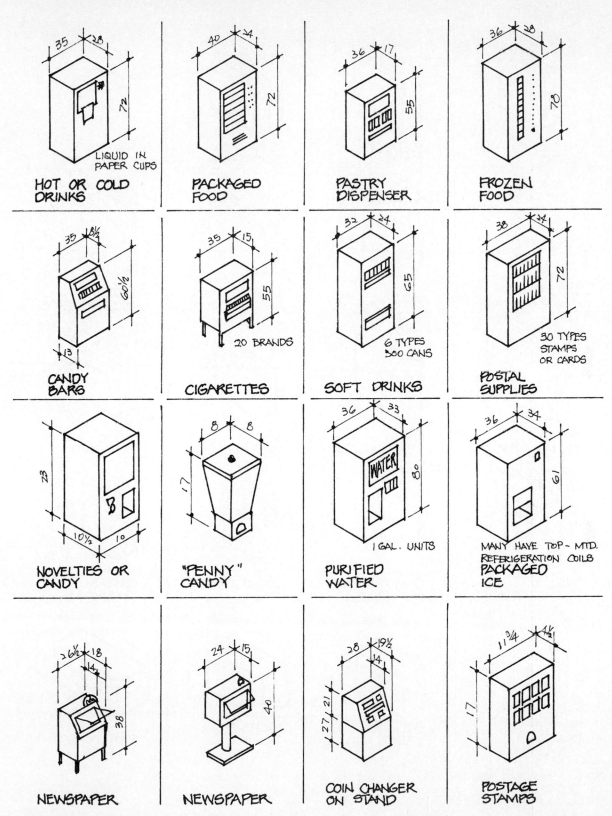

HOT OR COLD
DRINKS

PACKAGED
FOOD

PASTRY
DISPENSER

FROZEN
FOOD

CANDY
BARS

CIGARETTES

SOFT DRINKS

POSTAL
SUPPLIES

NOVELTIES OR
CANDY

"PENNY"
CANDY

PURIFIED
WATER

PACKAGED
ICE

NEWSPAPER

NEWSPAPER

COIN CHANGER
ON STAND

POSTAGE
STAMPS

DIMENSIONS ARE TYPICAL, CHECK WITH MANUFACTURER FOR SPECIFIC MODELS AND SIZES.

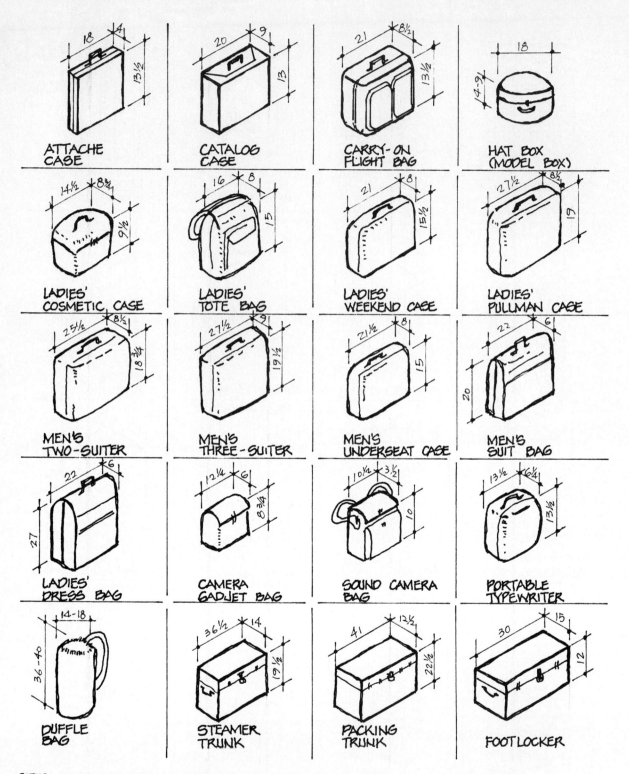

ATTACHE CASE

CATALOG CASE

CARRY-ON FLIGHT BAG

HAT BOX (MODEL BOX)

LADIES' COSMETIC CASE

LADIES' TOTE BAG

LADIES' WEEKEND CASE

LADIES' PULLMAN CASE

MEN'S TWO-SUITER

MEN'S THREE-SUITER

MEN'S UNDERSEAT CASE

MEN'S SUIT BAG

LADIES' DRESS BAG

CAMERA GADJET BAG

SOUND CAMERA BAG

PORTABLE TYPEWRITER

DUFFLE BAG

STEAMER TRUNK

PACKING TRUNK

FOOTLOCKER

SIZES SHOWN ARE AVERAGES AND WILL VARY WITH MANUFACTURER AND MATERIAL USED.

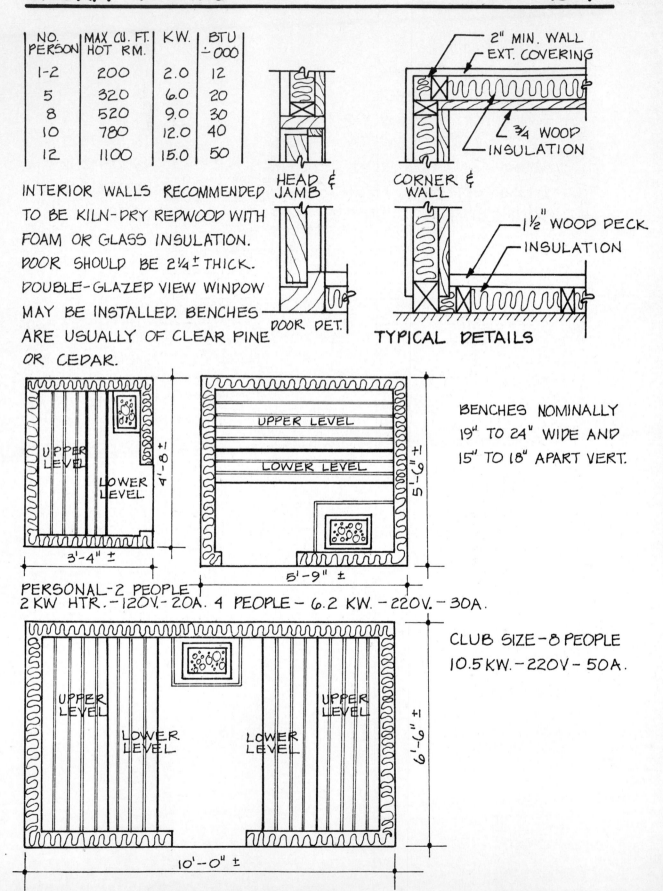

NO. PERSON	MAX CU. FT. HOT RM.	K.W.	BTU ÷ 000
1-2	200	2.0	12
5	320	6.0	20
8	520	9.0	30
10	780	12.0	40
12	1100	15.0	50

INTERIOR WALLS RECOMMENDED TO BE KILN-DRY REPWOOD WITH FOAM OR GLASS INSULATION. DOOR SHOULD BE 2¼ ± THICK. DOUBLE-GLAZED VIEW WINDOW MAY BE INSTALLED. BENCHES ARE USUALLY OF CLEAR PINE OR CEDAR.

HEAD & JAMB

DOOR DET.

CORNER & WALL

- 2" MIN. WALL
- EXT. COVERING
- ¾ WOOD INSULATION
- 1½" WOOD DECK
- INSULATION

TYPICAL DETAILS

PERSONAL-2 PEOPLE
2 KW HTR.-120V.-20A.

UPPER LEVEL

LOWER LEVEL

4'-8" ±

3'-4" ±

5'-9" ±

4 PEOPLE - 6.2 KW. - 220V. - 30A.

BENCHES NOMINALLY 19" TO 24" WIDE AND 15" TO 18" APART VERT.

CLUB SIZE - 8 PEOPLE
10.5 KW. - 220V - 50A.

UPPER LEVEL

LOWER LEVEL

LOWER LEVEL

UPPER LEVEL

6'-6" ±

10'-0" ±

HOT TUB SIZES								
SIZE	DIAMETER		HEIGHT			GAL.	WEIGHT (lbs.)	
	ID	OD	GRND.	STAVE	INSIDE		FULL	EMPTY
4 FT.	3'-9"	4'-0"	4'-0"	3'-11"	3'-7"	330	3,000	275
5 FT.	4'-11"	5'-2"	4'-0"	3'-11"	3'-7"	516	5,000	400
6 FT.	5'-9"	6'-0"	4'-0"	3'-11"	3'-7"	743	7,000	460
8 FT.	7'-9"	8'-0"	4'-0"	3'-11"	3'-7"	1332	12,000	800

TANK "FULL" APPROXIMATELY WITH WATER 4" TO 6" FROM TOP.

LOCATION OF 12" x 12" CONCRETE PIERS IF SOLID CONCRETE BASE NOT INSTALLED.

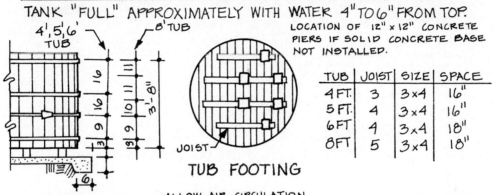

HOOP SPACING

TUB FOOTING

ALLOW AIR CIRCULATION UNDER AND AROUND TUB.

JOIST SPACING

TUB	JOIST	SIZE	SPACE
4 FT.	3	3x4	16"
5 FT.	4	3x4	16"
6 FT.	4	3x4	18"
8 FT.	5	3x4	18"

ELECTRICAL REQUIREMENTS

UNIT	SIZE	VOLTS	AMP
HEATER	12 KW	220	50
PUMP	1 HP	110	11
BLOWER		110	10

CALIFORNIA COOPERAGE

COMMON SOUND LEVELS (DECIBELS)

0	THRESHOLD OF HEARING
20	WHISPER
40	HOME NOISES
60	OFFICE NOISES
80	AVERAGE FACTORY NOISE
100	ROCK BAND
120	THRESHOLD OF PAIN
140	JET AIRPLANE TAKE-OFF

RECOMMENDED SOUND TRANSMISSION LEVELS — STC

PRIVATE RESIDENCE OR APARTMENT

	STC
LIVING AREA/BATHROOM	40
KITCHEN/LIVING AREA	38
KITCHEN/BEDROOM	38
BEDROOM/BEDROOM	32

APARTMENTS, MOTELS, HOSPITALS

	STC
LIVING AREA/BATHROOM	50
BATHROOM/BEDROOM	50
BATHROOM/BATHROOM	50
BEDROOM/BEDROOM	50
BEDROOM/CORRIDOR	42
SERVICE/CORRIDORS	45
KITCHEN/LIVING AREA	40

SCHOOLS

	STC
CLASSROOM/CLASSROOM	40
CLASSROOM/TOILET ROOMS	42
CLASSROOM/MECHANICAL SPACES	45
CLASSROOM/SHOPS	47
CLASSROOM/MUSIC ROOMS	50
CLASSROOM/CORRIDOR	50

OFFICES AND FACTORIES

	STC
GENERAL OFFICE/PRIVATE OFFICE	45
GENERAL OFFICE/WASHROOMS	40
PRIVATE OFFICE/PRIVATE OFFICE	45
PRIVATE OFFICE/WASHROOM	35
GENERAL OFFICE/SHOP AREA	50
LABORATORY/SHOP AREA	40
CONFERENCE ROOMS	40

IN CALCULATING SOUND TRANSMISSION IN STC, ATTENTION SHOULD BE ESPECIALLY GIVEN TO THE ATTIC OR ABOVE-PARTITION CONSTRUCTION TO REDUCE THE POSSIBILITY OF SOUND BEING CARRIED OVER THE PARTITION AS WELL AS THROUGH IT.

WOOD STUDS

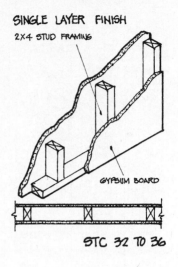

SINGLE LAYER FINISH

2×4 STUD FRAMING

GYPSUM BOARD

STC 32 TO 36

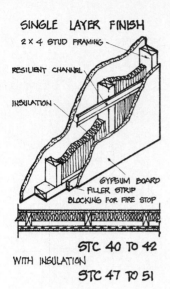

SINGLE LAYER FINISH

2 × 4 STUD FRAMING

RESILIENT CHANNEL

INSULATION

GYPSUM BOARD
FILLER STRIP
BLOCKING FOR FIRE STOP

STC 40 TO 42

WITH INSULATION

STC 47 TO 51

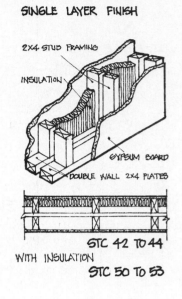

SINGLE LAYER FINISH

2×4 STUD FRAMING

INSULATION

GYPSUM BOARD
DOUBLE WALL 2×4 PLATES

STC 42 TO 44

WITH INSULATION

STC 50 TO 53

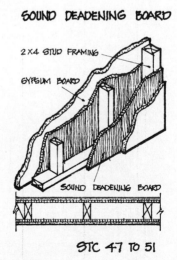

SOUND DEADENING BOARD

2×4 STUD FRAMING

GYPSUM BOARD

SOUND DEADENING BOARD

STC 47 TO 51

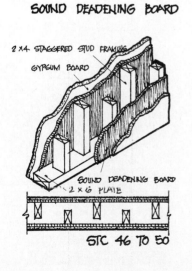

SOUND DEADENING BOARD

2×4 STAGGERED STUD FRAMING

GYPSUM BOARD

SOUND DEADENING BOARD
2×6 PLATE

STC 46 TO 50

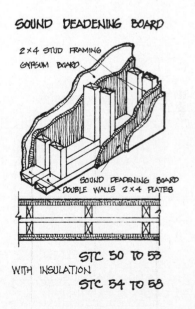

SOUND DEADENING BOARD

2×4 STUD FRAMING
GYPSUM BOARD

SOUND DEADENING BOARD
DOUBLE WALLS 2×4 PLATES

STC 50 TO 53

WITH INSULATION

STC 54 TO 58

FROM CONSTRUCTION: PRINCIPALS MATERIALS AND METHODS
UNITED STATES LEAGUE OF SAVINGS ASSOCIATIONS

WOOD STUDS

MULTILAYER FINISH

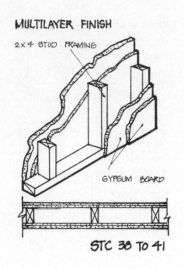

2 X 4 STUD FRAMING

GYPSUM BOARD

STC 38 TO 41

RESILIENT FINISH

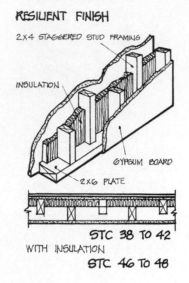

2 X 4 STAGGERED STUD FRAMING

INSULATION

GYPSUM BOARD

2 X 6 PLATE

STC 38 TO 42

WITH INSULATION
STC 46 TO 48

METAL LATH & PLASTER

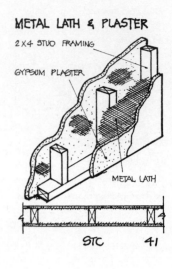

2 X 4 STUD FRAMING

GYPSUM PLASTER

METAL LATH

STC 41

GYPSUM LATH & PLASTER

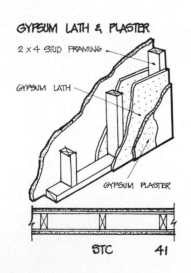

2 X 4 STUD FRAMING

GYPSUM LATH

GYPSUM PLASTER

STC 41

GYPSUM LATH & PLASTER

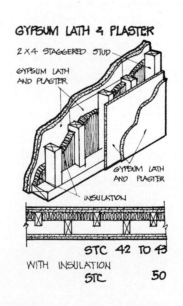

2 X 4 STAGGERED STUD

GYPSUM LATH AND PLASTER

GYPSUM LATH AND PLASTER

INSULATION

STC 42 TO 43

WITH INSULATION
STC 50

PLASTER BASE, VENEER PLASTER

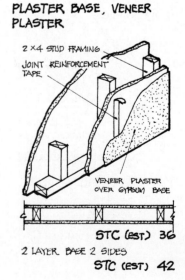

2 X 4 STUD FRAMING

JOINT REINFORCEMENT TAPE

VENEER PLASTER OVER GYPSUM BASE

STC (EST) 36

2 LAYER BASE 2 SIDES
STC (EST) 42

FROM CONSTRUCTION: PRINCIPALS MATERIALS AND METHODS
UNITED STATES LEAGUE OF SAVINGS ASSOCIATIONS

WOOD STUDS

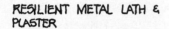

RESILIENT METAL LATH & PLASTER

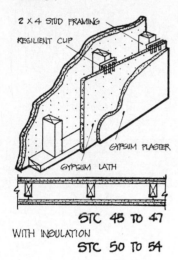

2 X 4 STUD FRAMING
RESILIENT CLIP
GYPSUM PLASTER
GYPSUM LATH

STC 45 TO 47
WITH INSULATION
STC 50 TO 54

RESILIENT PLASTER BASE, VENEER PLASTER

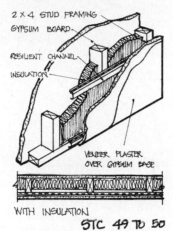

2 X 4 STUD FRAMING
GYPSUM BOARD
RESILIENT CHANNEL
INSULATION
VENEER PLASTER OVER GYPSUM BASE

WITH INSULATION
STC 49 TO 50

RESILIENT PLASTER BASE & MULTILAYER BASE, VENEER PLASTER

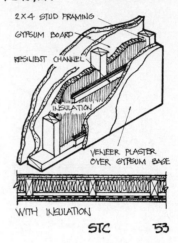

2 X 4 STUD FRAMING
GYPSUM BOARD
RESILIENT CHANNEL
INSULATION
VENEER PLASTER OVER GYPSUM BASE

WITH INSULATION
STC 53

RESILIENT GYPSUM LATH & PLASTER

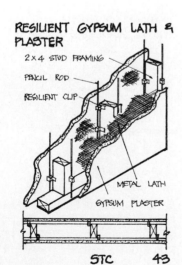

2 X 4 STUD FRAMING
PENCIL ROD
RESILIENT CLIP
METAL LATH
GYPSUM PLASTER

STC 43

FROM CONSTRUCTION: PRINCIPALS MATERIALS AND METHODS
UNITED STATES LEAGUE OF SAVINGS ASSOCIATIONS

METAL STUDS

SINGLE LAYER FINISH

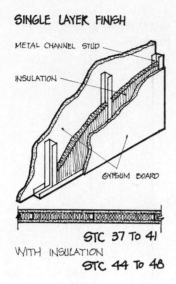

METAL CHANNEL STUD

INSULATION

GYPSUM BOARD

STC 37 TO 41

WITH INSULATION
STC 44 TO 48

SINGLE LAYER FINISH SOUND DEADENING BOARD

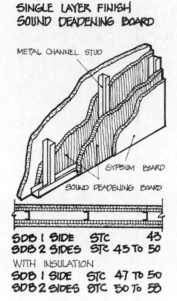

METAL CHANNEL STUD

GYPSUM BOARD

SOUND DEADENING BOARD

SDB 1 SIDE STC 43
SDB 2 SIDES STC 45 TO 50

WITH INSULATION
SDB 1 SIDE STC 47 TO 50
SDB 2 SIDES STC 50 TO 58

SINGLE LAYER FINISH SOUND DEADENING BOARD

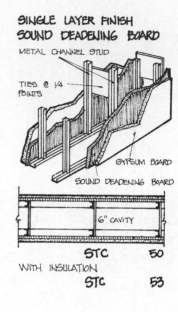

METAL CHANNEL STUD

TIES @ 1/4 POINTS

GYPSUM BOARD

SOUND DEADENING BOARD

6" CAVITY

STC 50

WITH INSULATION
STC 53

SINGLE LAYER FINISH

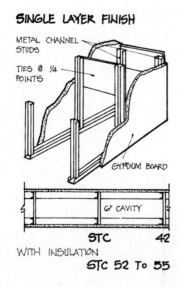

METAL CHANNEL STUDS

TIES @ 1/4 POINTS

GYPSUM BOARD

6" CAVITY

STC 42

WITH INSULATION
STC 52 TO 55

UNBALANCED FINISH

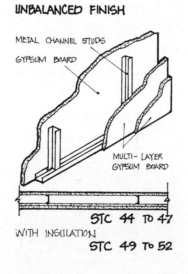

METAL CHANNEL STUDS

GYPSUM BOARD

MULTI-LAYER GYPSUM BOARD

STC 44 TO 47

WITH INSULATION
STC 49 TO 52

UNBALANCED FINISH SOUND DEADENING BOARD

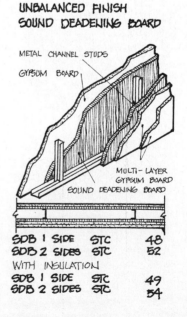

METAL CHANNEL STUDS

GYPSUM BOARD

MULTI-LAYER GYPSUM BOARD

SOUND DEADENING BOARD

SDB 1 SIDE STC 48
SDB 2 SIDES STC 52

WITH INSULATION
SDB 1 SIDE STC 49
SDB 2 SIDES STC 54

FROM CONSTRUCTION: PRINCIPALS MATERIALS AND METHODS
UNITED STATES LEAGUE OF SAVINGS ASSOCIATIONS

METAL STUDS

MULTILAYER FINISH

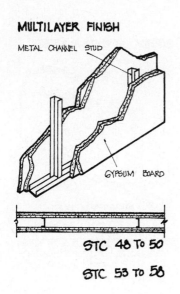

- METAL CHANNEL STUD
- GYPSUM BOARD

STC 48 TO 50

STC 53 TO 58

MULTILAYER FINISH SOUND DEADENING BOARD

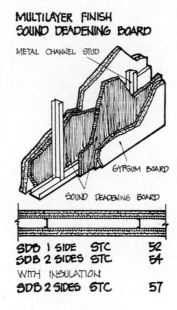

- METAL CHANNEL STUD
- GYPSUM BOARD
- SOUND DEADENING BOARD

SDB 1 SIDE STC 52
SDB 2 SIDES STC 54
WITH INSULATION
SDB 2 SIDES STC 57

GYPSUM LATH & PLASTER

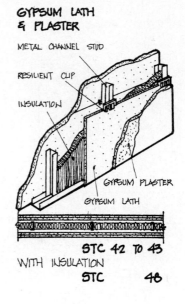

- METAL CHANNEL STUD
- RESILIENT CLIP
- INSULATION
- GYPSUM PLASTER
- GYPSUM LATH

STC 42 TO 43

WITH INSULATION
STC 48

PLASTER BASE & VENEER PLASTER

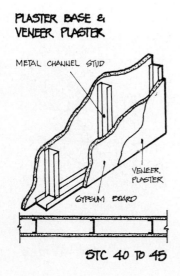

- METAL CHANNEL STUD
- VENEER PLASTER
- GYPSUM BOARD

STC 40 TO 45

MULTILAYER BASE & VENEER PLASTER

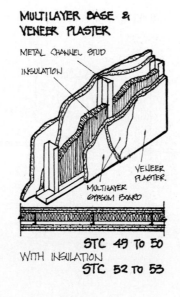

- METAL CHANNEL STUD
- INSULATION
- VENEER PLASTER.
- MULTILAYER GYPSUM BOARD

STC 49 TO 50
WITH INSULATION
STC 52 TO 53

RESILIENT GYPSUM LATH & PLASTER

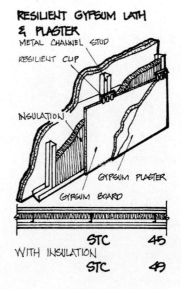

- METAL CHANNEL STUD
- RESILIENT CLIP
- INSULATION
- GYPSUM PLASTER
- GYPSUM BOARD

STC 45

WITH INSULATION
STC 49

FROM CONSTRUCTION: PRINCIPALS MATERIALS AND METHODS
UNITED STATES LEAGUE OF SAVINGS ASSOCIATIONS

METAL STUDS

MULTILAYER FINISH

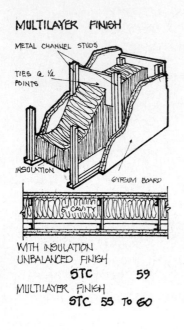

METAL CHANNEL STUDS

TIES @ 1/4 POINTS

INSULATION

GYPSUM BOARD

CAVITY

WITH INSULATION
UNBALANCED FINISH
STC   59
MULTILAYER FINISH
STC 55 TO 60

MULTILAYER FINISH
SOUND DEADENING BOARD

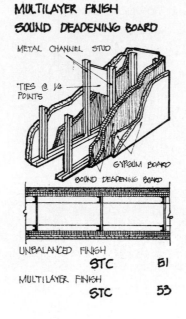

METAL CHANNEL STUD

TIES @ 1/4 POINTS

GYPSUM BOARD

SOUND DEADENING BOARD

UNBALANCED FINISH
STC   51
MULTILAYER FINISH
STC   53

GYPSUM LATH & PLASTER

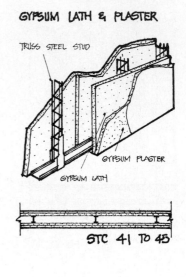

TRUSS STEEL STUD

GYPSUM PLASTER

GYPSUM LATH

STC 41 TO 45

METAL LATH & PLASTER

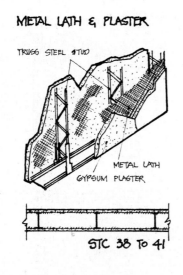

TRUSS STEEL STUD

METAL LATH

GYPSUM PLASTER

STC 38 TO 41

RESILIENT GYPSUM LATH & PLASTER

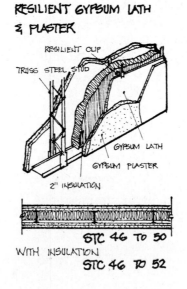

RESILIENT CLIP

TRUSS STEEL STUD

GYPSUM LATH

GYPSUM PLASTER

2" INSULATION

STC 46 TO 50
WITH INSULATION
STC 46 TO 52

RESILIENT METAL LATH & PLASTER

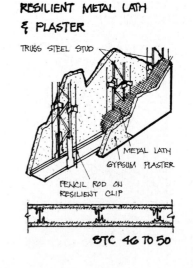

TRUSS STEEL STUD

METAL LATH

GYPSUM PLASTER

PENCIL ROD ON RESILIENT CLIP

STC 46 TO 50

FROM CONSTRUCTION: PRINCIPALS MATERIALS AND METHODS
UNITED STATES LEAGUE OF SAVINGS ASSOCIATIONS

CONCRETE MASONRY

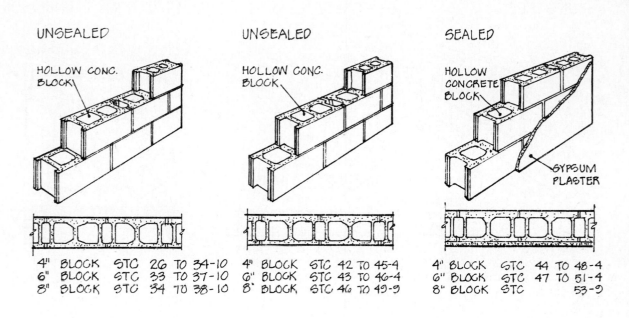

UNSEALED

HOLLOW CONC. BLOCK

4" BLOCK	STC	26 TO 34-10
6" BLOCK	STC	33 TO 37-10
8" BLOCK	STC	34 TO 38-10

UNSEALED

HOLLOW CONC. BLOCK

4" BLOCK	STC	42 TO 45-4
6" BLOCK	STC	43 TO 46-4
8" BLOCK	STC	46 TO 49-9

SEALED

HOLLOW CONCRETE BLOCK

GYPSUM PLASTER

4" BLOCK	STC	44 TO 48-4
6" BLOCK	STC	47 TO 51-4
8" BLOCK	STC	53-9

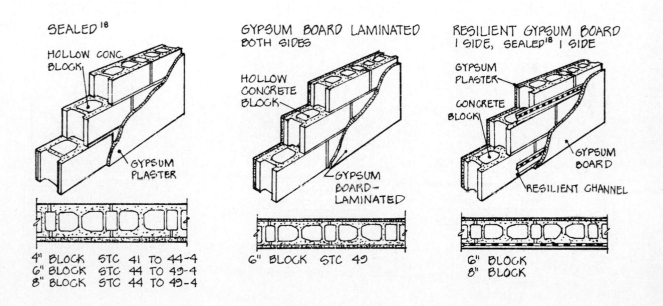

SEALED [18]

HOLLOW CONC. BLOCK

GYPSUM PLASTER

4" BLOCK	STC	41 TO 44-4
6" BLOCK	STC	44 TO 49-4
8" BLOCK	STC	44 TO 49-4

GYPSUM BOARD LAMINATED BOTH SIDES

HOLLOW CONCRETE BLOCK

GYPSUM BOARD-LAMINATED

6" BLOCK STC 49

RESILIENT GYPSUM BOARD 1 SIDE, SEALED [18] 1 SIDE

GYPSUM PLASTER

CONCRETE BLOCK

GYPSUM BOARD

RESILIENT CHANNEL

6" BLOCK
8" BLOCK

FROM CONSTRUCTION: PRINCIPALS, MATERIALS AND METHODS
UNITED STATES LEAGUE OF SAVINGS ASSOCIATIONS

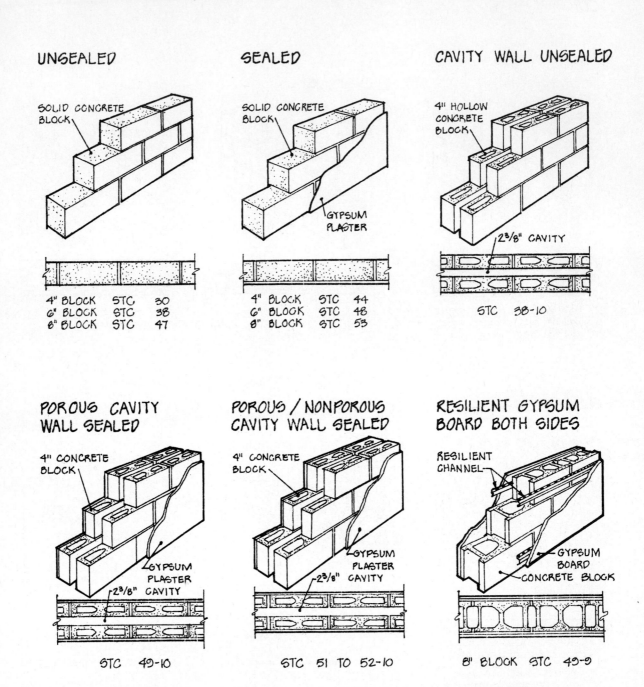

UNSEALED

SOLID CONCRETE BLOCK

4" BLOCK STC 30
6" BLOCK STC 38
8" BLOCK STC 47

SEALED

SOLID CONCRETE BLOCK

GYPSUM PLASTER

4" BLOCK STC 44
6" BLOCK STC 48
8" BLOCK STC 53

CAVITY WALL UNSEALED

4" HOLLOW CONCRETE BLOCK

2³/₈" CAVITY

STC 38-10

POROUS CAVITY WALL SEALED

4" CONCRETE BLOCK

GYPSUM PLASTER

2³/₈" CAVITY

STC 49-10

POROUS / NONPOROUS CAVITY WALL SEALED

4" CONCRETE BLOCK

GYPSUM PLASTER

2³/₈" CAVITY

STC 51 TO 52-10

RESILIENT GYPSUM BOARD BOTH SIDES

RESILIENT CHANNEL

GYPSUM BOARD
CONCRETE BLOCK

8" BLOCK STC 49-9

FROM CONSTRUCTION: PRINCIPALS, MATERIALS AND METHODS
UNITED STATES LEAGUE OF SAVINGS ASSOCIATIONS

CONCRETE MASONRY

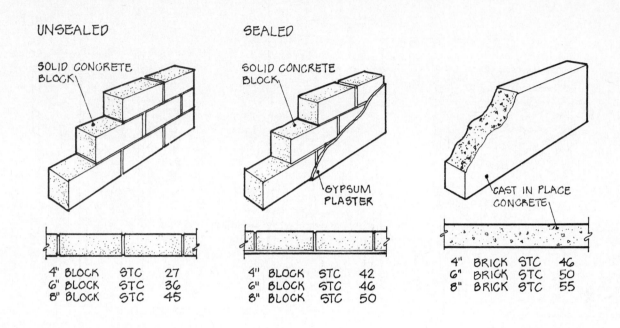

UNSEALED

SOLID CONCRETE BLOCK

4" BLOCK	STC	27
6" BLOCK	STC	36
8" BLOCK	STC	45

SEALED

SOLID CONCRETE BLOCK

GYPSUM PLASTER

4" BLOCK	STC	42
6" BLOCK	STC	46
8" BLOCK	STC	50

CAST IN PLACE CONCRETE

4" BRICK	STC	46
6" BRICK	STC	50
8" BRICK	STC	55

CLAY MASONRY

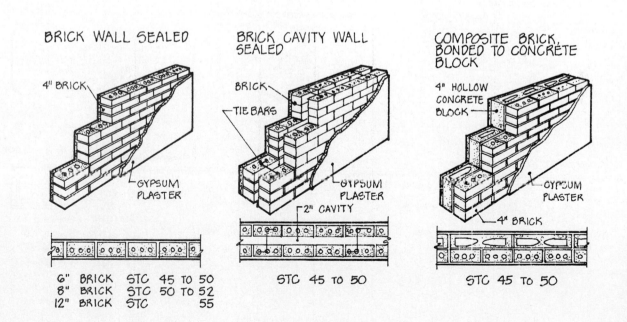

BRICK WALL SEALED

4" BRICK

GYPSUM PLASTER

6" BRICK	STC	45 TO 50
8" BRICK	STC	50 TO 52
12" BRICK	STC	55

BRICK CAVITY WALL SEALED

BRICK

TIE BARS

GYPSUM PLASTER

2" CAVITY

STC 45 TO 50

COMPOSITE BRICK, BONDED TO CONCRETE BLOCK

4" HOLLOW CONCRETE BLOCK

GYPSUM PLASTER

4" BRICK

STC 45 TO 50

FROM CONSTRUCTION: PRINCIPALS. MATERIALS AND METHODS
UNITED STATES LEAGUE OF SAVINGS ASSOCIATIONS

WOOD CONSTRUCTION

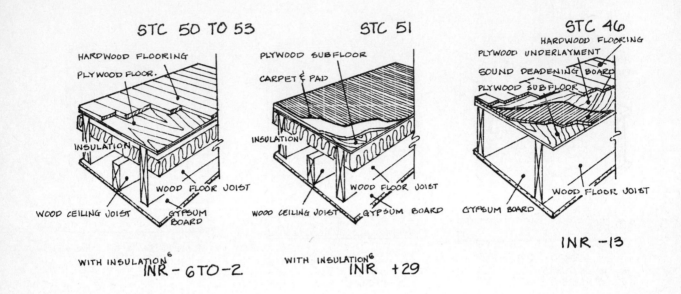

STC 50 TO 53

HARDWOOD FLOORING
PLYWOOD FLOOR.
INSULATION
WOOD CEILING JOIST
GYPSUM BOARD
WOOD FLOOR JOIST

WITH INSULATION[6]
INR - 6 TO -2

STC 51

PLYWOOD SUBFLOOR
CARPET & PAD
INSULATION
WOOD CEILING JOIST
GYPSUM BOARD
WOOD FLOOR JOIST

WITH INSULATION[6]
INR +29

STC 46

HARDWOOD FLOORING
PLYWOOD UNDERLAYMENT
SOUND DEADENING BOARD
PLYWOOD SUBFLOOR
GYPSUM BOARD
WOOD FLOOR JOIST

INR -13

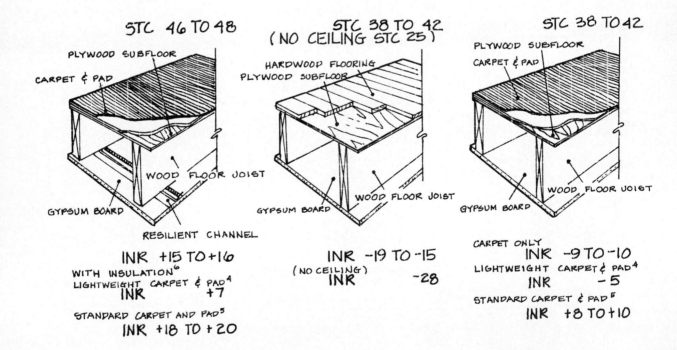

STC 46 TO 48

PLYWOOD SUBFLOOR
CARPET & PAD
GYPSUM BOARD
WOOD FLOOR JOIST
RESILIENT CHANNEL

INR +15 TO +16
WITH INSULATION[6]
LIGHTWEIGHT CARPET & PAD[4]
INR +7
STANDARD CARPET AND PAD[5]
INR +18 TO +20

STC 38 TO 42
(NO CEILING STC 25)

HARDWOOD FLOORING
PLYWOOD SUBFLOOR
GYPSUM BOARD
WOOD FLOOR JOIST

INR -19 TO -15
(NO CEILING)
INR -28

STC 38 TO 42

PLYWOOD SUBFLOOR
CARPET & PAD
GYPSUM BOARD
WOOD FLOOR JOIST

CARPET ONLY
INR -9 TO -10
LIGHTWEIGHT CARPET & PAD[4]
INR -5
STANDARD CARPET & PAD[5]
INR +8 TO +10

FROM CONSTRUCTION: PRINCIPALS MATERIALS AND METHODS.
UNITED STATES LEAGUE OF SAVINGS ASSOCIATIONS.

WOOD CONSTRUCTION

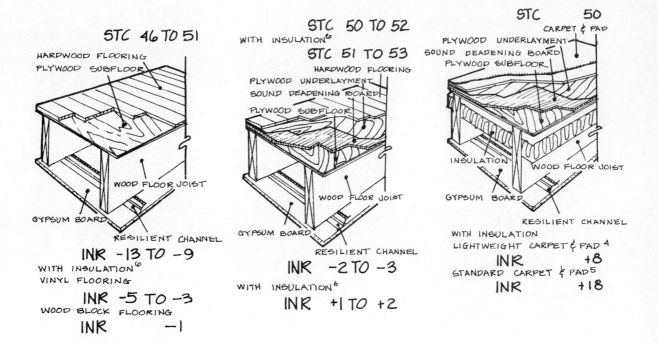

STC 46 TO 51

HARDWOOD FLOORING
PLYWOOD SUBFLOOR

WOOD FLOOR JOIST

GYPSUM BOARD

RESILIENT CHANNEL

INR -13 TO -9

WITH INSULATION[6]
VINYL FLOORING

INR -5 TO -3

WOOD BLOCK FLOORING

INR -1

STC 50 TO 52
WITH INSULATION[6]
STC 51 TO 53

HARDWOOD FLOORING
PLYWOOD UNDERLAYMENT
SOUND DEADENING BOARD
PLYWOOD SUBFLOOR

WOOD FLOOR JOIST

GYPSUM BOARD

RESILIENT CHANNEL

INR -2 TO -3

WITH INSULATION[6]

INR +1 TO +2

STC 50

CARPET & PAD
PLYWOOD UNDERLAYMENT
SOUND DEADENING BOARD
PLYWOOD SUBFLOOR

INSULATION

WOOD FLOOR JOIST

GYPSUM BOARD

RESILIENT CHANNEL

WITH INSULATION
LIGHTWEIGHT CARPET & PAD [4]

INR +8

STANDARD CARPET & PAD[5]

INR +18

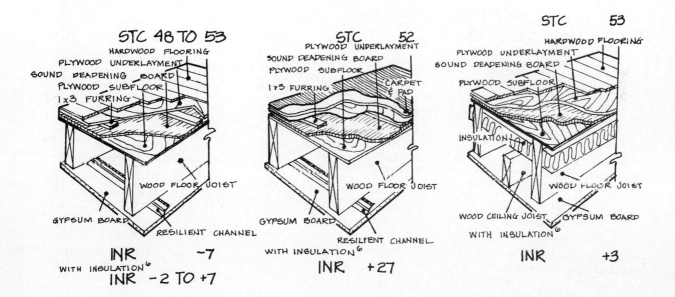

STC 48 TO 53

HARDWOOD FLOORING
PLYWOOD UNDERLAYMENT
SOUND DEADENING BOARD
PLYWOOD SUBFLOOR
1x3 FURRING

WOOD FLOOR JOIST

GYPSUM BOARD

RESILIENT CHANNEL

INR -7

WITH INSULATION[6]

INR -2 TO +7

STC 52

PLYWOOD UNDERLAYMENT
SOUND DEADENING BOARD
PLYWOOD SUBFLOOR
1x3 FURRING

CARPET & PAD

WOOD FLOOR JOIST

GYPSUM BOARD

RESILIENT CHANNEL

WITH INSULATION[6]

INR +27

STC 53

HARDWOOD FLOORING
PLYWOOD UNDERLAYMENT
SOUND DEADENING BOARD
PLYWOOD SUBFLOOR

INSULATION

WOOD FLOOR JOIST

WOOD CEILING JOIST   GYPSUM BOARD

WITH INSULATION[6]

INR +3

FROM CONSTRUCTION: PRINCIPALS MATERIALS AND METHODS.
UNITED STATES LEAGUE OF SAVINGS ASSOCIATIONS.

WOOD CONSTRUCTION

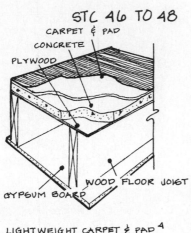

STC 46 TO 48

CARPET & PAD
CONCRETE
PLYWOOD

GYPSUM BOARD
WOOD FLOOR JOIST

LIGHTWEIGHT CARPET & PAD[4]
INR   -2
STANDARD CARPET & PAD[5]
INR   +10

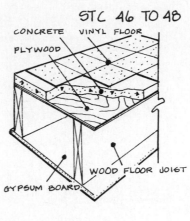

STC 46 TO 48

CONCRETE VINYL FLOOR
PLYWOOD

GYPSUM BOARD
WOOD FLOOR JOIST

INR -10 TO -14

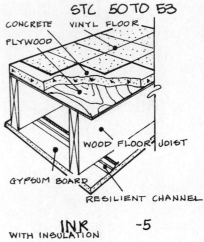

STC 50 TO 53

CONCRETE VINYL FLOOR
PLYWOOD

WOOD FLOOR JOIST
GYPSUM BOARD
RESILIENT CHANNEL

WITH INSULATION   INR   -5
WOOD BLOCK FLOORING
                         INR   +1
CUSHION BACKED VINYL
                         INR   +5

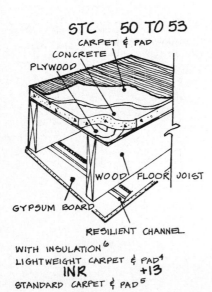

STC 50 TO 53

CARPET & PAD
CONCRETE
PLYWOOD

WOOD FLOOR JOIST
GYPSUM BOARD
RESILIENT CHANNEL

WITH INSULATION[6]
LIGHTWEIGHT CARPET & PAD[4]
INR   +13
STANDARD CARPET & PAD[5]

INR   +23

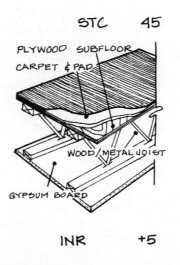

STC 45

PLYWOOD SUBFLOOR
CARPET & PAD

WOOD/METAL JOIST
GYPSUM BOARD

INR   +5

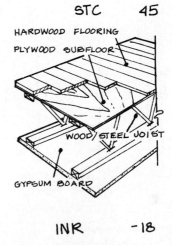

STC 45

HARDWOOD FLOORING
PLYWOOD SUBFLOOR

WOOD/STEEL JOIST
GYPSUM BOARD

INR   -18

FROM CONSTRUCTION: PRINCIPALS MATERIALS AND METHODS.
UNITED STATES LEAGUE OF SAVINGS ASSOCIATIONS.

WOOD CONSTRUCTION

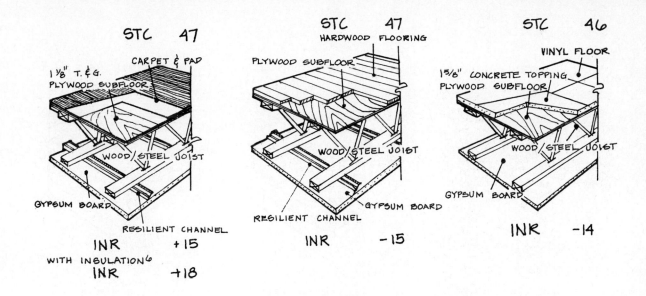

STC 47

1⅛" T. & G. PLYWOOD SUBFLOOR
CARPET & PAD
GYPSUM BOARD
WOOD/STEEL JOIST
RESILIENT CHANNEL

INR   +15
WITH INSULATION⁶
INR   +18

STC 47

HARDWOOD FLOORING
PLYWOOD SUBFLOOR
WOOD/STEEL JOIST
RESILIENT CHANNEL
GYPSUM BOARD

INR   -15

STC 46

VINYL FLOOR
1⅝" CONCRETE TOPPING
PLYWOOD SUBFLOOR
WOOD/STEEL JOIST
GYPSUM BOARD

INR   -14

CAST-IN-PLACE CONCRETE

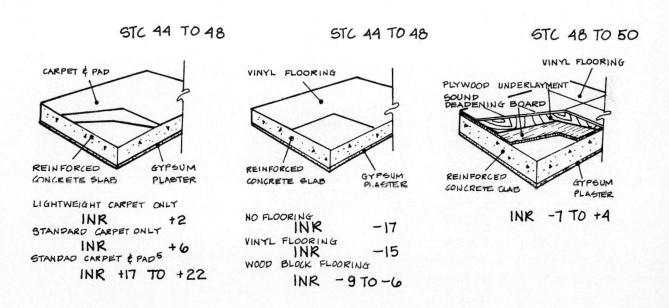

STC 44 TO 48

CARPET & PAD
REINFORCED CONCRETE SLAB
GYPSUM PLASTER

LIGHTWEIGHT CARPET ONLY
INR   +2
STANDARD CARPET ONLY
INR   +6
STANDAD CARPET & PAD⁵
INR +17 TO +22

STC 44 TO 48

VINYL FLOORING
REINFORCED CONCRETE SLAB
GYPSUM PLASTER

NO FLOORING
INR   -17
VINYL FLOORING
INR   -15
WOOD BLOCK FLOORING
INR -9 TO -6

STC 48 TO 50

VINYL FLOORING
PLYWOOD UNDERLAYMENT
SOUND DEADENING BOARD
REINFORCED CONCRETE SLAB
GYPSUM PLASTER

INR -7 TO +4

FROM CONSTRUCTION: PRINCIPALS MATERIALS AND METHODS.
UNITED STATES LEAGUE OF SAVINGS ASSOCIATIONS.

PRECAST CONCRETE FLOORS

STC   45

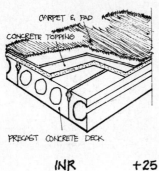

CARPET & PAD
CONCRETE TOPPING

PRECAST CONCRETE DECK

INR   +25

STC 45 TO 47

CARPET & PAD
CONCRETE TOPPING

PRECAST CONCRETE DECK

INR +18 TO +22

STC 45 TO 47

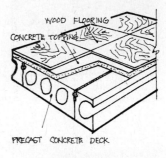

WOOD FLOORING
CONCRETE TOPPING

PRECAST CONCRETE DECK

VINYL FLOORING
        INR - 28 TO -23
WOOD BLOCK FLOORING
        INR -3 TO -4

STC   49

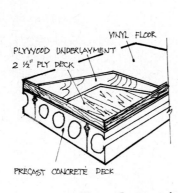

VINYL FLOOR
PLYWOOD UNDERLAYMENT
2 ½" PLY DECK

PRECAST CONCRETE DECK

INR +2 TO +4

STC 47 TO 51

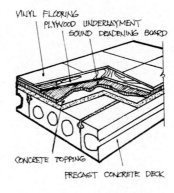

VINYL FLOORING
PLYWOOD UNDERLAYMENT
SOUND DEADENING BOARD

CONCRETE TOPPING

PRECAST CONCRETE DECK

INR +2 TO +4

FROM CONSTRUCTION: PRINCIPALS MATERIALS AND METHODS
UNITED STATES LEAGUE OF SAVINGS ASSOCIATIONS

BAR JOIST CONCRETE

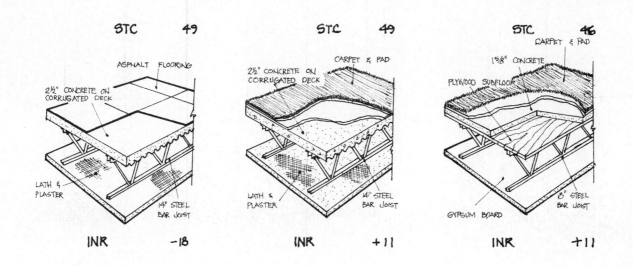

STC 49
ASPHALT FLOORING
2½" CONCRETE ON CORRUGATED DECK
LATH & PLASTER
14" STEEL BAR JOIST
INR −18

STC 49
CARPET & PAD
2½" CONCRETE ON CORRUGATED DECK
LATH & PLASTER
14" STEEL BAR JOIST
INR +11

STC 46
CARPET & PAD
1⅝" CONCRETE
PLYWOOD SUBFLOOR
GYPSUM BOARD
18" STEEL BAR JOIST
INR +11

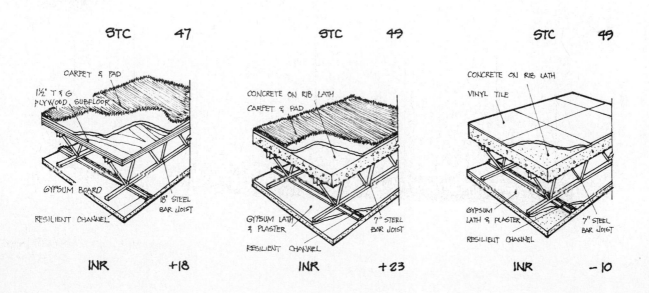

STC 47
CARPET & PAD
1½" T & G PLYWOOD SUBFLOOR
GYPSUM BOARD
RESILIENT CHANNEL
18" STEEL BAR JOIST
INR +18

STC 49
CONCRETE ON RIB LATH
CARPET & PAD
GYPSUM LATH & PLASTER
RESILIENT CHANNEL
7" STEEL BAR JOIST
INR +23

STC 49
CONCRETE ON RIB LATH
VINYL TILE
GYPSUM LATH & PLASTER
RESILIENT CHANNEL
7" STEEL BAR JOIST
INR −10

FROM CONSTRUCTION: PRINCIPALS MATERIALS AND METHODS
UNITED STATES LEAGUE OF SAVINGS ASSOCIATIONS

BAR JOIST CONCRETE

STC 47 TO 50   STC   47
                           WITH INSULATION
                                        STC   50

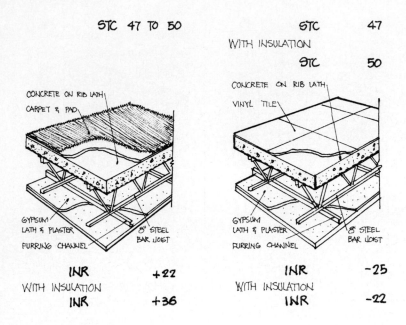

CONCRETE ON RIB LATH
CARPET & PAD

GYPSUM
LATH & PLASTER
FURRING CHANNEL   8" STEEL
                        BAR JOIST

CONCRETE ON RIB LATH
VINYL TILE

GYPSUM
LATH & PLASTER
FURRING CHANNEL   8" STEEL
                        BAR JOIST

INR   +22   INR   -25
WITH INSULATION   WITH INSULATION
INR   +36   INR   -22

FROM CONSTRUCTION: PRINCIPALS MATERIALS AND METHODS
UNITED STATES LEAGUE OF SAVINGS ASSOCIATIONS

FLOOR / CEILING SEPARATION RESIDENTIAL UNITS	GRADE I		GRADE II		GRADE III	
	STC	IIC	STC	IIC	STC	IIC
BEDROOM ABOVE BEDROOM	55	55	52	52	48	48
LIVINGROOM ABOVE BEDROOM	57	60	54	57	50	53
KITCHEN ABOVE BEDROOM	58	65	55	62	52	58
FAMILY ROOM ABOVE BEDROOM	60	65	56	62	52	58
CORRIDOR ABOVE BEDROOM	55	65	52	62	48	58
BEDROOM ABOVE LIVINGROOM	57	55	54	52	50	48
LIVINGROOM ABOVE LIVINGROOM	55	55	52	52	48	48
KITCHEN ABOVE LIVINGROOM	55	60	52	57	48	53
FAMILY ROOM ABOVE LIVINGROOM	58	62	54	60	52	56
CORRIDOR ABOVE LIVINGROOM	55	60	52	57	48	53
BEDROOM ABOVE KITCHEN	58	52	55	50	52	46
LIVING ROOM ABOVE KITCHEN	55	55	52	52	48	48
KITCHEN ABOVE KITCHEN	52	55	50	52	46	48
BATHROOM ABOVE KITCHEN	55	55	52	52	48	48
FAMILY ROOM ABOVE KITCHEN	55	60	52	58	48	54
CORRIDOR ABOVE KITCHEN	50	55	48	52	46	48
BEDROOM ABOVE FAMILY ROOM	60	50	56	48	52	46
LIVING ROOM ABOVE FAMILY ROOM	58	52	54	50	52	48
KITCHEN ABOVE FAMILY ROOM	55	55	52	52	48	50
BATHROOM ABOVE FAMILY ROOM	52	52	50	50	48	48
CORRIDOR ABOVE FAMILY ROOM	50	50	48	48	46	46
BATHROOM ABOVE BATHROOM	52	52	50	50	48	48
CORRIDOR ABOVE CORRIDOR	50	50	48	48	46	46

ADAPTED FROM FEDERAL HOUSING ADMINISTRATIONS
"GUIDE TO AIR BORNE NOISE IN DWELLINGS"

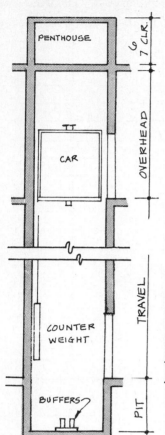

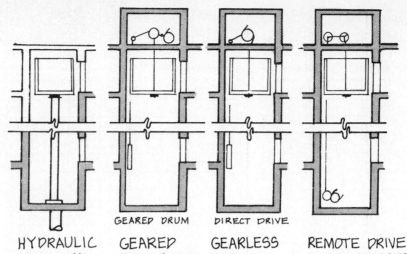

GEARED DRUM   DIRECT DRIVE

HYDRAULIC   GEARED   GEARLESS   REMOTE DRIVE

CHECK ANSI — A17.1 SAFETY CODE AND LOCAL ORDINANCES.

HYDRAULIC · RESIDENTIAL / SMALL COMERCIAL · 5 STORY - 75/200 FPM

CAPACITY	1200	2000	2500	3000	3500	4000
PLATFORM	$5^0 \times 4^0$	$6^4 \times 4^5$	$7^0 \times 5^0$	$7^0 \times 5^6$	$7^0 \times 6^2$	$5^8 \times 8^8$
HOISTWAY	$6^4 \times 4^3$	$7^8 \times 4^8$	$8^4 \times 5^3$	$8^4 \times 5^2$	$8^4 \times 6^5$	$7^6 \times 8^{11}$
ENTRANCE	$3^0 \times 7^0$	$3^0 \times 7^0$	$3^6 \times 7^0$	$3^6 \times 7^0$	$3^6 \times 7^0$	$4^0 \times 7^0$
PIT	4^0	4^6	5^0	5^0	5^6	5^6

SHAFT HOLE = TRAVEL + 6'-0" REQ. POWER RM. APPROX. $7^0 \times 9^0 \times 7^6$ HI.

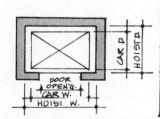

FREIGHT · LIGHT DUTY · GEARED · PIT 5^6 MIN. · 50/100 FPM

CAPACITY	2500 #	3000 #	6000 #	8000 #
CAR SIZE W x D	$5^4 \times 7^0$	$6^4 \times 8^0$	$8^4 \times 10^0$	$8^4 \times 10^0$
HOISTWAY W x D	$7^4 \times 7^6$	$8^4 \times 8^6$	$10^4 \times 10^6$	$10^{10} \times 10^6$
DOOR OP'NG W x H	$5^0 \times 7^0$	$6^0 \times 7^0$	$8^0 \times 7^0$	$8^0 \times 8^0$
OVERHEAD	16^0	16^0	16^4	16^8

FREIGHT · MEDIUM & HEAVY DUTY · GEARED · 50/200 FPM

CAPACITY	10000 #		12000 #		16000 #		18000 #		20000 #	
NO. DOORS	1	2	1	2	1	2	1	2	1	2
CAR SIZE W x D	$8^4 \times 12^0$	$8^4 \times 12^0$	$10^4 \times 14^0$	$10^4 \times 14^0$	$10^4 \times 14^0$	$10^4 \times 14^0$	$10^4 \times 16^0$	$10^4 \times 16^6$	$12^0 \times 20^0$	$12^0 \times 20^6$
HOIST WAY W x D	$11^8 \times 12^8$	$11^8 \times 12^8$	$13^8 \times 14^8$	$13^8 \times 14^{11}$	$13^8 \times 14^8$	$13^8 \times 14^{11}$	$13^8 \times 16^8$	$13^8 \times 16^{11}$	$15^4 \times 20^8$	$15^4 \times 20^8$
OVERHEAD	17^0	17^0	18^0	18^0	18^6	18^6	19^0	19^0	22^0	22^0
PIT	5^6	5^6	5^6	5^6	5^6	5^6	5^6	5^6	5^6	5^6
DOOR OP'NG. W x H	$8^0 \times 8^0$	$8^0 \times 8^0$	$10^0 \times 8^0$	$10^0 \times 8^0$	$10^0 \times 10^0$	$10^0 \times 10^0$	$10^0 \times 10^0$	$10^0 \times 10^0$	$11^8 \times 10^6$	$11^8 \times 10^6$

ALL INFORMATION IS TYPICAL. FOR DEFINITE REQUIREMENTS CONSULT ELEVATOR MANUFACTURERS.

GEARED ELEVATORS HAVE MOTOR AND BRAKE ON ONE SHAFT WHICH HAS GEARS TO DRIVE THE MAIN SHAFT. GEARLESS MACHINES HAVE MOTOR, DRUM AND BRAKE ALL MOUNTED ON ONE SHAFT THUS ONE MOTOR REVOLUTION TURNS SHAFT ONE TIME.

PASSENGER · GEARED · APARTMENT BLDGS. · SMALL HOTELS · OFFICES

CAPACITY LBS	1500	2000	2500	3000	3500
PERSONS	10	13	16	20	23
CAR W×D	$5^1 \times 4^5$	$6^1 \times 4^5$	$7^0 \times 5^0$	$7^0 \times 5^6$	$7^0 \times 6^2$
HOIST W×D	$6^8 \times 6^0$	$7^8 \times 5^0$	$8^4 \times 6^1$	$8^4 \times 6^{10}$	$8^4 \times 7^6$
ENT. DR. W×H	$2^8 \times 7^0$	$3^0 \times 7^0$	$3^6 \times 7^0$	$3^6 \times 7^0$	$3^6 \times 7^0$

SPEED FPM	1500 PIT	1500 O'HEAD	2000 PIT	2000 O'HEAD	2500 PIT	2500 O'HEAD	3000 PIT	3000 O'HEAD	3500 PIT	3500 O'HEAD
200	—	—	5^2	16^2	5^2	16^2	5^2	17^2	5^1	17^2
250	5^2	16^6	6^8	17^2	6^8	17^2	6^8	17^6	6^2	17^6
300	5^1	16^6	6^8	17^6	6^8	17^6	6^8	17^6	6^2	17^6
350	5^1	16^6	7^0	18^3	7^8	18^3	7^8	18^3	7^6	18^3

PASSENGER · GEARLESS · OFFICE BLDG · HOTELS · HI-RISE BLDGS.

CAPACITY LBS.	2000	2500	3000	3500	4000
PERSONS	13	16	20	23	26
CAR W×D	$6^1 \times 4^5$	$7^0 \times 5^0$	$7^0 \times 5^6$	$7^0 \times 6^2$	$8^0 \times 6^2$
HOIST W×D	$7^8 \times 5^0$	$8^4 \times 6^4$	$8^4 \times 6^{10}$	$8^4 \times 7^6$	$9^4 \times 7^6$
ENT. DR. W×H	$3^0 \times 7^0$	$3^6 \times 7^0$	$3^6 \times 7^0$	$3^6 \times 7^0$	$4^0 \times 7^0$

SPEED FPM	2000 PIT	2000 O'HEAD	2500 PIT	2500 O'HEAD	3000 PIT	3000 O'HEAD	3500 PIT	3500 O'HEAD	4000 PIT	4000 O'HEAD
500	8^4	15^2	8^4	16^1	8^4	16^1	8^4	17^1	8^6	17^2
600	9^2	18^2	9^2	18^1	9^2	16^{11}	9^2	16^{11}	9^4	17^0
700	10^2	19^2	10^2	19^1	10^2	16^{11}	10^2	16^{11}	10^2	17^2
800	10^2	20^1	10^2	20^5	10^2	18^3	10^2	18^3	10^{11}	18^4
1000	15^5	23^7	15^5	23^7	15^5	21^5	15^5	21^6	15^1	21^6
1200	15^5	23^7	15^5	23^7	15^5	21^3	15^5	21^6	15^1	21^6

HOSPITAL · GEARED

LBS.–PERSON	3500 · 23		4000 · 26		4500 · 30	
DOORS	1	2	1	2	1	2
CAR W×D	$5^1 \times 8^1$	$5^1 \times 8^{10}$	$5^8 \times 8^2$	$5^8 \times 9^2$	$5^8 \times 9^6$	$5^8 \times 9^{10}$
HOIST W×D	$7^4 \times 9^2$	$7^4 \times 10^1$	$7^8 \times 9^0$	$7^8 \times 9^1$	$7^{10} \times 9^{11}$	$7^{10} \times 10^1$
ENT. DR. W×H	$3^{10} \times 7^0$	$3^{10} \times 7^0$	$4^0 \times 7^0$	$4^0 \times 7^0$	$4^0 \times 7^0$	$4^0 \times 7^0$

SPEED FPM	1-PIT	1-O'HEAD	2-PIT	2-O'HEAD	1-PIT	1-O'HEAD	2-PIT	2-O'HEAD	1-PIT	1-O'HEAD	2-PIT	2-O'HEAD
200	5^0	16^6	5^0	16^6	5^2	17^0	5^2	17^0	5^8	17^2	5^2	18^0
250	5^2	16^6	5^2	16^6	6^2	17^6	6^2	19^6	6^2	17^6	6^2	19^6
300	6^2	16^6	6^2	16^6	6^2	17^6	6^2	19^6	6^2	17^6	6^2	19^6
350	7^8	17^0	7^8	17^0	7^8	18^3	7^8	19^6	7^8	18^3	7^8	19^6
500	—	—	—	—	10^6	21^{10}	10^6	27^6	10^6	21^{10}	10^6	27^6

ALL INFORMATION IS TYPICAL. FOR DEFINITE REQUIREMENTS CONSULT ELEVATOR MANUFACTURERS.

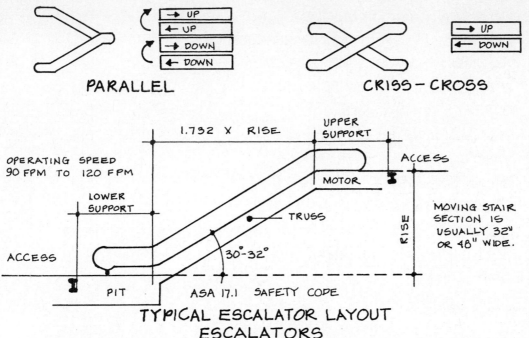

PARALLEL   CRISS-CROSS

TYPICAL ESCALATOR LAYOUT

ESCALATORS

WIDTH	SPEED (fpm)	MAX. CAPACITY	75% CAPACITY
32" (1.25 PERSON PER STEP)	90	425/5 MIN. 5,000 HR.	319/5 MIN. 3750 HR.
	120	566/5 MIN. 6,700 HR.	425/5 MIN. 5025 HR.
48" (2 PERSONS PER STEP)	90	680/5 MIN. 8,000 HR.	510/5 MIN. 6000 HR.
	120	891/5 MIN. 10,000 HR.	668/5 MIN. 8025 HR.

MOVING RAMPS

INCLINE	SPEED (fpm)	MAX. CAPACITY	75% CAPACITY
0°	180	1200/5 MIN. 14,400 HR	900/5 MIN. 10,000 HR.
5°	140	932/5 MIN. 11,180 HR.	700/5 MIN. 8,400 HR.
10°	130	867/5 MIN. 10,400 HR.	650/5 MIN. 7,800 HR.
15°	125	833/5 MIN. 10,000 HR.	625/5 MIN. 7,500 HR.

AMERICAN SAFETY CODE ALLOWS ONLY ONE HANDRAIL IF THE SLOPE IS 3° OR LESS, IF SPEED IS 70 FPM OR LESS, OR IF WIDTH IS NO MORE THAN 21". ALL ESCALATORS AND MOVING RAMPS MUST HAVE FACILITIES FOR CLOSING BETWEEN FLOORS IN CASE OF FIRE OR OTHER ACCIDENTS

MECHANICAL SYMBOLS   15.1

—— SOIL LINE	—A— COMRESSED AIR	—ACID— ACID WASTE
—-— COLD WATER	—V— VACUUM	—S— SPRINKLER MAIN
—--— HOT WATER	—+—+ REFRIGERANT	—FO— FUEL OIL
—G— FUEL GAS	—D— DRAIN LINE	—C— CONDENSATE
----- VENT	—CH— CHILLED WATER	—F— FIRE LINE

VALVE, CHECK	AUTOMATIC EXPANSION VALVE
VALVE, DIAPHRAGM	RETURN OR EXHAUST DUCT
VALVE, GATE	SUPPLY DUCT (SHOW SIZE)
VALVE, GLOBE	200/100 CFM CEILING AIR OUTLET
VALVE, LOCK AND SHIELD	20 x 12 / 100 CFM WALL AIR OUTLET
VALVE, MOTOR OPERATED	DUCT VOLUME DAMPER
VALVE, PRESSURE REDUCING	LIQUID PUMP
STRAINER	TANK, WATER OR FUEL
CO. CLEAN OUT	COMPRESSOR
HB HOSE BIBB	GAUGE
FLOOR DRAIN	SCALE TRAP
90° ELBOW	WATER CLOSET, TANK TYPE
45° ELBOW	WATER CLOSET, FLUSH VALVE
TEE CONNECTION	LAVATORY OR SINK
CROSS CONNECTION	URINAL
REDUCER	TUB - 4', 5', OR 5'-6"
STOP COCK	TUB, SQ. CORNER TYPE
SHOWER HEAD	SHOWER

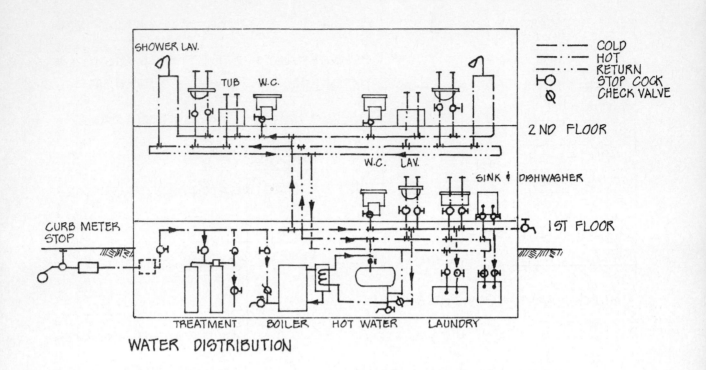

WATER DISTRIBUTION

COLD
HOT
RETURN
STOP COCK
CHECK VALVE

2 ND FLOOR

1 ST FLOOR

SHOWER LAV.

TUB   W.C.

W.C.   LAV.

SINK & DISHWASHER

CURB METER STOP

TREATMENT   BOILER   HOT WATER   LAUNDRY

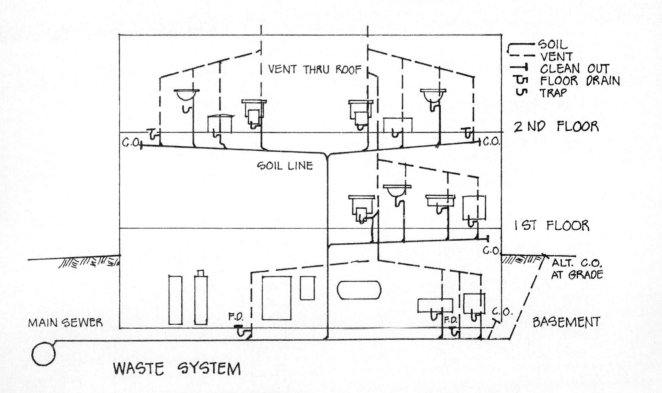

WASTE SYSTEM

SOIL
VENT
CLEAN OUT
FLOOR DRAIN
TRAP

VENT THRU ROOF

2 ND FLOOR

SOIL LINE

1 ST FLOOR

ALT. C.O. AT GRADE

MAIN SEWER

F.O.   F.O.   C.O.

BASEMENT

C.O.   C.O.

WATER CONSUMPTION REQUIRMENTS

	RESID.		APTS.		OFFICE		CLUB		GYMS		HOTEL		FACTORY		SCHOOL	
	CW	HW	CW	HW	CW	HW	CW	HW	CW	HW	CW	HW	CW	HW	CW	HW
WATERCLOSET FV	5		5		30		30		30		20		30		20	
WATERCLOSET TANK	8		8		15		15		50		35		50		35	
URINAL FV					20		20		20		14		20		20	
URINAL TANK					15		15		15		10		15		15	
URINAL AUTO. TANK					30		30		30		30		30		30	
URINAL PIPE / FT.													5		4	
LAVATORY	½	1	½	1	½	1	1	3	1	4	1	3	5	10	½	1
SHOWERS	10	20	10	20			100	200	25	250	35	70	125	250	25	75
BATH TUB	10	20	10	20			8	15	16	32	7	14				
KITCHEN SINK	5	10	4	8			10	30			10	30	10	30	10	30
DISHWASHER	5	15									35	35				
LAUNDRY TRAY	10	15	5	10			15	30			20	40				
LAUNDRY WASHER	15	35														

GALLONS PER HOUR DEMAND. DEMAND PER DAY IS USUALLY ABOUT TEN TIMES THE MAXIMUM HOUR DEMAND.

PRESSURES IN POUNDS PER SQUARE INCH, CORRESPONDING TO HEADS OF WATER IN FEET

HEAD FT.	0	1	2	3	4	5	6	7	8	9
0		0.433	0.866	1.299	1.732	2.165	2.598	3.031	3.464	3.987
10	4.330	4.763	5.196	5.629	6.062	6.495	6.928	7.361	7.794	8.277
20	8.660	9.093	9.526	9.959	10.392	10.825	11.258	11.691	12.124	12.557
30	12.990	13.423	13.856	14.289	14.722	14.722	15.588	16.021	16.454	16.877
40	17.320	17.753	18.186	18.619	19.052	19.052	19.918	20.351	20.784	21.217
50	21.650	22.083	22.516	22.949	23.382	23.815	24.248	24.681	25.114	25.547
60	25.980	26.413	26.846	27.279	27.712	28.145	28.578	29.001	29.444	29.877
70	30.310	30.743	31.176	31.609	32.042	32.475	32.908	33.341	33.774	34.207
80	34.640	35.073	35.506	35.939	36.372	36.805	37.238	37.671	38.104	38.537
90	38.970	39.403	39.836	40.269	40.702	41.135	41.568	42.001	42.436	42.867

HEADS OF WATER IN FEET CORRESPONDING TO PRESSURES IN POUNDS PER SQUARE INCH

PRESSURE LBS. PER SQ. IN.	0	1	2	3	4
0		2.309	4.619	6.928	9.238
10	23.095	25.404	27.714	30.023	32.333
20	46.189	48.499	50.808	53.118	55.427
30	69.284	71.594	73.903	76.213	78.522
40	92.379	94.688	96.998	99.307	101.62
50	115.47	117.78	120.09	122.40	124.71
60	138.57	140.88	143.19	145.50	147.81
70	161.66	163.97	166.28	168.59	170.90
80	184.76	187.07	189.38	191.69	194.00
90	207.85	210.16	212.47	214.78	217.09

	5	6	7	8	9
0	11.547	13.857	16.166	18.476	20.785
10	34.642	36.952	39.261	41.570	43.880
20	57.737	60.046	62.356	64.665	66.975
30	80.831	83.141	85.450	87.760	90.069
40	103.93	106.24	108.55	110.85	113.16
50	127.02	129.33	131.64	133.95	136.26
60	150.12	152.42	154.73	157.04	159.35
70	173.21	175.52	177.83	180.14	182.45
80	197.31	198.61	200.92	203.23	205.54
90	219.40	221.71	224.02	226.33	228.64

AT 62° F., 1 FOOT HEAD = 0.433 LB. PER SQUARE INCH; 0.433 × 144 = 0.433 × 144 = 62.355 LB. PER CUBIC FOOT. 1 LB. PER SQUARE INCH = 2.30947 FEET HEAD. 1 ATMOSPHERE = 14.7 LB. PER SQUARE INCH = 33.94 FEET HEAD.

CAST IRON PIPE ASSOCIATION

CONTENTS OF PIPE
CAPACITIES IN CUBIC FEET AND IN UNITED STATES GALLONS
(231 CUBIC INCHES) PER FOOT OF LENGTH

DIAMETER, INCHES	DIAMETER, FEET	FOR 1 FOOT LENGTH		DIAMETER, INCHES	DIAMETER, FEET	FOR 1 FOOT LENGTH		DIAMETER, INCHES	DIAMETER, FEET	FOR 1 FOOT LENGTH	
		CUBIC FT., ALSO AREA IN SQ. FEET	U.S. GAL. (231 CU. IN.)			CUBIC FT., ALSO AREA IN SQ. FEET	U.S. GAL. (231 CU. IN.)			CUBIC FT., ALSO AREA IN SQ. FEET	U.S. GAL. (231 CU. IN.)
1/4	.0208	.0003	.0026	6.75	.5625	.2485	1.859	19.0	1.583	1.969	14.73
5/16	.0260	.0005	.0040	7.00	.5833	.2673	1.999	19.5	1.625	2.074	15.52
3/8	.0313	.0008	.0057	7.25	.6042	.2868	2.144	20.0	1.666	2.182	16.32
7/16	.0365	.0010	.0078	7.50	.6250	.3068	2.295	20.5	1.708	2.292	17.15
1/2	.0417	.0014	.0102	7.75	.6458	.3275	2.450	21.0	1.750	2.405	17.99
9/16	.0469	.0017	.0129	8.00	.6667	.3490	2.611	21.5	1.792	2.521	18.86
5/8	.0521	.0021	.0159	8.25	.6875	.3713	2.777	22.0	1.833	2.640	19.65
11/16	.0573	.0026	.0193	8.50	.7083	.3940	2.948	22.5	1.875	2.761	20.75
3/4	.0625	.0031	.0230	8.75	.7292	.4175	3.125	23.0	1.917	2.885	21.58
15/16	.0677	.0036	.0270	9.00	.7500	.4418	3.305	23.5	1.958	3.012	22.53
7/8	.0729	.0042	.0312	9.25	.7708	.4668	3.492	24.0	2.000	3.142	23.50
15/16	.0781	.0048	.0359	9.50	.7917	.4923	3.682	25.0	2.083	3.409	25.50
1.00	.0833	.0055	.0408	9.75	.8125	.5185	3.879	26.0	2.166	3.687	27.58
1.25	.1042	.0085	.0638	10.00	.8333	.5455	4.081	27.0	2.250	3.976	29.74
1.50	.1250	.0123	.0918	10.25	.8542	.5730	4.286	28.0	2.333	4.276	31.99
1.75	.1458	.0168	.1250	10.50	.8750	.6013	4.498	29.0	2.416	4.587	34.31
2.00	.1667	.0218	.1632	10.75	.8958	.6303	4.714	30.0	2.500	4.909	36.72
2.25	.1875	.0276	.2066	11.00	.9167	.6600	4.937	31.0	2.583	5.241	39.21
2.50	.2083	.0341	.2550	11.25	.9375	.6903	5.163	32.0	2.666	5.585	41.78
2.75	.2292	.0413	.3085	11.50	.9583	.7213	5.397	33.0	2.750	5.940	44.43
3.00	.2500	.0491	.3673	11.75	.9792	.7530	5.633	34.0	2.833	6.305	47.17
3.25	.2708	.0576	.4310	12.00	1.000	.7854	5.876	35.0	2.916	6.681	49.98
3.50	.2917	.0668	.4998	12.50	1.042	.8523	6.375	36.0	3.000	7.069	52.88
3.75	.3125	.0767	.5738	13.00	1.083	.9218	6.895	37.0	3.083	7.486	55.86
4.00	.3333	.0873	.6528	13.50	1.125	.9940	7.435	38.0	3.166	7.876	58.92
4.25	.3542	.0985	.7370	14.00	1.167	1.069	7.997	39.0	3.250	8.296	62.06
4.50	.3750	.1105	.8263	14.50	1.208	1.147	8.578	40.0	3.333	8.728	65.29
4.75	.3958	.1231	.9205	15.00	1.250	1.227	9.180	41.0	3.416	9.168	68.58
5.00	.4167	.1364	1.020	15.50	1.292	1.310	9.801	42.0	3.500	9.620	71.96
5.25	.4375	.1503	1.124	16.00	1.333	1.396	10.44	43.0	3.583	10.084	75.43
5.50	.4583	.1650	1.234	16.50	1.375	1.485	11.11	44.0	3.666	10.560	79.00
5.75	.4792	.1803	1.349	17.00	1.417	1.576	11.79	45.0	3.750	11.044	82.62
6.00	.5000	.1963	1.469	17.50	1.458	1.670	12.50	46.0	3.833	11.540	86.32
6.25	.5208	.2130	1.594	18.00	1.500	1.767	13.22	47.0	3.916	12.048	90.12
6.50	.5417	.2305	1.724	18.50	1.542	1.867	13.97	48.0	4.000	12.566	94.02

1 CUBIC FOOT OF WATER WEIGHS 62.35 POUNDS; 1 GALLON (U.S.) WEIGHS 8.335 POUNDS.

CAST IRON PIPE RESEARCH ASSOCIATION

COMPARATIVE PIPE SIZES

NOM. PIPE SIZE	GALVANIZED STEEL			COPPER PIPE			COPPER TUBING TYPE L			CAST IRON PIPE STANDARD WT. BELL AND SPIGOT		
	OUT DI.	IN DI.	WT/FT.	OUT DI.	IN DI.	WT/FT.	OUT DI.	IN DI.	WT./FT.	OUT DI.	IN DI.	WT./FT.
¼	.540	.364	.42	.540	.375	.46	.375	.315	.126			
½	.640	.622	.85	.840	.625	.957	.625	.545	.285			
¾	1.050	.824	1.13	1.050	.822	1.30	.875	.785	455			
1	1.315	1.049	1.68	1.315	1.062	1.83	1.125	1.025	.655			
1¼	1.660	1.380	2.27	1.660	1.365	2.69	1.375	1.265	.884			
1½	1.900	1.610	2.72	1.900	1.600	3.20	1.625	1.505	1.14			
2	2.375	2.067	3.65	2.375	2.062	4.23	2.125	1.985	1.75	2.38	2.00	3.5
2½	2.875	2.469	5.79	2.875	2.500	6.14	2.265	2.105	2.48			
3	3.500	3.178	7.58	3.500	3.062	8.75	3.125	2.945	3.33	3.50	3.00	4.5
3½	4.000	3.645	9.11	4.000	3.500	11.41	3.625	3.425	4.29			
4	4.500	4.126	10.79	4.500	4.000	12.94	4.125	3.905	5.38	4.50	4.00	6.5
5	5.563	5.147	14.62	5.563	5.062	15.21	5.125	4.875	7.61	5.50	5.00	8.4
6	6.625	6.065	18.97	6.625	6.125	19.41	6.125	5.845	10.2	6.50	6.00	10.4
8	8.625	7.981	28.55	8.625	8.000	31.63	8.125	7.725	19.3	8.63	8.00	17.0
10	10.75	10.02	40.48	10.75	10.02	46.22	10.13	9.625	30.1	10.75	10.00	23.0
12	12.75	12.00	49.56				12.13	11.56	40.4	12.75	12.00	35.0

      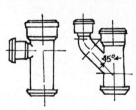

90° ELBOW   TEE   CROSS   45° ELBOW   90° ELBOW

TEE

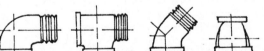   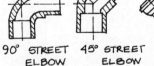 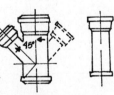

STREET ELBOW   STREET TEE   45° ST. ELL.   REDUCER

GALVANIZED STEEL OR BRASS

TYPICAL PIPE FITTINGS

90° STREET ELBOW   45° STREET ELBOW

COPPER TUBING   CAST IRON

125 LB. PER SQ. IN. BOLTED FLANGE

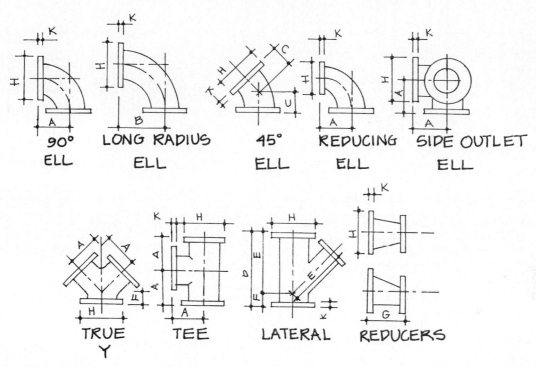

90° ELL LONG RADIUS ELL 45° ELL REDUCING ELL SIDE OUTLET ELL

TRUE Y TEE LATERAL REDUCERS

NOM. SIZE	A	B	C	D	E	F	G	H	K	L	M
1	3½	5	1¾	7½	5¾	1¾	—	4¼	7/16	3⅛	5/8
1¼	3¾	5½	2	8	6¼	1¾	—	4⅝	½	3½	5/8
1½	4	6	2¼	9	7	2	—	5	9/16	3⅞	5/8
2	4½	6½	2½	10½	8	2½	5	6	5/8	4¾	3/4
2½	5	7	3	12	9½	2½	5½	7	11/16	5½	3/4
3	5½	7¾	3	13	10	3	6	7½	3/4	6	3/4
3½	6	8½	3½	14½	11½	3	6½	8½	13/16	7	3/4
4	6½	9	4	15	12	3	7	9	15/16	7½	3/4
5	7½	10¼	4½	17	13½	3½	8	10	15/16	8½	7/8
6	8	11½	5	18	14½	3½	9	11	1	9½	7/8
8	9	14	5½	22	17½	4½	11	13½	1⅛	11¾	7/8
10	11	16½	6½	25½	20½	5	12	16	1 3/16	14¼	1
12	12	19	7½	30	24½	5½	14	19	1¼	17	1

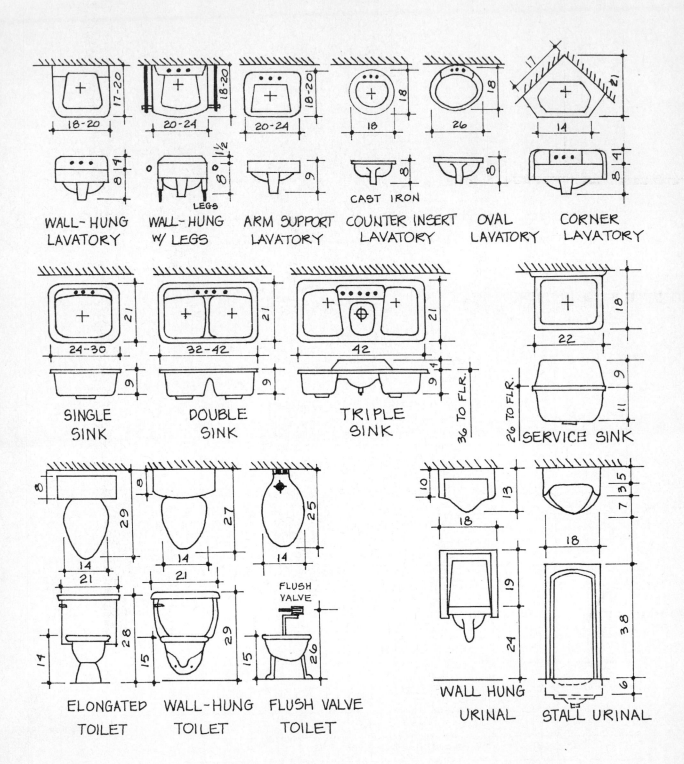

WALL-HUNG LAVATORY

WALL-HUNG W/ LEGS

ARM SUPPORT LAVATORY

COUNTER INSERT LAVATORY

OVAL LAVATORY

CORNER LAVATORY

SINGLE SINK

DOUBLE SINK

TRIPLE SINK

SERVICE SINK

ELONGATED TOILET

WALL-HUNG TOILET

FLUSH VALVE TOILET

WALL HUNG URINAL

STALL URINAL

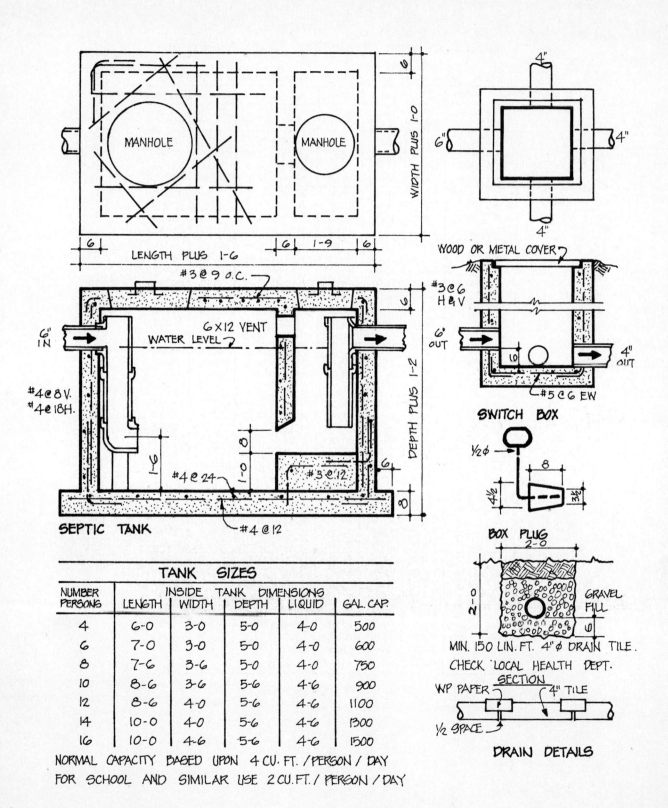

SEPTIC TANK

WOOD OR METAL COVER

SWITCH BOX

BOX PLUG

MIN. 150 LIN. FT. 4"ø DRAIN TILE.
CHECK LOCAL HEALTH DEPT.

GRAVEL FILL

SECTION

WP PAPER   4" TILE
½ SPACE

DRAIN DETAILS

TANK SIZES					
NUMBER PERSONS	INSIDE TANK DIMENSIONS				
	LENGTH	WIDTH	DEPTH	LIQUID	GAL. CAP.
4	6-0	3-0	5-0	4-0	500
6	7-0	3-0	5-0	4-0	600
8	7-6	3-6	5-0	4-0	750
10	8-6	3-6	5-6	4-6	900
12	8-6	4-0	5-6	4-6	1100
14	10-0	4-0	5-6	4-6	1300
16	10-0	4-6	5-6	4-6	1500

NORMAL CAPACITY BASED UPON 4 CU. FT./PERSON/DAY
FOR SCHOOL AND SIMILAR USE 2 CU. FT./PERSON/DAY

CONTENTS OF TANKS AND CISTERNS PER FOOT OF DEPTH

1 GALLON = 231 CUBIC INCHES = 1 CUBIC FOOT ÷ 7.4805 = 0.13368 CUBIC FEET.

DIAM. FT. IN.	AREA SQ. FT.	GAL. 1 FOOT DEPTH	DIAM. FT. IN.	AREA SQ. FT.	GAL. 1 FOOT DEPTH	DIAM. FT. IN.	AREA SQ. FT.	GAL. 1 FOOT DEPTH
4 - 0	12.57	94.00	10 - 3	82.52	617.26	20 - 3	322.06	2409.2
4 - 1	13.10	97.96	10 - 6	86.59	647.74	20 - 6	330.06	2469.1
4 - 2	13.64	102.00	10 - 9	90.76	678.95	20 - 9	338.16	2529.6
4 - 3	14.19	106.12	11 - 0	95.03	710.90	21 - 0	346.36	2591.0
4 - 4	14.75	110.32	11 - 3	99.40	743.58	21 - 3	354.66	2653.0
4 - 5	15.32	114.61	11 - 6	103.87	776.99	21 - 6	363.05	2715.8
4 - 6	15.90	118.97	11 - 9	108.48	811.14	21 - 9	371.54	2779.3
4 - 7	16.50	123.42	12 - 0	113.10	846.03	22 - 0	380.13	2843.6
4 - 8	17.10	127.95	12 - 3	117.86	881.65	22 - 3	388.82	2908.6
4 - 9	17.72	132.56	12 - 6	122.72	918.00	22 - 6	397.61	2974.3
4 - 10	18.35	137.25	12 - 9	127.68	955.09	22 - 9	406.49	3040.8
4 - 11	18.99	142.02	13 - 0	132.73	992.91	23 - 0	415.48	3108.0
5 - 0	19.63	146.88	13 - 3	137.89	1031.5	23 - 3	424.56	3175.9
5 - 1	20.29	151.82	13 - 6	143.14	1070.8	23 - 6	433.74	3244.6
5 - 2	20.97	156.83	13 - 9	148.49	1110.8	23 - 9	443.01	3314.0
5 - 3	21.65	161.93	14 - 0	153.94	1151.5	24 - 0	452.39	3384.1
5 - 4	22.34	167.12	14 - 3	159.48	1193.0	24 - 3	461.86	3455.0
5 - 5	23.04	172.38	14 - 6	165.13	1235.3	24 - 6	471.44	3526.6
5 - 6	23.76	177.72	14 - 9	170.87	1278.2	24 - 9	481.11	3598.9
5 - 7	24.48	183.75	15 - 0	176.71	1321.9	25 - 0	490.87	3672.0
5 - 8	25.72	188.66	15 - 3	182.65	1366.4	25 - 3	500.74	3745.8
5 - 9	25.97	194.25	15 - 6	188.69	1411.5	25 - 6	510.71	3820.3
5 - 10	26.73	199.92	15 - 9	194.83	1484.4	25 - 9	520.77	3895.6
5 - 11	27.49	205.67	16 - 0	201.06	1504.1	26 - 0	530.93	3971.6
6 - 0	28.27	211.51	16 - 3	207.39	1551.4	26 - 3	541.19	4048.4
6 - 3	30.68	229.50	16 - 6	213.82	1599.5	26 - 6	551.55	4125.9
6 - 6	33.18	248.23	16 - 9	220.35	1648.4	26 - 9	562.00	4204.1
6 - 9	35.78	267.69	17 - 0	226.98	1697.9	27 - 0	572.56	4283.0
7 - 0	38.48	287.88	17 - 3	233.71	1748.2	27 - 3	583.21	4362.7
7 - 3	41.28	308.81	17 - 6	240.53	1799.3	27 - 6	593.96	4443.1
7 - 6	44.18	330.48	17 - 9	247.45	1851.1	27 - 9	604.81	4524.3
7 - 9	47.17	352.88	18 - 0	254.47	1903.6	28 - 0	615.75	4606.2
8 - 0	50.27	376.00	18 - 3	261.59	1956.8	28 - 3	626.80	4688.8
8 - 3	53.46	399.88	18 - 6	268.80	2010.8	28 - 6	637.94	4772.1
8 - 6	56.75	424.48	18 - 9	276.12	2065.5	28 - 9	649.18	4856.2
8 - 9	60.13	449.82	19 - 0	283.53	2120.9	29 - 0	660.52	4941.0
9 - 0	63.62	475.89	19 - 3	291.04	2177.1	29 - 3	671.96	5026.6
9 - 3	67.20	502.70	19 - 6	298.65	2234.0	29 - 6	683.49	5112.0
9 - 6	70.88	530.24	19 - 9	306.35	2291.7	29 - 9	695.13	5199.9
9 - 9	74.66	558.51	20 - 0	314.16	2350.1	30 - 0	706.86	5287.7
10 - 0	78.54	587.52						

CAST IRON PIPE RESEARCH ASSOCIATION

% DEPTH FILLED	% CAPACITY	% DEPTH FILLED	% CAPACITY	% DEPTH FILLED	% CAPACITY	% DEPTH FILLED	% CAPACITY	% DEPTH FILLED	% CAPACITY
1	.20	21	15.26	41	38.64	61	63.86	81	86.77
2	.50	22	16.32	42	39.89	62	65.10	82	87.76
3	.90	23	17.40	43	41.14	63	66.34	83	88.73
4	1.34	24	18.50	44	42.40	64	67.56	84	89.68
5	1.87	25	19.61	45	43.66	65	68.81	85	90.60
6	2.45	26	20.73	46	44.92	66	69.97	86	91.50
7	3.07	27	21.86	47	46.19	67	71.16	87	92.36
8	3.74	28	23.00	48	47.45	68	72.34	88	93.20
9	4.45	29	24.07	49	48.73	69	73.52	89	94.02
10	5.20	30	25.31	50	50.00	70	74.69	90	94.80
11	5.98	31	26.48	51	51.27	71	75.93	91	95.55
12	6.80	32	27.46	52	52.55	72	77.00	92	96.26
13	7.64	33	28.84	53	53.81	73	78.14	93	96.93
14	8.50	34	30.03	54	55.08	74	79.27	94	97.55
15	9.40	35	31.19	55	56.34	75	80.39	95	98.13
16	10.32	36	32.44	56	57.60	76	81.50	96	98.66
17	11.27	37	33.66	57	58.86	77	82.60	97	99.10
18	12.24	38	34.90	58	60.11	78	83.68	98	99.50
19	13.23	39	36.14	59	61.36	79	84.74	99	99.80
20	14.23	40	37.39	60	62.61	80	85.77	100	100.00

DIAM. FT. IN.	GAL. 1 FT. DEEP	DIAM. FT. IN.	GAL. 1 FT. DEEP	DIAM. FT. IN.	GAL. 1 FT. DEEP	DIAM. FT. IN.	GAL. 1 FT. DEEP	DIAM. FT. IN.	GAL. 1 FT. DEEP
1-0	5.8	6-0	211.4	11-0	710.6	16-0	1503.6	21-0	2590.2
1-3	9.17	6-3	229.4	11-3	743.3	16-3	1550.9	21-3	2652.2
1-6	13.21	6-6	248.1	11-6	776.7	16-6	1599.0	21-6	2715.0
1-9	17.91	6-9	267.6	11-9	810.9	16-9	1647.8	21-9	2778.5
2-0	23.49	7-0	287.8	12-0	848.1	17-0	1697.4	22-0	2842.7
2-3	29.73	7-3	308.7	12-3	881.3	17-3	1747.7	22-3	2907.7
2-6	36.70	7-6	330.3	12-6	917.7	17-6	1798.7	22-6	2973.4
2-9	44.41	7-9	352.7	12-9	954.8	17-9	1850.5	22-9	3039.9
3-0	52.86	8-0	375.9	13-0	992.6	18-0	1903.0	23-0	3107.1
3-3	62.03	8-3	399.7	13-3	1031.1	18-3	1956.2	23-3	3175.0
3-6	73.15	8-6	424.3	13-6	1070.4	18-6	2010.2	23-6	3243.6
3-9	82.59	8-9	449.2	13-9	1108.0	18-9	2064.9	23-9	3313.0
4-0	93.97	9-0		14-0	1151.2	19-0		24-0	3383.1
4-3	106.12	9-3		14-3	1192.6	19-3		24-3	3454.0
4-6	118.9	9-6		14-6	1234.9	19-6		24-6	3525.5
4-9	132.5	9-9		14-9	1277.8	19-9		24-9	3597.9
5-0	146.8	10-0		15-0	1321.5	20-0		25-0	3670.9
5-3	161.8	10-3		15-3	1365.9	20-3		25-3	3744.7
5-6	177.7	10-6		15-6	1407.5	20-6		25-6	3819.2
5-9	194.1	10-9		15-9	1457.0	20-9		25-9	3894.5

MAXIMUM DUCT VELOCITIES						
APPLICATION	TYP. NOISE LEVEL (DECIBELS)	IF REGENERATED NOISE IS CONTROLLED	IF DUCT FRICTION IS CONTROLLED			
			MAIN DUCTS		BRANCH DUCTS	
			SUPPLY	RETURN	SUPPLY	RETURN
RESIDENTIAL	20-35	1000	1000	800	600	600
APARTMENTS HOTEL BEDROOMS HOSPITAL BEDROOMS	24-50	1200	1500	1300	1200	1000
PRIVATE OFFICES DIRECTORS' ROOMS LIBRARIES	35-45	1500	2000	1500	1600	1200
GENERAL OFFICES HIGH CLASS RESTAURANTS HIGH CLASS STORES BANKS	45-55	1700	2000	1500	1600	1200
AVERAGE STORES CAFETERIAS	50-70 55-70	2000	2000	1500	1600	1200
INDUSTRIAL	70 PLUS	2200	2500	1800	2000	1500

RETURN AIR OPENINGS: INDUSTRIAL 800 FPM; COMMERCIAL 700 FPM, RESIDENTIAL 400 FPM. AIR INTAKES 700 FPM. CORRIDORS 125 FPM.

DUCT CLASS	GALV. STL. GA.	ALUM. (IN.)	NOMINAL SECTION LENGTH	MAX. SIZE PERIM.	MAX. SIZE SIDE
1	24	.025	96"	47"	19
2	24	.025	96"	94"	12 to 24
3	24	.025	48"	95"	25 to 30
3	22	.032			31 to 40
4	24	.025	48"	190"	18 to 30
4	22	.032			31 to 40
4	22	.032			41 to 60
4	20	.040			61 to 80
5	22	.032	48"	360"	36 to 40
5	22	.032			41 to 60
5	20	.040			61 to 72
5	20	.040			73 to 90
6	18	.051	48"	361" UP	91 & UP

ALL STEEL DUCTS TO BE CROSS-BROKEN UNLESS INSULATED. ALL ALUMINUM DUCTS TO BE CROSS-BROKEN. MINIMUM DIMENSION OF ANY DUCT NOT LESS THAN 6".

DUCT CLASS, DIMENSION AND SECTION AREA

DUCT DIMENSION IN INCHES — CLASS AND AREA OF DUCT IN SQ. FT.

(Left column: DUCT DIMENSION IN INCHES)

Dim	10	12	14	16	17½	18	19½	20	22	24	26	28	30	32	34	36	38	40	42	44	46	48	50	52
6				.67	.73	.75		.83	.91	1.0	1.1	1.2	1.3	1.3	1.4	1.5	1.6	1.7	1.8	1.8	1.9	2.0	2.1	2.2
7			.68	.78																				
8		.67	.78	.88		1.0		1.1	1.2	1.3	1.4	1.6	1.7	1.8	1.9	2.0	2.1	2.2	2.3	2.4	2.6	2.7	2.8	2.9
9		.75	.88																					
10	.69	.83	.97	1.1		1.3		1.4	1.5	1.7	1.8	1.9	2.1	2.2	2.4	2.5	2.6	2.8	2.9	3.1	3.2	3.3	3.5	3.6
11	.76	.92																						
12		1.0	1.2	1.3		1.5		1.7	1.8	2.0	2.2	2.3	2.5	2.7	2.8	3.0	3.2	3.3	3.5	3.7	3.8	4.0	4.2	4.3
14			1.3	1.6		1.8		1.9	2.1	2.3	2.5	2.7	2.9	3.1	3.3	3.5	3.7	3.9	4.1	4.3	4.5	4.7	4.9	5.1
16				1.8		2.0		2.2	2.4	2.7	2.9	3.1	3.3	3.6	3.8	4.0	4.2	4.5	4.7	4.9	5.1	5.3	5.6	5.8
17½					2.2			2.4	2.7	2.9														
18						2.3		2.5	2.8	3.0	3.3	3.5	3.8	4.0	4.3	4.5	4.8	5.0	5.3	5.5	5.8	6.0	6.3	6.5
20								2.8	3.1	3.3	3.6	3.9	4.2	4.5	4.7	5.0	5.3	5.6	5.8	6.1	6.4	6.7	7.0	7.2
22									3.4	3.7	4.0	4.3	4.6	4.9	5.2	5.5	5.8	6.1	6.4	6.7	7.0	7.3	7.6	8.0
24										4.0	4.3	4.7	5.0	5.3	5.7	6.0	6.3	6.7	7.0	7.3	7.7	8.0	8.3	8.7
26											4.7	5.1	5.4	5.8	6.1	6.5	6.9	7.2	7.6	8.0	8.3	8.7	9.0	9.4
28												5.5	5.8	6.2	6.6	7.0	7.4	7.8	8.2	8.6	9.0	9.3	9.7	10
30													6.3	6.7	7.1	7.5	7.9	8.3	8.8	9.2	9.6	10	10	11
32														7.1	7.6	8.0	8.4	8.9	9.3	9.8	10	11	11	12
34															8.0	8.5	9.0	9.5	9.9	10	11	11	12	12
36																9.0	9.5	10	11	11	12	12	13	13
38																	10	11	11	12	12	13	13	14
40																		11	12	12	13	13	14	14
42																			12	13	13	14	15	15
44																				13	14	15	15	16
46																					15	15	16	17
48																						16	17	17
50																							17	18
52																								19

CARRIER CORP.

DUCT DIMENSION IN INCHES (top) / **DUCT DIMENSION IN INCHES** (left)

CLASS AND AREA OF DUCT IN SQ. FT.

	54	56	58	60	64	68	72	76	80	84	88	92	96	100	104	108	112	116	120	124	128	132	136	140
6	2.3	2.3	2.4	2.5	2.7	2.8	3.0	3.2	3.3	3.5	3.7	3.8	4.0	4.1	4.3	4.5	4.7	4.8	5.0	5.2	5.3	5.5	5.7	5.8
8	3.0	3.1	3.2	3.3	3.6	3.8	40	4.2	4.4	4.7	4.9	5.1	5.3	5.6	5.8	6.0	6.2	6.5	6.7	6.9	7.1	7.3	7.6	7.8
10	3.8	3.9	4.0	4.2	4.5	4.7	50	5.3	5.6	5.8	6.1	6.4	6.7	6.9	7.2	7.5	7.8	8.1	8.3	8.6	8.9	9.2	9.4	9.7
12	4.5	4.7	4.8	5.0	5.3	5.7	6.0	6.3	6.7	7.0	7.4	7.6	8.0	8.3	8.7	9.0	9.3	9.7	10	10	11	11	11	12
14	5.3	5.4	5.6	5.8	6.2	6.6	7.0	7.4	7.8	8.2	8.6	8.9	9.3	9.7	10	11	11	11	12	12	12	13	13	14
16	6.0	6.2	6.5	6.7	7.1	7.6	8.0	8.5	8.9	9.3	9.8	10	11	11	12	12	12	13	13	14	14	15	15	16
18	6.8	70	7.3	7.5	80	8.5	9.0	9.5	10	11	11	12	12	13	13	14	14	15	16	16	16	17	17	18
20	7.5	78	8.1	8.3	8.9	9.5	10	11	11	12	12	13	13	14	15	15	16	16	17	17	18	18	19	19
22	8.3	8.6	8.9	9.2	9.8	10	11	12	12	13	13	14	14	15	16	17	17	18	18	19	20	20	21	21
24	9.0	9.3	9.7	10	11	11	12	13	13	14	15	15	16	17	17	18	19	19	20	21	21	22	23	23
26	9.8	10	11	11	12	12	13	14	14	15	16	17	17	18	19	20	20	21	22	22	23	24	25	25
28	11	11	11	12	12	13	14	15	16	16	17	18	19	19	20	21	22	23	23	24	25	26	27	27
30	11	12	12	13	13	14	15	16	17	18	18	19	20	21	22	23	23	24	25	26	27	28	28	29
32	12	13	13	13	14	15	16	17	18	19	20	20	21	22	23	24	25	26	27	28	29	29	30	31
34	13	13	14	14	15	16	17	18	19	20	21	22	23	24	25	26	26	27	28	30	30	31	32	33
36	14	14	15	15	16	17	18	19	20	21	22	23	24	25	26	27	28	29	30	31	32	33	34	35
38	14	15	15	16	17	18	19	20	21	22	23	24	26	26	27	29	30	31	32	33	34	35	36	37
40	15	16	16	17	18	19	20	21	22	23	24	26	27	28	29	30	31	32	33	34	36	37	38	39
42	16	16	17	18	19	20	21	22	23	25	26	27	28	29	30	32	33	34	35	36	37	39	40	41
44	17	17	18	18	20	21	22	23	24	26	27	28	29	31	32	33	34	35	37	38	39	40	42	43
46	17	18	19	19	20	22	23	24	26	27	28	29	31	32	33	35	36	37	38	40	41	42	44	45
48	18	19	19	20	21	23	24	25	27	28	29	31	32	33	35	36	37	39	40	41	43	44	45	47
50	19	19	20	21	22	24	25	26	28	29	31	32	33	35	36	38	39	40	42	43	44	46	47	49
52	20	20	21	22	23	25	26	27	29	30	32	33	35	36	38	39	40	42	43	45	46	48	49	51
54	20	21	22	23	24	26	27	29	30	32	33	35	36	38	39	41	42	44	45	47	48	50	51	53
56		22	23	23	25	27	28	30	31	33	34	36	37	39	40	42	44	45	47	48	50	51	53	54
58			23	24	26	27	29	31	32	34	35	37	39	40	42	44	45	47	48	50	52	53	55	56
60				25	27	28	30	32	33	35	37	38	40	42	43	45	47	48	50	52	53	55	57	58
64					28	30	32	34	36	37	39	41	43	44	46	48	50	52	53	55	57	59	60	62
68						32	34	36	38	40	42	44	45	47	49	51	53	55	57	59	60	62	64	66
72								38	40	42	44	46	48	50	52	54	56	58	60	62	64	66	68	70
76								40	42	44	47	49	51	53	55	57	59	61	63	66	68	70	72	74
80									45	47	49	51	53	56	58	60	62	65	67	69	71	73	76	78
84										49	51	54	56	58	61	63	65	68	70	72	75	77	79	82
88											54	56	59	61	64	66	69	71	73	76	78	81	83	86
92												59	61	64	67	69	72	74	77	79	82	84	87	89

CARRIER CORP.

ELECTRICAL   DIVISION 16

————	WIRING IN WALL OR CEILING	⌇⌒₆	SINGLE POLE SWITCH
– – –	WIRING IN FLOOR	⌇⌒₃	THREE-WAY SWITCH
- - - - -	WIRING EXPOSED	⌇⌒ᴸ	LOCK OR KEY SWITCH
—///—	CONDUIT WITH NUMBER OF WIRES	⌇⌒ᴾ	SWITCH AND PILOT LIGHT
—⊃	SERVICE WEATHER HEAD	⌇⊖ˢ	SWITCH AND DUPLEX RECEPTACLE
⌀	STREET LIGHT AND BRACKET	⊘	CEILING PAN
△	TRANSFORMER	◔	CLOCK RECEPTACLE
▬	PANELBOARD OR MAIN SWITCH	◀	TELEPHONE
⌇⊖	DUPLEX RECEPTACLE	▣ ⊙	SIGNAL PUSH BUTTON
⌇⊖	TRIPLEX RECEPTACLE	▽	BUZZER
⌇⬤	DUPLEX SPLIT-WIRED	◯▢	BELL
⌇▲	SPECIAL-PURPOSE OUTLET	R	RADIO OUTLET
⌇⊖ᴿ	RANGE OUTLET	TV	TELEVISION OUTLET
⌀	CEILING LIGHT FIXTURE	⟲	ELECTRIC MOTOR
⌇⌀	WALL BRACKET LIGHT FIXTURE	⌒	CIRCUT BREAKER
▭	FLUORESCENT LIGHT FIXTURE	⌁	FUSIBLE ELEMENT
EXIT	EXIT LIGHT	⊢◯	NURSE CALL SYSTEM
Ⓑ	BLANKED OUTLET	⊢◇	PAGING SYSTEM
Ⓙ	JUNCTION BOX	⊢◁	SOUND SYSTEM

	WATTS	VOLTS	WIRES	CIRCUIT BREAKER OR FUSE
RANGE	12,000	120/240	3 #6	60 A.
OVEN	5,000	120/240	3 #8	30 A.
RANGE TOP (UNIT)	7,000	120/240	3 #8	40 A.
BROILER	1,500	120	2 #12	20 A.
DEEP FRYER	1,300	120	2 #12	20 A.
MICROWAVE OVEN		120	2 #12	20 A.
REFRIGERATOR	400	120	2 #12	20 A.
FREEZER	400	120	2 #12	20 A.
COFFEEMAKER	1,000	120	2 #12	20 A.
DISPOSAL UNIT	400	120	2 #12	20 A.
DISHWASHER	1,800	120	2 #12	20 A.
LAUNDRY WASHER	1,200	120	2 #12	20 A.
LAUNDRY DRYER	5,000	120/240	3 #10	30 A.
TELEVISION	300	120	2 #12	20 A.
FIXED LIGHT	150	120	2 #14	15 A.
AIR CONDITIONER	2,400	120	3 #10	30 A.
CENTRAL FURNACE	600	120	2 #12	20 A.
FIXED BATH HEATER	1,500	120	2 #12	20 A.
PORTABLE HEATER	1,500	120	2 #12	20 A.
WATER PUMP	500	120/240	3 #12	20 A.
DUPLEX OUTLET	150	120	2 #14	15 A.

WATTAGE LOADS VARY WITH EQUIPMENT SO CHECK CAREFULLY
IF EQUIPMENT MFGR. IS KNOWN. FOR CALCULATING WATT
LOADS FOR FIXED LIGHTS AND DUPLEX OUTLETS, 150 WATTS-
PER-UNIT IS MINIMUM.

TO SIZE MAIN SAFETY SWITCH:

$$\frac{\text{TOTAL WATTS}}{\text{VOLTAGE}} = \text{SWITCH AMPS.}$$

NEW WORK OR REWIRING: TYPES RF-2, RFH-2, R, RH, RW, RHN, RHW, RH-RW
NEW WORK: FEP, FEBP, RUN, RUW, T, TF, THHN, THW, THWN, TW

WIRE SIZE	MAXIMUM NUMBER OF CONDUCTORS IN CONDUIT AND TUBING											
	½	¾	1	1¼	1½	2	2½	3	3½	4	5	6
18	7	12	20	35	49	80	115	176				
16	6	10	17	30	41	68	98	150				
14	4	6	10	18	25	41	58	90	121	155		
12	3	5	8	15	21	34	50	76	103	132	208	
10	1	4	7	13	17	29	41	64	86	110	173	
8	1	3	4	7	10	17	25	38	52	67	105	152
6	1	1	3	4	6	10	15	23	32	41	64	93
4	1	1	1	3	5	8	12	17	24	31	49	72
3		1	1	3	4	7	10	16	21	28	44	63
2		1	1	3	3	6	9	14	19	24	38	55
1		1	1	1	3	4	7	10	14	18	29	42
0			1	1	2	4	6	9	12	16	25	37
00			1	1	1	3	5	8	11	14	22	32
000			1	1	1	3	4	7	9	12	19	27
0000				1	1	2	3	6	8	10	16	23
250				1	1	1	3	5	6	8	13	19
300				1	1	1	3	4	5	7	11	16
350				1	1	1	1	3	5	6	10	15
400					1	1	1	3	4	6	9	13
500					1	1	1	3	4	5	8	11

REWIRING: TYPES TF, T, THW, TW, RUH, RUW

WIRE SIZE	MAXIMUM NUMBER OF CONDUCTORS IN CONDUIT OR TUBING											
	½	¾	1	1¼	1½	2	2½	3	3½	4	5	6
18	13	24	38	68	93	152						
16	11	19	31	55	75	123	176	270				
14	5	10	16	29	40	65	93	143	192			
12	4	8	13	24	32	53	76	117	157	202		
10	4	6	11	19	26	43	61	95	127	163	257	
8	1	4	6	11	15	25	36	56	75	96	152	219
6	1	2	4	7	10	16	23	36	48	62	97	141
4	1	1	3	5	7	12	17	27	36	46	73	106
3	1	1	2	4	6	10	15	23	31	40	63	91
2	1	1	1	4	5	9	15	20	27	34	54	78
1		1	1	2	4	6	9	14	19	25	39	57
0		1	1	2	3	5	8	12	16	21	33	48
00		1	1	1	3	4	7	10	14	18	28	41
000		1	1	1	2	4	5	9	12	15	24	35
0000			1	1	1	3	5	7	10	13	20	29
250				1	1	2	4	6	8	10	16	23
300				1	1	2	3	5	7	9	14	20
350				1	1	1	3	4	6	8	12	18
400					1	1	2	4	5	7	11	16
500					1	1	1	3	4	6	9	14

CONDUIT INFORMATION

TRADE SIZE INCHES	NORMAL EXTERIOR DIAMETER			NORMAL INTERIOR DIAMETER			WEIGHT LBS. PER 100 LIN. FT.		
	STEEL CONDUIT	ALUM. CONDUIT	ELECT. MET. TUBE	STEEL CONDUIT	ALUM. CONDUIT	ELECT. MET. TUBE	STEEL CONDUIT	ALUM. CONDUIT	ELECT. MET. TUBE
½	0.840	0.840	0.706	0.622	0.622	0.622	79.0	27.4	28.5
¾	1.050	1.050	0.921	0.824	0.824	0.824	105.0	36.4	43.5
1	1.315	1.315	1.163	1.049	1.049	1.049	153.0	53.0	64.0
1¼	1.660	1.660	1.510	1.380	1.380	1.380	201.0	69.6	95.0
1½	1.900	1.900	1.740	1.610	1.610	1.610	249.0	86.2	110.0
2	2.375	2.375	2.197	2.067	2.067	2.067	332.0	115.7	140.0
2½	2.875	2.875	2.875	2.469	2.469	2.731	527.0	182.5	220.0
3	3.500	3.500	3.500	3.068	3.068	3.356	682.6	238.9	260.0
3½	4.000	4.000	4.000	3.548	3.548	3.834	831.0	287.7	365.0
4	4.500	4.500	4.500	4.026	4.026	4.334	972.3	340.0	400.0
5	5.563	5.563		5.047	5.047		1313.6	465.4	
6	6.625	6.625		6.065	6.065		1745.3	612.5	

WIRE INFORMATION

TYPE LETTER	TRADE NAME	MAX. OP. TEMP.	USE	TYPE LETTER	TRADE NAME	MAX. OP. TEMP.	USE
AF	ASBESTOS HEAT RESIST.	150°C 302°F	FIXTURE	SA	SILICONE ASBESTOS	90°C 194°F	DRY
AVA	ASBESTOS VAR. CAMBRIC	110°C 230°F	DRY	SF-1	SILICONE RUBBER	200°C 392°F	FIXTURE 300V. MAX.
AVB	ASBESTOS VAR. CAMBRIC	90°C 194°F	DRY	SF-2	SILICONE RUBBER	200°C 392°F	FIXTURE 7 STRAND
AVL	ASBESTOS VAR. CAMBRIC	110°C 230°F	WET & DRY	T	THERMOPLASTIC	60°C 140°F	DRY
MI	MINERAL INSULATED	85°C 185°F	WET & DRY	TA	THERMOPLASTIC ASBESTOS	90°C 194°F	SW'BD.
RF-1	RUBBER COVER	60°C 140°F	FIXTURE 300V MAX.	TF	THERMOPLASTIC SOLID OR STRAND	60°C 140°C	FIXTURE
RF-2	RUBBER COVER	60°C 140°F	FIXTURE 7 STRAND	TFN	THERMOPLASTIC HEAT RESIST.	90°C	FIXTURE
RFH-1	RUBBER COVER HEAT RESIST.	75°C 167°F	FIXTURE 300V. MAX.	THHU	THERMOPLASTIC HEAT RESIST.	90°C 194°F	DRY
RFH-2	RUBBER COVER HEAT RESIST.	75°C 167°F	FIXTURE 7 STRAND	THW	THERMO. MOIST. & HEAT RESIST.	75°C 167°F	WET & DRY
RH	RUBBER COVER HEAT RESIST.	75°C 167°F	DRY	THWN	THERMO. MOIST. & HEAT RESIST.	75°C 167°F	WET & DRY
RHH	RUBBER COVER HEAT RESIST.	90°C 194°F	DRY	TW	THERMOPLASTIC MOIST. RESIST.	60°C 140°F	WET & DRY
RHW	RUBBER, MOIST, & HEAT RESIST.	75°C 167°F	WET & DRY	V	VARNISH CAMBRIC	85°C 185°F	DRY
RUH	LATEX HEAT RESIST.	75°C	DRY	XRHW	THERMO.—POLY X-LINK-RESIST.	75°C 167°F	WET & DRY
RUW	LATEX MOIST. RESIST.	60°C 146°F	WET & DRY		PAPER COVER	85°C 185°F	U'GRND.

RECOMMENDED FOOTCANDLES			
AREA	FOOT CANDLES REC.	AREA	FOOT CANDLES REC.
AUDITORIUMS	15-30	LIBRARY - READING	30-70
CASHIER STATION	50-70	STACKS	10-30
CLUBS / LODGE RMS.	30	DESK	70
CONFERENCE RMS.	100	OFFICES: GENERAL	70-150
DANCE HALLS	5	PRIVATE	100-150
DORMATORIES	30-70	SCHOOL; CLASS RM.	50-70
DRAFTING ROOMS	100-150	SEWING	150
FOOD: DINING RM.	10-30	LECTURE	70
KITCHEN	70	SHOP	100
GARAGE: INDOOR	10-50	STAIRS / HALLS	20-30
EXT. LOT	.5-1	TELEVISION VIEWING	20-70
LABORATORIES	100	TOILETS / WASH RMS.	10-30
LOCKER ROOMS	20	WAREHOUSES	10-50

SPORTS LIGHTING

ARCHERY	50	HANDBALL	50
BADMINTON	30	ICE HOCKEY	100
BASEBALL	100-150	RACING, ALL TYPES	5-30
BASKETBALL	50	RIFLE, PISTOL RANGE	20-100
BOWLING	10-50	SKATING, INDOORS	10
BOXING / WRESTLING	100-200	SWIMMING, INDOORS	30-50
FOOTBALL	50-100	TENNIS	30-50
GOLF	5-10	VOLLEYBALL	20

TO CALCULATE AVERAGE FOOTCANDLE ILLUMINATION ON WORK LEVEL, MULTIPLY NUMBER OF LUMINAIRES X LAMPS PER LUMINAIRE X INITIAL LUMENS PER LAMP X COEFFICIENT OF UTILIZATION X MAINTENANCE FACTOR. DIVIDE THIS PRODUCT BY AREA IN SQUARE FEET TO OBTAIN FOOTCANDLE.

COEFFICIENTS OF UTILIZATION

EFFECTIVE CEILING CAVITY REFLECTANCE (CCR) = 70% EFFECTIVE WALL CAVITY REFLECTANCE (WCR) = 50, 30, 10% EFFECTIVE FLOOR CAVITY REFLECTANCE (FCR) = 20%	TYPICAL DISTRIBUTION AND PER CENT LAMP LUMENS		COEFFICIENT OF UTILIZATION WCR		
			50	30	10
TYPICAL LUMINAIRE	MAXIMUM S/MH GUIDE[d]	RCR[c] ↓			
1 — PENDANT DIFFUSING SPHERE WITH INCANDESCENT LAMP	1.5 — 35½% ↑ 45% ↓	0	.81	.81	.81
		1	.66	.62	.59
		2	.56	.50	.46
		3	.48	.42	.37
		4	.42	.36	.30
		5	.37	.30	.25
		6	.33	.26	.21
		7	.29	.23	.18
		8	.27	.20	.16
		9	.24	.18	.14
		10	.22	.16	.12
2 — PORCELAIN-ENAMELED VENTILATED STANDARD DOME WITH INCANDESCENT LAMP	1.3 — 0% ↑ 83½% ↓	0	.97	.97	.97
		1	.86	.83	.81
		2	.76	.72	.67
		3	.67	.61	.57
		4	.60	.53	.48
		5	.53	.46	.41
		6	.47	.40	.35
		7	.42	.35	.30
		8	.38	.31	.26
		9	.34	.27	.23
		10	.31	.24	.20
3 — R40 FLOOD WITH SPECULAR ANODIZED REFLECTOR SKIRT; 45° CUTOFF	0.7 — 0% ↑ 85% ↓	0	.98	.98	.98
		1	.94	.92	.91
		2	.90	.87	.85
		3	.86	.83	.81
		4	.82	.79	.77
		5	.79	.75	.73
		6	.76	.72	.70
		7	.73	.69	.66
		8	.70	.66	.63
		9	.67	.63	.60
		10	.64	.60	.58
4 — REFLECTOR DOWNLIGHT WITH BAFFLES AND INSIDE FROSTED LAMP	0.7 — 0% ↑ 44½% ↓	0	.52	.52	.52
		1	.50	.49	.48
		2	.48	.48	.45
		3	.46	.45	.43
		4	.44	.43	.42
		5	.43	.41	.40
		6	.41	.40	.38
		7	.40	.38	.37
		8	.38	.37	.36
		9	.37	.35	.34
		10	.36	.34	.38

CONSTRUCTION SPECIFICATIONS INSTITUTE

EFFECTIVE CEILING CAVITY REFLECTANCE (CCR) = 70% EFFECTIVE WALL CAVITY REFLECTANCE (WCR)=30,50,10% EFFECTIVE FLOOR CAVITY REFLECTANCE (FCR) = 20%	TYPICAL DISTRIBUTION AND PER CENT LAMP LUMENS		COEFFICIENT OF UTILIZATION		
			WCR		
			50	30	10
TYPICAL LUMINAIRE	MAXIMUM S/MH GUIDE	RCR^c ↓			
MEDIUM DISTRIBUTION UNIT WITH LENS PLATE AND INSIDE FROST LAMP.	1.0 0%↑ 54½%↓	0	.63	.63	.63
		1	.58	.57	.56
		2	.54	.52	.50
		3	.50	.47	.45
		4	.47	.44	.41
		5	.43	.40	.38
		6	.40	.37	.35
		7	.37	.34	.32
		8	.35	.31	.30
		9	.32	.30	.27
		10	.30	.27	.24
1" WIDE ALUMINUM TROFFER WITH 40° CW x 45° LW SHIELDING AND SINGLE EXTRA-HIGH-OUTPUT LAMP	1.1 / 0.8 0%↑ 42½%↓	0	.49	.49	.49
		1	.45	.44	.43
		2	.42	.40	.38
		3	.39	.36	.34
		4	.35	.33	.31
		5	.33	.30	.28
		6	.30	.28	.26
		7	.28	.25	.23
		8	.26	.23	.21
		9	.24	.21	.19
		10	.22	.19	.17
2-LAMP, SURFACE MOUNTED, BARE LAMP UNIT—PHOTO-METRY WITH 18" WIDE PANEL ABOVE LUMINAIRE (LAMPS ON 6" CENTERS)	1.3 9½%↑ 78%↓	0	.98	.98	.98
		1	.85	.79	.75
		2	.71	.65	.60
		3	.62	.55	.49
		4	.55	.47	.41
		5	.48	.40	.34
		6	.43	.35	.29
		7	.38	.30	.25
		8	.34	.27	.22
		9	.31	.23	.18
		10	.28	.21	.16
LUMINOUS BOTTOM SUSPENDED UNIT WITH EXTRA-HIGH-OUTPUT LAMP	1.5 66%↑ 12%↓	0	.67	.67	.67
		1	.59	.57	.54
		2	.51	.48	.45
		3	.45	.41	.37
		4	.40	.35	.31
		5	.35	.30	.27
		6	.32	.27	.23
		7	.28	.23	.30
		8	.25	.21	.17
		9	.23	.18	.15
		10	.21	.16	.13

CONSTRUCTION SPECIFICATIONS INSTITUTE

EFFECTIVE CEILING CAVITY REFLECTANCE (CCR)=70% EFFECTIVE WALL CAVITY REFLECTANCE(WCR)=50,30,10% EFFECTIVE FLOOR CAVITY REFLECTANCE(FCR)=20% TYPICAL LUMINAIRE	TYPICAL DISTRIBUTION AND PER CENT LAMP LUMENS / MAXIMUM S/MH GUIDE 4	RCR ↓	COEFFICIENT OF UTILIZATION WCR		
			50	30	10
PRISMATIC BOTTOM AND SIDES, OPEN TOP, 4 LAMP SUSPENDED UNIT—MULTIPLY BY 1.05 FOR 2 LAMPS	1.4/1.2 33%↑ 50%↓	0	.84	.84	.84
		1	.75	.73	.73
		2	.67	.63	.63
		3	.60	.55	.50
		4	.53	.48	.43
		5	.48	.42	.37
		6	.43	.37	.33
		7	.39	.33	.28
		8	.35	.29	.25
		9	.31	.26	.23
		10	.28	.23	.19
2 LAMP PRISMATIC WRAPAROUND — MULTIPLY BY 0.95 FOR 4 LAMPS	1.2 24%↑ 50%↓	0	.77	.77	.77
		1	.67	.65	.62
		2	.59	.55	.52
		3	.53	.45	.44
		4	.45	.42	.38
		5	.43	.37	.33
		6	.39	.32	.29
		7	.35	.39	.26
		8	.32	.36	.23
		9	.29	.23	.20
		10	.26	.21	.18
FLUORESCENT UNIT WITH FLAT PRISMATIC LENS, 4 LAMP 2' WIDE—MULTIPLY BY 1.10 FOR 2 LAMP	1.4/1.2 0%↑ 62%↓ 60°	0	.72	.72	.72
		1	.65	.63	.61
		2	.58	.54	.52
		3	.52	.48	.44
		4	.48	.42	.38
		5	.41	.37	.33
		6	.37	.32	.29
		7	.33	.29	.26
		8	.30	.25	.22
		9	.27	.22	.19
		10	.24	.20	.16
CEILING CAVITY REFLECTANCE = 50% ρCC FROM BELOW ~65% DIFFUSING PLASTIC OR GLASS 1) CEILING EFFICIENCY ~60%, DIFFUSER TRANSMITTANCE ~50%, DIFFUSER REFLECTANCE ~40%. CAVITY WITH MIN. OBSTRUCTIONS AND PAINTED WITH 80% REFLECTANCE PAINT—USE ρc = 70. 2) FOR LOWER REFLECTANCE PAINT OR OBSTRUCTIONS — USE ρc = 50.		1	.58	.50	.54
		2	.51	.47	.43
		3	.45	.41	.36
		4	.39	.35	.31
		5	.35	.30	.26
		6	.31	.26	.23
		7	.28	.23	.20
		8	.25	.20	.17
		9	.23	.18	.15
		10	.21	.16	.13

CONSTRUCTION SPECIFICATIONS INSTITUTE

APPENDIXES

CONSTRUCTION SPECIFICATIONS INSTITUTE

CSI FORMAT—
MASTER LIST OF SPECIFICATION SECTION TITLES*

The CSI Format has been established as a recognized industry standard. It has resolved the need for consistent arrangement for construction documents. Widespread acceptance of The CSI Format has helped contractors and increased accuracy of bids while reducing the efforts normally associated with bidding. Contractors find projects easier to control. Architects and engineers have greater assurance that specifications are complete. The building owner stands to reduce his expenditures through increased efficiencies. Of special interest to specifiers is the ability to relate all files, product literature references, and specifications to a single unified system.

The real benefits are derived from widespread use of this single system. Just as one would find it confusing to use a dictionary that was not arranged in the customary alphabetical order, so do difficulties arise from myriad construction specifications that do not follow a recognizable, established pattern. The construction industry has decided that it can no longer afford the luxury of several thousand specification systems.

Using the CSI Format and This Document

The CSI Format is sometimes construed to describe only the arrangement of specifications. The CSI Format is comprised of four major groupings of documents. Only one of these groupings is the specifications.

The CSI Format groupings are:

    BIDDING REQUIREMENTS
    CONTRACT FORMS
    GENERAL CONDITIONS
    and
    SPECIFICATIONS

The following Reference Sheet contains the current CSI Format for Construction Specifications as contained in the 1972 edition of The Uniform Constructions Index: it contains the 16 Divisions and the arrangement and preferred wording for the Broadscope Section Titles.

This document, The CSI Format-Master List of Specification Section Titles, provides both a flexible specification system and a standard framework for fixed specification sections facilitating automated processing. The decision between fixed or flexible specification Section Titles remains the prerogative of the specifier. In the interest of consistency and standardization, this document recommends—for either a fixed or flexible system—the inclusion of the Broadscope Section Titles, with the wording and in the sequence proposed whenever the project requires their use. The Broadscope Section Titles in this publication are printed entirely in capital letters. The Keyword Index references these Broadscope Section Titles. The Narrowscope Section Titles are also presented with preferred wording and in preferred sequence.

Designating Sections

A random designation system may be ideal for certain practices. However, it may not completely fulfill the needs of those who wish to standardize portions of their specifications, nor those who utilize the advantages of automated printing and data retrieval systems. Within this document, a 5-digit numbering system is used for the designation of all sections, Broadscope and Narrowscope. This numerical classification system has been adopted and is recommended by the Technical Documents Committee of the Construction Specifications Institute.

Separate Contracts

The publication of The CSI Format has raised questions about whether The CSI Format implies CSI preference for single contract work. It does not. The Institute's position is that the merits of single vs. separate contracts cannot be arbitrarily decided by decree. The design professional has the responsibility to determine which is preferable when a choice is necessary.

In many areas, separate contracts are required by law. Statutes may require mechanical and electrical work to be separated, or more complex variations may be required. In other instances, separate contracts may be desired by the owner, or recommended by the design professional.

The CSI Format can readily be used to advantage under either circumstance—single or separate contracts. The division grouping does not preclude the preparation of separate contracts. In fact, The CSI Format can actually facilitate such preparation when good specification principles are observed.

This discussion does not encompass the entire range of specification principles. The Institute's Manual of Practice is devoted to the subject, of which this document is only a part. However, the following considerations are significant:

● Whenever separate contracts are used, they should be prepared and let under similar contract conditions. This can be accomplished by preparing only one set of general conditions, whether a single contract or several contracts are involved.

● The CSI Format should be followed in preparing specification sections, whether single or multiple contracts are involved.

● When separate contracts are required, state the fact within Division 1, Summary of the Work, and identify the work that is to be a part of each contract.

● Include pertinent information within the Bidding Requirements.

CONSTRUCTION SPECIFICATIONS INSTITUTE

Each prime contractor will require at least one set of contract documents, including portions of all other prime contracts relating his work to that of others. Additional copies can be assembled on the basis of specification sections included in the prime contract. For example, extra copies for a separate plumbing contract might consist of Bidding Requirements, Contract Forms, General Conditions, Supplementary Conditions, and applicable sections of the specifications.

Section Titles for the Specification Format

To readily use this document as a method of organizing project or master specifications, you will need to know just what each division contains. The information following is presented as a list of preferred section titles in each division. These lists are prepared with the following considerations:

- Each division is identified by division number and title. These divisions are fixed in number and in name. As titles they appear only in the Table of Contents. Even so, their influence will be seen throughout the specifications. The divisions are the alphabet of The CSI Format for Construction Specifications. They indicate the location of sections just as letters indicate the location of words in a dictionary.

- Each division contains a group of related section titles. The bold face type identifies "Broadscope" Section Titles. The identified listings which in most cases follows the Broadscope title heading are preferred Narrowscope section titles. These are the coverage of the particular "Broadscope" title. The alphabetical Keyword Index will enable the user to find the proper division and proper Broadscope heading for most items specified as part of a project specification.

- To specify a particular type of work, the specifier may use (1) a Broadscope title, (2) Narrowscope titles, or (3) a combination of Broadscope and Narrowscope titles.

- Less complex work requires fewer sections and uses mainly Broadscope Section Titles.

- More complex work requires a greater number of sections for clarity; hence, the use of Narrowscope Section Titles. You can make a section all-inclusive, or you can write several shorter sections and still be assured that they will be together in the finished specification. This is a basic advantage of the use of this document; separate sections can be written and reproduced at any time with no fear they will lose their physical grouping; this document assigns a constant location for each section. There are advantages in splitting longer sections into shorter ones. The contractor can exercise greater control. Specifications become easier to use, easier to coordinate during writing, and easier to reproduce and assemble. The task of assembling a project specification is made easier, whether the specifier uses automated, semi-automated, or manual techniques.

- All section titles, Broadscope and Narrowscope, are presented as "preferred titles" presented in "preferred sequence" and identified in a "preferred numerical classification arrangement".

- The specifier striving for a high degree of uniformity within construction specifications will attempt to use the titles and numbers as shown. However, there will be times when it is necessary to add titles to convey a particular meaning for a particular project.

DIVISION 0—BIDDING AND CONTRACT REQUIREMENTS

00010	PRE-BID INFORMATION
00100	INSTRUCTIONS TO BIDDERS
00200	INFORMATION AVAILABLE TO BIDDERS
00300	BID/TENDER FORMS
00400	SUPPLEMENTS TO BID/TENDER FORMS
00500	AGREEMENT FORMS
00600	BONDS AND CERTIFICATES
00700	GENERAL CONDITIONS OF THE CONTRACT
00800	SUPPLEMENTARY CONDITIONS
00950	DRAWINGS INDEX
00900	ADDENDA AND MODIFICATIONS

DIVISION 1—GENERAL REQUIREMENTS

01010	SUMMARY OF WORK
01020	ALLOWANCES
01030	SPECIAL PROJECT PROCEDURES
01040	COORDINATION
01050	FIELD ENGINEERING
01060	REGULATORY REQUIREMENTS
01070	ABBREVIATIONS AND SYMBOLS
01080	IDENTIFICATION SYSTEMS
01100	ALTERNATES/ALTERNATIVES
01150	MEASUREMENT AND PAYMENT
01200	PROJECT MEETINGS
01300	SUBMITTALS
01400	QUALITY CONTROL
01500	CONSTRUCTION FACILITIES AND TEMPORARY CONTROLS
01600	MATERIAL AND EQUIPMENT
01650	STARTING OF SYSTEMS
01660	TESTING, ADJUSTING, AND BALANCING OF SYSTEMS
01700	CONTRACT CLOSEOUT

DIVISION 2—SITE WORK

02010	SUBSURFACE INVESTIGATION
02050	DEMOLITION
02100	SITE PREPARATION
02150	UNDERPINNING
02200	EARTHWORK
02300	TUNNELLING
02350	PILES, CAISSONS AND COFFERDAMS
02400	DRAINAGE
02440	SITE IMPROVEMENTS
02480	LANDSCAPING
02500	PAVING AND SURFACING
02590	PONDS AND RESERVOIRS
02600	PIPED UTILITY MATERIALS AND METHODS
02700	PIPED UTILITIES
02800	POWER AND COMMUNICATION UTILITIES
02850	RAILROAD WORK
02880	MARINE WORK

DIVISION 3—CONCRETE

03050	CONCRETING PROCEDURES
03100	CONCRETE FORMWORK
03150	FORMS
03180	FORM TIES AND ACCESSORIES
03200	CONCRETE REINFORCEMENT
03250	CONCRETE ACCESSORIES
03300	CAST-IN-PLACE CONCRETE
03350	SPECIAL CONCRETE FINISHES
03360	SPECIALLY PLACED CONCRETE
03370	CONCRETE CURING
03400	PRECAST CONCRETE
03500	CEMENTITIOUS DECKS
03600	GROUT
03700	CONCRETE RESTORATION AND CLEANING

DIVISION 4—MASONRY

04050	MASONRY PROCEDURES
04100	MORTAR
04150	MASONRY ACCESSORIES
04200	UNIT MASONRY
04400	STONE
04500	MASONRY RESTORATION AND CLEANING
04550	REFRACTORIES
04600	CORROSION RESISTANT MASONRY

DIVISION 5—METALS

05010	METAL MATERIALS AND METHODS
05050	METAL FASTENING
05100	STRUCTURAL METAL FRAMING
05200	METAL JOISTS
05300	METAL DECKING
05400	COLD-FORMED METAL FRAMING
05500	METAL FABRICATIONS
05700	ORNAMENTAL METAL
05800	EXPANSION CONTROL
05900	METAL FINISHES

DIVISION 6—WOOD AND PLASTICS

06050	FASTENERS AND SUPPORTS
06100	ROUGH CARPENTRY
06130	HEAVY TIMBER CONSTRUCTION
06150	WOOD-METAL SYSTEMS
06170	PREFABRICATED STRUCTURAL WOOD
06200	FINISH CARPENTRY
06300	WOOD TREATMENT
06400	ARCHITECTURAL WOODWORK
06500	PREFABRICATED STRUCTURAL PLASTICS
06600	PLASTIC FABRICATIONS

DIVISION 7—THERMAL AND MOISTURE PROTECTION

07100	WATERPROOFING
07150	DAMPPROOFING
07200	INSULATION
07250	FIREPROOFING
07300	SHINGLES AND ROOFING TILES
07400	PREFORMED ROOFING AND SIDING
07500	MEMBRANE ROOFING
07570	TRAFFIC TOPPING
07600	FLASHING AND SHEET METAL
07800	ROOF ACCESSORIES
07900	JOINT SEALANTS

DIVISION 8—DOORS AND WINDOWS

08100	METAL DOORS AND FRAMES
08200	WOOD AND PLASTIC DOORS
08250	DOOR OPENING ASSEMBLIES
08300	SPECIAL DOORS
08400	ENTRANCES AND STOREFRONTS
08500	METAL WINDOWS
08600	WOOD AND PLASTIC WINDOWS
08650	SPECIAL WINDOWS
08700	HARDWARE
08800	GLAZING
08900	GLAZED CURTAIN WALLS

DIVISION 9—FINISHES

09100	METAL SUPPORT SYSTEMS
09200	LATH AND PLASTER
09230	AGGREGATE COATINGS
09250	GYPSUM WALLBOARD
09300	TILE
09400	TERRAZZO
09500	ACOUSTICAL TREATMENT
09550	WOOD FLOORING
09600	STONE AND BRICK FLOORING
09650	RESILIENT FLOORING
09680	CARPETING
09700	SPECIAL FLOORING
09760	FLOOR TREATMENT
09800	SPECIAL COATINGS
09900	PAINTING
09950	WALL COVERING

DIVISION 10—SPECIALITIES

10100	CHALKBOARDS AND TACKBOARDS
10150	COMPARTMENTS AND CUBICLES
10200	LOUVERS AND VENTS
10240	GRILLES AND SCREENS
10250	SERVICE WALL SYSTEMS
10260	WALL AND CORNER GUARDS
10270	ACCESS FLOORING
10280	SPECIALTY MODULES

CONSTRUCTION SPECIFICATIONS INSTITUTE

10290	PEST CONTROL		13110	OBSERVATORIES
10300	FIREPLACES AND STOVES		13120	PRE-ENGINEERED STRUCTURES
10340	PREFABRICATED STEEPLES, SPIRES, AND CUPOLAS		13130	SPECIAL PURPOSE ROOMS AND BUILDINGS
10350	FLAGPOLES		13140	VAULTS
10400	IDENTIFYING DEVICES		13150	POOLS
10450	PEDESTRIAN CONTROL DEVICES		13160	ICE RINKS
10500	LOCKERS		13170	KENNELS AND ANIMAL SHELTERS
10520	FIRE EXTINGUISHERS, CABINETS, AND ACCESSORIES		13200	SEISMOGRAPHIC INSTRUMENTATION
			13210	STRESS RECORDING INSTRUMENTATION
10530	PROTECTIVE COVERS		13220	SOLAR AND WIND INSTRUMENTATION
10550	POSTAL SPECIALTIES		13410	LIQUID AND GAS STORAGE TANKS
10600	PARTITIONS		13510	RESTORATION OF UNDERGROUND PIPELINES
10650	SCALES		13520	FILTER UNDERDRAINS AND MEDIA
10670	STORAGE SHELVING		13530	DIGESTION TANK COVERS AND APPURTENANCES
10700	EXTERIOR SUN CONTROL DEVICES		13540	OXYGENATION SYSTEMS
10750	TELEPHONE ENCLOSURES		13550	THERMAL SLUDGE CONDITIONING SYSTEMS
10800	TOILET AND BATH ACCESSORIES		13560	SITE CONSTRUCTED INCINERATORS
10900	WARDROBE SPECIALTIES		13600	UTILITY CONTROL SYSTEMS
			13700	INDUSTRIAL AND PROCESS CONTROL SYSTEMS

DIVISION 11—EQUIPMENT

11010	MAINTENANCE EQUIPMENT		13800	OIL AND GAS REFINING INSTALLATIONS AND CONTROL SYSTEMS
11020	SECURITY AND VAULT EQUIPMENT		13900	TRANSPORTATION INSTRUMENTATION
11030	CHECKROOM EQUIPMENT		13940	BUILDING AUTOMATION SYSTEMS
11040	ECCLESIASTICAL EQUIPMENT		13970	FIRE SUPPRESSION AND SUPERVISORY SYSTEMS
11050	LIBRARY EQUIPMENT		13980	SOLAR ENERGY SYSTEMS
11060	THEATER AND STAGE EQUIPMENT		13990	WIND ENERGY SYSTEMS
11070	MUSICAL EQUIPMENT			
11080	REGISTRATION EQUIPMENT			
11100	MERCANTILE EQUIPMENT			
11110	COMMERCIAL LAUNDRY AND DRY CLEANING EQUIPMENT			**DIVISION 14—CONVEYING SYSTEMS**
11120	VENDING EQUIPMENT		14100	DUMBWAITERS
11130	AUDIO-VISUAL EQUIPMENT		14200	ELEVATORS
11140	SERVICE STATION EQUIPMENT		14300	HOISTS AND CRANES
11150	PARKING EQUIPMENT		14400	LIFTS
11160	LOADING DOCK EQUIPMENT		14500	MATERIAL HANDLING SYSTEMS
11170	WASTE HANDLING EQUIPMENT		14600	TURNTABLES
11190	DETENTION EQUIPMENT		14700	MOVING STAIRS AND WALKS
11200	WATER SUPPLY AND TREATMENT EQUIPMENT		14800	POWERED SCAFFOLDING
11300	FLUID WASTE DISPOSAL AND TREATMENT EQUIPMENT		14900	TRANSPORTATION SYSTEMS
11400	FOOD SERVICE EQUIPMENT			
11450	RESIDENTIAL EQUIPMENT			**DIVISION 15—MECHANICAL**
11460	UNIT KITCHENS		15050	BASIC MATERIALS AND METHODS
11470	DARKROOM EQUIPMENT		15200	NOISE, VIBRATION, AND SEISMIC CONTROL
11480	ATHLETIC, RECREATIONAL, AND THERAPEUTIC EQUIPMENT		15250	INSULATION
			15300	SPECIAL PIPING SYSTEMS
11500	INDUSTRIAL AND PROCESS EQUIPMENT		15400	PLUMBING SYSTEMS
11600	LABORATORY EQUIPMENT		15450	PLUMBING FIXTURES AND TRIM
11650	PLANETARIUM AND OBSERVATORY EQUIPMENT		15500	FIRE PROTECTION
			15600	POWER OR HEAT GENERATION
11700	MEDICAL EQUIPMENT		15650	REFRIGERATION
11780	MORTUARY EQUIPMENT		15700	LIQUID HEAT TRANSFER
11800	TELECOMMUNICATION EQUIPMENT		15800	AIR DISTRIBUTION
11850	NAVIGATION EQUIPMENT		15900	CONTROLS AND INSTRUMENTATION

DIVISION 12—FURNISHINGS

DIVISION 16—ELECTRICAL

12100	ARTWORK		16050	BASIC MATERIALS AND METHODS
12300	MANUFACTURED CABINETS AND CASEWORK		16200	POWER GENERATION
12500	WINDOW TREATMENT		16300	POWER TRANSMISSION
12550	FABRICS		16400	SERVICE AND DISTRIBUTION
12600	FURNITURE AND ACCESSORIES		16500	LIGHTING
12670	RUGS AND MATS		16600	SPECIAL SYSTEMS
12700	MULTIPLE SEATING		16700	COMMUNICATIONS
12800	INTERIOR PLANTS AND PLANTINGS		16850	HEATING AND COOLING
			16900	CONTROLS AND INSTRUMENTATION

DIVISION 13—SPECIAL CONSTRUCTION

13010	AIR SUPPORTED STRUCTURES
13020	INTEGRATED ASSEMBLIES
13030	AUDIOMETRIC ROOMS
13040	CLEAN ROOMS
13050	HYPERBARIC ROOMS
13060	INSULATED ROOMS
13070	INTEGRATED CEILINGS
13080	SOUND, VIBRATION, AND SEISMIC CONTROL
13090	RADIATION PROTECTION
13100	NUCLEAR REACTORS

CONSTRUCTION SPECIFICATIONS INSTITUTE

DIVISION 1—GENERAL REQUIREMENTS

01010	**SUMMARY OF WORK**
	Work Covered by Contract Documents
	Contracts
	Work by Others
	Owner-furnished items
	Future Work
	Work Sequence
	Contractor use of Premises
	Partial Owner Occupancy
01020	Allowances
01030	Field Engineering
01031	Grades, Lines, & Levels
01050	Coordination
01051	Project Coordination
01052	Mechanical & Electrical Coordination
01070	Cutting and Patching
01080	Applicable Codes
01090	Abbreviations and Symbols
01091	Definitions
01100	**ALTERNATIVES**
01150	**MEASUREMENT & PAYMENT**
01200	**PROJECT MEETINGS**
01210	Preconstruction Conferences
01220	Progress Meetings
01230	Job Site Administration
01300	**SUBMITTALS**
01310	Construction Schedules
01311	Network Analysis
01320	Progress Reports
01330	Survey Data
01340	Shop Drawings, Product Data & Samples
01360	Layout Data
01370	Schedule of Values
01380	Construction Photographs
01400	**QUALITY CONTROL**
01410	Testing Laboratory Services
01420	Inspection Services
01500	**TEMPORARY FACILITIES AND CONTROLS**
01510	Temporary Utilities
01511	Temporary Electricity
01512	Temporary Lighting
01513	Temporary Heat & Ventilation
01514	Temporary Telephone Service
01515	Temporary Water
01516	Temporary Sanitary Facilities
01517	Temporary First Aid Facilities
01518	Temporary Fire Protection
01520	Construction Aids
01521	Construction Elevators and Hoists
01522	Temporary Enclosure
01523	Swing Staging
01530	Barriers
01531	Fences
01532	Tree and Plant Protection
01533	Guardrails & Barricades
01540	Security
01550	Access Roads & Parking Areas
01560	Special Controls
01561	Noise Control
01562	Dust Control
01563	Water Control
01564	Pest Control
01565	Rodent Control
01567	Pollution Control
01570	Traffic Regulation
01571	Traffic Signals
01572	Flagmen
01573	Flares and Lights
01574	Parking
01580	Project Identification
01590	Field Offices and Sheds
01600	**MATERIAL AND EQUIPMENT**
01620	Transportation & Handling
01630	Storage & Protection
01640	Substitutions & Product Options

01700	**PROJECT CLOSEOUT**
01710	Cleaning
01720	Project Record Documents
01730	Operations & Maintenance Data
01740	Guarantees, Warranties, & Bonds
01750	Spare Parts & Maintenance Materials

DIVISION 2—SITE WORK

02010	**SUBSURFACE EXPLORATION**
02011	Borings
02012	Core Drilling
02013	Standard Penetration Tests
02014	Seismic Exploration
02100	**CLEARING**
02101	Structure Moving
02102	Clearing and Grubbing
02103	Tree Pruning
02104	Shrub and Tree Relocation
02110	**DEMOLITION**
02111	Building Demolition
02112	Selective Demolition
02200	**EARTHWORK**
02210	Site Grading
02211	Rock Removal
02212	Embankment
02220	Excavating and Backfilling
02221	Trenching, Backfilling, and Compacting
02222	Structural Excavation, Backfill and Compaction
02223	Roadway Excavation, Backfill, and Compaction
02224	Pipe Boring and Jacking
02227	Waste Material Disposal
02230	Soil Compaction Control
02240	Soil Stabilization
02241	Soil Stabilization, Lime Slurry Injection
02243	Soil Stabilization Vibro-Flotation
02245	Finish Grading
02250	**SOIL TREATMENT**
02251	Termite Control
02252	Vegetation Control
02300	**PILE FOUNDATIONS**
02308	Pile Load Tests
02310	Piles
02311	Wood Piles
02312	Precast Concrete Piles
02313	Prestressed Concrete Piles
02314	Compacted Concrete Piles
02315	Steel H-Section Piles
02316	Steel Pipe Piles
02317	Concrete-Filled Steel Shell Piles
02350	**CAISSONS**
02351	Drilled Caissons
02352	Excavated Caissons
02400	**SHORING**
02411	Steel Sheeting
02413	Walers and Shores
02414	Cribbing
02415	Piling with Intermediate Lagging
02420	Underpinning
02500	**SITE DRAINAGE**
02510	Subdrainage Systems
02511	Foundation Drainage
02512	Underslab Drainage
02513	Drainage Structures
02520	Drainage Pipe
02530	Dewatering
02531	Sand Drains
02532	Wellpoints
02533	Relief Wells
02540	Erosion Control
02550	**SITE UTILITIES**
02551	Gas Distribution System
02552	Gas Transmission Lines

02553	Oil Distribution System
02554	Oil Transmission Lines
02555	Water Distribution System
02556	Water Transmission Lines
02557	Steam Distribution
02558	Hot Water Distribution
02559	Chilled Water Distribution
02560	Waste Water Collection
02580	Water Wells
02590	Sewage Lagoons
02600	**PAVING AND SURFACING**
02605	Mudjacking
02610	Paving
02611	Crushed Stone Paving
02612	Asphalt Concrete Paving
02613	Brick Paving
02614	Portland Cement Concrete Paving
02615	Bituminous Brick Paving
02616	Repair and Resurfacing
02617	Pavement Sealing
02618	Pavement Marking
02620	Curbs and Gutters
02630	Walks
02640	Synthetic Surfacing
02641	Synthetic Grass
02642	Synthetic Cinders
02643	Synthetic Resilient Matting
02700	**SITE IMPROVEMENTS**
02710	Fences and Gates
02711	Chain Link Fences
02712	Wire Fences
02713	Wood Fences
02720	Road and Parking Appurtenances
02721	Guardrails
02722	Signs
02723	Traffic Signals
02724	Culvert Pipe Underpasses
02730	Playing Fields
02731	Recreational Facilities
02740	Fountains
02741	Fountain Structures
02742	Fountain Equipment
02750	Irrigation System
02751	Underground Sprinkler Systems
02752	Aboveground Sprinkler Systems
02760	Site Furnishings
02765	Rubble Site Structures
02766	Railroad Tie Structures
02770	Lighting
02800	**LANDSCAPING**
02810	Soil Preparation
02820	Lawns
02821	Seeding
02822	Sodding
02823	Plugging
02824	Sprigging
02830	Trees, Shrubs, and Ground Cover
02831	Trees and Shrubs
02832	Ground Cover
02833	Plants
02835	Aggregate Beds
02836	Wood Chip Beds
02850	**RAILROAD WORK**
02851	Trackwork
02852	Ballasting
02870	Service Facilities
02880	Traffic Control
02900	**MARINE WORK**
02910	Docks
02920	Boat Facilities
02930	Protective Marine Structures
02931	Fenders
02932	Seawalls
02933	Groins
02934	Jettys
02940	Dredging
02950	**TUNNELING**
02960	Tunnel Excavation
02970	Tunnel Grouting
02980	Support Systems
02981	Rock Bolting

CONSTRUCTION SPECIFICATIONS INSTITUTE

DIVISION 3—CONCRETE

03100	**CONCRETE FORMWORK**
03110	Formwork for Structural Cast-in-Place Concrete
03120	Formwork for Architectural Cast-in-Place Concrete
03130	Formwork for Structural Precast Concrete
03140	Formwork for Architectural Precast Concrete
03150	**FORMS**
03151	Formliners and Coatings
03152	Wood Forms
03153	Prefabricated Forms
03154	Panel Forms
03155	Pan Forms
03156	Steel Forms
03157	Fiberglass Forms
03158	Prefabricated Stair Forms
03200	**CONCRETE REINFORCE-MENT**
03210	Reinforcing Steel
03220	Welded Wire Fabric
03230	Stressing Tendons
03250	**CONCRETE ACCESSORIES**
03251	Expansion and Contraction Joints
03252	Anchors and Inserts
03253	Waterstops
03300	**CAST-IN-PLACE CONCRETE**
03310	Structural Concrete
03311	Normalweight Structural Concrete
03312	Heavyweight Structural Concrete
03313	Lightweight Structural Concrete
03314	Prestressed Structural Contrete
03330	Architectural Concrete
03331	Normalweight Architectural Concrete
03332	Lightweight Architectural Concrete
03334	Prestressed Architectural Concrete
03340	Low Density Concrete
03341	Insulating Concrete
03350	**SPECIALLY FINISHED (ARCHITECTURAL) CONCRETE**
03351	Exposed Aggregate Concrete
03352	Tooled Concrete
03353	Blasted Concrete
03354	Grooved Surface Concrete
03360	**SPECIALLY PLACED CONCRETE**
03361	Shotcrete
03400	**PRECAST CONCRETE**
03410	Structural Precast Concrete
03411	Precast Wall Panels
03412	Precast Deck
03413	Precast Structural Sections
03420	Precast Prestressed Sections
03250	Architectural Precast Concrete
04351	Architectural Wall Panels
03500	**CEMENTITIOUS DECKS**
03510	Gypsum Concrete
03530	Cementitious Wood Fiber Deck
03600	**GROUT**
03601	Catalyzed Metallic Grout
03602	Nonmetallic Grout
03603	Epoxy Grout

DIVISION 4—MASONRY

04100	**MORTAR**
04110	Cement and Line Mortars
04120	Acid Resisting Mortars
04130	Premixed Mortars
04150	**MASONRY ACCESSORIES**
04160	Joint Reinforcement
04170	Anchors and Tie Systems
04180	Control Joints
04200	**UNIT MASONRY**
04210	Brick Masonry
04212	Adobe Masonry
04220	Concrete Unit Masonry
04225	Defaced Concrete Unit Masonry
04230	Reinforced Unit Masonry
04232	High-Lift Grouted Masonry
04233	High-Lift Grouted Concrete Block
04235	Preassembled Masonry Panels
04240	Clay Backing Tile
04245	Clay Facing Tile
04250	Ceramic Veneer
04251	Terra Cotta Veneer
04252	Mechanically Supported Masonry Veneer
04270	Glass Unit Masonry
04280	Gypsum Unit Masonry
04285	Sound Absorbing Perforated Hollow Masonry Units
04400	**STONE**
04410	Rough Stone
04420	Cut Stone
04422	Marble
04423	Limestone
04424	Granite
04425	Sandstone
04426	Slate
04430	Simulated Masonry
04435	Cast Stone
04440	Flagstone
04450	Natural Stone Veneer
04500	**MASONRY RESTORATION AND CLEANING**
04510	Masonry Cleaning
04520	Masonry Restoration
04550	**REFRACTORIES**
04551	Flue Liners
04552	Corrosion Resistant Brick Lining
04553	Combustion Chambers

DIVISION 5—METALS

05100	**STRUCTURAL METAL FRAMING**
05120	Structural Steel
05130	Structural Aluminum
05200	**METAL JOISTS**
05210	Steel Joists
05211	Standard Steel Joists
05212	Custom Fabricated Steel Joists
05220	Aluminum Joists
05250	Framing Systems
05251	Space Frames
05252	Geodesic Structures
05300	**METAL DECKING**
05310	Metal Roof Deck
05320	Metal Floor Deck
05400	**LIGHTGAGE FRAMING**
05410	Metal Stud System
05420	Metal Joist System
05500	**METAL FABRICATIONS**
05501	Anchor Bolts
05502	Expansion Bolts
05510	Metal Stairs
05520	Handrails and Railings
05521	Pipe and Tube Railings
05530	Gratings
05540	Castings
05700	**ORNAMENTAL METAL**
05710	Ornamental Stairs
05720	Ornamental Handrails and Railings
05730	Ornamental Sheet Metal
05800	**EXPANSION CONTROL**

CONSTRUCTION SPECIFICATIONS INSTITUTE

DIVISION 6—WOOD & PLASTICS

06100	**ROUGH CARPENTRY**
06110	Framing and Sheathing
06111	Light Wooden Structures Framing
06112	Preassembled Components
06113	Sheathing
06114	Diaphragms
06130	**HEAVY TIMBER CONSTRUCTION**
06131	Timber Trusses
06132	Mill-Framed Structures
06133	Pole Construction
06150	**TRESTLES**
06170	**PREFABRICATED STRUCTURAL WOOD**
06180	Glued Laminated Construction
06181	Glue-Laminated Structural Units
06182	Glue-Laminated Decking
06190	Wood Trusses
06191	Wood-Metal Joists
06200	**FINISH CARPENTRY**
06220	Millwork
06240	Laminated Plastic
06300	**WOOD TREATMENT**
06310	Pressure Treated Lumber
06311	Preservative Treated Lumber
06312	Fire Retardant Treated Lumber
06400	**ARCHITECTURAL WOODWORK**
06410	Cabinetwork
06411	Wood Cabinets: Unfinished
06420	Paneling
06421	Hardwood Plywood Paneling
06422	Softwood Plywood Paneling
06430	Stairwork
06431	Wood Stairs and Railings
06500	**PREFABRICATED STRUCTURAL PLASTICS**
06600	**PLASTIC FABRICATIONS**

DIVISION 7—THERMAL AND MOISTURE PROTECTION

07100	**WATERPROOFING**
07110	Membrane Waterproofing
07111	Elastomeric Membrane Waterproofing
07112	Bituminous Membrane Waterproofing
07120	Fluid Applied Waterproofing
07121	Liquid Waterproofing
07130	Bentonite Waterproofing
07140	Metal Oxide Waterproofing
07150	**DAMPPROOFING**
07160	Bituminous Dampproofing
07170	Silicone Dampproofing
07175	Water Repellant Coatings
07180	Cementitious Dampproofing
07190	Vapor Barriers/Retardants
07191	Bituminous Vapor Barrier/Retardants
07192	Laminated Vapor Barrier/Retardants
07193	Plastic Vapor Barrier/Retardants
07200	**INSULATION**
07210	Building Insulation
07211	Loose Fill Insulation
07212	Rigid Insulation
07213	Fibrous and Reflective Insulation
07214	Foamed-in-Place Insulation
07215	Sprayed-On Insulation
07230	High and Low Temperature Insulation
07240	Roof and Deck Insulation
07250	Perimeter and Under-Slab Insulation
07300	Shingles and Roofing Tiles
07310	Shingles
07311	Asphalt Shingles
07312	Asbestos-Cement Shingles
07313	Wood Shingles and Shakes
07314	Slate Shingles
07315	Porcelain Enamel Shingles
07316	Metal Shingles
07320	Roofing Tiles
07321	Clay Roofing Tiles
07322	Concrete Roofing Tiles
07400	**PREFORMED ROOFING AND SIDING**
07410	Preformed Wall and Roof Panels
07411	Preformed Metal Siding
07420	Composite Building Panels
07440	Preformed Plastic Panels
07460	Cladding/Siding
07461	Wood Siding
07462	Composition Siding
07463	Asbestos-Cement Siding
07464	Plastic Siding
07500	**MEMBRANE ROOFING**
07510	Built-Up Bituminous Roofing
07520	Prepared Roll Roofing
07530	Elastic Sheet Roofing
07540	Fluid Applied Roofing
07570	**TRAFFIC TOPPING**
07600	**FLASHING AND SHEET METAL**
07610	Sheet Metal Roofing
07620	Flashing and Trim
07630	Roofing Specialties
07631	Gutters and Downspouts
07660	Gravel Stops
07800	**ROOF ACCESSORIES**
07810	Skylights
07811	Plastic Skylights
07812	Metal-Framed Skylights
07830	Hatches
07840	Gravity Ventilators (not connected to ductwork)
07850	Prefabricated Curbs
07860	Prefabricated Expansion Joints
07900	**SEALANTS**
07950	Joint Fillers and Gaskets
07951	Sealants and Calking

DIVISION 8—DOORS & WINDOWS

08100	**METAL DOORS AND FRAMES**
08110	Hollow Metal Work
08111	Stock Hollow Metal Work
08112	Custom Hollow Metal Work
08120	Aluminum Doors and Frames
08130	Stainless Steel Doors and Frames
08140	Bronze Doors and Frames
08200	**WOOD AND PLASTIC DOORS**
08210	Wood Doors
08211	Flush Wood Doors
08212	Panel Wood Doors
08213	Plastic Faced Wood Doors
08220	Plastic Doors
08300	**SPECIAL DOORS**
08310	Sliding Metal Fire Doors
08320	Metal-Clad Doors
08330	Coiling Doors
08340	Coiling Grilles
08350	Folding Doors
08351	Folding Doors: Panel
08353	Accordion Folding Doors
08355	Flexible Doors
08360	Overhead Doors
08370	Sliding Glass Doors
08375	Safety Glass Doors
08380	Sound Retardant Doors
08390	Screen and Storm Doors
08400	**ENTRANCES & STORE-FRONTS**
08450	Revolving Doors
08500	**METAL WINDOWS**
08510	Steel Windows
08520	Aluminum Windows
08530	Stainless Steel Windows
08540	Bronze Windows
08600	**WOOD & PLASTIC WINDOWS**
08610	Wood Windows
08620	Plastic Windows
08621	Reinforced Plastic Windows
08650	**SPECIAL WINDOWS**
08700	**HARDWARE & SPECIALTIES**
08710	Finish Hardware
08720	Operators
08721	Automatic Door Equipment
08725	Window Operators
08730	Weatherstripping & Seals
08740	Thresholds
08800	**GLAZING**
08810	Glass
08811	Plate Glass & Float Glass
08812	Sheet Glass
08813	Tempered Glass
08814	Wired Glass
08815	Rough and Figured Glass
08816	Bullet Resistance Glass
08817	Spandrel Glass
08820	Processed Glass
08821	Coated Glass
08822	Laminated Glass
08823	Insulating Glass
08830	Mirror Glass
08840	Glazing Plastics
08850	Glazing Accessories
08900	**WINDOW WALLS/CURTAIN WALLS**
08910	Window Walls
08911	Steel Window Walls
08912	Aluminum Window Walls
08913	Stainless Steel Window Walls
08914	Bronze Window Walls
08915	Wood Window Walls

CONSTRUCTION SPECIFICATIONS INSTITUTE

DIVISION 9—FINISHES

09100	**LATH AND PLASTER**
09110	Furring and Lathing
09150	Gypsum Plaster
09180	Cement Plaster
09190	Acoustical Plaster
09195	Plaster Accessories
09250	**GYPSUM WALLBOARD**
09260	Gypsum Wallboard Systems
09280	Gypsum Wallboard Accessories
09300	**TILE**
09310	Ceramic Tile
09320	Ceramic Mosaics
09330	Quarry Tile
09340	Marble Tile
09350	Glass Mosaics
09360	Plastic Tile
09370	Metal Tile
09380	Conductive Tile
09400	**TERRAZZO**
09410	Portland Cement Terrazzo
09420	Precast Terrazzo
09430	Conductive Terrazzo
09440	Plastic Matrix Terrazzo
09500	**ACOUSTICAL TREATMENT**
09510	Acoustical Ceilings
09511	Acoustical Panels
09512	Acoustical Tiles
09520	Acoustical Wall Treatment
09530	Acoustical Insulation and Barriers
09540	**CEILING SUSPENSION SYSTEMS**
09550	**WOOD FLOORING**
09560	Wood Strip Flooring
09670	Wood Parquet Flooring
09580	Plywood Block Flooring
09590	Resilient Wood Flooring System
09600	Wood Block Industrial Flooring
09650	**RESILIENT FLOORING**
09651	Cementitious Underlayment
09660	Resilient Tile Flooring
09665	Resilient Sheet Flooring
09670	Fluid Applied Resilient Flooring
09675	Conductive Resilient Flooring
09680	**CARPETING**
09681	Carpet Cushion
09682	Carpet
09683	Bonded Cushion Carpet
09684	Custom Carpet
09690	Carpet Tile
09700	**SPECIAL FLOORING**
09710	Magnesium Oxychloride Floors
09720	Epoxy-Marble Chip Flooring
09730	Elastomeric Liquid Flooring
09731	Conductive Elastomeric Liquid Flooring
09740	Heavy-Duty Concrete Toppings
09741	Armored Floors
09750	Brick Flooring
09755	Laminated Plastic Flooring
09760	**FLOOR TREATMENT**
09800	**SPECIAL COATINGS**
09810	Abrasion Resistant Coatings
09820	Cementitious Coatings
09830	Elastomeric Coatings
09840	Fire-Resistant Coatings
09841	Sprayed Fireproofing
09850	Aggregate Wall Coatings
09900	**PAINTING**
09910	Exterior Painting
09920	Interior Painting
09930	Transparent Finishes
09950	**WALL COVERING**
09951	Vinyl-Coated Fabric Wall Covering
09952	Vinyl Wall Covering
09953	Cork Wall Covering
09954	Wallpaper
09955	Wall Fabrics
09956	Asbestos Wall Covering
09960	Flexible Wood Sheets
09970	Prefinished Panels
09990	Adhesives

DIVISION 10—SPECIALTIES

10100	**CHALKBOARDS & TACKBOARDS**
10110	Chalkboards
10120	Tackboards
10150	**COMPARTMENTS & CUBICLES**
10151	Hospital Cubicles
10160	Toilet Partitions and Urinal Screens
10161	Laminated Plastic Toilet Partitions and Urinal Screens
10162	Metal Toilet Partitions and Urinal Screens
10163	Stone Partitions
10170	Shower & Dressing Compartments
10200	**LOUVERS & VENT (not connected to ductwork)**
10240	**GRILLES & SCREENS (not connected to ductwork)**
10260	**WALL & CORNER GUARDS**
10270	**ACCESS FLOORING**
10280	**SPECIALTY MODULES**
10290	**PEST CONTROL**
10300	**FIREPLACES**
10301	Prefabricated Fireplaces
10302	Prefabricated Fireplace Forms
10310	Fireplace Accessories
10350	**FLAGPOLES**
10400	**IDENTIFYING DEVICES**
10410	Directories and Bulletin Boards
10411	Directories
10420	Plaques
10440	Signs
10450	**PEDESTRIAN CONTROL DEVICES**
10500	**LOCKERS**
10501	Wardrobe Lockers
10502	Box Lockers
10503	Basket Lockers
10530	**PROTECTIVE COVERS**
10531	Walkway Covers
10532	Car Shelters
10550	**POSTAL SPECIALTIES**
10551	Mail Chutes
10552	Mail Boxes
10600	**PARTITIONS**
10601	Mesh Partitions
10610	Demountable Partitions
10616	Movable Gypsum Partitions
10620	Folding Partitions
10623	Accordion Folding Partitions
10650	**SCALES**
10670	**STORAGE SHELVING**
10700	**SUN CONTROL DEVICES (EXTERIOR)**
10750	**TELEPHONE ENCLOSURES**
10751	Telephone Booths
10752	Telephone Directory Units
10753	Telephone Shelves
10800	**TOILET & BATH ACCESSORIES**
10900	**WARDROBE SPECIALTIES**

DIVISION 11—EQUIPMENT

11050	**BUILT-IN MAINTENANCE EQUIPMENT**
11051	Vacuum Cleaning System
11052	Powered Window Washing
11100	**BANK AND VAULT EQUIPMENT**
11150	**COMMERCIAL EQUIPMENT**
11170	**CHECKROOM EQUIPMENT**
11180	**DARKROOM EQUIPMENT**
11200	**ECCLESIASTICAL EQUIPMENT**
11260	Pews
11270	Ecclesiastical Furniture
11300	**EDUCATIONAL EQUIPMENT**
11400	**FOOD SERVICE EQUIPMENT**
11401	Food Service Equipment: Custom Fabricated
11410	Bar Units
11420	Cooking Equipment
11430	Dishwashing Equipment
11435	Garbage Disposers
11440	Food Preparation Machines
11450	Food Preparation Tables
11460	Food Serving Units
11470	Refrigerated Cases
11471	Refrigerated Boxes
11480	**VENDING EQUIPMENT**
11500	**ATHLETIC EQUIPMENT**
11550	**INDUSTRIAL EQUIPMENT**
11600	**LABORATORY EQUIPMENT**
11610	Laboratory Furniture
11611	Steel Laboratory Furniture
11612	Wood Laboratory Furniture
11630	**LAUNDRY EQUIPMENT**
11650	**LIBRARY EQUIPMENT**
11700	**MEDICAL EQUIPMENT**
11800	**MORTUARY EQUIPMENT**
11830	**MUSICAL EQUIPMENT**
11850	**PARKING EQUIPMENT**
11860	**WASTE HANDLING EQUIPMENT**
11861	Packaged Incinerators
11862	Waste Compactors
11863	Bins
11864	Pulping Machines & Systems
11865	Chutes and Collectors
11870	**LOADING DOCK EQUIPMENT**
11871	Dock Levelers
11872	Leveling Platforms
11873	Portable Ramps, Bridges & Platforms
11874	Seals & Shelters
11875	Dock Bumpers
11880	**DETENTION EQUIPMENT**
11900	**RESIDENTIAL EQUIPMENT**
11970	**THEATER AND STAGE EQUIPMENT**
11990	**REGISTRATION EQUIPMENT**

CONSTRUCTION SPECIFICATIONS INSTITUTE

DIVISION 12—FURNISHINGS

12100	**ARTWORK**
	Murals
	Photo Murals
	Carved or Cast Statuary
	Carved or Cast Relief Work
	Custom Altar Vestments
	Custom Chancel Fittings
12300	**CABINETS AND STORAGE**
12310	Classroom Cabinets
12320	Dormitory Units
12330	Metal Casework
12340	Wood Casework
12341	Educational Casework
12342	Hospital Casework
12500	**WINDOW TREATMENT**
12501	Blinds & Shades
12502	Shutters
12560	**FABRICS**
12600	**FURNITURE**
12670	**RUGS AND MATS**
12675	Floor Mats
12700	**SEATING**
12710	Auditorium Seating
12730	Stadium Seating
12735	Telescoping Bleachers
12800	**FURNISHING ACCESSORIES**

DIVISION 13—SPECIAL CONSTRUCTION

13010	**AIR SUPPORTED STRUCTURES**
13050	**INTEGRATED ASSEMBLIES**
13100	**AUDIOMETRIC ROOM**
13250	**CLEAN ROOM**
13350	**HYPERBARIC ROOM**
13400	**INCINERATORS**
13440	**INSTRUMENTATION**
13460	**INSULATED ROOM**
13500	**INTEGRATED CEILING**
13540	**NUCLEAR REACTORS**
13550	**OBSERVATORY**
13600	**PREFABRICATED STRUCTURES**
13601	Prefabricated Buildings
13700	**SPECIAL PURPOSE ROOMS & BUILDINGS**
13710	Prefabricated Rooms
13750	**RADIATION PROTECTION**
13751	Lead Radiation Shielding
13760	Radio Frequency Shielding
13770	**SOUND AND VIBRATION CONTROL**
13800	**VAULTS**
13850	**SWIMMING POOL**

DIVISION 14—CONVEYING SYSTEMS

14100	**DUMBWAITERS**
14200	**ELEVATORS**
14210	Passenger
14230	Freight
14300	**HOISTS AND CRANES**
14400	**LIFTS**
14410	People Lifts
14420	Aerial Tramways
14430	Platform and Stage Lifts
14440	Funiculars
14500	**MATERIAL HANDLING SYSTEMS**
14550	Conveyors & Chutes
14551	Conveyors
14555	Chutes
14570	**TURNTABLES**
14600	**MOVING STAIRS AND WALKS**
14610	Escalators
14620	Moving Walks
14700	**TUBE SYSTEMS**
14800	**POWERED SCAFFOLDING**

CONSTRUCTION SPECIFICATIONS INSTITUTE

DIVISION 15—MECHANICAL

15010	**GENERAL PROVISIONS**
15015	Mechanical Reference Symbols
15020	Work Included
15021	Work Not Included
15023	Codes, Fees, and Lateral Costs
15040	Starting the Piping Systems
15041	Chlorination of Domestic Water Lines
15042	Tests
15043	Balancing of Air Systems
15044	General Completion
15045	Results Expected
15046	Demonstration
15047	Identification
15048	Maintenance Contracts
15049	Materials Manufacturers
15050	**BASIC MATERIALS AND METHODS**
15060	Pipe and Pipe Fittings
15061	Steel Pipe
15062	Cast Iron Pipe
15063	Copper Pipe
15064	Plastic Pipe
15065	Glass Pipe
15066	Stainless Steel Pipe
15067	Aluminum Pipe
15075	Hose
15080	Piping Specialties
15081	Gaskets
15082	Swivel Joints
15083	Strainers, Filters, and Driers
15084	Vent Caps
15085	Traps
15086	Vacuum Breakers
15087	Shock Absorbers
15090	Supports, Anchors, and Seals
15091	Anchors
15092	Wall Seal
15093	Flashing and Safing
15094	Hangers and Supports
15100	Valves, Cocks, and Faucets (Manual)
15101	Gate Valves
15102	Blowdown Valves
15103	Butterfly Valves
15104	Ball Valves
15105	Globe Valves
15106	Refrigerant Valves
15107	Stop Cocks
15108	Curb Stops
15109	Hydrants
15110	Check Valves
15111	Swing Check Valves
15112	Backwater Valves
15113	Vertical Check Valves
15114	Stop and Check Valves
15115	Faucets
15116	Washer Outlets
15120	Self Contained Control Valves
15121	Pressure Regulating Valves
15122	Pressure Relief Valves
15123	Automatic Temperature and Pressure Relief Valves
15124	Solenoid Valves
15125	Steam Traps
15130	Tempering Controllers
15131	Photo Lab Tempering Controller
15132	Mixing Station
15133	Refrigerant Control Valves and Specialties
15134	Feed Water Regulator
15140	Pumps
15141	Centrifugal
15142	Rotary
15143	Turbine
15144	Reciprocating
15145	Sump Pump
15146	Submersible Pump
15147	Pneumatic Ejector
15150	Compressors
15151	Vacuum Pumps

15152	Air Compressors
15160	Vibration Isolation and Expansion Compensation
15161	Vibration Isolation
15162	Expansion Joints
15164	Flexible Connections
15170	Meters and Gages
15171	Temperature Gages
15172	Pressure Gages
15173	Flow Measuring Devices
15174	Liquid Level Gages
15175	Tanks
15176	Steel Tanks
15177	Plastic Tanks
15178	Cast Iron Tanks
15180	**INSULATION**
15181	General
15182	Cold Water Piping
15183	Chilled Water Piping
15184	Refrigerant Piping
15185	Hot Water Piping
15186	Steam and Condensate Return Piping
15187	Underground Piping
15188	Outside Piping
15190	Duct
15195	Breeching
15196	Equipment
15200	**WATER SUPPLY AND TREATMENT**
15201	General (To include descriptions of all systems involved) (Coordinate with Division 2)
15220	Pump and Piping System
15230	Booster Pumping Equipment
15240	Water Reservoirs and Tanks
15250	Water Treatment
15251	Filtration Equipment
15252	Aeration Equipment
15253	Water Softening Equipment
15260	Chemical Feeding Equipment
15261	Chlorinating Equipment
15270	Metering and Related Piping
15300	**WASTE WATER DISPOSAL AND TREATMENT**
15301	General (To include descriptions of all systems, including sewerage, septic tank systems and sewage treatment) (Coordinate with Division 2)
15310	Sewage Ejectors
15320	Grease Interceptors
15350	Lift Stations
15361	Septic Tanks
15362	Drainage Fields
15380	Sewage Treatment Equipment
15381	Screens and Skimming Tanks
15382	Sedimentation Tanks
15385	Filtration Equipment
15390	Aeration Equipment
15395	Sludge Digestion Equipment
15400	**PLUMBING**
15401	General; to include descriptions of all systems, including:
	Water Supply System
	Chilled Water Piping Systems
	Distilled Water Piping Systems
	Compressed Air Piping System
	Oxygen Piping System
	Helium Piping System
	Nitrous Oxide Piping System
	Vacuum Piping System
	Laboratory Gas Piping System
	Compressed Industrial Gas Piping Systems
	Central Soap Piping System
	Soil Piping System
	Waste Piping System
	Roof Drainage System
	Chemical Waste Drainage System
	Industrial Waste Drainage System

	Process Piping Systems
15420	Equipment
15421	Floor and Shower Drains
15422	Roof Drains
15423	Cleanouts and Cleanout Access Covers
15424	Domestic Water Heaters
15425	Aftercoolers & Separators
15426	Stills
15427	Anti-syphon Equipment
15428	Sediment Interceptors
15429	Laundry/Utility Units
15430	Packaged Waste, Vent, or Water Piping Units
15435	Domestic Water Conditioners
15440	Special System Accessories
15441	Soap System Accessories
15442	Gas Accessories
15443	Compressed Air Equipment
15450	Plumbing Fixtures and Trim
15451	Special Fixtures & Trim
15452	Fixture Carriers
15455	Domestic Watercoolers
15456	Washfountains Check
15457	Showers
15458	Receptors
15470	Pool Equipment
15471	Circulation and Filtration Equipment
15472	Pool Drains, Inlets, and Outlets
15473	Pool Cleaning Equipment
15475	Chemical Treatment Equipment
15480	Fountain Piping and Nozzles
15490	Special Equipment
15500	**FIRE PROTECTION**
15501	General (To include a description of all systems)
15510	Sprinkler Equipment
15521	Foam Equipment
15522	Carbon Dioxide Equipment
15530	Standpipe and Fire Hose Equipment
15531	Fire Hose Connections
15532	Fire Hose Cabinets and Accessories
15533	Fire Hose Reels
15534	Fire Hose
15540	Portable Extinguishers
15541	Fire Blankets
15550	Fire Extinguisher Cabinets and Accessories
15560	Hood and Duct Fire Protection
15570	Non-electrical Alarm Equipment
15600	**POWER OR HEAT GENERATION**
15601	General (To include descriptions of all systems)
15605	Fuel Handling Equipment
15606	Oil Storage Tanks, Controls, and Piping
15607	L-P Gas Tanks, Controls, and Piping
15610	Ash Removal System
15615	Lined Breechings
15616	Lined Prefabricated Chimneys and Stacks
15617	Exhaust Equipment
15618	Draft Control Equipment
15620	Boilers
15621	Cast Iron Boiler
15622	Firebox Boiler
15623	Scotch Marine Boiler
15624	Water Tube Boilers
15625	Absorption Boiler
15630	Burners and Controls
15635	Stokers
15638	Fuel Preheaters
15639	Boiler Accessories
15640	Boiler Feedwater Equipment
15641	Packaged Boiler Feed Pump System

CONSTRUCTION SPECIFICATIONS INSTITUTE

15642	Deaerators	15754	Radiators	15861	Manual Dampers
15650	**REFRIGERATION**	15760	Unit Heaters	15862	Gravity Backdraft Dampers
15651	General (Descriptions of all systems including Refrigeration Piping System)	15761	Fan Coil Units	15863	Barometric Dampers
		15762	Unit Ventilators	15864	Fire Dampers
		15763	Air Handling Units (with coils)	15865	Smoke Dampers
15655	Refrigerant Compressors	15770	Packaged Heating and Cooling	15866	Turning Vanes
15656	Centrifugal Compressors	15772	Packaged Heat Pump	15867	Distribution Device
15657	Rotary Compressors	15780	Humidity Control	15868	Duct Access Panels and Test Holes
15658	Reciprocating Compressors	15781	Humidifiers		
15660	Condensing Units	15783	Centrifugal Type Humidifier	15870	Outlets
15661	Air Cooled Condensing Units	15785	Dehumidifiers	15871	Wall and Floor Diffusers
15662	Water Cooled Condensing Units	15786	Desiccant Dehumidifiers	15972	Ceiling Diffusers
		15790	Process Heating	15873	Ceiling Air Distribution System
15663	Evaporative Condensing Units	15795	Storage Cells	15874	Light Troffer-Diffusers
15670	Chillers	15799	Special Devices	15875	Warm Air Baseboard
15671	Reciprocating Chillers	**15800**	**AIR DISTRIBUTION**	15876	Cabinet Diffusers
15672	Air Cooled Chillers	15801	General	15877	Air Floors
15673	Ethylene Glycol Chillers	15810	Furnaces	15878	Roof Mounted Air Inlets & Outlets
15674	Centrifugal Chillers	15811	Direct Fired Furnaces		
15675	Absorption Chillers	15812	Cast Iron Furnaces	15879	Air Inlet and Outlet Louvers (connected to ductwork)
15676	Rotary Chillers	15813	Steel Furnaces		
15680	Cooling Tower (Propeller type)	15814	Rooftop Furnaces	15880	Air Treatment Equipment
15681	Cooling Tower (Centrifugal type)	15815	Direct Fired Unit Heaters	15881	Disposable Filters
		15816	Direct Fired Duct Heaters, Reheaters	15882	Permanent Filters
15685	Ice Bank			15883	High Efficiency Filters
15686	Special Ice Making Equipment	15820	Fans	15884	Roll Filters
15687	Commercial Ice Making Equipment	15821	Centrifugal Fans	15885	Oil Bath Air Filters
		15824	Propeller Fans	15886	Electronic Air Filters
15690	Evaporators	15825	Attic Exhaust Fans	15887	Air Washers
15691	Unit Coolers	15826	Fly Fans	15888	Dust Collectors
15695	Condensers	15827	Axial Flow Fans	15889	Fume Collectors or Dispensers
15699	Refrigeration Accessories	15828	Induced Draft Fans	15890	Sound Attenuators
15700	**LIQUID HEAT TRANSFER**	15829	Exhaust Fans	15895	Special Devices
15701	General; to include descriptions of all systems, including:	15830	Power Roof Ventilators	**15900**	**CONTROLS AND INSTRUMENTATION**
		15831	Power Wall Ventilators		
		15832	Roof Ventilators (connected to ductwork)	15901	General
	Hot Water Piping System			15902	Electrical and Interlocks
	Chilled Water Piping System	15834	Air Handling Units (without coils)	15906	Identification
	Steam Supply and Return Piping System			15907	Inspection, Testing, and Balancing
		15835	Air Curtains		
	Radiant Heat System	15840	Ductwork	15910	Control Piping, Tubing, and Wiring
	Snow Melting System	15841	Low Pressure Steel Ductwork		
15710	Hot Water Specialties	15842	High Pressure Steel Ductwork	15915	Control Air Compressor and Dryer
15715	Steam Specialties	15843	Nonmetallic Ductwork		
15720	Condensate Pump and Receiver Set	15844	Special Ductwork	15920	Control Panels
		15846	Prefabricated Insulated Ductwork	15925	Instrument Panelboard
15730	Heat Exchangers			15930	Primary Control Devices
15731	Storage Water Heater	15847	Flexible Ductwork	15931	Thermostats
15732	Converter	15848	Duct Lining	15932	Humidistats
15734	Clean Steam Heat Exchanger	15849	Duct Hangers and Supports	15934	Aquastats
15735	Water Heat Reclaim Equipment	15850	Special Ductwork Systems	15935	Relays and Switches
		15851	Tailpipe Exhaust Equipment	15936	Timers
15740	Terminal Units	15852	Dust Collection Equipment	15937	Control Dampers
15741	Induction Units	15853	Paint Spray Booth System Equipment	15938	Control Valves
15745	Radiant Panels			15939	Control Motors
15750	Coils	15854	Fume Collection System Equipment	15950	Sequence of Operation
15751	Baseboard Units			15960	Recording Devices
15752	Finned Tube	15855	Breeching and Smokepipe	15970	Alarm Devices
15753	Convectors	15860	Duct Accessories	15980	Special Process Controls

CONSTRUCTION SPECIFICATIONS INSTITUTE

DIVISION 16—ELECTRICAL

16010	**GENERAL PROVISIONS**
16015	Electrical Reference Symbols
16020	Work Included
16021	Work Not included
16025	Codes and Fees
16030	Tests
16031	Demonstration of Completed Electrical Systems
16040	Identification
16100	**BASIC MATERIALS AND METHODS**
16101	General
16110	Raceways
16111	Conduits
16112	Bus Ducts
16113	Underfloor Ducts
16114	Cable Trays
16120	Wires and Cables
16121	Wire Connections and Devices
16125	Pulling Cables
16130	Outlet Boxes
16131	Pull and Junction Boxes
16132	Floor Boxes
16133	Cabinets
16134	Panelboards
16140	Switches and Receptacles
16150	Motors
16160	Motor Starters
16170	Disconnects (motor and circuit)
16180	Overcurrent Protective Devices
16181	Fuses
16182	Circuit Breakers
16190	Supporting Devices
16199	Electronic Devices
16200	**POWER GENERATION**
16201	General
16210	Generator
16220	Engine
16221	Reciprocating Engine
16224	Turbine
16230	Cooling Equipment
16240	Exhaust Equipment
16250	Starting Equipment
16260	Automatic Transfer Equipment
16300	**POWER TRANSMISSION**
16301	General
16310	Substation
16320	Switchgear
16330	Transformer
16340	Vaults
16350	Manholes
16360	Rectifier
16370	Converter
16380	Capacitor
16400	**SERVICE AND DISTRIBUTION**
16401	General (To include descriptions of all wiring systems)
16410	Electric Service
16411	Underground Service
16420	Service Entrance
16421	Emergency Service
16430	Service Disconnect
16431	Primary Load Interrupter
16440	Metering
16450	Grounding
16460	Transformers
16470	Distribution Switchboards
16471	Branch Circuit Panelboard
16480	Feeder Circuit
16490	Converters
16491	Rectifiers
16500	**LIGHTING**
16501	General
16510	Interior Lighting Fixtures
16511	Luminous Ceiling
16515	Signal Lighting
16530	Exterior Lighting Fixtures
16531	Stadium Lighting
16532	Roadway Lighting
16550	Accessories
16551	Lamps
16552	Ballasts and Accessories
16570	Poles and Standards
16600	**SPECIAL SYSTEMS**
16601	General (To include descriptions of all systems involved)
16610	Lightning Protection
16620	Emergency Light and Power
16621	Storage Batteries
16622	Battery Charging Equipment
16640	Cathodic Protection
16650	Electromagnetic Shielding
16700	**COMMUNICATIONS**
16701	General (To include descriptions of all systems involved)
16710	Radio Transmission
16711	Shortwave Transmission
16712	Microwave Transmission
16720	Alarm and Detection
16721	Fire Alarm and Detection
16725	Smoke Detector
16727	Burglar Alarm
16730	Clock and Program Equipment
16740	Telephone
16750	Telegraph
16760	Intercommunication Equipment
16770	Public Address Equipment
16780	Television Systems
16781	Master TV Antenna Equipment
16790	Learning Laboratories
16850	**HEATING AND COOLING**
16851	General
16858	Snow Melting Cable and Mat
16859	Heating Cable
16860	Electric Heating Coil
16865	Electric Baseboard
16870	Packaged Room Air Conditioners
16880	Radiant Heaters
16881	Duct Heaters
16890	Electric Heaters (Prop Fan Type)
16900	**CONTROLS AND INSTRUMENTATION**
16901	General
16910	Recording and Indicating Devices
16920	Motor Control Centers
16930	Lighting Control Equipment
16940	Electrical Interlock
16950	Control of Electric Heating
16960	Limit Switches
16970	Urinal Flush Valve

CONSTRUCTION SPECIFICATIONS INSTITUTE

Acoustical Society of America
335 East 45th Street
New York, N.Y. 10017

Air-Conditioning & Refrigeration Institute
1815 North Fort Meyer Drive
Arlington, Virginia 22209

American Arbitration Association
140 West 51st Street
New York, N.Y. 10020

American Concrete Institute
P.O. Box 4754 Bedford Station
Detroit, Michigan 48217

American Hospital Association
840 North Lake Shore Drive
Chicago, Illinois 60611

American Institute of Architects
1735 New York Avenue, N.W.
Washington, D.C. 20006

American Institute of Consulting Engineers
345 East 47th Street
New York, N.Y. 10017

American Institute of Landscape Architects
501 East San Juan Avenue
Phoenix, Arizona 85012

American Institute of Steel Construction
101 Park Avenue
New York, N.Y. 10017

American Institute of Timber Construction
1657 K Street, N.W.
Washington, D.C. 20006

American National Standards Institute
1430 Broadway
New York, N.Y. 10018

American Plywood Association
1119 A Street
Tacoma, Washington 98401

American Society of Architectural
    Hardware Consultants
P.O. Box 599
Mill Valley, California 94941

American Society of Heating, Refrigeration and
    Air Conditioning Engineers Inc.
345 East 47th Street
New York, N.Y. 10017

American Society of Professional Estimators
14918 Burbank Boulevard
Van Nuys, California 91401

American Society for Testing and Materials
1916 Race Street
Philadelphia, Pennsylvania 19103

Associated General Contractors of America
1957 E Street, N.W.
Washington, D.C. 20006

Building Officials and Code Administrators
    International
1313 East 60th Street
Chicago, Illinois 60637

California Redwood Association
617 Montgomery Street
San Francisco, California 94111

Ceramic Tile Institute
3415 West Eighth Street
Los Angeles, California 90005

Concrete Reinforcing Steel Institute
228 North La Salle Street
Chicago, Illinois 60601

Construction Specifications Institute
1150 Seventeenth Street, N.W.
Washington, D.C. 20036

Consulting Engineers Council of the U.S.
1155 Fifteenth Street, N.W.
Washington, D.C. 20005

Copper Institute
50 Broadway
New York, N.Y. 10004

Drywall Industry Trust Fund
9800 South Sepulvada Boulevard
Los Angeles, California 90045

Earthquake Engineering Research Institute
424 Fourtieth Street
Oakland, California 94609

Engineers Joint Council
345 East 47th Street
New York, N.Y. 10017

Flat Glass Jobbers Association
6210 West 10th Street
Topeka, Kansas 66615

Gypsum Association
201 North Wells Street
Chicago, Illinois 60606

Hardware Association
205 West Wacker Drive
Chicago, Illinois 60606

Hardwood Plywood Institute
2301 South Walter Reed Drive
Arlington, Virginia 22206

International Conference of Building Officials
5360 South Workman Mill Road
Whittier, California 90601

Marble Institute of America Inc.
Pennsylvania Building
Washington, D.C. 20005

National Architectural Accrediting Board
1785 Massachusetts Avenue, N.W.
Washington, D.C. 20036

National Association of Architectural
    Metal Manufacturers
228 North La Salle Street
Chicago, Illinois 60601

National Association of Home Builders
1625 L Street, N.W.
Washington, D.C. 20036

National Association of Plumbing, Heating
    and Cooling Contractors
1016 20th Street, N.W.
Washington, D.C. 20005

National Concrete Masonry Association
P.O Box 9185 Rosslyn Station
Arlington, Virginia 22209

National Council of Architectural
    Registration Boards
2100 M St. N.W. Suite 706
Washington, D.C. 20037

National Electrical Contractors' Association
1730 Rhode Island Avenue, N.W.
Washington, D.C. 20036

National Fire Protection Association
60 Batterymarch Street
Boston, Massachusetts 02110

National Terrazzo and Mosaic Association Inc.
716 Church Street
Arlington, Virginia 22314

National Woodwork Manufacturers' Association
400 West Madison Street
Chicago, Illinois 60606

Painting and Decorating Contractors of America
2625 West Peterson Avenue
Chicago, Illinois 60645

Perlite Institute
45 West 45th Street
New York, N.Y. 10036

Plastering Information Bureau
11520 San Vicente Boulevard
Los Angeles, California 90049

Portland Cement Association
33 West Grand Avenue
Chicago, Illinois 60610

Prestressed Concrete Institute
205 West Wacker Drive
Chicago, Illinois 60606

The Producers Council
1717 Massachusetts Avenue, N.W.
Washington, D.C. 20036

Red Cedar Shingle and Handsplit Shake Bureau
5510 White Building
Seattle, Washington 98101

Sheet Metal and Air Conditioning Contractors'
    National Association
1611 North Kent Street
Arlington, Virginia 22209

Southern Building Code Congress
3617 8th Avenue
Birmingham, Alabama 35203

Southern Pine Association
P.O. Box 52468
New Orleans, Louisiana 70150

Steel Deck Institute
9836 West Roosevelt Road
Westchester, Illinois 60153

Steel Door Institute
2130 Keith Building
Cleveland, Ohio 44115

Steel Joist Institute
2001 Jefferson Davis Highway
Arlington, Virginia 22202

Steel Window Institute
18445 Harvest Lane
Brookfield, Wisconsin 53005

Structural Clay Products Institute
1520 28th Street, N.W.
Washington, D.C. 20036

Tile Council of America Inc.
360 Lexington Avenue
New York, N.Y. 10017

Underwriters' Laboratories Inc.
207 East Ohio Street
Chicago, Illinois 60611

Urban Land Institute
1200 Eighteenth Street, N.W.
Washington, D.C. 20036

U.S. Department of Commerce
Commodity Standards Division
Washington, D.C. 20025

Vermiculite Institute
141 West Jackson Boulevard
Chicago, Illinois 60604

West Coast Lumber Inspection Bureau
1410 Southwest Morrison Street
Portland, Oregon 97250

Western Red Cedar Lumber Association
Yeon Building
Portland, Oregon 97204

Western Wood Products Association
Yeon Building
Portland, Oregon 97204

Wood Flooring Institute of America
201 North Wells Street
Chicago, Illinois 60606

Woodwork Institute of California
1833 Broadway
Fresno, California 93721